Ethical Prophets along the Way

"This book is a timely and urgent wake-up call to critical educators, liberation theologians, and all concerned with justice. Through the prophetic voices who speak truth to power, Rufus Burrow challenges the political and religious establishment with insightful analysis and compassionate heart. His voice comes out like 'a sharp razor,' evoking and provoking our conscious response. A courageous book that appeals to the sacredness of all human beings against all that is inhuman, a remarkable account of God's graciousness."

—**Débora B. Agra Junker,** Assistant Professor of Christian Education, Garrett-Evangelical Theological Seminary

"Rufus Burrow Jr. has crafted a multivalent profile of the 'ethical prophet' through a striking array of leaders who exhibit divergent expressions of political courage, intellectual creativity, and bold faith. Each one inspires. Collectively they expand our imaginations about the ethical contours of individual leadership committed to anti-racism and spirituality."

—**Traci C. West,** author of *Solidarity and Defiant Spirituality: Africana Lessons on Racism, Religion, and Ending Gender Violence*

"Burrow Jr. points us to the essence of God-centered living: to stand with and fight for mistreated and powerless people, such as children, women, the poor, and refugees. The manifesto is poignant and life-giving all at once, an antidote to social atrocities and the promise of social redemption. Burrow renders the ethical prophet as vital for churches, synagogues, and mosques."

—**Timothy A. Knight,** Knight Life Solutions (KLS)

"*Ethical Prophets* is strong evidence that Rufus Burrow Jr. belongs in the hall of fame for social ethicists who give voice to the voiceless and who inspire and instruct those wishing to embody the ethical prophecy exemplified by the brave souls depicted in these powerful pages. A magisterial study and, best of all, an enlightening read for those of us stuck in troubling times."

—**Michael G. Long,** editor of *We the Resistance: Documenting a History of Nonviolent Protest in the United States*

"Burrow Jr. uses Abraham Heschel's theoretical constructions to assert that prophets respond to divine calling through maladjustment to routinized practices of dehumanization. . . . This book is a signpost and an important read for all who actively pursue justice."

—**Rosetta E. Ross,** Professor of Religion, Spelman College

Ethical Prophets along the Way

Those Hall of Famers

RUFUS BURROW JR.

Foreword by Susannah Heschel
Afterword by Mary Alice Mulligan

CASCADE *Books* • Eugene, Oregon

ETHICAL PROPHETS ALONG THE WAY
Those Hall of Famers

Copyright © 2020 Rufus Burrow Jr. All rights reserved. Except for brief quotations in critical publications or reviews, no part of this book may be reproduced in any manner without prior written permission from the publisher. Write: Permissions, Wipf and Stock Publishers, 199 W. 8th Ave., Suite 3, Eugene, OR 97401.

Cascade Books
An Imprint of Wipf and Stock Publishers
199 W. 8th Ave., Suite 3
Eugene, OR 97401

www.wipfandstock.com

PAPERBACK ISBN: 978-1-5326-7779-3
HARDCOVER ISBN: 978-1-5326-7780-9
EBOOK ISBN: 978-1-5326-7781-6

Cataloguing-in-Publication data:

Names: Burrow, Rufus, 1951–, author. | Heschel, Susannah, foreword. | Mulligan, Mary Alice, 1952–, afterword.

Title: Ethical prophets along the way : those hall of famers / Rufus Burrow Jr. ; foreword by Susannah Heschel ; afterword by Mary Alice Mulligan.

Description: Eugene, OR : Cascade Books, 2020 | Includes bibliographical references and index.

Identifiers: ISBN 978-1-5326-7779-3 (paperback) | ISBN 978-1-5326-7780-9 (hardcover) | ISBN 978-1-5326-7781-6 (ebook)

Subjects: LCSH: Prophets. | Church and social problems—History—20th century. | Heschel, Abraham Joshua,—1907–1972. | Grimké, Angelina Emily, 1807–1879. | Wells-Barnett, Ida B., 1862–1931. | Baldwin, James—1924–1987. | X, Malcolm—1925–1965. | King Martin Luther—Jr.—1929–1968. | Romero, Óscar A.—(Óscar Arnulfo)—Saint—1917–1980. | Walker, Alice, 1944–.

Classification: BR1700.2 .B87 2020 (print) | BR1700.2 .B87 (ebook)

Scripture quotations are from New Revised Standard Version Bible, copyright © 1989 National Council of the Churches of Christ in the United States of America. Used by permission. All rights reserved worldwide.

Manufactured in the U.S.A.   DECEMBER 26, 2019

For Mom (Mrs. Fannie B. Burkhalter Burrow) and Aunt Gara (Mrs. Gara Mae Burkhalter Harrell), both for the love they were and the unrelenting love, compassion, understanding, and encouragement they unselfishly gave a son and nephew who was sometimes lost, but has never stopped trying to find his way.

Contents

Foreword by Susannah Heschel | ix
Acknowledgments | xiii

Introduction | 1

Part 1—The Nature of Ethical Prophecy
1. Setting the Stage: Contributions of Abraham J. Heschel | 23

Part 2—Ethical Prophets along the Way
2. Angelina Grimké as Ethical Prophet | 55
3. Ida B. Wells-Barnett as Ethical Prophet | 81
4. James Baldwin as Ethical Prophet | 107
5. Malcolm X as Ethical Prophet | 136
6. Martin Luther King Jr. as Ethical Prophet | 159
7. Óscar Romero as Ethical Prophet | 186
8. Alice Walker as Ethical Prophet | 215

Afterword by Mary Alice Mulligan | 239
Bibliography | 247
Index | 261

Foreword

A threat is hanging over our heads around the world: the very concept of democracy is being repudiated, and religion does not seem to be effective in halting the growing hatred, selfishness, cruelty, and vulgarity. Racism, bigotry, and anti-Semitism are everywhere on the rise, and hatred of Muslims is a scourge from India, China, and Myanmar to Europe and the United States. Authoritarian regimes are being elected, and neo-Nazi groups are growing. We are losing a basic commitment to human life, to human dignity, and to God as creator of all. We are becoming callous and indifferent, turning away from the suffering and destruction that our governments are creating. Into this horrible cauldron comes a book by Rufus Burrow Jr., *Ethical Prophets along the Way*, that offers us hope and guidance.

"The world does not like prophets," writes the Rev. Otis Moss Jr. perceptively. Burrow cites Moss in presenting extraordinary religious figures whom he calls "ethical prophets." Angelina Grimké, Óscar Romero, Ida B. Wells, Alice Walker, Malcolm X, Martin Luther King Jr., Abraham Joshua Heschel, and James Baldwin are the extraordinary prophetic "sheroes" and heroes whose lives and ideas Burrow lifts up and urges us to emulate. Crucial figures of ancient biblical history, the Hebrew prophets came alive again in the last two centuries to arouse the conscience of the world for social and political change.

A remarkable theological convergence occurred in the United States in the late nineteenth century: the writings of the Hebrew prophets inspired a reshaping of the liberal Protestant church and Reform Judaism. Ministers and rabbis now called their congregations to philanthropy, political change, and social activism. No longer narrowly focused on defining doctrine, these clergy wanted prophetic religion: faith in action, justice in the land, an end to poverty and a new spirit of responsibility for society.

The prophetic message had always been central to the black church; now white Protestants, Catholics, and Jews were starting to catch up. A new boost came with the civil rights and peace movements, whose leaders were imbued with prophetic enthusiasm and fearlessness. One voice that articulated the theology of the prophets was the Jewish theologian and refugee from Nazi Europe, Abraham Joshua Heschel, whose 1962 book, *The Prophets*, gave a new formulation of the nature of the prophet:

> What manner of man is the prophet? The prophet is a man who feels fiercely. God has thrust a burden upon his soul, and he is bowed and stunned at man's fierce greed. Frightful is the agony of man; no human voice can convey its full terror. Prophecy is the voice that God has lent to the silent agony, a voice to the plundered poor, to the profaned riches of the world. It is a form of living, a crossing point of God and man. God is raging in the prophet's words.

"Heschel's theology of prophecy," Burrow writes, "is amazingly similar to that found in the black religious tradition." The prophets' emphasis on justice and liberation that constitutes the "prophetic drama" results not from "human beings' initiative, but God's." Prophecy is not a negation of humanity in favor of God; on the contrary, Heschel writes, "Never in history has man been taken as seriously as in prophetic thinking." God's responsiveness to human beings is called "divine pathos" by Heschel, signifying that God is deeply affected by human suffering and by the misdeeds of one person to another. The prophets act in sympathy with God, conveying God's passion in their pleas and demands for justice. Burrow cites Heschel's formulation that "in prophetic sympathy, man is open to the presence and emotion of the transcendent Subject. He carries within himself the awareness of what is happening to God."

For Burrow, it is precisely this understanding of God and human beings to which "other ethical prophet hall of fame candidates appeal." His "candidates" are "ethical prophets" who seek to transform the hearts of human beings and, with them, society itself.

In his beautiful portrayals of the passionate "ethical prophets" he calls members of the "ethical prophet hall of fame," Burrow gives us figures of inspiration and calls on us, whether Jewish, Christian, Muslim, agnostic, or atheist, to go forth and do likewise. Act with "courage, integrity, the highest respect for the dignity and sacredness of human beings and with eyes on the highest ideals": that is his message to us, his call to our prophetic action.

There are certain eras when the words of the prophets fall on receptive ears and open our hearts. Heschel once wrote that the opposite of good is not evil but indifference; let us open our hearts and hear the prophetic message Burrow is presenting and strive to emulate and perhaps even become members of the prophetic hall of fame. I cannot imagine a more needed book for this desperate era.

—Susannah Heschel

Acknowledgments

When the late Richard D. N. Dickinson (former dean and, later, president) of Christian Theological Seminary (CTS) announced in the early 1980s that he was going on sabbatical he informed me that I had been assigned to teach Prophetic and Ethical Witness of the Church, a required Master of Divinity course taught annually by him. This caused me some consternation since this was my first faculty appointment, and I had only been on the CTS faculty two years. Fortunately I had carte blanche in how to structure and teach the course. Although I was not excited about having to develop yet another new course, the whole thing turned out to be a blessing, which began to take shape after a surprise discovery in the seminary library.

While browsing in the stacks one day, I happened upon Abraham Joshua Heschel's book *The Prophets*. A thick volume, I pulled it from the shelf, immediately perused the table of contents, and then began reading the introduction. I read much of chapter 1, and before I knew it I had stood in the same spot for more than two hours scanning that book. I was fascinated with Heschel's focus on *divine pathos* and could not seem to put the book down. It then occurred to me that I had found the primary text to use in the course, for it had the strong theological and ethical focus I wanted to incorporate.

I was thoroughly intrigued by Heschel's lively discussions on the mind, consciousness, and practice of the Hebrew prophets and how he was able to ferret out basic elements of prophecy in each. As I thought more about developing the course syllabus I decided that students would be required to read *The Prophets* in its entirety. In addition, because I wanted to know whether students not only understood the approach and nature of prophecy as expounded by Heschel, but whether they were also able to determine who was a prophet in the tradition of Hebrew prophecy and who was not, I decided that in addition to a final paper they would be required to write several summary-analysis papers on at least three select personalities. Because CTS is a predominantly white institution I decided that the personalities I selected would primarily consist of persons of color and women (of all races). Students would read works by Malcolm X, Martin Luther King Jr., James Cone, Angelina and Sarah Grimké, Sojourner Truth, David Walker, Anna Julia Cooper, Fannie Lou Hamer, Ida B. Wells, Dorothy Day, James Baldwin, Rigoberta Menchú, Óscar Romero, Alice Walker, Robert McAfee Brown, Ada María Isasi-Díaz, etc., in an attempt to determine whether they met the criteria for ethical prophet. This was an important exercise, since most students—especially white ones—had not heard of or been introduced to works by most of the select personalities.

To my surprise, when Dickinson returned from sabbatical he again assigned me to teach the course. From that point forward it was my course to teach, and I taught it—enthusiastically—for more than two decades. Although books by Bruce C. Birch (*Let Justice Roll Down*, 1991) and Marvin McMickle (*Where Have All the Prophets Gone?*, 2006) were important supplementary volumes, Heschel's profound book was always the primary text. I quickly came to love teaching Prophetic and Ethical Witness of the Church, and I became—and remain—enamored with Heschel's approach to prophecy. This was the unexpected blessing.

All of this is to say that I am deeply appreciative for the surprise discovery in the CTS library. In addition, I am grateful for the more than two decades of mostly awestruck students who grappled with the Hebrew prophets and what God requires of human beings. To be sure, not all students agreed with Heschel's and the professor's interpretation of what they came to know as *ethical prophecy*. Indeed, I shall never forget the time—on two different occasions—when a student was so angered by what was being taught about the significance of the prophets and the failure of Christians and others to take it seriously that he jumped up from his desk and left the classroom, slamming the door on his way out. He dropped out of the course. The other student, who also left the classroom angrily during a lecture, not only returned after a few minutes, but years later came back to apologize, saying that her long-held conservative views were being challenged so severely that she simply could not stand it that day. Nevertheless, she confessed that she was a better person and that her faith and fortitude for ministry were strengthened because she remained in the class to learn the lessons of ethical prophecy.

There are no words to adequately express my gratitude and respect for two truly superb teacher-scholar-author-activists who have read, thought, and written much about ethical prophecy. They have been courageous prophetic witnesses in their own right. Moreover, they have modeled ethical prophecy for their students, colleagues, and others.

Professor Mary Alice Mulligan teaches at CTS and is a senior pastor in the Christian Church (Disciples of Christ). Mary Alice was among my first students in Prophetic and Ethical Witness of the Church. After graduating from seminary she earned the PhD degree in homiletics and ethics at Vanderbilt University. Not long thereafter she began teaching at CTS, and we later coauthored two books on ethical prophecy: *Daring to Speak in God's Name: Ethical Prophecy in Ministry* (2002) and *Standing in the Margin* (2004). Needless to say, I am pleased that she agreed to write the afterword for *Ethical Prophets along the Way*.

And then there is Professor Susannah Heschel, daughter and only child of the inimitable Rabbi Abraham Joshua Heschel. An outstanding and renowned teacher, scholar, and public lecturer, as well as a prolific writer, Susannah is Eli Black Professor of Jewish Studies at Dartmouth College. She has made significant contributions to Martin Luther King Jr. and Heschel studies, focusing on the strong relationship and theological affinities between her father and King. Her work on King and Heschel as prophet is foundational for future contributions in this area.

I knew from the beginning that I wanted Susannah to write the foreword to my book. She was the closest connection to Heschel himself. In addition, I consider her to be a distinguished celebrity scholar. I met Susannah at the beginning of my career (and hers) when the Lecture Committee at CTS invited her to campus. I felt ever so special after meeting and shaking hands with Susannah. Later I had the good fortune to read a number of her writings and was particularly instructed by what she wrote and published about her father and his work, as well as his relationship with King, their civil rights and anti-Vietnam War activism together, and their mutual respect and admiration for each other. When I finally mustered sufficient courage to invite Susannah to write the foreword, I sent her a letter, along with the introduction and first chapter of the manuscript. She apologized for the delay in responding, and said, "If you still want me to write a short foreword, I would be honored to do so." I then sent the entire manuscript. I was ecstatic. I was pleased beyond words. I remain convinced that *I* am the one who was honored—by her acceptance. This book, with its strong

Heschellian influence, needed a word from Professor Susannah Heschel, and to my utter delight we have it.

My longtime colleague in Martin Luther King Jr. studies, Lewis V. Baldwin, Emeritus Professor of Religious Studies at Vanderbilt University, and arguably the top King scholar in the world, has conversed with me many times about Heschel and ethical prophecy. He eagerly endorsed my first solo-authored book on this type of prophecy: *God and Human Responsibility: David Walker and Ethical Prophecy* (2003), where Heschel's influence was apparent even then. All the time I have known and been in dialogue with Lewis, he has been a wise, honest, forthright, hardheaded, diplomatic critic and supporter of my work. For all these years Lewis Baldwin has been a true colleague, but more important, a faithful friend.

I would be remiss if I failed to name and thank five outstanding and distinguished scholar-professors who generously sacrificed time and energy to graciously read my book in manuscript form and to write endorsements. These include Professors Rosetta Ross (Spelman College), Timothy A. Knight (Martin University), Traci C. West (Drew University Theological School), Michael G. Long (Elizabethtown College), and Debora B. A. Junker (Garrett-Evangelical Theological Seminary). Nothing I could say here would fully convey the depth, breadth, and height of my appreciation, admiration, and respect for these colleagues.

I credit two women in the *womanist* tradition, my mother, Mrs. Fannie B. Burkhalter Burrow, and her oldest sister, Mrs. Gara Mae Burkhalter Harrell, for instilling in me the spirit of ethical prophecy from the time I was a boy, and insisting on the need and importance of having the courage to be a truth-teller in the face of wrongdoing and injustice. The example, strength, and witness of those two smart, bodacious, sassy, talk-back women is why I zealously dedicate *Ethical Prophets along the Way* to them and their memory.

Introduction

While writing *Daring to Speak in God's Name: Ethical Prophecy in Ministry* (2002), Mary Alice Mulligan[1] and I enthusiastically decided that the language in our book should be gender-inclusive. We accomplished this, in part, by alternating the use of feminine and masculine references by chapter. This allowed us to avoid the frequent use of the awkward "he-she" construction. I continue this approach in the current volume, beginning with the feminine in this Introduction. As in the previous text, however, I allow gender-specific references in direct quotes to remain as originally written.

In the course of writing *Daring*, Mulligan and I introduced the term *ethical prophecy* to describe that type of prophecy that is most consistent with that represented in the Hebrew prophets of ancient Israel. At the time we had no idea that Old Testament scholar Norman Snaith had actually used the term in *The Distinctive Ideas of the Old Testament* (1944). We later discovered that his understanding of the term was similar to ours. Snaith equated the term with eighth-century Hebrew prophecy, with its heavy emphasis on speaking God's truth to power and doing justice in righteous ways. Although strongly focused on ethical behavior, ethics as such was not the primary concern. To be sure, ethical teaching was significant, but it seemed to us that the greater emphasis was on the theological nature of the prophet's vocation. We and Snaith agreed that the ground of the prophets'

---

1. Mary Alice Mulligan, PhD, is an Affiliate Professor of Homiletics and Ethics at Christian Theological Seminary in Indianapolis, Indiana, and a senior minister in the Christian Church (Disciples of Christ).

teaching is found not in ethics but in theology. In other words, God is the fundamental source of ethical prophecy. The primary focus is on God, and only secondarily on right conduct or ethics. What do human beings mean to God, and what does God require of them? This is a basic question for the ethical prophet.

In yet another coauthored book with Mulligan, *Standing in the Margin* (2004), we devoted several pages to a brief discussion on six persons we believed to have been in the ethical prophet tradition: Menno Simons, Zilpha Elaw, Maria W. Stewart, Angelina E. Grimké, Martin Luther King Jr., and Óscar Romero.[2] We had plans of developing this into a much broader treatment of some of these and other select personalities. When our plans did not materialize as a coauthored project, I decided to take it up, and Mulligan graciously agreed to contribute the afterword.

What is an ethical prophet and what are some traits that characterize her? At least since the time of the eighth-century prophets of Israel the ethical prophet has been among the most peculiar personalities in history. Indeed, Abraham Joshua Heschel, an exemplary ethical prophet in his own right, whose theology of prophecy has much influenced this book, described the Hebrew prophets as "some of the most disturbing people"[3] to appear on the stage of history. More than their contemporaries, prophets are the personification of what may be referred to as the *ethics of maladjustment*. They reject anything in their society that is out of step with God's point of view. This stance may well contribute to the prophet's seeming peculiarity. The way Heschel put it is what should be remembered while reading this book: "The prophet is a person who suffers from a profound maladjustment to the spirit of society, with its conventional lies, with its concessions to man's weakness. Compromise is an attitude the prophet abhors. . . . The prophet's maladaptation to his environment may be characterized as *moral madness*."[4] Moreover, as far back as 1957 Martin Luther King Jr., also a paragon of ethical prophecy, declared that there were certain things—racism, economic injustice, and the madness of militarism, for example—that he absolutely would not adjust to, preferring instead to be "as maladjusted as the prophet Amos, who in the midst of the injustices of his day could cry out in words that echo across the centuries: 'Let justice roll down like waters and righteousness like a mighty stream.'"[5] The mind of the ethical prophet

---

2. Mulligan and Burrow, *Standing in the Margin*, 28–45.
3. Heschel, *Prophets*, xiii.
4. Heschel, *Prophets*, 408.
5. Carson et al., *Papers*, 6:475. See also 327.

appears to be in a realm that is different from that of most people, which is why she can say that she hears and sees what others do not.

The ethical prophet is less concerned about saving souls for heaven than speaking God's truth about sociopolitical and religious policies and practices that crush and demean human beings and the image of God in them. Prophets are concerned about the blood-and-guts, life-and-death issues of the world, not whether there is a heaven or hell on the other side of the grave. They see God's inexhaustible compassion, love, and concern for justice as grounded in God's concern for and involvement with human beings and what happens in the here and now. Indeed, the prophet's eye is always focused on the big, the small, and even the seemingly trivial sociopolitical issues of the day, not whether there might be streets of gold and lavish furniture in heaven. "This is why," said Heschel, "it is not enough for a prophet to be inspired by God; *he also must be informed about the world. The world and its fate are very dear to him*,"[6] as it is to God. The ethical prophet is not concerned about "the spiritual realities of the Beyond, but the life of the people; not the glories of eternity, but the blights of society. He addresses himself to those who trample upon the needy and destroy the poor of the land; who increase the price of grain, use dishonest scales, and sell the refuse of the corn (Amos 8:4–6). What the prophet's ear perceives is the word of God, but what the word contains is God's concern for the world."[7] Not heaven, but the margin or gutters of the world—that is the domain of the ethical prophet, who denounces all practices that diminish the sense of the dignity of persons and undermine the significance of the image of God in them. So let's be clear: the ethical prophet contends that God's special concern is not for the strong, the wealthy, and the powerful. Rather, the heart of God is on the side of the poor, weak, disinherited, downtrodden, and forgotten. God privileges these over their oppressors. This is but one way in which Heschel's theology of prophecy was a precursor to what came to be known in the 1970s as liberation theology.

The ethical prophet possesses the highest conceivable reverence for the worth and sacredness of persons as such and teaches that God imbues all persons with the divine image and creates them such that their very existence is based on their interrelationship with other persons and with God. Persons mean nothing if not viewed in terms of relationship with other persons and God. The relational element is inherent in human beings. To be a person is to be in relationship with other persons—human and divine. It is highly questionable that one can even be a person without other

6. Heschel, *Prophets*, 364 (my italics).
7. Heschel, *Prophets*, 364.

persons. Invoking the southern Bantu word *ubuntu* (meaning "humanity" and suggesting "personhood"), retired South Afrikan Archbishop Desmond Tutu contends that the term suggests that human beings are fundamentally "set in a delicate network of interdependence with our fellow human beings, and with the rest of God's creation. . . . It speaks of the fact that my humanity is caught up and inextricably bound up in yours. I am human because I belong."[8] The individual has been created such that she cannot exist alone. We can only be human together. Human beings are fundamentally "persons-in-community,"[9] or persons-in-relationship.

Going forward there are several traits of ethical prophecy that should be kept in mind, characteristics shared by our hall of fame candidates. First, the prophet's task is to convey God's point of view, to denounce everything that dehumanizes persons and forces them out of relationship with each other and with God. Failure in this regard requires that the prophet announce divine judgment, although such announcements are conditional upon humans' response to God's will and purpose. If the people hear God's word and respond appropriately, they will escape destruction.

Second, ethical prophets are committed to being the voice of the voiceless. This is clearly evident in the prophecy of Amos. His was not a voice that made uncertain or muffled sounds; neither was it a voice that could be terrorized into silence. Amos was clear about what God required him to do for those who had no voice in the presence of the powers and the privileged. Like other ethical prophets his voice was "often like thunder" and his words sounded "as if he were in a state of hysteria."[10] He had no interest in being subtle or equivocal in his speech; he was not concerned that some might be offended by God's razor-sharp truth or that he might incur their wrath. What mattered to him was making all aware of God's distaste for purely religious ceremony, since God privileges justice and righteousness over ritual,

---

8. Tutu, *God Has a Dream*, 25, 26. Similarly, Afrikan philosopher John S. Mbiti writes, "The individual can only say: 'I am, because we are; and since we are, therefore I am'" (*African Religions and Philosophy*, 106). The reader will note that throughout the book (except in direct quotations) I have consistently used the letter *k* in *Afrika* and *Afrikan* rather than the conventional *c*. It has been my practice to use these spellings in all published writings since the publication of my second book in 1999. I have done so out of respect for those who struggled for freedom in the United States and on the Afrikan continent in the 1960s, and because the use of the letter *c* reflects the Anglicized spellings; that letter does not exist in West Afrikan languages. Moreover, during the Black Consciousness Movement of the 1960s, a number of people adopted the use of *k*, which was consistent with the usage of many groups on the Afrikan continent and in diaspora.

9. Muelder, *Moral Law*, 29, 46, 113, entirety of chapter 2.

10. Heschel, *Prophets*, 308.

sacraments, and ceremony. The prophet's task is to convey this truth to the people and the powers.

Third, in her dealings with the powerful and privileged the ethical prophet always retains her autonomy. By doing so her prophetic and ethical edge is less likely to be blunted. Only as the prophet retains her sense of autonomy is it possible for her to be the conscience of a society and world that functions outside God's will. To retain her sense of autonomy and her commitment to God's expectations only, the prophet must be constantly vigilant about how she relates to the powers, the wealthy, and the privileged.

Fourth, at bottom the ethical prophet is always the servant of God, the poor, the oppressed, and others among the forgotten. She does not live above the people and does not accept rewards, favors, or even protection—things that are denied the people. Furthermore, the prophet generally lives among the people; she is one of (or with) the people.

Finally, and especially true of the Afrikan American religious and cultural tradition, ethical prophets are witnesses—witnesses to all that has happened to a people and to the vision of what they can be despite being dealt a poor hand by the powers. As witness the prophet is more than a messenger who conveys God's truth. Rather, "as a witness, he must bear testimony that the word is divine."[11] The prophet, knowing that there will be consequences and a price to pay, persists in bearing witness to the truth. She courageously tells the story of what God's word requires and bears witness to the truth of what human beings can become when they submit to, seek to understand, and live according to God's perspective and demands.

What Walter Rauschenbusch (1861–1918)—church historian, Christian ethicist, and leader of the white Social Gospel movement—said about Hebrew prophecy did much to further clarify the nature and meaning of ethical prophecy. Although Rauschenbusch did not use my nomenclature (i.e., *ethical prophet*) to describe the Hebrew prophets, he rightly saw them as religious reformers who unceasingly remonstrated against injustice and told the people and the powers what God required. In *Christianizing the Social Order* he had this to say about the role of the prophets:

> They were not discussing holiness in the abstract, but dealt with concrete, present-day situations in the life of the people which were sometimes due to the faults of the people themselves, but usually to the sins of the ruling classes. They demanded neighborly good will and humane care of the helpless. But their most persistent and categorical demand was that the men in power

---

11. Heschel, *Prophets*, 22.

should quit their extortion and judicial graft. They were trying to beat back the hand of tyranny from the throat of the people.[12]

Historically, the spirit of Hebrew prophecy has emerged whenever there was clear antagonism between the present order and what God requires.[13]

This view of the Hebrew prophets and their significance in the Jewish and Christian traditions had a strong influence on Martin Luther King Jr., one of our candidates for the ethical prophet hall of fame. In addition, Heschel, another of the hall of fame candidates, espoused ideas about the prophets that are similar to Rauschenbusch's, although I have as yet found no evidence that he actually read or was influenced by Rauschenbusch's writings. More importantly, there is no question that Heschel and Rauschenbusch had similar understandings of the prophets and their historical significance. For example, both were certain that a basic conviction of the prophets was that God demanded justice and righteousness, and only justice and righteousness. In addition, each was convinced that the prophets sought to convey the fundamental truth that religion and ethics are inseparable, a theme that is prominent throughout their writings. Furthermore, both men were adamant that right living is the true worship of God, not adherence solely to the sacraments, ritual, and formal worship. Also, for both men injustice and oppression were the twin evils that the Hebrew prophets fought so fervently and persistently against and for which they took the people and the powers to task. Eradicating injustice and oppression was uppermost in the mind of the prophets. The issue for them was not formal worship or ritualism, and it most assuredly was not those cute, fuzzy-warm, feel-good but unchallenging sermons that most church people expect to hear on Sunday morning and that preachers continue to preach as if their own and the people's salvation depend on it. The issue was God's demand that justice be done in righteous ways—ways that respect the dignity of the forgotten and left-outs.

And finally, suffice to say that Heschel and Rauschenbusch believed that the prophets were more concerned about the social morality of the nation than the morality of pious individuals. There is no question that the Bible and Jewish and Christian history provide many examples of concern for personal or private morality and religion. Moreover, there is no reason to doubt that the Hebrew prophets themselves saw the importance of formal worship, ritualism, and the sacraments, despite their staunch criticisms. The point is that the prophets did not see these as substitutes for seeking justice and righteousness. They were critical of ritualism and worship only

12. Rauschenbusch, *Christianizing*, 51.
13. Rauschenbusch, *Theology*, 195.

when these were made to appear more important to God than protesting against injustice, poverty, oppression, and other social ills. The response that Rauschenbusch gave to those who focus primarily on ritual, the sacraments, worship, and individual morality is consistent with the line of argument in this book: "If anyone holds that religion is essentially ritual and sacramental; or that it is purely personal; or that God is on the side of the rich; or that social interest is likely to lead preachers astray; he must prove his case with his eye on the Hebrew prophets, and the burden of proof is with him."[14]

The most striking difference between Heschel and Rauschenbusch is that Heschel grounded his entire theology of prophecy on the principle of *divine pathos*, the idea that God is deeply and irrevocably concerned about what happens to human beings. God is intimately and profoundly involved in what Heschel called the "everydayness" of human life. God is utterly preoccupied with human beings and all things—both weighty and trivial—that affect them. So profound is Heschel's doctrine of divine pathos that I have adopted, adapted, and incorporated it as the framework through which the meaning and importance of ethical prophecy is unfolded and advanced in this book.

Many may reject this interpretation of ethical prophecy and its significance. However, we will see that it is consistent with the understanding of the Hebrew prophets and the prophetic tradition as advocated throughout this text. Ethical prophecy has been dormant for much too long and needs to be liberated from the closets of the theological academy and religious institutions. The basic ideas of the prophetic tradition should be taught whether believers want to learn them or not; taught regardless of the amount of discomfort they may generate; taught because God requires that human beings see the world as God sees it.

As seen above, the Hebrew prophets focused on public or social morality more than on the private morality of individuals (e.g., "cussing," drinking, dancing, and premarital or extramarital sex). The criterion for true worship was not church membership or frequency of church attendance. *Instead, right living, ethical living was the true test of worship.* More than anyone before their time the prophets came preaching the inseparability of religion and ethics. Consequently, ethical prophets tended not to be among the most popular people of their day—and that same unpopularity besets the ethical prophets of our day.

Unpopularity of Ethical Prophets

While lamenting how unpopular prophets are, Otis Moss Jr.—pastor, activist, and close associate of Martin Luther King—gave an excellent description

14. Rauschenbusch, *Christianity and the Social Crisis*, 31.

of the type of prophet that inspired the writing of this book. Certain types of prophets are quite popular in religious institutions and society, but that is not the case with the prophet in the tradition of Jeremiah, Amos, Micah, Hosea, and Isaiah. The personalities discussed in this book stand squarely in the tradition of these prophets, and therefore have at one time or another been disliked, despised, excoriated, hated, and even killed.[15] Amos made the point when he declared, "They hate the one who reproves in the gate, and they abhor the one who speaks the truth" (Amos 5:10).

Reflecting on Martin Luther King Jr. as prophet, Moss rightly asserts what has long been true about the prophet's relation to the world: "The world does not like prophets. Prophets disturb us. They shake us out of our dogmatic slumber. So we prefer comfort to commitment. The world does not like prophets. Prophets override our creeds and our half-truths. Prophets expose our injustices and our contradictions and put to shame our mediocrity. The world does not like prophets and the church often refuses to celebrate them."[16] Indeed, Moss would have been just as accurate had he said that the church and other religious institutions often dislike prophets even more than the secular world does.

Most people use the word *prophet* rather loosely, implying that one can be a prophet of virtually anything—wealth, the economy, or politics. However, the focus of this book is on a particular type of prophet. Such ones are ethical prophets in the sense that they claim to be called as spokespersons for God; they courageously persist in speaking truth to power; and they relentlessly declare God's absolute concern and compassion for human beings and how they fare in the world. They are ethical prophets, but they are much more than this, since they believe that God *calls* them to declare God's unrelenting and overwhelming preoccupation with human beings.

The English word *prophet* is derived from the Greek word *prophētēs* (one who speaks for another). The Hebrew term for prophet in the Hebrew Bible is *nabi*, which is related to the Akkadian verb *nabu*, meaning "to call" or "to announce." There is no unanimity of agreement as to whether nabi has an *active* meaning (i.e., one who does the calling or announcing) or a *passive* meaning (i.e., one who is called to do the announcing). However, there is evidence that both the active and passive meanings are relevant for the type of prophecy and prophet under consideration. The prophet understood herself to be called and sent by God to deliver God's message to the people and the nation. There is therefore evidence of both the active and the passive meaning of nabi for the type of prophet discussed here. In addition,

---

15. Heschel, *Prophets*, 18.
16. Moss, "Prophetic Witness," 778.

the authority of the prophet lay not in herself but in God, who calls and commissions her to speak. Hebrew Bible scholar Bernhard Anderson made the point in a helpful way:

> The prophets understood themselves to be *sent*. They had received Yahweh's commission, "Go and say to my people." Moreover, a prophetic message often begins with the formula "Thus says Yahweh" and concludes with "the oracle of Yahweh" or "says Yahweh" (e.g., Amos 1:3-5; Jer 2:1-3; Isa 45:11-13). All of this indicates that the prophets thought of themselves as *messengers* sent to communicate "the word of Yahweh" to the people. Their authority lay not in themselves—in their religious experience or in their opinions—but in the One who had sent them.[17]

The ethical prophet answers first and last to the One who calls her, and she always has a sense of being committed to a higher purpose—to something much larger than herself. She has a strong sense that what she is doing is less about her and much more about the One who called and commissioned her.

The prophets were not concerned about the past or future as much as the present. They were interested in how the future or some prediction they announced might influence or impinge on the present. Therefore, their real concern was the here and now, that is, what happens in this world. They were not particularly concerned about what happens on the other side of the grave. The task of the prophet "was to communicate God's message for *now*, and to summon the people to respond *today*."[18] On some level the women and men discussed in this book believed themselves to be messengers of God's truth for their day.

For our purpose, *prophet* or *prophecy* means something much more substantial than what it seems to mean to most people, including many so-called born-again evangelical Christians and their leaders, who seem wholly unaware that Amos, Micah, Hosea, Jeremiah, and Isaiah ever existed. Indeed, according to the type of prophecy examined in this book God is "the supreme Subject, the One to Whom all prophetic events are referred as their source and initiator; the 'I' Who calls, questions, demands, and acts."[19] The God of the Hebrew prophets is the source of the call—the One to whom the called is ultimately responsible. As supreme Subject, the biblical God is preoccupied with human beings, concerned about and affected by all that happens to them.

17. Anderson, *Understanding the Old Testament*, 248-49.
18. Anderson, *Understanding the Old Testament*, 249.
19. Heschel, *Prophets*, 485.

Which God?

The Hebrew prophets revealed that the God of the Bible is wholly different from the god espoused by ancient Greek and Roman philosophers such as Plato, Aristotle, Epicurus, Epictetus, and Cicero. These held that inasmuch as the Good differs in nature from all else, it has no need for anything else, nor is it concerned about anything outside itself.[20] And yet, Plato's view of God is different from Aristotle's and Cicero's. Plato's description of the Idea of the Good resembles that of the Christian God (but is not synonymous with it) when he writes in the *Republic* that "for all things, this [the Form of the Good] is the cause of whatever is right and good; in the visible world it gives birth to light and to the lord of light, while it is itself sovereign in the intelligible world and the parent of intelligence and truth. Without having had a vision of this Form no one can act with wisdom, either in his own life or in matters of state."[21] According to Plato, God is creator, good, has perfect moral character, and is not indifferent to the world. This is similar to the Christian conception of God, but it falls way short because there is no evidence in Plato's doctrine that God is fully personal. Raphael Demos made the point when he wrote, "Plato's God is endowed with moral perfection. His god is not explicitly conceived as a person, it is true; nevertheless, he is a God of loving care for the world, and a God who takes sides in the moral conflict."[22] This god not only "observes the world" but "is aware of it in its details as well as in its general character, cherishes it, works on it."[23] These are traits of the Christian God as well. Still insisting that Plato's God is not personal to the degree that the Christian God is, Demos nevertheless writes that Plato's "God is a father and loving to his children, gentle, and using persuasion instead of compulsion. Also he rules by reason, not by law; he takes account of individual differences. Such a relation is that of person to person. It is not suggested that Plato conceived of God in terms of personality. For example, there is no trace of the idea of freedom of choice in Plato's account of God."[24] Freedom of choice is a fundamental trait of what it means to be a person. As much as Plato's God is similar to the Christian God, it is neither the Christian God nor the God of the Hebrew prophets.

Likewise, the self-sufficient "unmoved mover" of Aristotle who thinks only its own thoughts, is completely immutable, impassive, wholly actual, wholly separated from all else in life, and has no need of anything not itself

---

20. Heschel, *Prophets*, 234–35.
21. Plato, *Republic*, VII.517 (231).
22. Demos, *Philosophy of Plato*, 101.
23. Demos, *Philosophy of Plato*, 108.
24. Demos, *Philosophy of Plato*, 119.

is far from being the Jewish or Christian God. Aristotle's god, unlike the God of the prophets, did not create the universe and is not concerned about the world and the welfare of human beings. There is no divine providence. The object of this god's thought is itself, and therefore it thinks only of itself, not of human beings.[25]

For Cicero, god is in no way concerned about small matters, but only "attend[s] to great matters."[26] Similarly, the (slave) stoic philosopher Epictetus referenced this class of thinkers (i.e., Plato, Aristotle, and Cicero) when he said that they are clear that god exists and exhibits concern, "but only in respect of great and heavenly things, but of nothing that is on the earth."[27] Although aware of human beings' existence, such a god is at best indifferent to their daily experiences in the world. But once again, this is not the God of the Bible generally, or of the Hebrew prophets in particular. Instead, the God of the prophets is supremely good and unremittingly concerned about human beings and all—including small matters—that affects them. This is the central principle in Heschel's theology of prophecy. No subject is as worthy of consideration by God as are human beings. It is to this God that the one who is called owes her utmost loyalty and allegiance. Heschel rightly declares that the very mind of the God of the Hebrew prophets is "preoccupied with man, with the concrete actualities of history rather than with the timeless issues of thought."[28]

The type of prophecy reflected in the witness and work of the persons discussed in this book requires that one believe in God as the highest good; be able to hear and see what others do not; be a sharp social critic in light of God's demand that justice should be done in righteous ways; be in step with God's relentless care, compassion, and concern for human beings and the world; and be aware that God and human beings need each other to achieve God's purpose. It is not a one-way relationship. Human beings need God, but God—unlike the god of the philosophers—also needs human beings. Candidates for the ethical prophet hall of fame are quite certain of the mutual relationship between God and human beings—that God cannot and will not do for human beings what they can and must do for themselves and that human beings need God's assistance.

We will see that ethical prophecy makes the absolute sacredness of human beings a fundamental concern. The ethical prophet is deeply concerned

---

25. Gilson, *God and Philosophy*, 34. See also Jones, *History of Western Philosophy*, 231.
26. Heschel, *Prophets*, 5.
27. Epictetus, *Teaching*, 193.
28. Heschel, *Insecurity of Freedom*, 102.

about anything that undermines the worth of persons. But in an even more profound sense, she wishes to convey to the world that the value of human beings is grounded in the goodness, love, and compassion of God and that human beings are infinitely valuable because they are called into existence, sustained, and loved by the highest good in the universe—the God of the Hebrew prophets.

When we acknowledge God as the highest good, it should not be difficult to develop a sense of moral outrage against injustices that are done to human beings—who are immeasurably precious to God. This awareness opens up an entirely new world of knowing, for it means that human beings—insofar as they are capable—are now (to some degree) able to see and think of the world as God does. God is concerned about the massive numbers of poor people who are displaced and made homeless in order to satisfy the selfish desires of the well-to-do. As the highest good, God is that for which human beings ought to live and toward which they ought to strive in all that they do. In this regard, God has the prophet Jeremiah remind us that if we must boast about anything at all, let it not be material things such as wealth and power. Instead, let us boast that we know and are faithful to the God of the universe, the greatest and highest good who acts and delights in "steadfast love, justice, and righteousness" (Jer 9:23–24).

The Keenness of the Prophet's Hearing and Seeing

The ethical prophet is able to hear and see what others do not. Her ear is "attuned to a cry imperceptible to others."[29] This means, in part, that she is able to detect and is concerned about the smallest matters that adversely affect human beings. Heschel argued convincingly that the sensitivity and perceptivity of the prophet's ear is such that she is able (and willing!) to hear what others do not. Accordingly, the notes sounded by the prophet are one octave too high for most to hear and decipher. However, the prophet has the ear, voice, and sensitivity of God, and therefore is able not only to hear but also to understand and withstand what is heard and to communicate this to the people and the powers.

Just what is it that the prophet hears and sees that others do not? The prophet perceives and hears the silent agony of the poor and the oppressed and cannot hold her peace or remain silent. The presence of even the slightest amount of suffering and social evil is neither tolerable nor acceptable to her. She knows that it is not abstract human beings who are being oppressed and treated unjustly but flesh-and-blood individuals who have names and actual lives and who belong to and are loved by God. So, even when it seems

---

29. Heschel, *Prophets*, 7.

that the United States is having a good year economically, the prophet is gravely disturbed because of her keen awareness of the existence of unnecessary pain and suffering within certain groups of human beings because they are denied adequate financial and other life-sustaining resources. Although the U.S. stock market in 2018 reached its highest levels in history, it benefited the poor and the middle class only slightly, if at all. The prophet cries out loudly and agonizingly against the suffering that many people (usually the rich and powerful) find to be "acceptable." Heschel tells us that "we and the prophet have no language in common. To us the moral state of society, for all its stains and spots, seems fair and trim; to the prophet it is dreadful."[30] To most people a little crime here, a little injustice there, and a little mistreatment of children, the elderly and others among the most vulnerable is not the worst state of affairs, is not a state of emergency at all, but rather is thought to be tolerable. But to the ethical prophet it is not in the least tolerable. *It is catastrophic.* That the prophet employs notes that are one octave too high for others to hear and interpret makes her both sensitive and outraged at what others frequently do not hear or see in society. If they do see and hear they—like Donald J. Trump, his unthinking followers, and virtually all congressional Republicans—pretend that they do not. But most often they simply fail to see, or ignore, what is staring them in the face. They choose to be indifferent, a most dreadful evil in itself, of which the prophets of old were sharply critical.

Not only does the ethical prophet see and hear what others do not, she also possesses keen socio-analytical skills, a point borne out by each of the candidates for the ethical prophet hall of fame. For example, at a time when it was not popular to criticize United States foreign policy, Heschel and King were among the most courageous, outspoken, passionate, incisive critics of the war in Vietnam, and both paid a heavy price for their outspokenness. When religious leaders and politicians were soft-spoken or even silent on racism, poverty, and war, Heschel's and King's voices boomed thunderously and persistently against them. They were men of deep religious convictions whose faithfulness to God and their call led them to be outspoken social critics. They were true "profiles in courage."[31] The ethical prophet does not remain silent in the face of social injustice and other wrongdoing. She finds a way to express God's displeasure, which is also *her* displeasure. Each of our hall of fame candidates courageously spoke truth to power while conveying God's message. When the prophet rails against injustice in light of God's understanding and perspective regarding human existence, she does so without expecting to receive societal or religious accolades.

30. Heschel, *Prophets*, 9.
31. John F. Kennedy wrote a popular book by this title.

The ethical prophet challenges attitudes, traditions, and practices that have been uncritically accepted by people and society: "Beliefs cherished as certainties, institutions endowed with supreme sanctity, he exposes as scandalous pretensions."[32] How is it that institutions and buildings—including churches, synagogues, and mosques—are in themselves touted as possessing sacredness and dignity? Nowhere in the Bible, nowhere in the best of Jewish and Christian history and tradition, nowhere in the Qur'an are we told that God created institutions and buildings in God's image and infused them with ineradicable sacredness. This is said only of human beings. Because the ethical prophet realizes that she is not involved in a popularity contest—that her obligation is to obey God's commands first and last—she is not hesitant to criticize any and all who seem to behave contrary to what God requires. And what does God require, but that we do justice, love mercy, and walk humbly with God (Mic 6:8)? The ethical prophet always criticizes things as they are, in light of her understanding of what God requires.

The *ethical prophet hall of famer* lives by the conviction that God and human beings need each other. She has no patience for the long-held traditional view that there is a one-way relationship between God and human beings. That God also needs human beings says something about how significant and valuable human beings are to God. God not only creates human beings but also remains near enough to them to reveal God's concern and God's need of their help in achieving God's purpose in the world. That God needs human beings says less about a lack of divine power and more about the reciprocal nature of the divine-human relationship.

God in Search of Human Beings

The ethical prophet is certain that God is always in search of human beings, in the hope that they will hear and obey God's summons to return to covenant relationship with God and with each other. This is reminiscent of the idea that God is always turning toward human beings—what Heschel calls *anthropotropism*. Accordingly, the Bible is not human beings' story about God but God's story about human beings in the world. It is the story of God's initiative in persistently pursuing and searching for human beings.[33] The Bible and the prophets especially depict God as always taking the initiative in this regard. This means that human beings *respond* to God's initiative. The

---

32. Heschel, *Prophets*, 10.

33. God in search of human beings is a fundamental theme in Heschel's theology of prophecy. Readers get a good sense of this subject in *The Prophets* and in other of his writings as well. In addition, Heschel addresses this theme systematically in *God in Search of Man*.

chief example in the Bible of God turning toward human beings is God's call to the prophets to accept the prophetic mission and to proclaim God's truth. This is all wholly initiated by God.[34] More than Friedrich Schleiermacher's doctrine of the "feeling of absolute dependence"[35] on God, the most unique quality of awareness that characterizes biblical religion is, according to Heschel, "an awareness of a God who helps, demands, and calls upon man. It is a sense of being pursued, being found, and being reached by God."[36] Without using the term *anthropotropism*, Martin Luther King characterized it as the prophet (e.g., Micah) taking God to the people and pleading for God.[37] But also like Heschel, King insisted that it was not a matter of human beings searching for God but of God "unwearily" and persistently searching for human beings, so that even when human beings pray they are responding to some action by God.[38]

The Bible also teaches—and we will see that the personalities discussed in this book agree—that God's turning toward human beings was only part of the story. Human beings also turn toward God—what Heschel calls *theotropism*. This is what happens when human beings seek communion with God through worship, the sacraments, praise, and/or prayer—what King referred to as the priest (e.g., Moses) taking the people to God and pleading on their behalf.[39] It is important to remember that it is never God who actually turns away from human beings, no matter what we do to shame ourselves, others, the rest of the created order, and God. God steadfastly turns toward human beings and thus is always present and concerned—and never indifferent—to what happens to us. Although when things get difficult our inclination is to say that God has turned away from us, the argument of this book is that it is truer to say that human beings, by our choices and behavior, turn away from God. For this is a God who totally and relentlessly searches for human beings in the hope that they will return to covenant relation. This is the God of ethical prophecy.

A Forward Look

My thinking about ethical prophecy is much influenced by the theology of prophecy so admirably developed and lived by Rabbi Abraham Joshua

---

34. Heschel, *Prophets*, 440.
35. Schleiermacher, *Christian Faith*, 12–18.
36. Heschel, *Prophets*, 440.
37. King, "Speech at Staff Retreat, Penn Center," 30.
38. Carson et al., *Papers*, 6:409, 410.
39. King, "Speech at Staff Retreat, Penn Center," 30.

Heschel, and the reader will see his influence throughout. The book is divided into two parts. Part 1 focuses on the nature and meaning of ethical prophecy and consists of one chapter. I consider this the pivotal chapter since it lays out the meaning of the type of prophecy under consideration and discusses its criteria.

It was by sheer accident that I discovered Heschel's amazing book *The Prophets* (1962) as I was browsing in the stacks at the Christian Theological Seminary (CTS) library in Indianapolis, Indiana, not long after I began teaching there. It was also during this period that I met Heschel's only child, Professor Susannah Heschel, who kindly and enthusiastically agreed to write the foreword to this book. In any case, I made Heschel's book required reading for more than two decades in a required course for Master of Divinity students titled Prophetic and Ethical Witness of the Church. The book was a revision and expansion of Heschel's doctoral dissertation. I later learned from an article by Susannah Heschel that the book also influenced several of King's lieutenants and close advisors, including Andrew Young, James Lawson, Bayard Rustin, C. T. Vivian, and Vincent Harding. She said that these carried around a copy of the book for inspiration.[40] Edward Kaplan observes that as a seminary student Young was introduced to Heschel's book and later was impressed that an academic of Heschel's stature agreed to march with them from Selma to Montgomery, Alabama.[41] Looking back, Young referred to Heschel as one of his heroes.[42] At any rate, when I read in Heschel's book that the prophets came to teach human beings that God is preeminently concerned about what happens to them and is affected by it all, I was completely sold on the type of prophecy he was writing about. When I taught at United Theological Seminary of the Twin Cities during the 2016–17 school year I taught Ethical Prophecy. *The Prophets* was required reading in that course as well, and its impact on the students was no less profound than on those at CTS.

Chapter 1 of *Ethical Prophets along the Way* presents a theology of ethical prophecy and how it may be witnessed to and lived out. To this end the chapter examines the theology of prophecy developed by Heschel, who, in 1963, became a close friend of Martin Luther King. In addition to allowing so much of his adult public life to be guided and influenced by the teachings and example of the Hebrew prophets, Heschel did not pass up opportunities to tell the people and the powers about the God of the prophets, as well as what God expected of them. Like the prophets, Heschel

40. S. Heschel, "Two Friends, Two Prophets," 4.
41. Kaplan, *Spiritual Radical*, 222.
42. Young, *Easy Burden*, 364.

exemplified courage and character the likes of which eluded most of his contemporaries. Without question, he paid dearly for declaring "thus says the Lord" about racism, war, anti-Semitism, economic exploitation, injustice, and other social evils in the world and the demand to eradicate them. As in subsequent chapters, this one provides brief biographical information on the hall of fame candidate under discussion. In addition, the chapter cites and discusses criteria that position Heschel well as a candidate for the ethical prophet hall of fame.

This first chapter also names and discusses a number of elements of ethical prophecy that Heschel identified and discussed during his study of the prophets: the call, the importance of speaking truth to power, the inestimable sacredness of persons, the use of sweeping allegations, the place of divine judgment, the cost of prophecy, and hope. While a similar pattern is followed in the remaining chapters, the aim in each is to discuss the criteria that seem most relevant in the work of the candidate being discussed. Knowing what the meaning and criteria of ethical prophecy are makes it possible to identify ethical prophets, as well as pretenders.

Part 2 focuses on other select candidates for the ethical prophet hall of fame and is comprised of seven chapters, roughly arranged in historical order. Ethical prophets may be found among both women and men, as well as in each racial-ethnic group. Consequently, although frequently the tendency has been to exclude women when discussing ethical prophecy, readers will see that historically some of the greatest, most courageous representatives of this type of prophecy have been women. When I finally made the decision to write this book, I took as a given that women must necessarily be included, not in passing or peripherally, but as major characters and contributors to the ethical prophet tradition and the effort to make people and the world better than they are. I examine the ethical prophetic witness of three women—one white and two Afrikan American—in different periods of United States history. Angelina E. Grimké's prophetic and ethical witness is the subject of chapter 2. A nineteenth-century abolitionist and feminist who grew up in Charleston, South Carolina, Grimké, even as a young girl, rejected the enslavement of the Afrikans. She and her sister, Sarah, became leaders in the women's rights movement and staunch advocates for the immediate abolition of enslaved Afrikans. The chapter names and discusses elements of ethical prophecy such as the call; speaking the truth in love; the sacredness of persons; the demand for justice; and the importance of divine judgment. These and other traits are examined to show how they were manifested in Angelina Grimké's life and work.

Yet another woman in the ethical prophet tradition, Ida B. Wells-Barnett, is the subject of chapter 3. She was born just months before President

Abraham Lincoln issued the Emancipation Proclamation. When her parents and baby brother died during a yellow fever epidemic she insisted on becoming the guardian and primary caregiver of her siblings. Taking charge in this way proved to be a defining trait that remained with her throughout her career. This was especially important because she was both black and a woman and therefore was expected to be submissive to whites and to all men. Much like Angelina Grimké, Wells-Barnett early discovered the power of the pen and the power of voice as potential weapons in the struggle for her people's freedom. While still a young woman, her "deep and abiding love for people" in general, and her own people more particularly, led her to become a virtual one-woman crusader against lynching.

Chapter 4 introduces the reader to James Baldwin, who ultimately became so disillusioned with the church that he was compelled to leave it in order to learn what it truly meant to be a Christian. Baldwin's appreciation for theological matters, especially his belief about what God requires of those who claim to be religious, never diminished. He remained what may be characterized as an armchair theologian whose writings and speeches sought to show that human beings can be better than they are. The chapter reveals Baldwin's God to be one who privileges the oppressed, downtrodden, and forgotten over the rich and powerful. His is a God of love-justice and liberation. It will also be seen that like most literary artists of his type, Baldwin thought of himself as an artist or poet. The significance of this for our purpose is that he thought of the artist and poet in ways that are similar to my portrayal of the ethical prophet. We will also see that while Baldwin provides no explicit call narrative, the evidence is overwhelming that he was called to his work as artist and witness. The inclusion of Baldwin (and, in chapter 8, Alice Walker) is a reminder that the God of the Hebrew prophets can choose whoever God wills to be messenger to the people and the nations. No matter the prophet's vocation or profession, God calls her to be God's voice from wherever she is stationed, including within the ranks of literary artists.

Malcolm X is best remembered for his controversial phrases "by any means necessary" and "the white man is the devil." Although as a boy he was taught the fundamentalist Christianity of his father, who was a Pentecostal minister and follower of Marcus Garvey, Malcolm did not take this faith as his own. Rather, while in prison in Massachusetts, he accepted the Islamic faith as interpreted by Elijah Muhammad. Malcolm became one of the most severe critics of Christianity. Although other hall of fame candidates were also strong critics of Christianity, they did not, like Malcolm, reject it entirely. And yet, chapter 5 reveals that many of the criteria for ethical prophecy are just as prominent in Malcolm's Muslim ministry. Some of these—the emphasis on the sacredness of *all* persons, for example—attain prominence only *after* his break with the Nation of Islam and his religious pilgrimage to Mecca. It will be seen that some of the elements of ethical prophecy came to light only after Malcolm began doing his own thinking and after he broke with Elijah Muhammad. We will see that Malcolm took the idea of making sweeping generalizations or exaggerations, especially regarding one's opponent or the nation, to an entirely new level in comparison with other hall of fame candidates. "The white man" (not "some" white men) "is the devil," he declared. Malcolm also exhibited a strong belief in divine judgment if racist whites did not cease their devilish behavior and work instead for the elimination of racism and economic injustice.

Chapter 6 focuses on Martin Luther King Jr., his understanding of ethical prophecy, and how its elements were manifested in his civil rights and antiwar ministries. It will be seen that from the time he was a boy, King heard his father and other black ministers preach about the prophets and their understanding of what God required of the people and the nations. These ministers were concerned about what was happening in God's world and were committed to conveying their sense of what God required. By the time King began full-time ministry in Montgomery, Alabama, he was already fully committed to ethical prophecy and its importance for the work that lay ahead. This chapter reveals that Martin Luther King Jr. understood prophecy in much the same way as Heschel and explained and literally applied its principles in the hot, even deadly cauldron of the civil rights and peace movements. The chapter depicts a King who frequently stressed, indeed lived out, a number of the traits of ethical prophecy, not least his emphasis on the divine call, the sacredness of persons, the divine command to do justice, the importance of divine judgment, the cost of prophecy, and hope for a better world as articulated through his doctrine of the *beloved community*.

Unlike the other ethical prophet hall of fame candidates, the one discussed in chapter 7 was not a citizen of the United States. Óscar Arnulfo Romero was a Roman Catholic archbishop in El Salvador. When he was appointed, the powers believed that he could be easily manipulated and controlled and therefore would not be a threat to the oligarchs and the rulers. But God apparently also had a plan to be enacted, one that did not include Romero in the role of patsy to the ruling class and the military junta. Indeed, the murder of Father Rutilio Grande not long after Romero's appointment as archbishop turned out to be the occasion for his own conversion to the poor and the prophetic church. Subsequently, for the next three years—what would be the last three years of his life—Romero's witness was that of ethical prophet extraordinaire. We will see that Romero, like King and Malcolm, remained faithful to God's call, spoke truth to power, insisted on the sacredness of all persons, warned of God's judgment for social wrongdoing, and retained a strong sense of hope right up to the time his voice was silenced by an assassin's bullet.

Chapter 8 is the final chapter of this book. The reader is introduced to another outstanding representative of ethical prophecy among literary artists, the distinguished, Pulitzer Prize–winning writer Alice Walker. Similar to James Baldwin, Walker thinks of herself as artist or poet and understands this in much the same way as Baldwin. Having grown up in a Methodist church in rural Georgia, as a college student she came to reject much of Christianity as taught and lived by her parents, although she remains a woman of deep spirituality and religious faith. Her views on God are nontraditional and provocative, and this includes how she names God—as, for example, "Mother," "Nature," and "It." Walker is certain that human beings are not in life's struggle alone—that they are always in the care of something larger than themselves.

Concerned about the plight of the human race in general and black women more especially, Walker took the lead in helping black women name themselves and their sociopolitical project. Focusing on black women's bold self-determination, sassiness, and their propensity to talk back, she settled on the term *womanist*. In addition, she is concerned to highlight the significance of the sacredness of human beings generally and black women especially. She insists on the need to treat black women justly and to speak truth to the people and to power. Moreover, the chapter reveals Walker's sense of divine judgment and her awareness of the cost of witnessing against injustice. But Walker, too, leaves us with a vision of hope, such that doom and judgment do not get the last word.

In the life and witness of each of the hall of fame candidates discussed in this book the reader is introduced to an example of what an ethical prophet looks like. Such a prophet, like the prophet Micah, is generally a member of the community and close to the common, ordinary people who are systematically oppressed by the privileged and powerful. This is an important trait of the hall of fame candidates. The hope is that readers will allow the witness and example of these personalities to so influence their lives that they, too, will develop the courage to speak truth to power and to recognize that they need not leave the world as it was when they were born into it—and that they will begin doing all they can to make persons and the world better than they are.

PART 1

The Nature of Ethical Prophecy

1

Setting the Stage: Contributions of Abraham J. Heschel

My understanding of ethical prophecy[1] is much influenced by the teaching, witness, and prophetic social activism of Rabbi Abraham Joshua Heschel (1907–72), longtime professor at the Jewish Theological Seminary in New York City. He championed interfaith dialogue at a time when it was not popular to do so; he was an official observer at the Second Vatican Council; he challenged the long legacy of anti-Semitism in the Catholic Church and its desire to proselytize the Jews, and sent a letter to Augustin Cardinal Bea suggesting that "the formulation of the dogmas of biblical inspiration within the church were influenced by Jewish perspectives."[2] In addition, and significantly, Heschel greatly anticipated what came to be known as liberation theology in the 1970s, with his emphasis on liberation and justice for the poor and oppressed; his accent on knowing what one sees rather than seeing what one knows; his stressing the deed rather than words, or actions rather than thought;[3] and his frequent insistence that God privileges the poor and oppressed over the rich and powerful, as expressed in his statement in 1963 that

---

1. Mary Alice Mulligan and I introduced the term *ethical prophecy* in our book *Daring to Speak in God's Name* (2002). Norman Snaith cited the term in *The Distinctive Ideas of the Old Testament* (59), but we came to this nomenclature on our own, prior to reading his book.

2. Quoted in S. Heschel, foreword to *Heavenly Torah*, xix.

3. Rothschild, *Between God and Man*, 81–82.

"the Bible insists that the interests of the poor have precedence over the interests of the rich. The prophets have a bias in favor of the poor."[4] This latter was a clear anticipation of liberation theology's concept of God's "preferential option" for the poor.[5] Without question, and so clearly implied in these four emphases, the liberation theme is one that begs for attention in Heschel studies.

Furthermore, Heschel and Martin Luther King Jr. shared many important ideas in common; both were strongly influenced by the eighth-century prophets and applied their teachings to the civil, human rights, and peace movements. The two men became fast and close friends after first meeting at the Conference on Race in Chicago in 1963 where each gave outstanding keynote addresses. Nearly two years later, at King's urgent request, Heschel marched with him after the tragic "bloody Sunday" march in Selma, Alabama, in 1965. He was seated near King on the dais at Riverside Church on April 4, 1967, when King delivered his famous address against the war in Vietnam precisely one year before he was assassinated. Heschel was a cofounder of Clergy Concerned about Vietnam, the organization that invited King to give the Riverside speech. The two men also stood next to each other during a prayer vigil-protest at Arlington National Cemetery on February 6, 1968, two months before King was assassinated. Just like King, Heschel was staunchly and passionately critical of the injustices to which blacks were subjected, such as racism and economic exploitation.

Heschel's sixtieth birthday was the occasion for what became a famous conversation between Conservative rabbis and Martin Luther King Jr. just two weeks before King was assassinated. During that event King and Heschel praised each other. King referred to Heschel as "one of the truly great men of our day and age. . . . He is indeed a truly great prophet."[6] King did not consider Heschel to be one of those many religious leaders who stand in the face of injustice and other social evils while "mouthing pious irrelevancies and sanctimonious trivialities." Instead, he said, "I feel that Rabbi Heschel is one of the persons who is relevant at all times, always

---

4. Heschel, *Insecurity of Freedom*, 95. Interestingly enough, a dozen or so years before the emergence of liberation theology, Karl Barth stressed this very idea when he wrote that "God always takes His stand unconditionally and passionately on this side and on this side alone: against the lofty and on behalf of the lowly; against those who already enjoy right and privilege and on behalf of those who are denied it and deprived of it" (*Church Dogmatics*, 2/1:386).

5. See the important discussion by Gutiérrez where he interprets the meaning of "preferential option" ("Liberation and the Poor," 22–63). See also Eagleson and Scharper, *Puebla and Beyond*, for the complete document titled "A Preferential Option for the Poor," 264–67.

6. King, "Conversation," 658.

standing with prophetic insights to guide us through these difficult days."[7] King also acknowledged that Heschel had been with them in many of their campaigns for civil rights. We will see in chapter 6 that Heschel was equally commendatory of King. Susannah Heschel rightly observes that more than any other Jewish leader Heschel "brought King and his message to a wide Jewish audience, and King made Heschel a central figure in the struggle for civil rights."[8]

Interestingly enough, Heschel and King referred to each other as a prophet, although neither made a habit of referring to himself that way. To an extent that we do not find in many in the ethical prophet tradition, these two men often explicitly acknowledged how they were influenced by the Hebrew prophets. They frequently quoted the prophets and their demand that justice should be done and were convinced that divine judgment was the price for failure to do so. They also spoke and wrote about the prophets in order to teach about their meaning and expectations.

I begin with this chapter on Heschel because he actually developed a viable and quite profound theology of prophecy based on his research and reflections on the Hebrew prophets and his experience in Nazi Europe. He grounded his theology of prophecy on the doctrine of *divine pathos*, the idea that God is preeminently concerned about human beings and is always searching for them to return to covenant relationship with God and each other. The approach to prophecy in this book, then, is unapologetically Heschellian, as seen and interpreted through the cultural lens and experience of an Afrikan American theological social ethicist.

I do not pretend that Heschel's theology of prophecy is the only approach to prophecy. It is not. However, in my own work I have found his approach to be the most consistent with my reading and understanding of the Hebrew prophets of ancient Israel and what that type of prophecy should mean for individuals, religious institutions, and the world today. In addition, I find that Heschel's theology of prophecy is amazingly similar to that found in the black religious tradition and among blacks who frequently invoked the prophets' theme of justice and righteousness from the time of American slavery to the civil and human rights movements and beyond. The prophets stressed the need to convey God's point of view to the people and the powers regarding the divine requirement to do justice in the world. Moreover, they came to tell the people about God's unrelenting compassion and concern for their welfare.

---

7. King, "Conversation," 659.
8. S. Heschel, "Two Friends, Two Prophets," 2.

Who was Rabbi Abraham Joshua Heschel, and why are he and his ideas about prophecy so important for us today? The biographical information that follows is largely provided by Heschel's only child, Susannah Heschel, a prominent Jewish feminist theologian, teacher, and publishing scholar who has taught at a number of colleges, and presently is Eli Black Professor of Jewish Studies at Dartmouth College. After providing a sense of who Rabbi Heschel was, I turn to a brief discussion of his theology of divine pathos, which I consider to be the touchstone of his theology of prophecy. Afterward, I discuss a number of specific elements of ethical prophecy that one finds in his work. My argument is that when these elements are present in the life and work of a person, he is quite likely an ethical prophet. Since this is (in the social science sense) a *type* of prophecy, we should not expect to find perfect manifestations of its elements in any of the personalities discussed in this book. Some of the elements will be more obviously present in the witness and work of some personalities than in others. In the chapters that follow, I apply these elements to the women and men considered for induction into the ethical prophet hall of fame. We begin with a consideration of who Heschel was and some of the basic principles of ethical prophecy in his teaching and writing.

Who Was Abraham Joshua Heschel?

Abraham Joshua Heschel was a revered Jewish rabbi, civil rights and antiwar activist, theologian, and prolific publishing scholar. He knew that it was not possible for human beings to attain final Truth, but he believed there was much to be said for the sense of wonder about Truth. There was much to be said about the desire, the spirit, the quest, and the journey toward Truth. Heschel was certain that the quest for Truth itself is a lifetime journey and adventure. Anyone who reads and ponders his writings knows that he spent his life journeying toward Truth, and, along the way, he shared with others aspects of the Truth that were revealed to him through study, meditation, prayer, and social activism.

Heschel was adamant that human beings' concern ought to be with "the everydayness" of life on earth—its joys, hopes, frustrations, and disappointments. In this, he would have agreed with James Baldwin, who held that it would be the gravest mistake not to live life to the fullest. One lives life to the fullest, and most effectively, *by living according to God's understanding and expectations of human beings in the world.* This means, minimally, that God expects that human beings will lead lives exemplified by service and by reverence to and for persons, for every person is inestimably precious and sacred to God.

One senses in Heschel's writings an overwhelming concern and passion for living life to the fullest, for living life well and for doing all that he could to make life both worth living and worthy of redemption by God. I know of no greater authority, living or dead, who has not only written bounteously, passionately, and profoundly on what this book calls *ethical prophecy*, but who also sees prophecy as the most religious way of living in the world, than Abraham Joshua Heschel.

Prophetic ethics is generally relegated to a footnote in ministry and in theological social ethics, if it gets mentioned at all. In part, my aim is to contribute to reversing the long-standing practice of addressing ethical prophecy in seminaries and in ministry as if it were only an addendum to be considered *if* time and space permits. The only ministry and the only theological ethics that makes sense to me is that which takes seriously the Hebrew prophetic tradition. Once one comes to this conclusion, it will be necessary to work tirelessly and continuously to apply the teachings and principles of prophecy to what is happening in all areas of life and the world.

On a number of occasions Heschel wrote and spoke of his early desire that his would be a life of reading, study, teaching, writing, and publishing—a life of privacy and peace of mind, devoted to trying to unravel the mystery of the meaning of life and the ultimate issues of philosophy and theology. It was his intention to be a teacher and scholar. We will see, however, that the God of his faith, and the events of his day, prompted a different path, although inclusive of teaching and scholarship.

In retrospect, Heschel said that three experiences forced him to take a different path. The first was his experiences in Germany, including Hitler's rise to power and the failure of Christian scholars in Germany to stand up and support the Jews. This failure hurt him deeply and violated his sense of peace of mind that was needed to be a first-rate scholar. The second experience was his discovery that "indifference to evil" was no solution, but rather was worse than evil itself,[9] a conviction he arrived at largely through systematic study of the Hebrew prophets. "All prophecy is one great exclamation," Heschel wrote. "*God is not indifferent to evil!* He is always concerned. He is personally affected by what man does to man. He is a God of pathos"[10]—concerned about even the most trivial things that happen to human beings. Therefore, those who claim to serve God must not be indifferent to evil. Heschel came to see that no matter how important the work of scholarship is one's participation in it must never be a justification or excuse for cool

9. Heschel, *Prophets*, 284.
10. Heschel, *Prophets*, 284 (my italics).

indifference in the face of injustice and other forms of cruelty to human beings.

The third thing that led Heschel to change his mind and drove him from the comfort and isolation of the scholar's study was his decision to undertake an intensive and critical study of the Hebrew prophets. He had in fact written his doctoral dissertation on the consciousness of the prophets. His renewed interest and study of these most peculiar biblical personalities led to the publication in 1962 of what is arguably his most important work, *The Prophets*. This book, as much as any, led to Heschel's involvement in the civil rights and antiwar movements of the 1960s. In addition, the book was reportedly influential to a number of Martin Luther King Jr.'s associates.

In part, the reason that Heschel turned to an intensive study of the Hebrew prophets was his disenchantment with the way philosophy was being taught at the university in Berlin. As a doctoral student, who also had his feet firmly on the ground, he came to the conclusion that philosophy was being taught in ways that did not provide answers to the real issues of life and death that adversely affected the lives of flesh-and-blood human beings. Abstract philosophy had no answers to the plight of his people. His study of the prophets was an important corrective, inasmuch as it helped him understand that God was not pleased about what was happening to the Jews and other innocent, defenseless people; that God was not indifferent to but rather cared deeply about persons and what was happening to them; and that every person shares in responsibility for what happens in God's world, even if particular persons are not guilty of the actual causes of specific social evils. By virtue of being moral agents created in freedom, every person is at least responsible for how he responds to what happens in the world. In part, this stance led to Heschel's oft-stated view that "few are guilty, but all are responsible."[11] It may be that only a few are guilty of causing a specific social evil, but all are responsible for how they respond to it. Indeed, "in a free society," Heschel often proclaimed, "All are involved in what some are doing."[12] Heschel's study of the prophets led him to the renewed conviction that God is immanent in, and intimately involved in, the everyday affairs of human beings and cares about it all. Heschel, against much of ancient philosophy and theology, did not see God as being deaf or indifferent to the plight of human beings.

The prophets taught Heschel that the moral comprehension of human beings is frequently impoverished to the point that they easily tolerate what they deem to be minor injustices and assaults on human dignity. The

---

11. Heschel, *Prophets*, 16.
12. Heschel, "Moral Outrage of Vietnam," 50.

prophet denounces injustice on any level, as well as the assailing of human worth. In addition, so out of touch is the moral sense of many individuals that they readily tolerate injustices done to certain groups of people, such as the poor and people of color, as if these are not as important as their group. Heschel insisted that every human being is important and that one who takes seriously the Hebrew prophetic tradition knows without doubt that *every* human life is significant and precious to God.

By immersing himself in the study of the prophets, Heschel underwent a radical conversion that transformed him to the uttermost depths of his being. The words and lives of the prophets helped him see clearly that "morally speaking there is no limit to the concern one must feel for the suffering of human beings."[13] One who gives serious attention to the message of the prophets cannot avoid being deeply troubled about injustice and oppression, whether committed against an individual or a group. Such a one no longer finds even minor infractions or violations of human dignity to be permissible or tolerable. Rather, he is sensitive to the divine perspective and is therefore outraged at *every* insult to human dignity.

Heschel through the Eyes of His Daughter

Most of the biographical information that follows is based on four informative biographical sketches written by Susannah Heschel. These are not identical, and therefore each should be read by anyone who is truly interested in the life and work of Rabbi Heschel. One of these appears as the introduction to Heschel's reissued book *God in Search of Man* (1987),[14] originally published in 1955; it was also published in *To Grow in Wisdom: An Anthology of Abraham Joshua Heschel*, edited by Jacob Neusner with Noam M. M. Neusner (1990). Yet another appears as the introduction to Susannah Heschel's collection of some of her father's hard-to-find shorter writings, *Moral Grandeur and Spiritual Audacity* (1996).[15] A third biographical essay written by Susannah Heschel is in the introduction to her compilation *Abraham Joshua Heschel: Essential Writings* (2011).[16] Finally, some additional biographical information appears in her introduction to the HarperPerennial edition of *The Prophets* (2001).[17]

13. Heschel, *Moral Grandeur*, 225.
14. S. Heschel, foreword to *God in Search of Man*, xix–xxxviii; see also Neusner and Neusner, *To Grow in Wisdom*, 195–211.
15. S. Heschel, introduction to *Moral Grandeur*, vi–xxx.
16. S. Heschel, introduction to *Abraham Joshua Heschel*, 17–44.
17. S. Heschel, introduction to *The Prophets* (2001), xiii–xx. After I completed my book a collection of Heschel's shorter writings while he was in Nazi Germany and then

Heschel was of East European descent, born in Warsaw, Poland, in 1907. He was a descendant in a long line of distinguished Hasidic rabbis on the maternal and paternal sides of his family. "His mother, Rivka Reizl, descended from the famed Rabbi Levi Yitzhak of Berdichev, was known for her piety, and women clustered near her in the synagogue, inspired by her praying. His father, Moshe Mordecai, raised in the large, majestic court of his grandfather, the Ruzhines rebbe in Sadegora, had become a rebbe in an impoverished neighborhood in Warsaw, Pelzovizna."[18] The youngest of six children (four sisters and one brother), Heschel was nine years old when his father died during a flu epidemic in 1916. He received a great deal of attention as a child, not only because he was the youngest but also because early on he exhibited signs of brilliance and being special. Susannah Heschel has commented on this, saying, "My father's childhood education was traditional and rigorous in the study of Hebrew texts and immersed in the holiness of Hasidic life. Everyone assumed he would one day become a rebbe. His mind was recognized as extraordinary even when he was a child, and to honor his position as son of the rebbe, adults would rise when he entered the room, even when he was a small boy."[19]

At the age of twenty-two Heschel left Warsaw for Berlin, where he studied for the PhD degree in philosophy at the Humboldt University. He simultaneously enrolled at the nearby Reform rabbinical seminary and lectured frequently at the nearby Orthodox seminary. Unlike most students, Heschel was comfortable in both seminary settings. In these as well as the university environment he excelled. He completed his dissertation (published as *Die Prophetie* in 1936), a phenomenological study of the consciousness of the Hebrew prophets, and was awarded his doctorate in 1933, just a few weeks after Hitler came to power.

Arrested by the Gestapo in the middle of the night in the fall of 1938, Heschel was allowed to pack only two suitcases, which he filled with a number of manuscripts he was working on. He was then made to walk to the police station, dragging along the two heavy suitcases. He was confined to a small cell. The next day he was deported to Poland along with many other Jews holding Polish passports. He had to stand during the entire train trip. To add insult to injury, when the train arrived, the Polish people refused to allow the Jews to reenter Poland. They were then placed in a detention camp near the border. More fortunate than most, Heschel received help

---

exiled in London was published. Susannah Heschel contributed the foreword and provided more biographical information on her father's years in Germany and London when he was in his twenties. See Heschel, *In This Hour*, xi–xiv.

18. S. Heschel, introduction to *Abraham Joshua Heschel*, 19.
19. S. Heschel, foreword to *God in Search of Man*, xxii.

from his family and was allowed to return to Warsaw. In July 1939, just six weeks before the Nazis invaded Poland, he received word that Julian Morgenstern, president of Hebrew Union College in Cincinnati, Ohio, would be sending him a visa. He managed to flee to England, and in 1940 arrived in the United States to assume his appointment as assistant professor on the faculty at Hebrew Union.

Heschel remained at Hebrew Union for five of the loneliest, most painful years of his life. Although it was all he could do to get himself out of Eastern Europe, he worked frantically, tirelessly, and unsuccessfully to get his mother and sister (Gittel) out. His level of discomfort was exacerbated even more because he could barely speak English when he arrived in the United States. To make things worse, he found that he could not even depend on the support of the American Jewish community, which seemed unconcerned about the plight of European Jews. Susannah Heschel put it bluntly when she said that her father was "shocked by the complacency and even hostility toward the fate of the European Jews that he encountered among some American Jews."[20]

The letters from Heschel's mother and sister that reached him in the United States broke his heart; his attempts to get them out of Poland came to nothing. And here he was, alone in Cincinnati, unable to speak English very well, without the sympathy and encouragement of American Jews, and living each day with the knowledge that his mother and sister could be killed at any moment. And yet, in letters to him, his mother and his sister expressed worry over *his* safety. He was still alone in Cincinnati when he received word of their murders. Words cannot possibly convey how deeply this affected Heschel. What we do know is that he could not bring himself to return to Poland or to Germany again, a point confirmed by his daughter.[21] Heschel himself reflected that he could not bear such a return: "If I should go to Poland or Germany, every stone, every tree would remind me of contempt, hatred, murder, of children killed, of mothers burned alive, of human beings asphyxiated."[22] But we also know that Heschel dedicated *Heavenly Torah*, "the book he hoped his readers would study the most thoroughly,"[23] to the memory of his three sisters and his mother. Heschel's oldest sister, Sarah Bracha, died in New York in 1964. His older brother, Rabbi Jacob Heschel, died in London at age 67.

20. S. Heschel, foreword to *God in Search of Man*, xxiv.
21. S. Heschel, introduction to *Moral Grandeur*, xix.
22. Heschel, *Israel: An Echo*, 113.
23. S. Heschel, foreword to *Heavenly Torah*, xx.

The woman who became Heschel's wife, Sylvia Straus, was born in Philadelphia and grew up in Cleveland. She was a talented pianist and was studying in Cincinnati when she and Heschel met and developed "an instant rapport." Susannah Heschel said that her parents' meeting was "the most significant encounter of those years"[24] for her father especially. The next time they met was in New York City in 1945, where Heschel was teaching at the Jewish Theological Seminary, and Sylvia Straus, having been auditioned by virtuoso pianist Arthur Rubinstein, was studying piano with Edward Steuermann and taking philosophy courses at Columbia University.[25] Heschel and Straus were married in Los Angeles on December 10, 1946, and were a perfect match. According to Susannah Heschel, "He fell in love with her artistry, her mind, her gentleness, and her soul."[26] Straus had studied literature and philosophy and was a gentle and religious person who would frequently serve as reader and critic of Heschel's lectures and speeches.

Ten days before Abraham Joshua Heschel failed to awaken on the Sabbath, December 23, 1972, he taped an informative and fascinating televised interview with NBC correspondent Carl Stern. Those who had never seen or heard Heschel speak were now able to get a sense of the man, the lover of God, humanity, and all other things divine. In this interview one sees a spirited, passionate, earthy, sensitive, and committed man who sought to convey God's point of view to a troubled country and world. One sees a man of deep religious faith who was committed to sharing with the world *his understanding of God's understanding and expectation of human beings in the world.* One cannot miss (in that interview) Heschel's passion, energy, respect for life generally, and for human life more specifically. I showed the video to more than two decades of my students, who were awed by the man and his commitment to his faith and ideals.

Heschel was the quintessential teacher and man of faith, who began to sense during the writing of *The Prophets* that it was no longer appropriate, nor morally acceptable, to be so devoted to study and writing that he permitted himself to be out of touch with the need to be concerned about, and involved in, what he liked to refer to as the "everydayness" of life—the concrete issues and problems that affect human beings. Nothing, he came to believe, should so isolate him or any person of religious faith from issues of injustice that he could not speak God's truth about injustice and other social evils. Heschel's study of the Hebrew prophets drove him from the privacy and comfort of his study and convinced him that God is always concerned

---

24. S. Heschel, foreword to *God in Search of Man*, xxv.
25. Kaplan, *Spiritual Radical*, 83.
26. S. Heschel, foreword to *God in Search of Man*, xxv.

about human beings and all that adversely affects them. He also came to see that because human beings are so important to God, so too must they be important to Abraham Joshua Heschel and to every other person.

A man of deep spirituality and faith who possessed an unending love for learning, Heschel came to be, in what may be viewed as the third major phase of his American career,[27] just as deeply committed (and more so) to the well-being of persons in their daily existence. Better than most, he was able to retain a sense of balance between matters of the spirit and the more mundane but important things of the world.

Edward Kaplan reports that when Heschel—who had never actually seen a black person in Europe—first arrived in the United States he was "startled to see an African American kneeling to polish the shoes of a white man."[28] He was from the beginning deeply troubled by segregation and the racial hierarchy in this country. Heschel's focus on racism and other sociopolitical issues in the United States began in earnest during the early 1960s,[29] roughly around the time of the publication of *The Prophets*. Not long thereafter he met and befriended Martin Luther King Jr.

Heschel and King

Heschel's first explicit involvement with the civil rights movement began when he agreed to appear with Martin Luther King Jr. (whom he had not previously met) and others at the National Conference on Religion and Race in Chicago in 1963.[30] The keynote addresses by King and Heschel were nothing short of ethical prophetic speeches against racism at all costs and at all levels.

Heschel's was the opening address at the conference, in which he asserted, "At the first conference on religion and race, the main participants were Pharaoh and Moses. Moses's words were: 'Thus says the Lord, the God of Israel, let My people go that they may celebrate a feast to Me' . . . The outcome of that summit meeting has not come to an end. Pharaoh is not ready

---

27. Kaplan, *Holiness in Words*, 11.

28. Kaplan, *Spiritual Radical*, 5. See also page 10, where the reader is told of Heschel's befriending of the black matron at Hebrew Union.

29. See S. Heschel, introduction to *Moral Grandeur*, xxii–xxiii.

30. Interestingly, Taylor Branch reports that Heschel was initially somewhat skeptical about participating in the conference because of rumors or criticisms about King that reached him at the Jewish Theological Seminary. "Could it be true, asked Heschel, that King was a shallow, hack politician for Negroes, a troublemaker of hidden and perhaps Communist motives who might belong in the jail cells he frequented?" (*Pillar of Fire*, 23–24). Heschel quickly came to the conclusion that this did not apply to King.

to capitulate. The exodus began, but is far from having been completed. In fact, it was easier for the children of Israel to cross the Red Sea than for a Negro to cross certain university campuses."[31] Indeed, Heschel went on to question how a person of faith could, in good conscience, even utter the words "religion" and "race" in the same sentence. He put it this way:

> To act in the spirit of religion is to unite what lies apart, to remember that humanity as a whole is God's beloved child. To act in the spirit of race is to sunder, to slash, to dismember the flesh of living humanity. Is this the way to honor a father: to torture his child? How can we hear the word "race" and feel no self-reproach?[32]

Susannah Heschel has written that racism in the United States "horrified my father."[33] He called racism "an 'eye disease' of white Americans."[34] Heschel was one of the *very* few white people in the entire history of this country to be so repulsed by racism that he simply could not hold his peace about it and unashamedly and passionately fought against it at every turn. In any event, as it turned out, the concerns raised by Heschel and King at the Chicago conference were remarkably similar, including their direct appeal to the prophet Amos: "Let justice roll down like waters, and righteousness like a mighty stream" (5:24). It was here, too, that Heschel proclaimed that the prophet is *never* tolerant of wrongs done to others and that the prophet's great contribution to humanity was his discovery of the evil of indifference.[35]

Susannah Heschel described her father's and King's relationship as "an extraordinary friendship." And more: "The bond my father felt with Dr. King was religious, and what linked them was the Bible, especially the prophets. Theirs was a relationship on the level of what my father called 'depth theology,' the fear and trembling in the hearts of pious people, regardless of their religion."[36] The two men were guided by the life and witness of the prophets to a degree that eluded most. Without question, each allowed the teachings of the prophets to guide his sense of call. Moreover, each spoke prophetically as boldly and courageously as the Hebrew prophets.

When King planned the march in Selma after the one that resulted in the "bloody Sunday" tragedy, he called on Heschel to join the front rank of the marchers along with other leaders. Around this time Heschel was

---

31. Heschel, *Insecurity of Freedom*, 85.
32. Heschel, *Insecurity of Freedom*, 85–86.
33. S. Heschel, introduction to *Abraham Joshua Heschel*, 35.
34. S. Heschel, introduction to *Abraham Joshua Heschel*, 18.
35. Heschel, *Insecurity of Freedom*, 92.
36. S. Heschel, introduction to *Abraham Joshua Heschel*, 35.

ill, which caused his daughter and wife considerable concern. But Heschel decided that so important was this invitation from King that he *had* to go to Selma. This goes to the issue of the depth of Heschel's commitment and his stance against racism. Furthermore, he had been strongly encouraged by a former student, Rabbi Everett Gendler, to join the march.[37] Reflecting on the Selma march later, Heschel's daughter pointed to the symbolic and practical significance of his placement among the leaders of the march, saying, "Heschel's presence in the front row of marchers was a visual symbol of religious Jewish commitment to civil rights, and 'stirred not only the Jewish religious community but Jews young and old into direct action, galvanizing the whole spectrum of activists from fundraisers to lawyers.'"[38] So he had to go, despite his illness and his awareness of the strong possibility of anti-Semitic verbal abuse or other violence during the march.[39] Susannah Heschel contends that fundamentally the Selma march was, for her father, not a sociopolitical event but "a religious moment." Reflecting on the march, Heschel himself said, "I thought of my having walked with Hasidic rabbis on various occasions. I felt a sense of the Holy in what I was doing."[40] Furthermore, Heschel spoke of his deep appreciation for King's expression of gratitude that he had joined them in Selma. "Later," his daughter said, "my father told us how he had experienced the march: he said, 'I felt my legs were praying.'"[41] In another place Rabbi Heschel reflected that it is sometimes necessary to go into harm's way but that it is also important to "learn how to stand before God."[42] Reflecting further on the Selma experience he said, "For many of us the march from Selma to Montgomery was both protest and prayer. Legs are not lips, and walking is not kneeling. And yet our legs uttered songs. Even without words, our march was worship."[43] However, Susannah Heschel recalls that after Selma her father also expressed disappointment that Jewish institutions failed "to interpret a civil-rights movement in terms of Judaism. The vast number of Jews participating actively in it are totally unaware of what the movement means in terms of the prophetic traditions."[44] In any case, Heschel was certain that praying, worship

37. Kaplan, *Spiritual Radical*, 222.
38. S. Heschel, "Two Friends, Two Prophets," 6–7, quoting Friedman, *What Went Wrong?*, 191.
39. Kaplan, *Spiritual Radical*, 223.
40. Quoted in S. Heschel, introduction to *Moral Grandeur*, xxiii.
41. S. Heschel, "Heschel as *Mensch*," 206.
42. Heschel, "What We Might Do Together," 135.
43. Heschel, "What We Might Do Together," 135.
44. Quoted in S. Heschel, introduction to *The Prophets* (2001), xiv.

of God, is not all in the singing, preaching, and praying that one does during a formal worship service. He viewed nonviolent demonstration for human dignity and against racial injustice as a significant form of worshipping the God who cares.

Significance of Divine Pathos

When he was studying the prophets, Heschel learned that although a major role of the Hebrew prophets was that of advocate for the weak, the poor, and the voiceless, they were not the first to implement the practice of remonstrating on their behalf, either in the presence of oppressors (demanding that justice be done) or in the presence of God (pleading for divine tolerance and patience). Indeed, the practice of "interfering in a case in which a wrong was inflicted upon someone else is reported from the time of David. For example, after King David's sin with Bathsheba, the wife of Uriah, the prophet Nathan went to David and told him a parable [2 Sam 12:1–6]."[45]

According to Heschel, the human being and the ethical are in the forefront and have the right-of-way in prophecy.[46] But this idea must be understood as being caused by a deeper principle and should be seen to be in dialectical relation with that principle. That is, according to Heschel, the moralizing effect of prophecy is a result of the divine pathos, of God's inexhaustible care, compassion, and concern for human beings. The emphasis on divine pathos actually serves to ground prophecy theologically. In this regard, Heschel's is a staunchly theocentric view of prophecy. That is, he sees God as the ground of prophecy. God is at the center of ethical prophecy. The entire prophetic drama, then, is a result of God's initiative, not human beings'. It is a result of the divinely initiated search for human beings to return to covenant relation with God. God initiates or acts and human beings respond.

Divine pathos is the regulating ideal or central element in Heschel's theology of prophecy. Accordingly, it is the chief category of prophetic understanding of God and is echoed in virtually all prophetic pronouncements. It is the touchstone of all communication of divine attitudes to

---

45. Heschel, *Prophets*, 206. In this regard, Albert C. Knudson wrote that goodness is the essence of religion and that "the idea that righteousness is an essential element in religion goes back to the time of Moses and was dramatically reaffirmed by the prophets Nathan and Elijah as against David . . . and Ahab. . . . But it was the eighth-century prophets who first elevated the idea into a position of exclusive significance" (*Prophetic Movement in Israel*, 111).

46. S. Heschel, *Abraham Joshua Heschel*, 47.

prophetic consciousness.⁴⁷ Divine pathos conveys the idea of a God who is endlessly compassionate and concerned about human beings.⁴⁸ The God of the prophets is not the Wholly Other of Karl Barth—not the Remote One. Rather, God is the One who is near, concerned, and involved in human affairs.

> Never in history has man been taken as seriously as in prophetic thinking. Man is not only an image of God; he is a perpetual concern of God. The idea of pathos adds a new dimension to human existence. Whatever man does affects not only his own life, but also the life of God insofar as it is directed to man. The import of man raises him beyond the level of mere creature. He is a consort, a partner, a factor in the life of God.⁴⁹

The heart of God is on the side of the weak and downtrodden. God's special concern is not for the strong, powerful, and privileged but for the lowly and disinherited, the forgotten, the stranger, the poor, the widow, the orphan, and the homeless.⁵⁰ God privileges these over the wealthy, privileged, and powerful. We will see that this is the same God to which other ethical prophet hall of fame candidates appeal.

One can detect more than a dozen elements of ethical prophecy in the writings of Heschel. I focus on six of these and their manifestation in the life and witness of Angelina Grimké, Ida B. Wells-Barnett, James A. Baldwin, Malcolm X, Martin Luther King Jr., Óscar A. Romero, and Alice Walker. The six factors highlighted in the discussion that follows include the call, emphasis on the sacredness of persons, speaking truth to power, God's judgment, the cost of prophecy, and a vision of hope. When these traits of prophecy are present in one's life and work, one is in the camp of ethical prophecy, indeed, is most likely an ethical prophet. The discussion of these criteria is seen through the interpretation of Heschel and the cultural lens of an Afrikan American male who has been much influenced by his witness, teaching, and example.

The Call

One is not born an ethical prophet. Rather, he is called. Heschel maintains that there is a prophetic element in every high calling, whether in teaching,

---

47. Heschel, *Prophets*, 223.
48. Heschel, *Prophets*, 257.
49. Heschel, *Prophets*, 226.
50. Heschel, *Prophets*, 167.

medicine, education, or art.[51] Such callings require loyalty and complete devotion to one's calling and its requirements. So we see at the outset that the call is of utmost importance in ethical prophecy.

C. H. Spurgeon gave wise counsel to those who claim the certainty of a divine call for no other reason than they have tried and failed at everything else, and therefore it must be the case that God has called them to ministry. Spurgeon gave this poignant reply to his students:

> My answer generally is, "Yes, I see; you have failed in everything else, and therefore you think the Lord has especially endowed you for his service; but I fear you have forgotten that the *ministry needs the very best of men, and not those who cannot do anything else*." A man who would succeed as a preacher would probably do right well either as a grocer, or a lawyer, or anything else. A really valuable minister would have excelled at anything. There is scarcely anything impossible to a man who can keep a congregation together for years, and be the means of edifying them for hundreds of consecutive Sabbaths; he must be possessed of some abilities, and be by no means a fool or ne'er-do-well. Jesus Christ deserves the best men to preach his cross, and not the empty-headed and the shiftless.[52]

If ministry is the greatest vocation in the world, as Reinhold Niebuhr and Martin Luther King claimed, why would God not call forth the best for that work? This is what Niebuhr had in mind when he wrote in his journal, "Here is a task [ministry] which requires the knowledge of a social scientist and the insight and imagination of a poet, the executive talents of a business man and the mental discipline of a philosopher."[53] Surely such a vocation requires people who have done more in life than fail.

Coming from different walks of life, the Hebrew prophets came to their vocation through an experience of a divine call.[54] Those in the tradition of Jeremiah, Amos, Isaiah, Hosea, and Micah are not born prophets. They are called. However, one cannot always detect in the writings of the prophets an explicit call narrative. Indeed, although there is no obvious call narrative in the book of Micah, for example, we can be sure from the prophetic utterances throughout that book that Micah met the criteria for being called by God. But how may one discern whether one is being called, since not everybody has that direct, dramatic, unmistakable experience of being called by

---

51. Heschel, *Insecurity of Freedom*, 28.
52. Spurgeon, "Call to the Ministry," 36 (my italics).
53. Niebuhr, *Leaves from the Notebook*, 174.
54. See Bright, *History of Israel*, 246.

God that Saul of Tarsus and Protestant reformer Martin Luther reportedly experienced? Indeed, many people experience a less dramatic call, similar to that of Martin Luther King Jr., to be discussed in chapter 6. Not everybody's call experience is of the riveting and obvious type. So what can a person do, in addition to praying, reflecting, and seeking the counsel of his pastor or spiritual advisor, to help discern whether God may be calling him to ministry?

Many years ago, Hebrew Bible scholars Charles Foster Kent and Robert Seneca Smith gave a helpful suggestion to assist in discerning whether one is experiencing a divine call. In this regard they wrote, "If your heart ever aches because of the cry of the needy or the despised, and your eyes behold a vision of God's infinite love and tenderness, put the two together; they are God's method of calling you to His service."[55] In other words, one who is tormented by the abuse, injustice, oppression, and pain inflicted upon others, and has a deep sense of God's expectation that love-justice be done to and for all people, is quite possibly being called to prophetic ministry. Since in most instances the hall of fame candidates discussed in this book do not provide a formal call narrative, it will be important to keep in mind the two minimal criteria provided by Kent and Smith: experience of an aching heart because of abuse and injustice done to others and an awareness of God's tender loving care and compassion. We will see that the candidates for the ethical prophet hall of fame had a burning desire to address and eradicate injustice and to uphold the dignity and sacredness of the oppressed. They also had a strong awareness of a higher being who is concerned that people be treated a certain way.

The experience of the divine call is what *commissions* the prophet to be God's messenger.[56] During the time of the Hebrew prophets the call was in fact a new mode or literary device for introducing YHWH's prophet. This is what made the call so important—that it was written down, and at a time in the ancient East when people did not write things down merely for the sake of writing them down. In those days, when something was written down, it was considered to be of utmost importance. The written record had a definite purpose. Gerhard von Rad argued that "the very fact that a call was recorded in writing shows that it was regarded at the time it occurred as something unusual."[57] Still, we should remember that the written account of the call was not as important as the call itself, since the call commissioned the prophet and gave him the authority to convey God's message to

---

55. Kent and Smith, *Earlier Prophets*, 1.
56. Rad, *Old Testament Theology*, 2:55.
57. Rad, *Old Testament Theology*, 2:54.

the people and the powers. The prophet was required to *do* something, for which he felt completely burdened and obligated.

One has to be clear about the source and authority of one's call. It is God who is the initiator and commissioner of the call and who therefore gives one authority to convey God's point of view. For example, Jeremiah 1:4 reports that God initiated the call, not Jeremiah. Indeed, Jeremiah was predestined even before birth to be a prophet; God overruled his objections and promised to provide what he needed; and significantly, God placed the divine word in his mouth (Jer 1:9). It was an instance of God taking the initiative to turn toward and to summon Jeremiah. Jeremiah responded to God's action. God spoke first. It was not Jeremiah's meeting, nor his word. It was God's project, one might say, and Jeremiah had only to respond appropriately to God's initiative.

Heschel's Contribution to Understanding the Call

Heschel saw much in Jeremiah 20:7 that helped him understand and convey the seriousness of the call. He renders the verse as follows: "O Lord, Thou hast seduced me, and I am seduced; Thou hast raped me and I am overcome."[58] Heschel was struck by the use of both *patah* ("seduce") and *hazak* ("rape") in the verse. The New Revised Standard Version (NRSV) does not use the term "rape" in the text, but it does imply a taking by force in the phrase "you have overpowered me." This implies that not only has something of great value been taken away, but *violently* so. Heschel gives further explanation of the use of "seduce" and "rape" in the passage, saying, "These terms used in immediate juxtaposition forcefully convey the complexity of the divine-human relationship: sweetness of enticement as well as violence of rape. Jeremiah, who like Hosea thought of the relationship between God and Israel in the image of love, interpreted his own involvement in the same image. This interpretation betrays an ambivalence in the prophet's understanding of his own experience."[59]

Heschel's interpretation of Jeremiah 20:7 exposes the complexity, indeed, the mystery, of the phenomenon of the divine call. Heschel did not solve the mystery by any means, nor did he provide an easy rendering of the *dialectic of seduction and rape* that we find in the text—the sense of being lured or seduced and, on some level, even enjoying some aspects of the seduction. On another level, however, there is the feeling of being completely overwhelmed and overpowered, so that one has no choice but to give in. As

---

58. Heschel, *Prophets*, 113.
59. Heschel, *Prophets*, 114.

complex and mysterious as this dialectic is, and as questionable and morally unacceptable as is the language of seduction, deceit, and rape in this verse, we are nonetheless left with a sense of the importance and profundity of the divine call. *This is what I want to stress in the verse—the seriousness and indispensableness of the call.* In addition, the passage conveys a sense of how determined God is that the one called should respond affirmatively and take up the call to prophesy God's truth. This too is an important point disclosed in the passage. One can see in these words the seriousness with which the call should be taken, and this is the chief purpose of this discussion. *However*—and this is absolutely critical—the seduction-rape language, the use of "entice" and "overpower" in the verse, is without question problematic to any who take seriously the ethical content of the type of prophecy being discussed, and the conviction that God calls persons into existence in freedom and genuinely loves each and every one. In addition, in light of my understanding of God as fundamentally love and compassion, I personally find the language of *persuasive love* to be both more morally credible and palatable, as well as more intelligible than the regrettable language of "enticing" and "overpowering force" that we find in the text. A God whose essential nature is love would not commit violence against human beings. Moreover, I am in complete agreement with womanist biblical theologian Renita Weems,[60] as well as biblical theologian Walter Brueggemann,[61] who express concern about the language of divine seduction and violent force in the text.[62]

I next turn to a consideration of five other elements of ethical prophecy in the work of Heschel. The prophet is charged with speaking the truth to the people and the nation. This means that he must be in step with God's requirements, in addition to mustering the courage to speak what thus says the Lord.

---

60. See Weems, *Battered Love*, ch. 4

61. See Brueggemann, *Theology of the Old Testament*, 359–62.

62. See the instructive discussion on 20:7 in Bracke, *Jeremiah 1–29*, 163–64. Bracke supports the interpretation in my book. J. A. Thompson does so as well; see Thompson, *Book of Jeremiah*, 459. The commentary of Jack R. Lundbom is also in agreement. See his book *Jeremiah 1–20*, 854–55. Other scholars render a much different interpretation of the verse, suggesting that there are no sexual connotations and that there is no evidence that YHWH deceived Jeremiah. See Craigie, Kelley, and Drinkard, *Jeremiah 1–25*, 273.

Speaking Truth to the People and the Powers

This criterion requires the prophet to convey to the people and the nations God's perspective on what is occurring in the world. The prophet is engaged in an exegesis of day-to-day existence from God's point of view. "Understanding prophecy," Heschel maintains, "is an understanding of understanding rather than an understanding of knowledge; it is exegesis of exegesis. It involves sharing the perspective from which the original understanding is done."[63] The prophet speaks to God's point of view on things, but as a human being he necessarily does so from his own viewpoint and sociocultural location. By virtue of conveying God's message the ethical prophet always speaks the truth to the people, for God requires that the truth, and only the truth, be conveyed. Nevertheless, it is not the prophet's truth but God's, and the true prophet dares not repress, water down, or otherwise defile God's message. He is accountable only to God, and, like Jeremiah, he expresses the intensity of the desire to speak God's truth (Jer 20:8, 9). He is compelled to speak, so much so that his very soul feels like it is on fire. He cannot hold it in but must speak it even at the risk of torture and death itself.

God gives the prophet the word to speak to the people and the nation, and the prophet accepts the call to deliver it. In this regard, God and the prophet are in mutual sympathy. That is, each is open to the presence and feelings of the other. Heschel is instructive when he writes, "Sympathy is an act in which a person is open to the presence of another person. It is a feeling which feels the feeling to which it reacts; the opposite of emotional solitariness. In prophetic sympathy, man is open to the presence and emotion of the transcendent Subject. He carries within himself the awareness of what is happening to God."[64] He also carries within himself what God requires of the people and the powers.

When standing before the people, the Hebrew prophets sought to convey to them God's point of view on what was happening in the world and what God required of them. In this regard, the prophet is a person of vision. He "learns to read events and see them in God's way.... Where others have a complacent or disillusioned view, the prophet presents a view which is both critical and refreshing."[65] Depending on the situation, the prophet expresses God's love, or God's anger and wrath, but in each instance the aim is to get the people to return to covenant relation with God.

Heschel was certain that in carrying forth God's mission the ethical prophet also suffered the harms done to the people. After all, like Micah, he

63. Heschel, *Prophets*, xviii.
64. Rothschild, *Between God and Man*, 126.
65. Prévost, *How to Read the Prophets*, 14.

is one of them, a member of the community, and as much affected as they. "Whenever a crime is committed," Heschel writes, "it is as if the prophet were the victim and the prey."[66] The prophet is never tolerant of injustices and wrongs done to human beings. "He even calls upon others to be the champions of the poor."[67]

God commissions the prophet to speak the truth to the people, and during times of worship especially, when too little truth is spoken in pulpits around the nation and around the world. Marvin McMickle drives home the point in his book *Where Have All the Prophets Gone?*: "The fiery words of the prophets . . . go unspoken in most pulpits across America. There is very little likelihood that the vast majority of those who hear sermons today will come out of their churches saying to one another, 'The land is not able to bear all his words' (Amos 7:10)."[68] The prophet is not interested in entertaining the people but only in speaking God's truth.

In chapter 6 we will see that Martin Luther King was courageous enough to criticize his own community, including his ministerial colleagues. This was no less true of Heschel, and like King this practice made him unpopular in some circles, even among his own people. On one occasion Heschel declared, "On every Sabbath multitudes of Jews gather in the synagogues, and they often depart as they have entered."[69] Heschel knew that the prophet is called to speak truth not only to the powers but to the people as well. Moreover, he knew that in either case the prophet pays.

God alone puts the message into the prophet's mouth. We find evidence of this in a number of places in the Bible. It is graphically illustrated in several of the Hebrew prophets. Jeremiah, for example, had a vision of God touching his mouth and saying, "Behold, I have put my words in your mouth. See, I have set you this day over nations and over kingdoms, to pluck up and to break down, to destroy and to overthrow, to build and to plant" (Jer 1:9-10). It was not Jeremiah's word but God's. Similarly, Deutero-Isaiah reported that God chose him from his mother's womb (Isa 49:1). He was called by God to convey God's word. "He made my mouth like a sharp sword . . . ; he made me a polished arrow" (Isa 49:2). This prophet had some incisive truths to convey to the people. Accordingly, Johannes Lindblom writes, "The active power of the divine words in the mouth of this prophet is expressed by the figurative terms 'sword' and 'arrow' just as Jeremiah by means of his words had effective power to root up and to pull down, to build

---

66. Heschel, *Insecurity of Freedom*, 92.
67. Heschel, *Insecurity of Freedom*, 92.
68. McMickle, *Where Have All the Prophets Gone?*, 7.
69. Quoted in S. Heschel, introduction to *The Prophets* (2001), xix.

and to plant."⁷⁰ The prophetic word does not come from the prophet as such. It comes from God and is conveyed through the prophet, who is the conduit through which the divine word is spoken to the people and the powers. God's message is so precious that the prophet is admonished to be careful when handling and conveying it to others.

When the prophet hears God's word and fails to convey it to the people, God holds him accountable for what happens to them (cf. Ezek 3:16–21; 33:6–7; Jer 25:3–7). God designates the prophet as watchman. As watchman, Ezekiel was charged to warn the people whenever he received word from God (Ezek 3:17). The prophet so commanded was obligated and therefore was responsible for the very lives of the people—lives that belong only to God. Failure to warn the people when God revealed truths to the prophet, then, meant that their blood was on his hands. For this, the prophet would have to answer to God, for human beings are precious and invaluable to God.

The Sacredness of Persons

When the prophet Ezekiel proclaimed that all life belongs to God, he most especially had in mind the lives of human beings (Ezek 18:4). Ezekiel and Jeremiah both stressed the individuality and worth of human beings to a degree that others did not. Their teaching heightened the preciousness of persons. Indeed, Ezekiel has been referred to as "pre-eminently the prophet of individualism."⁷¹ In addition, Jeremiah proclaimed that the children will no longer be punished for the sins of their parents, but only for their own sins (Jer 31:30), and under the new covenant God's law will be written on the heart of each individual (Jer 31:33). Each human being is of immeasurable value to God. Susannah Heschel reminds us that for her father the same cannot be said about books and scholarship. Few loved books and scholarship more than Heschel, but he absolutely rejected the idea of placing these on the same level of importance and worth as human beings.⁷² The prophets came to teach us that God cares deeply not about things and impersonal objects but about human beings and human suffering. The acknowledgment of and respect for the inherent sacredness of human beings and their absolute dignity is a chief test of ethical prophecy. If the presumed prophet does not acknowledge and respect the inherent preciousness of human beings in both words and deeds he fails to meet even the minimal requirement

---

70. Lindblom, *Prophecy in Ancient Israel*, 191.
71. Strahan, *God in History*, 140.
72. S. Heschel, foreword to *God in Search of Man*, xxx.

of what it means to be an ethical prophet. Furthermore, we may go so far to say that he is a false prophet. One cannot be an ethical prophet and not love God's people—*all* people—and acknowledge in word and deed their absolute sacredness. Moreover, in Hebrew prophecy we are constantly reminded that *all* people—without qualification—are God's people. God cannot possibly *like* many of the things we humans do, since so much of what we do undermines the worth of self, other human beings, and other life forms. However, God loves persons, regardless of sexual orientation, race, class, gender, age, health, or religion. The prophet Hosea showed us that God's love for Israel was inexhaustible, and so too is God's love for us today. God loves people so absolutely that God cannot—indeed, will not—give them up. "How can I give you up, Ephraim? How can I hand you over, O Israel?" (Hos 11:8). Truly, God loves us even though we commit the most heinous crimes against human and nonhuman life forms and nature. However, God's love for us does not mean that we can commit such crimes with impunity, for God is also preeminently the God of justice.

So special and valuable is every person to God that God does not, under any circumstance, give up on any one of us.[73] Therefore, it has been rightly said that in God's family there are *no outsiders*. Rather, every person is an insider in the divine family.[74] Without question, the ethical prophet contends that every person is imbued with the image or likeness of God and is infinitely sacred to God. This must be the case, for the Bible tells us that God knows the number of hairs on our heads (Matt 10:30) and even calls us by name (Isa 43:1). So important is every person that God is personally and intimately acquainted with each and every one.

The Hebrew prophets strongly convey the idea that the source of the dignity and sacredness of human beings is YHWH. This means that dignity and sacredness are constitutive of what it means to be a person. Theologically, human beings are precious because they are created and loved by God. Because every human being carries a trace of the divine within him, we may say that each of us is a God-carrier. In other words, all human beings share a common parentage, which implies a unity (not uniformity) between human beings and the Creator. Heschel put it nicely: "God is every man's pedigree. He is either the Father of all men or of no man. The image of God is either in every man or in no man."[75] In an amazingly similar vein, and as far back as 1954, Benjamin E. Mays, longtime president of Morehouse College and mentor to Martin Luther King, said, "If God is Creator and

---

73. Tutu, *God Has a Dream*, 96.
74. Tutu, *God Has a Dream*, 20.
75. Heschel, *Insecurity of Freedom*, 95.

Father, then it must be that white men, black men, yellow men and brown men are brothers. Either all or none. Either God is the father of all men, or He is the father of none. Either the lives of all children are sacred, or the life of no child is sacred."[76] Indeed, Malachi asks, "Have we not all one father? Has not one God created us?" (Mal 2:10) Accordingly, one cannot reasonably claim to love God while simultaneously dishonoring and disrespecting human beings, whom God loves. One cannot presume to honor God while also torturing God's children.

The Hebrew prophets do not stress human beings' concern for God but God's concern for human beings. It is all about how God perceives human beings and what God thinks about them. That's an important foundation stone in ethical prophecy. *God cares about persons.* Because God is concerned about human beings, it is possible for us to exhibit concern for God and for each other.[77] Human beings have concern for each other and for God not because of their initiative but because of God's initiative and God's persistent and profound compassion and faithfulness. Although deemed worthless by the powerful and privileged,[78] every human being is so precious to God that God is involved in everything that happens to each one.[79] The God of ethical prophecy is personal, loving, and compassionate, and is therefore the Parent of all human beings—without exception. This God is active, present in every moment, central in the everyday affairs of human beings. Even when God is silent, God is nevertheless present in the lives of human beings.

The absoluteness of human dignity and sacredness is of critical significance in ethical prophecy. Absolute dignity has nothing to do with who one is based on one's social status, sexual orientation, class, race, religion, health, or other social identity. Neither is dignity relative; rather, it is grounded in the conviction that God willingly, thoughtfully, and lovingly chooses to call persons into existence and imbues each with the divine image, so that every person is sacred because every person is a child of God.

Theologically, the sacredness of human beings consists in having been called into existence by the God of the Hebrew prophets, who infused them with the indestructible image of God, which envelops the entire person, *mind and body*. That the entire human being is the image of God means that both their spiritual and their bodily needs should be addressed in prophetic ministry. One who does not acknowledge the sacredness of the entire

---

76. Mays, "Brotherhood," 116.
77. Heschel, *God in Search of Man*, 413.
78. Heschel, *Prophets*, 142.
79. Heschel, *Moral Grandeur*, 218.

person—soul and body—and treat him accordingly may be a prophet, but not an ethical prophet.

The Dialectic of Divine Judgment and Hope

Heschel's theology of prophecy also posits that divine judgment is an important element. Divine judgment is not an end in itself. Rather, it is depicted "as a refining fire for salvific purposes—in the service of the word of promise."[80] A good, loving, and just God, a God who is inexhaustibly compassionate and caring, would in no way *want* to punish people. And yet, when the Hebrew prophets appeared on the stage of history they introduced a new element into prophecy, that YHWH was not pleased with Israel's behavior and their breach of the covenant. This is what von Rad meant when he said that "the new feature in their preaching, and the one which shocked their hearers, was the message that Yahweh was summoning Israel before his judgment seat, and that he had in fact already pronounced sentence upon her: 'The end has come upon my people Israel.'"[81] This is not to say that prior to the eighth century there had been no prophecy of judgment in Israel. The difference is that prior to Amos there had been "no accusation against Israel as a whole nation," which in itself was "an added stress."[82] What was new, von Rad asserted, was "the prophets' zeal in laying bare man's innate tendency to oppose God, their endeavour to comprehend Israel's conduct in its entirety, and to bring out what, all historical contingency apart, might be taken as typical of that conduct."[83]

Contrary to what the official and professional prophets of the empire preached, the literary prophets of the eighth century came declaring that what had occurred in Israel up to their time was anything but salvific. Salvation lay in the future, and beyond God's judgment. Once again von Rad is helpful here: "The old traditions said that Yahweh led Israel into her land, founded Zion, and established the throne of David, and this was sufficient. No prophet could any longer believe this; for between him and those founding acts hung a fiery curtain of dire judgments upon Israel, judgments which, in the prophets' opinion, had already begun."[84] In other words, the Hebrew prophets emphatically proclaimed that while Israel will experience salvation,

---

80. Birch et al., *Theological Introduction to the Old Testament*, 278.
81. Rad, *Message of the Prophets*, 147.
82. Westermann, *What Does the Old Testament Say?*, 56.
83. Rad, *Message of the Prophets*, 149.
84. Rad, *Message of the Prophets*, 154.

it will come only beyond judgment, or "in the shadow of judgment."[85] Judgment of the nation was imminent. Anyone who preached otherwise, as Hananiah and Amaziah did, spoke about his own program or that of the ruling authorities, and not YHWH's—consequently, they were deemed by Jeremiah, Amos, and others to be false prophets. The Hebrew prophets held that brighter days were indeed coming, but only *after* the storm of judgment passed. And yet, God's business with Israel was not finished after the judgment. Brighter days were coming, but only on the other side of judgment.

The prophets did not come solely to castigate and prophesy destruction and doom, for these were not God's last words. They also uttered words of hope—hope that at least a remnant would return to covenant relation with God, even if things had degenerated to the point that they had first to go through the devastation or destruction. "Almost every prophet brings consolation, promise, and the hope of reconciliation along with censure and castigation," Heschel writes. "He begins with *a message of doom*; he concludes with *a message of hope*."[86] No matter how harsh or stinging the prophet's words might be, behind those words is God's ever-present love and compassion. The prophets sought to convey the truth that God was not merely love, mercy, and compassion. Heschel was adamant that the God of the Bible was more than that. "We must be reminded," he said, "that the God of the Bible is both Judge and Father, severe as well as compassionate"[87]— God of love *and* God of justice. Through Amos, God demanded that justice be done, but Hosea came along to remind the people of God's deep, indestructible love. This did not mean, however, that the people could continue their wrongdoing with impunity, for as much as God loved them God also detested wrongdoing and injustice. Reflecting on Hosea, Heschel asserts that God's "is not a love that is exclusive and that ignores the wickedness of the beloved, forgiving carelessly every fault. Here is a love grown bitter with the waywardness of man. The Lord is in love with Israel, but He also has a passionate love of right and a burning hatred of wrong."[88]

Accordingly, God (Love) never leaves or gives up on human beings, no matter how disobedient we are. And even in the most inhumane of circumstances, God is with us. The story is told of a Jewish prisoner who was forced to clean toilets in a Nazi death camp and was taunted by a guard, who asked repeatedly, "Where is your God now?"—to which the prisoner

---

85. Rad, *Message of the Prophets*, 154.
86. Heschel, *Prophets*, 12.
87. S. Heschel, *Abraham Joshua Heschel*, 175.
88. Heschel, *Prophets*, 50.

replied, "Right here in the muck and mire with me."[89] Even when some choose to subject others to massive destruction of human life, as the Nazis did, rather than obedience and faithfulness to God, God is never absent, but is present with the victims in the devastation. The prophet Isaiah assures us that God's wrath lasts only for a moment, but God's loyalty and steadfast love last forever (Isa 54:7–8, 10). Likewise, Jeremiah reminded the people of God's everlasting love and unrelenting faithfulness to them (Jer 31:3).

What Bernhard Anderson said about the book of Hosea is just as applicable to other Hebrew prophets: "The deepest note struck in the book of Hosea," he wrote, "is the proclamation that *God's 'wrath' or judgment is redemptive.*"[90] If we truly believe that God is love, and know what love means in the religious sense, then we have to conclude that God's purpose and will is never to destroy human beings or to permit their destruction, even when they choose it. Because of God's persistent love, faithfulness, and loyalty, God is always, *always* pursuing human beings in the hope of restoring us to healthy community—indeed, to the beloved community where every person will be respected by virtue of being a person and child of God.

When conveying God's truth the prophets spared no one. In their speech they had little concern for the exception. Rather, their prophecies tended to be all-inclusive. They were masters of what Heschel called sweeping allegations. What is the meaning of such generalizations, and what purpose do they serve in ethical prophecy?

Making Sweeping Allegations

Heschel characterizes the sweeping generalizations of the Hebrew prophets by saying, "The prophets were unfair to the people of Israel. Their sweeping allegations, overstatements, and generalizations defied standards of accuracy."[91] Hosea made sweeping allegations against the people of Israel: "Hear the word of the Lord, O people of Israel; for the Lord has an indictment against the inhabitants of the land. There is no faithfulness or loyalty, and no knowledge of God in the land" (4:1). There must have been some exceptions to this blanket charge, and Hosea must have known it. But accuracy, or even sparing the feelings of the few who were actually on the right side of justice, was not his concern. His aim was to get the attention of the people and the nation and to force them to think. In the same manner, Isaiah accused not *some* members but the entire nation of Judah of being a

---

89. This is a paraphrase of Tutu, *God Has a Dream*, 17.
90. Anderson, *Understanding the Old Testament*, 312 (my italics).
91. Heschel, *Prophets*, 13.

"sinful nation, people laden with iniquity, offspring who do evil, children who deal corruptly, who have forsaken the LORD, who have despised the Holy One of Israel, who are utterly estranged!" (Isa 1:4). *All*, according to the prophet, were guilty of this behavior, not *some*. Were the prophets aware that there were exceptions? Yes. But in order to get the people's attention, to force them to think, and to make the point that they were out of sorts with God and that judgment was on the horizon, they had to cut a wide swath with the allegations being made. We will see this tendency in all of the candidates for the ethical prophet hall of fame as well, and none were more proficient at making sweeping exaggerations and arousing the people, including the powers, than Ida B. Wells-Barnett and Malcolm X.

Heschel reminds us that "what seems to be exaggeration is often only a deeper penetration, for the prophets see the world from the point of view of God, as transcendent, not immanent truth."[92] Because the prophet sees and hears from God's perspective, what the people hear through his prophecy may be, indeed often is, perceived as exaggeration. In the mind of the prophet, however, he speaks only God's truth to the people. Thus the prophet does not merely call out individuals, but entire groups, communities, and nations.

It is difficult to imagine the prophetic sweeping allegation being anything but an urgent and stinging word, too heavy for the audience to contain. "Reading [and hearing] the words of the prophets is a strain on the emotions, wrenching one's conscience from the state of suspended animation,"[93] writes Heschel. Is it any wonder that the prophet's words were "often slashing, even horrid—designed to shock rather than to edify"?[94] Ethical prophets, then, are concerned to criticize not only individuals but entire groups of people and nations. In addition, their sweeping generalizations are actually part of the power of their prophetic critique. As noted before, they are not particularly concerned about the accuracy of their charges or the facts as such. Rather, they are concerned about "the meaning of the facts" for concrete human beings who are victims of injustice.

Conclusion

As seen in the foregoing discussion, the ethical prophet is one who prophesies in the spirit of the Hebrew prophets of ancient Israel. He exhibits specific characteristics, including a strong sense of call; an insistence on speaking

---

92. Heschel, *Prophets*, 14.
93. Heschel, *Prophets*, 7.
94. Heschel, *Prophets*, 7.

truth to the people and the nation; a firm belief in the sacredness of every human being; a desire to warn the people and the nation of impending judgment and destruction (though he ends with words of hope); and a penchant for making sweeping generalizations. These traits, along with the demand to do justice and a strong awareness of the cost of prophecy, provide a good sense of who the ethical prophet truly is every day of his life. These criteria are not traits that come to light only in one speech in which one musters the courage to softly criticize the powers that be. Rather, they tell us precisely the type of prophet such one is—an ethical prophet.

This book focuses on ethical prophecy, and the remaining seven personalities to be discussed are some of its important representatives. Because it is a *type* of prophecy and we are dealing with finite and limited beings, there are no perfect representatives—only human ones. Some of the traits will be more clearly evident in some representatives than in others, but to some degree each of the traits will be evident in the personalities discussed.

PART 2

Ethical Prophets along the Way

2

Angelina Grimké as Ethical Prophet

What literary artist and activist Alice Walker told Ellen Bring about the genuine feminist white woman and slavery in the United States is an excellent description of the nineteenth-century feminist-abolitionist Angelina Grimké and her sister Sarah: "A brave white woman looking at slavery would have had to try to see herself as one of the people enslaved. She would have had to know from her own suffering that there was a connection between herself and the slaves. She would have had to bond with the slaves and not with her husband."[1] In this chapter we will see that Angelina Grimké was just such a woman.

Angelina Emily Grimké (1805–79) was the youngest of fourteen children born to wealthy, aristocratic, slaveholding parents in Charleston, South Carolina. When Angelina was born her thirteen-year-old sister, Sarah, pleaded with their parents to allow her to be the child's godmother. Catherine Birney, a close friend of the sisters, wrote that Angelina was "the pet and darling of Sarah from the moment the light dawned upon her blue eyes."[2] Sarah's affection for Angelina was like "the yearning tenderness of a mother."[3] While growing up, Angelina affectionately referred to Sarah as her "sister-mother."[4]

---

1. "'Moving toward Coexistence': An Interview with Ellen Bring," in Byrd, *World Has Changed*, 76.
2. Birney, *Grimké Sisters*, 12.
3. Birney, *Grimké Sisters*, 12.
4. Weld, *In Memory*, 21.

Grimké's parents were John Faucheraud Grimké and Mary Smith Grimké. Mrs. Grimké's father was a wealthy financier. She enjoyed reading theology books and was known to be "a very devout woman, of rather narrow views, and undemonstrative in her affections."[5] She was impatient with the family's enslaved Afrikans as well as her own children. She had a particularly hard time with her oldest and youngest daughters, Sarah and Angelina. Without doubt, both had minds of their own and were not hesitant to speak their views. Even as young girls and adolescents they fought with their mother about both presuming to "own" the Afrikans and treating them harshly and violently.[6]

Mr. Grimké was an intellectual, politician, and state supreme court judge. His daughter Sarah was his favorite, and he loved her most of all.[7] When judge Grimké died in 1819, he left the family very well provided for.

Angelina Grimké left her Charleston, South Carolina, home in November 1829 at age twenty-three, as a protest against her family's presumed "ownership" of the Afrikans and the attitude of some family members (not least her mother) toward slavery. In addition, Grimké's religious affiliation with the Quakers made it impossible for her to remain in the slaveholding South. Early on she had been affiliated with the Episcopal church. She left it because it did not meet her spiritual needs and it advocated and supported slavery. Against her mother's wishes she then joined the Presbyterian church, but soon left because of its proslavery stance.

By leaving Charleston, Grimké effectively became an exile who was committed to witnessing against slavery, even if it meant forsaking family and friends. Already, at an early age, she was an emerging voice of conscience and showed signs of being called to a higher purpose. Later, when she published the powerful pamphlet *Appeal to the Christian Women of the South* (1836), she planned to spend the winter with her mother and sisters in Charleston. Prior to the planned visit, however, copies of her treatise were sent to Charleston and were detected by postal officials, who were on the lookout for antislavery and abolitionist literature entering the city. The mayor immediately banned Grimké from ever returning to Charleston. If she returned she was to be arrested on sight.[8] We will see that such tactics against those called to prophesy go to the issue of *cost*, for those in the tradition of the Hebrew prophets most certainly pay a price for speaking God's truth to the people and to power. Before discussing Angelina Grimké as

---

5. Birney, *Grimké Sisters*, 14.
6. Perry, *Lift Up Thy Voice*, 21, 22, 78–82.
7. Perry, *Lift Up Thy Voice*, 43.
8. Birney, *Grimké Sisters*, 149–50.

ethical prophet, it will be instructive to consider the relationship between her and her "dear sister Sarah," and how well they complemented each other in the struggle for women's rights and the abolition of slavery. We will see that both women stood squarely in the tradition of ethical prophecy.

Sarah and Angelina Grimké

The lives of Sarah and Angelina Grimké exemplified the principle that no matter her race, gender, and socioeconomic status, a woman could—had she courage and integrity—criticize and protest the shortcomings of her race, class, family, and religion. The Grimké sisters gave the lie once and for all to the claim of those of lesser character and courage that it was not possible to stand against slavery, patriarchy, and those who were its chief beneficiaries. Indeed, feminist Christian ethicist Barbara Hilkert Andolsen has rightly observed, "The example of white female abolitionists Angelina and Sarah Grimké shows that white women from slaveholding families did have a choice. They could have actively resisted slavery, although at great personal cost."[9] One of the things we learn from ethical prophecy is that frequently the prophet insists, often at great risk, that God requires that justice be done. She *chooses* to make that witness. No matter the situation she confronts, she always has a choice, even when it is known at the outset that any one of the available choices will end in unfavorable, undesirable consequences. Although one hopes to be able to make the choice that will lead to the least unfavorable and devastating results, a choice must be made. Indeed, one chooses one way or the other, for we are—to recall Jean-Paul Sartre—"condemned" to choose, "condemned forever to be free."[10] As fundamentally free beings it is not possible to not choose. As Sartre said classically, "I can always choose, but I ought to know that if I do not choose, I am still choosing."[11] Moreover, I am responsible for whatever choice I make. If, in the face of harm being done to another, I decide to do nothing, I am morally complicit. If I simply turn away, I am, by virtue of having been created-in-community, metaphysically complicit. In this regard, I simply cannot escape responsibility for how I respond to what happened, even if I am not guilty of the cause. In short, *the Grimké sisters proved that it was never the case that circumstances prevented white women (and white men!) from standing firmly against slavery. They always had a choice.*

---

9. Andolsen, *"Daughters of Jefferson"*, 115.
10. Sartre, *Age of Reason*, 276.
11. Sartre, "Existentialism," 41.

Historian Gerda Lerna claims that the sisters were "the *only* Southern white *women* in the abolition movement."[12] Without question, the sisters were the two most dynamic and forceful white abolitionists during the period of 1834–39, the period of their public years in the struggle. There were a number of white abolitionists during this period but few were as passionately and persistently outspoken against the enslavement of blacks as the sisters. Among the few other white abolitionists who exhibited such genuineness and awareness of the importance of socializing with their black abolitionist peers was Angelina's future husband, Theodore Dwight Weld (of the famous Lane Theological Seminary antislavery debates in Cincinnati that led his fellow students and him to indict the American Colonization Society in 1834).[13] Historian Benjamin Quarles observes, "A few white abolitionists, troubled because their colored fellow workers faced discrimination in public places, made it a point to appear with them, courting their lot. Still fewer, like Weld, ate at Negro homes and attended their parties, weddings, and funerals. At the marriage of Weld and Angelina Grimké on May 14, 1838, Grace Douglass and Sarah M. Douglass [mother and daughter, and both black] were among the nearly fifty guests and Theodore S. Wright [also black] was one of the two clergymen offering prayers."[14]

There were also growing numbers of white women feminists during the period of the sisters' public ministry. What set the sisters apart was that they were among the first white abolitionists, female or male, to link slavery with the struggle for women's rights—to see that justice is indivisible and that a threat to justice for black people was a threat to justice for *all* women and everybody else. Since many abolitionists insisted that the eradication of slavery must be their sole concern, and many white feminists held the same view about women's rights, the Grimkés were something of an anomaly, since they saw almost from the beginning that injustice must be addressed whenever and wherever it appears, for justice is indivisible. Both blacks and women of all races were treated unjustly and immorally by white society, causing the Grimkés to reason that as individuals who claimed to be members of the Christian community they were morally obligated to fight for the freedom of both blacks and all women. Indeed, we will see that they, unlike most white feminists, insisted on speaking explicitly and courageously to the unjust and horrific condition of black enslaved and also nominally free black women and how their oppression was so much worse than that of white women in general. The sisters persistently argued that "as

---

12. Lerner, *Feminist Thought*, 158.
13. See Ahlstrom, *Religious History*, 652–53.
14. Quarles, *Black Abolitionists*, 38.

women, white females bore a special obligation to their black sisters to oppose the desecration of family life and womanhood under slavery."[15] Indeed, Angelina argued in her pamphlet *An Appeal to the Women of the Nominally Free States* (1837) that enslaved women were their sisters, and all the more reason white women should identify with them.

Their persistence in exposing injustice and insisting that human relations must conform to the teachings of the prophets and Jesus places the sisters squarely in the tradition of ethical prophecy. They were well grounded in Christian principles and the Bible[16] and skillfully used these in their abolition and women's rights ministry. Angelina even declared that the Bible was her dictionary, that her "standard authors" were the prophets and the apostles,[17] and that she and Sarah grounded their social activism in the best of Jewish and Christian teachings about the oneness of the human family under God. In addition, Angelina was certain that when God told Pharaoh to let God's people go, they were to be liberated immediately. The prophets intended this as well. Accordingly, she told Catherine Beecher that when Jeremiah said, "Execute judgment in the morning, and deliver him that is spoiled out of the hand of the oppressor," he did not mean gradual but immediate liberation.[18]

Even as young girls the sisters, most especially Angelina, displayed an unmistakable resentment toward slavery and their family's arrogance of presuming to own human beings. The younger Grimké was in fact so repulsed by the practice that as a young woman she challenged her Presbyterian pastor and other leaders of her church to declare slavery a sin against God and humanity.[19] Ultimately, what the sisters effectively did was to remove all excuses from white women and white men who professed to be Christian, liberal-minded, and egalitarian while simultaneously failing to stand against slavery. The witness of the sisters essentially conveyed the message that one cannot claim to be committed to basic Christian principles while failing to acknowledge and fight for the human and political rights of all persons, regardless of race, gender, and class. The Grimké sisters had grown up in a family with vast financial resources and were among the very first well-to-do whites to be abolitionists who fought for the immediate emancipation

15. Boydston, Kelley, and Margolis, *Limits of Sisterhood*, 5–6.
16. Unfortunately, there is evidence of supersessionism in the sisters. They uncritically believed with so many in their day—and since—that with the coming of Jesus Christianity superseded Israel as God's chosen people. See Ceplair, *Public Years*, 39, 59, 99.
17. A. Grimké, *Letters to Catherine E. Beecher*, 11.
18. A. Grimké, *Letters to Catherine E. Beecher*, 11.
19. Lerner, *Grimké Sisters*, 70–73.

of the enslaved Afrikans. The sisters also rejected the colonization schemes of the American Colonization Society (ACS) to send blacks back to Afrika.

Looking back, Barbara Hilkert Andolsen reminded the white community that it was not only white men who were implicated in slavery and brutality against the enslaved Afrikans, but white women too.[20] Consequently, she refused to let white women off the moral hook. Like the Grimkés she knew full well that inasmuch as persons are moral agents they invariably make choices, and the only question is, What will they choose, and what will be the consequences of their choice? Moreover, would they be willing to endure the cost?

Not surprisingly, the sisters received much criticism from the clergy, the press, and the white community generally. This occurred when they were drawn into the struggle for women's rights as a means of justifying their stance against slavery[21] and their right as human beings to speak against it in mixed public audiences (of men and women), despite the male expectation (and that of many women as well) that they remain silent regarding such issues, and most particularly in public. And yet, because of their sense of being *called* to speak and to advocate for justice for women and for enslaved blacks, the sisters could not remain silent or hold their peace.

Consequently, some of the sisters' sharpest criticisms were directed at the clergy and the church. Clergy strongly denounced and spoke against them from their pulpits and urged their female members to avoid them. "Women were reminded that their power was in their dependence; that God had given them their weakness for their protection; and that when they assumed the tone and place of man, as public reformers, they made the care and protection of man seem unnecessary."[22] This was the sentiment expressed in the infamous "Pastoral Letter of the General Association of Massachusetts to the Congregational Churches Under their Care," issued on July 28, 1837. The letter did not name the sisters, but the criticisms against women in ministry and as public speakers was without question directed at them.[23] Sarah shared her reactions with their Afrikan American friend Sarah Douglass, saying, "They think to frighten us from the field of duty; but they do not move us. God is our shield, and we do not fear what man can do unto us. . . . It is really amusing to see how the clergy are arrayed against two women who are telling the story of the slaves' wrongs."[24] The

---

20. Andolsen, "*Daughters of Jefferson*", ch. 1.
21. Spender, *Women of Ideas*, 219.
22. Birney, *Grimké Sisters*, 185.
23. Lerner, *Grimké Sisters*, 189–92.
24. Quoted in Birney, *Grimké Sisters*, 183–84.

clergy tried to shout the sisters into silence, but still they spoke what they believed to be God's truth about abolition and women's rights. They were certain that ministry as done by most clergymen was contrary to what God required[25]—that God called ministers to be advocates for the sacredness of persons.

Called by God

The criteria that Charles Foster Kent and Robert Seneca Smith proposed for helping one discern whether one is being called by God—namely, the experience of a deep feeling that injustice is being done, the strong desire to do something about it, and the awareness that God requires its eradication—applies to Angelina Grimké. Although there is evidence in her letters and private diary (1828–35) of her belief that God was calling her to ministry of some sort, there is no extant detailed account of a call narrative. However, in Grimké's case it is easy to piece together elements of a call. In addition, the minimal criteria suggested by Kent and Smith support the idea that she was called to abolition and women's rights ministry. Without question, Angelina Grimké believed she was called by God to enter the cause of the abolition of enslaved Afrikans and to fight for the rights of *all* women.[26] We will see that at times she even invoked the phrase *"the work to which I believed myself called."*[27] In any event, hers was a long process of discernment. She had learned from Sarah to pray and wait for God's plan to be revealed to her. "She never lost faith in the power of prayer, the power of faith itself, nor did she ever lose faith in the clear sound of her own 'inner voice,' or her sense of destiny."[28] Not only did she believe God had a special work for her to do, she also believed that God wanted her to do that work in the North.

In one of the earliest entries in her diary (January 11, 1828) Grimké, then twenty-three years old, wrote of her displeasure with her mother's abusive treatment of one of their enslaved Afrikans. By this time, she was repulsed by the idea of "owning" the girl but preferred this to her mother's abuse of her. Angelina observed an injustice being done and was determined to do something about it. Moreover, she believed that slavery contradicted God's purpose. Nearly a decade later, the sisters recounted the incident in the *National Enquirer*. They related that Angelina "returned her to the

25. See Barnes and Dumond, *Weld-Grimké Letters*, 1:447.

26. It is no small matter to say that Grimké and her sister differed from most white feminists in that they persistently and passionately advocated for the rights of black women as well.

27. Barnes and Dumond, *Weld-Grimké Letters*, 2:537 (my italics).

28. Perry, *Lift Up Thy Voice*, 129.

donor" and that no money was involved in the transaction. In her naiveté, "she at that time only saw men as trees walking, and was not sensible of the sin she was committing in returning a fellow creature into bondage. She only felt that she did not want the responsibility of such an ownership, but had no clear conception of the intrinsic principles of slavery."[29] When Grimké began reading antislavery literature a few years later, she discovered for the first time the sinfulness of enslavement, under any circumstance. Only then did she realize the gravity of her earlier decision to return the enslaved girl to the donor. When this was revealed to Grimké she was left with extreme heaviness of heart and conscience and sought, albeit unsuccessfully, to rectify her error.[30]

Although no reference was made in the January 11, 1828, diary entry to God calling her to abolition work, what is important for our purpose is that Grimké early exhibited a strong displeasure and sense of injustice regarding the enslavement and inhumane treatment of the Afrikans. She believed that slavery contradicted God's will, and she possessed a burning desire to do something about it.

A few years later, writing to her good friend Jane Smith in 1836 about how comforting and supportive Sarah had been, Grimké reported that there was "strong evidence that my heavenly [Father] has *called* me into the Anti Slavery field."[31] When Angelina wrote a letter in 1835 to encourage William Lloyd Garrison in his abolition work and he published the letter in *The Liberator*, Sarah was initially against her leaning toward abolition work, largely because she knew the Quakers of the Arch Street Meeting in Philadelphia (where they had taken up membership) disapproved.[32] However, Sarah gradually saw the wisdom of her sister's decision and came to believe that God was calling her to that work.[33] Angelina Grimké prayed long and hard to God to open the way for her to do a great work that would contribute to the liberation of blacks. She was certain that she was "willing to bear any suffering" toward this end, declaring in a diary entry of October 1835, "O I sometimes feel as if I am willing to do anything if the Lord will only purify and refine & make us useful in his Church militant & prepare me at last for

---

29. Barnes and Dumond, *Weld-Grimké Letters*, 1:471.
30. Barnes and Dumond, *Weld-Grimké Letters*, 1:471.
31. Ceplair, *Public Years*, 82 (my italics).
32. Bushkovitch, *Grimkés of Charleston*, 578, 581, 584.
33. Bushkovitch, *Grimkés of Charleston*, 584.

him."[34] Her abolition and women's rights work was less a result of her own interests than her desire to be "in simple obedience to [God's] commands."[35]

As we can see, Grimké did not simply awaken one day and decide that abolition and women's rights ministry would be her life's work. Everything that happened—from the time she was a little girl—seemed to prepare her for that work. But there was also the awareness that abolition work was not her project alone, that something much higher was at the bottom of it all, that somehow it was all a part of God's plan. Ultimately, it was God's project. Moreover, by the time Grimké wrote to Jane Smith, she had a growing, overwhelming sense of being called to some great work, and asserted that any true minister is—indeed, must be—*called* to the task by God. In an 1828 diary entry she wrote, "I have no idea what it is [that I am being called to], and I may be mistaken, but it does seem that if I am obedient to the 'still small voice' in my heart, ... it will lead me and cause me to glorify my Master in a more honorable work than any in which I have been yet engaged."[36] Grimké became convinced that any true Christian minister, "like Elisha from the plough & Amos from gathering sycamore fruit, Matthew from the receipt of custom & Peter & John from their fishing nets," is called by God.[37] Sarah was also convinced that her younger sister had been called to preach the gospel, telling Henry C. Wright in August 1837, "I do most fully believe she has been called to the work of preaching the gospel."[38] On another occasion Sarah referred to her sister as "my precious Angelina one of the master's chosen vessels."[39]

While spending a second summer with her friend Margaret Parker in Shrewsbury, New Jersey, in 1836, and before she answered her call, Grimké's spirit was sorely tested over what she should be doing with her life. One night she became overwhelmed. Parker observed that Grimké kept asking what she could do and where she should go. She finally convinced Grimké that her "fertile intelligence" would show her which path to follow. With a smile on her face as she entered the dining room the next morning, Grimké joyously declared, "It has come to me. God has shown me what I can do; I can write an appeal to the Southern women."[40] In doing so, she would challenge the conscience of well-meaning Southern white women to use

34. Wilbanks, *Walking by Faith*, 213.
35. Quoted in McMillen, *Seneca Falls*, 66.
36. Quoted in Perry, *Lift Up Thy Voice*, 77.
37. Ceplair, *Public Years*, 285.
38. Barnes and Dumond, *Weld-Grimké Letters*, 1:437.
39. Quoted in Birney, *Grimké Sisters*, 45.
40. Quoted in Birney, *Grimké Sisters*, 138.

their influence with their husbands, sons, fathers, brothers, and uncles to abolish slavery and emancipate the Afrikans. She completed the treatise in two weeks, and then reflected in a letter to Sarah on how long she allowed herself to be stymied by her involvement with the Arch Street Meeting.

> I sometimes feel frightened to think that I was standing idle so long in the market place, and cannot help attributing it in a great measure to the doctrine of nothingness so constantly preached in our Society. It is the most paralyzing, zeal-quenching doctrine that ever was preached in a Church, and I believe it has produced its legitimate fruit of nothingness in reducing us to nothing, when we ought to have been a light in the Christian Church.[41]

Grimké was also resentful of the Arch Street Meeting's practice of reserving a race bench for black members. Among these were her friends Sarah and Grace Douglass. The sisters developed the practice of sitting "demonstratively on the 'colored bench'" at Arch Street.[42] When told that it was inappropriate for them to sit with the Douglasses and other blacks on the "colored bench," they replied that as long as the practice continued they would bear that humiliation with them.[43] The "colored bench" became their permanent seat and their persistent "public protest against that unchristian abomination. This was ever after their invariable rule. Whenever, in city or country, they entered a church having a negro seat . . . , they found their way to it, and shared with the occupants that spurning thus meted out to them."[44] In early January 1837, the sisters wrote to Sarah Douglass to say, "I feel deeply for thee in thy sufferings on account of the cruel and unchristian prejudice which thou hast suffered so much from."[45] However, Douglass, a schoolteacher before the Civil War, and antebellum cochair of the Women's Pennsylvania Branch of the American Freedman's Aid Association, acknowledged that there were a "noble few" white Quakers, most notably her close friends, Sarah and Angelina Grimké, "who have cleansed their garments from the foul stain of prejudice."[46] Douglass wrote more extensively of this in a letter to William Basset in December 1837, in which she described the sisters as

---

41. Quoted in Bushkovitch, *Grimkés of Charleston*, 585.
42. Lerner, *Grimké Sisters*, 132.
43. Bushkovitch, *Grimkés of Charleston*, 580.
44. Weld, *In Memory*, 22.
45. Barnes and Dumond, *Weld-Grimké Letters*, 1:363.
46. Quoted in Quarles, *Black Abolitionists*, 73.

"blessed among women."[47] She saw a level of genuineness in Angelina and Sarah that eluded most whites of her day, and any day since then.

Angelina understood what many white abolitionists, including white feminists, did not. When God calls one to ministry she must be totally committed and willing to sacrifice her all, including her reputation and even her life. In the letter to Garrison that effectively started her abolitionist work, Grimké made it clear that she understood that persecution might be the price of involvement in the work of abolition. She would depend solely upon God for strength to bear all consequences. So she said in the letter to Garrison: "LET IT COME; for it is my deep, solemn, deliberate conviction, that *this is a cause worth dying for.*"[48] She reminded Garrison that one "must be willing to suffer the loss of all things"[49] in carrying out God's will. The divine call places one under just such a burden. Angelina Grimké chose to bear the burden of God's call not least because of her staunch belief in the sacredness and preciousness of every human being in the sight of God.

The Sacredness of Persons

From childhood, Angelina Grimké was tormented by the inhumane treatment and injustice toward the enslaved Afrikans. With a deeper sense of obligation to the humanity and dignity of the Afrikans and to the Bible than to the Quakers, Grimké saw with clarity the sin[50] and "the enormous crime of slavery."[51] In a different place than many abolitionists—for example, Catherine Beecher—Grimké said that she had seen too much of the cruelty of slavery to be a gradualist. In addition, and similar to the Hebrew prophets, she told Beecher, "*Our* immediate emancipation means, doing justice and loving mercy *today*—and this is what we call upon every slaveholder to do."[52] The Hebrew prophets declared that God required that justice be done immediately—not gradually. Grimké never lost sight of this fact.

Implied in Grimké's stance was her undisputed sense of the humanity and sacredness of all people, not least the enslaved Afrikans. Many white people believed that the Afrikans were not as fully human as they, but Angelina Grimké took every opportunity to teach her people God's truth about

---

47. Barnes and Dumond, *Weld-Grimké Letters*, 2:832.
48. "Slavery and the Boston Riot," in Grimké and Grimké, *On Slavery and Abolitionism*, 125.
49. "Slavery and the Boston Riot," in Grimké and Grimké, *On Slavery and Abolitionism*, 124.
50. Ceplair, *Public Years*, 56, 71.
51. Ceplair, *Public Years*, 201.
52. A. Grimké, *Letters to Catherine E. Beecher*, 12–13.

the matter. She worked steadily to get family members to see that blacks were fully human and warranted utmost respect.[53] Grimké knew that one who advocates the sacredness of persons cannot truly support the idea of gradual emancipation, for such a one knows that sacred beings should not be enslaved in the first place. Moreover, she saw slavery as "that curse of nations" and insisted that there is no neutral ground regarding the subject of slavery.[54] "He that is not for us is against us," she declared, "and he that gathereth not with us, scattereth abroad."[55] God required that justice be done to the enslaved blacks immediately, not gradually.

Angelina Grimké argued that God loves all persons equally. So deeply troubled was she over the plight of the Afrikans that on May 12, 1835, she wrote in her journal, "Truly, I often feel ready to go to prison or to death in this cause of justice, mercy, and love."[56] She was prepared to sacrifice everything, including life itself, for the cause of the liberation of the enslaved Afrikans. Indeed, in 1828 Grimké wrote of anticipating that God would call her to a great work, for which all of her "other duties and trials were only preparatory."[57] She knew that many of the truths she would speak, both to white women of the South and North as well as to enslavers, would be unwelcome, tough, and difficult to receive. However, she made the point that she intended to speak those truths as lovingly as she could, but she meant to speak them, no matter the consequences or the cost.

In the *Appeal*, Grimké, unlike most white abolitionists, insisted that the enslavement of the Afrikans was a national sin *and* a sin before God[58]—the "master sin" of the nation and the church.[59] Slavery was both a political and a theological problem. She pushed and challenged white women to see that slavery and race prejudice was not just a problem for politics and politicians but for theology and morality.[60] It most assuredly should have been a problem for Christian and other religious women. Grimké's reading and study of the Bible convinced her that God did not command that any group of people be subject to any other. She was immovable from her stance that human beings were created in God's image and therefore "never can properly be termed a *thing*, though the laws of Slave States do call [the

---

53. Bushkovitch, *Grimkés of Charleston*, 665–66.
54. Ceplair, *Public Years*, 321.
55. Ceplair, *Public Years*, 321.
56. Quoted in Birney, *Grimké Sisters*, 123.
57. Quoted in Birney, *Grimké Sisters*, 55–56.
58. Ceplair, *Public Years*, 56, 71.
59. Grimké and Grimké, *On Slavery and Abolitionism*, 239.
60. Ceplair, *Public Years*, 66.

enslaved Afrikan] a 'chattel personal'; *man* then, I assert *never* was put *under the feet of man*, by that first charter of human rights which was given by God."[61] Human beings are not called into existence as slaves, to be slaves, or to enslave others. Furthermore, she told her white sisters,

> "*God never made a slave*," he made man upright; his back was *not* made to carry burdens, nor his neck to wear a yoke, and the *man* must be crushed within him, before *his* back can be *fitted* to the burden of perpetual slavery; and that his back is *not* fitted to it, is manifested by the insurrections that so often disturb the peace and security of slaveholding countries. Who ever heard of a rebellion of the beasts of the field; and why not? Simply because *they* were all placed *under the feet of man*, into whose hand they were delivered; it was originally designed that they should serve him, therefore their necks have been formed for the yoke, and their backs for the burden; but *not so with man*, intellectual, immortal man![62]

Grimké advocated the principle of measuring and judging human beings not by the color of their skin or their gender "but by their intellectual and moral worth."[63] This is yet another reminder of her deep awareness of the sacredness of human beings and their supreme value to God. This is why she could not bear the thought of gradual emancipation and/or colonization. Rather, she declared that "it is because I love the colored Americans, that I want them to stay in this country; and in order to make it a happy home to them, I am trying to talk down, and write down, and live down this horrible prejudice."[64]

Grimké not only chided and challenged whites in the South and North about their race prejudice and their unwillingness to acknowledge the humanity and sacredness of the Afrikans. On multiple occasions she expressed to blacks her awareness of their fundamental equality with whites, the underlying unity they share under God, and her belief that blacks had much to contribute to this country, notwithstanding all they had already contributed and not been given credit. Grimké was convinced of blacks' equality with whites on the basis of their humanity, which led her to conclude that equality for blacks was an irrevocable right and not a privilege to be bestowed at the discretion of whites.[65]

61. Ceplair, *Public Years*, 39.
62. Ceplair, *Public Years*, 51.
63. Ceplair, *Public Years*, 125.
64. A. Grimké, *Letters to Catherine E. Beecher*, 40.
65. A. Grimké, *Letters to Catherine E. Beecher*, 4, 5, 114.

Grimké was not hesitant but was courageous and forthright in criticizing her people for denying blacks their freedom, human and civil rights, and opportunities to make a life worth living. "In the sight of God, and in our own estimation, we have no superiority over you," she told a black audience in her "Address to the Free Colored People of the United States" in 1837. "We are all children of one Father, who has endowed us with equal capabilities for usefulness, improvement, and happiness; but the customs of society founded in violence, and perpetuated by pride, operate generally to deprive you of full and free opportunities to develop your moral and intellectual gifts."[66] Without question Grimké was in the tradition of the ethical prophet.

Angelina Grimké was certain that she had never known a happy enslaved person. God had not created human beings to be enslaved. In her famous speech at Pennsylvania Hall on May 16, 1838, she uttered these powerful words:

> It is admitted by some that the slave is not happy under the *worst* forms of slavery. But I have *never* seen a happy slave. I have seen him dance in his chains, it is true; but he was not happy. There is a wide difference between happiness and mirth. Man cannot enjoy the former while his manhood is destroyed, and that part of the being which is necessary to the making, and to the enjoyment of happiness, is completely blotted out.[67]

Indicators are that Angelina Grimké truly loved and respected blacks and sought to be humane and genuine toward them in every way. Moreover, it pleased her deeply when blacks showed their appreciation for her courage and willingness to speak truth to power on their behalf. On one occasion, referring to her "colored friends" and their support and reactions to her speeches on antislavery, she said, "O! when they come up after my meetings and press my hand in gratitude and love, I feel as if I was *overpaid* indeed. How much *sweeter* this than the attention of the rich and great."[68] Furthermore, blacks detected and appreciated her genuineness toward them and their cause. Black abolitionist and women's rights activist Sarah Forten expressed blacks' appreciation of Grimké's advocacy for them in a letter, saying, "We *all* feel deeply sensible of your labors of love for our people."[69] Previously we saw that Sarah Douglass expressed a similar sentiment.

To her credit, Angelina Grimké did not hesitate to express to black women her dismay and shame about racial prejudice. In a letter to Sarah

---

66. Ceplair, *Public Years*, 132.
67. Ceplair, *Public Years*, 319.
68. Barnes and Dumond, *Weld-Grimké Letters*, 2:566 (Grimké's italics).
69. Barnes and Dumond, *Weld-Grimké Letters*, 1:381.

Douglass she lamented, "Whenever allusion is made to that distinction which American prejudice has made between those who wear a darker skin than we do, I feel ashamed for my country, ashamed for the church, but the time is coming when such 'respect for persons' will no more be known in our land, & the children of the Lord will think no more of a difference in the color of the skin than of that of the hair or the eyes."[70] In a letter to another friend she and Sarah complained that Philadelphia Quakers had done nothing for its black members: "We attended their last Monthly Meeting of Managers and believed it right to throw before them our views on prejudice," they wrote. "No colored sister has ever been on the board and they have hardly had any colored men."[71] Writing to her friend Jane Smith, Grimké was even critical of the members of the Lady's Anti-Slavery Society for their entrenched racial prejudice and their failure to do anything at all for blacks. In addition, the Society had no black women on its board.[72] As noted earlier, white feminists failed miserably in their responsibility to lift up and demand the rights of black women—enslaved and nominally free. Angelina Grimké did not hesitate to speak the truth about this.

Speaking the Truth in Love

Angelina Grimké was committed to speaking the truth about slavery and women's rights. She knew that a heavy price would be exacted for accepting God's call to work for these causes. One gets a sense of this from a testimony she gave against slavery in a letter in which she said, "I give it with a heavy heart. My flesh crieth out, 'If it be possible, let this cup pass from me'; but, 'Father, thy will be done,' is, I trust, the breathing of my spirit."[73] She went on to say, "While I live, and slavery lives, I must testify against it. If I should hold my peace, the stone would cry out of the wall, and the beam out of the timber would answer it. But though I feel a necessity upon me, and a 'woe unto me,' if I withhold my testimony, I give it with a heavy heart."[74] She simply had to testify against the injustice of slavery and would not be silenced. Once convinced that God called her, Grimké let no opportunity pass to speak God's truth to power. She was right in step with her sister, who

---

70. Ceplair, *Public Years*, 126.
71. Quoted in Lerner, *Feminist Thought*, 165.
72. Ceplair, *Public Years*, 126.
73. Quoted in Weld, *In Memory*, 6.
74. Quoted in Weld, *In Memory*, 16.

told Sarah Douglass that "we must preach the truth even to the last hour as did the prophets in Jerusalem."[75]

Although Grimké was an accomplished orator, described as possessing "theatrical eloquence,"[76] it is not the argument here that the ethical prophet must be an orator, or even one who articulates the language well. Rather, she is charged by the God of the Hebrew prophets to convey to the people and the powers God's point of view and what God requires of them. One can be an incurable stutterer and still be summoned by God to speak God's truth. To have been summoned by God is the most important criterion, not one's gift of oratory or lack thereof. So, to not be able to speak well and eloquently is no excuse for not speaking when God calls. YHWH surely did not accept Moses' excuse that because he was not eloquent but was "slow of speech and slow of tongue" (Exod 4:10), he could not do as God commanded. Nor did YHWH accept Jeremiah's excuse that he knew not how to speak because he was only a boy (Jer 1:6).

Angelina Grimké spoke truth to power, regardless of the cost.[77] This is what Christians frequently and conveniently fail to understand and to do. Being a Christian will have consequences, at times costly ones. Christians are obligated to convey God's point of view to the people and the powers—regardless. One who claims to live in accordance with the agape imperative, as Christians do, must know, as young Angelina Grimké knew, that this cannot be done without great commitment and sacrifice. Grimké had no doubt that God commissioned her, was her ever-present help, and would provide what she needed. But she was just as certain that like the prophets of old she was obligated to "show the people their transgressions" and the nation its sins.[78]

Angelina Grimké was nothing short of maladjusted to the practice of enslaving her Afrikan sisters and brothers and to the denial of women's rights. She knew that she had to declare God's expectation that justice should be done in righteous ways. It was not possible for her to adjust in any case, since her aim was to see the world from God's point of view.[79] But to do this virtually guaranteed that she would be persecuted. This was no less the case with the Apostles, Grimké proclaimed in the *Appeal*. They were persecuted, stoned, jailed, and beaten because "they dared to *speak the truth*."[80] She also

---

75. Barnes and Dumond, *Weld-Grimké-Letters*, 1:469.
76. Dorr, *Susan B. Anthony*, 37.
77. Ceplair, *Public Years*, 37.
78. Grimké and Grimké, *On Slavery and Abolitionism*, 239.
79. Heschel, *Prophets*, xviii, 138, 212.
80. Ceplair, *Public Years*, 59.

warned white women about the injustice and sin of slavery, asking them if they, like women prophets of the Bible, could "see the sword of retributive justice hanging over the South."[81] Her challenge to Southern white women was profound and courageous. She expressed this in an important passage in the *Appeal*.

> Are there no Shiphrahs, no Puahs among you, who will dare in Christian firmness and Christian meekness, to refuse to obey the *wicked laws* which require *woman to enslave, to degrade and to brutalize woman?* Are there no Miriams, who would rejoice to lead out the captive daughters of the Southern States to liberty and light? Are there no Huldahs there who will dare to *speak the truth* concerning the sins of the people and those judgments, which it requires no prophet's eye to see must follow if repentance is not speedily sought? Is there no Esther among you who will plead for the poor devoted slave? Read the history of this Persian queen, it is full of instruction; she at first refused to plead for the Jews: but hear the words of Mordecai, "Think not within thyself, that *thou* shalt escape in the king's house more than all the Jews, for *if thou altogether holdest thy peace at this time*, then shall there enlargement and deliverance arise to the Jews, from another place: but *thou and thy father's house shall be destroyed.*" Listen, too, to her magnanimous reply to this powerful appeal; "*I will* go in unto the king, which is not according to law, and if I perish, I perish." Yes! if there were but *one* Esther at the South, she *might* save her country from ruin; but let the Christian women there arise, as the Christian women of Great Britain did, in the majesty of moral power, and that salvation is certain.[82]

Angelina had no doubt that white women of the South could go a long way toward eradicating the system of slavery if only they had the will and the courage to do so.

To her credit, Angelina Grimké did not just point fingers at other white people who were on the wrong side of the slavery question. Rather, she publicly named herself as "a repentant slaveholder." She courageously and publicly acknowledged her own role as a "man stealer," repented, sought forgiveness, and endeavored to dismantle the system of slavery. She said that as a moral being she was obligated to resist a system of human ownership and to do all in her power to eliminate it.

---

81. Grimké and Grimké, *On Slavery and Abolitionism*, 159.
82. Ceplair, *Public Years*, 65–66.

Declaring that the universe is based on a moral foundation,[83] Grimké argued for the rights of all human beings regardless of race-ethnicity and/or gender. We have seen that from the time she was a child she was aware of the sacredness of all human beings as advocated in the Bible and Christian teachings, and therefore was uncomfortable with the practice of holding blacks in bondage. Her efforts to eradicate slavery and also discrimination against women demanded a heavy price, not least having to endure name-calling. Indeed, newspapers in Richmond, Virginia, described the sisters as "the two 'fanatical women,'" which they, in fact, took as a compliment.[84]

Grimké was convinced that her dual advocacy for abolition and the rights of all women was a most important step in her maturation as a Christian social activist. There was no question in her mind that her work as abolitionist and fighter for women's rights was that to which the God of the Hebrew prophets called her. Her acceptance of the call was important for all concerned. She knew that she could not do it alone and that God gave her the power and strength to do what she otherwise could not. "I know that of myself," she told Jane Smith, "I can do nothing, but thro' Christ strengthening me, I can do all things."[85] She felt that she had to speak God's truth. "But I am calm, my soul is staid on God, & I wait his time & way, feeling that it will be 'woe unto me' if I open not my mouth for the dumb now & just in this way."[86] Like the prophets of old, she refused to hold back God's truth. All were responsible for how they responded to slavery and women's rights.

Grimké's speech at Pennsylvania Hall prompted many outside the building to throw rocks, breaking windows. She spoke truth about the North's complicity in slavery, telling of her own deepening hatred for slavery, until it finally became apparent that she had to leave her beloved South because she "could no longer bear to hear the wailing of the slave. I fled to the land of Penn;[87] for here, thought I, sympathy for the slave will surely be found. But I found it not. The people were kind and hospitable, but the slave had no place in their thoughts."[88] She soon saw the North's complicity in slavery. To the question, "What has the North to do?" Grimké replied that it could "cast out first the spirit of slavery from your own hearts, and then lend your aid to convert the South. Each one present has a work to

---

83. Ceplair, *Public Years*, 37.

84. Barnes and Dumond, *Weld-Grimké Letters*, 1:364.

85. Ceplair, *Public Years*, 307.

86. Ceplair, *Public Years*, 307.

87. The reference is to William Penn (1644–1718), a British Quaker leader who founded Pennsylvania.

88. Ceplair, *Public Years*, 321.

do. . . . The great men of this country will not do this work; the church will never do it. A desire to please the world, to keep the favor of all parties and of all conditions, makes them dumb on this and every other unpopular subject."[89] Grimké told the crowd in Pennsylvania Hall that it was her duty as a Southerner to stand before them and bear witness against slavery and all the atrocities associated with it. There could be no neutrality in the matter. As for her part, she would not hold her peace and would not dilute God's truth. She vowed to lift up her voice like a trumpet, "and show this people their transgression, their sins of omission towards the slave, and what they can do towards affecting Southern mind[s], and overthrowing Southern oppression."[90] Grimké was just as confident that those who fail to heed the words of the prophet are susceptible to divine judgment, but she also believed that God did not *want* to subject enslavers and violators of women's rights to judgment. But because she was just as convinced that God loves human beings and is also the God of justice, she knew that there would be consequences for injustice.

God's Judgment

We also see in ethical prophecy an emphasis on the dialectic of judgment and hope. Because the people persistently violated the covenant with YHWH, the Hebrew prophets generally began by prophesying divine judgment. They made it crystal clear that as much as God loved the people, God would not be mocked. If God's expectations about doing justice were not met there would be devastating consequences. Because of God's love the people and the nation would have ample opportunity to do what was required of them. But God's love did not diminish the requirement to do justice, and the consequences for failure thereof.

Over the course of her four-year public ministry, Angelina Grimké constantly warned white enslavers and violators of women's rights that their behavior was contrary to biblical principles and Christianity's emphasis on the absolute sacredness of persons. Like other hall of fame candidates Grimké insisted not on success but on unrelenting faithfulness to God's requirement to actualize justice. One was required to be faithful by trying daily to do and live in accordance with what God required. The prophet was to speak truth to the powers, for example, even if her actions did not succeed in getting them to come into line with divine expectations. She was to have the courage to speak about God's impending judgment against wrongdoing.

89. Ceplair, *Public Years*, 319.
90. Ceplair, *Public Years*, 321.

In addition, she was to be mindful that because the universe is established on a moral foundation and because of God's overwhelming love, concern, and compassion for human beings, judgment could not be the last word. The last word must be a word of hope—a reminder that if the people and the nations cease their unjust and inhumane practices and return to covenant relationship with each other and with God, great will be their reward.

Grimké sought to arouse white women of the South from their moral slumber regarding slavery. We saw before that she warned them of the "thunders of Divine anger" and "the sword of retributive justice hanging over the South,"[91] and she forewarned them that God was not pleased with their behavior. "Perceive you not that dark cloud of vengeance which hangs over our boasting Republic?" she asked. "Saw you not the lightnings [sic] of Heaven's wrath, in the flame which leaped from the Indian's torch to the roof of yonder dwelling, and lighted with its horrid glare the darkness of midnight?"[92]

The enormity of the sin of slavery and the need for whites to repent of their involvement, to pull up the weeds by the roots in an effort to abolish the whole sordid practice of enslaving human beings, was clear to Angelina Grimké. Like Thomas Jefferson, who wrote that "nothing is more certainly written in the book of fate, than that these people are to be free,"[93] Grimké was convinced that freedom was coming for blacks, regardless of what whites did. She was just as certain that failure to emancipate the enslaved Afrikans could mean harsh consequences for the nation, not least being subjected to the "vials of divine wrath." Furthermore, she believed that circumstances were such that solving the slavery problem could not be done short of devastating violence. At one time she lamented, "There seems to be no peaceful solution to the problem."[94] This could be read as a forewarning of impending civil war. Angelina Grimké agreed with Jefferson's claim that the liberties of a country are gifts of God and that violation of these can only be met with the wrath of God. Indeed, Jefferson trembled for his country when he reflected "that God is just; that his justice cannot sleep forever" and that "the Almighty has no attribute which can take side with [the whites] in such a contest."[95]

Throughout this discussion we have seen that those who answer the call to ethical prophecy are generally subjected to almost unbearable

---

91. Ceplair, *Public Years*, 65.
92. Ceplair, *Public Years*, 65.
93. Jefferson, *Autobiography*, 51.
94. Quoted in Bushkovitch, *Grimkés of Charleston*, 647.
95. Jefferson, *Notes on Virginia*, 279.

stresses and strains, including threats of death. Grimké herself endured name-calling, numerous threats of physical harm, and even severe health problems. Notwithstanding this, she, unlike most whites of her day, not only acknowledged the sinfulness of slavery but also exhibited the courage to speak and act against it. A most courageous woman, Angelina Grimké was both able and willing to endure the cost and perils of prophecy.

The Cost of Prophecy

Previously we saw that the witness of Angelina Grimké made it virtually impossible for white women to legitimately make excuses for their racism and failure to work toward the liberation and empowerment of their sisters and brothers of color. Essentially, Grimké's witness was a reminder that white women could behave differently, but there will be consequences. This is the nature of ethical prophecy, and it is this aspect that has posed the greatest challenge for most, then and now. The stance and actions of the Grimkés is proof positive that one who truly intends to be faithful to Christian teachings relative to race and women's rights can be faithful; one must simply be aware that it will be costly.

The life of the prophet is not one that she boasts about. She knows what such a life means in terms of cost. No prophet expressed this idea more clearly and emphatically than Jeremiah, who lamented, "Cursed be the day on which I was born! The day when my mother bore me . . . Why did I come forth from the womb to see toil and sorrow, and spend my days in shame?" (20:14, 18).

The ethical prophet understands that she is not engaged in a popularity contest, that she will not be well received by those to whom she speaks God's point of view about the need to do justice in righteous ways. Heschel reminds us that "over the life of a prophet words are invisibly inscribed: All flattery abandon, ye who enter here."[96] But there is more: "To be a prophet is both a distinction and an affliction. The mission he performs is distasteful to him and repugnant to others; no reward is promised him and no reward could temper its bitterness. The prophet bears scorn and reproach (Jer 15:15). He is stigmatized as a madman by his contemporaries, and, by some modern scholars, as abnormal."[97] Heschel turns to the prophet Amos to further illustrate the point: "They hate the one who reproves in the gate, and they abhor the one who speaks the truth" (5:10). As a human being the prophet understandably desires to be accepted and liked by others. She

---

96. Heschel, *Prophets*, 17.
97. Heschel, *Prophets*, 17–18.

often finds that the nature of her call tends only to alienate her from others, both the wicked and the pious: "the cynics as well as the believers, the priests and the princes, the judges and the false prophets," said Heschel. "But to be a prophet means to challenge and to defy and to cast out fear."[98] By definition, then, the ethical prophet will be rejected by those to whom she prophesies, as well as many otherwise good people who may find her strong words to be uncouth. Fortunately, the prophet knows that even though others will fight against her, God, the one who calls her, has promised to be with her every step of the way, so that the evildoers will not prevail over her. Therefore the life of the ethical prophet is not solely one of affliction. She also experiences moments of joy. Once again, the prophet Jeremiah makes the point: "Your words were found, and I ate them, and your words became to me a joy and the delight of my heart; for I am called by your name" (15:16).

The letter that Grimké wrote to William Lloyd Garrison was the occasion for her conversion to abolition work. We saw previously that in that early missive she expressed that she was prepared to pay the cost of the dangerous work that lay ahead. No matter what the price, she felt prepared to pay the bill. Her strength came from the Lord God. The cause of the liberation of the enslaved Afrikans was one worth dying for. Angelina had no martyr complex. She simply knew that those who stood against slavery would be persecuted. Reflecting on the work of the prophets and the apostles, she told white women, "For the bold utterance of the truth, and delivering the message to the people which was entrusted to them, they have been traduced and persecuted even unto strange cities."[99] No less would this be the case in her day.

In her diary, Grimké wrote that if God called her to return to her native South Carolina she would gladly go, realizing that "it will not be long before I shall suffer persecution of some kind or other."[100] She had no romantic ideas about what was involved in witnessing for God's truth. Rather, she was aware that accepting God's call necessarily meant that difficult challenges lay ahead, not least having to figure out how to live through the criticisms and feelings of being alienated. She was hurt by her Quaker friends, for example, when she refused to retract the letter she wrote to Garrison. And yet, she bore that as part of the cost for the work she was engaged in. She could do this all the more because she believed God called and commissioned her to do that work. Grimké chose to "act independently of consequences

---

98. Heschel, *Prophets*, 18.
99. Grimké and Grimké, *On Slavery and Abolitionism*, 239.
100. Wilbanks, *Walking by Faith*, 209.

to" herself.¹⁰¹ At Grimké's funeral, the abolitionist Elizur Wright reflected that "she not only faced death at the hands of stealthy assassins and howling mobs, in her loyalty to truth, duty, and humanity, but she encountered unflinchingly the awful frowns of the mighty consecrated leaders of society, the scoffs and sneers of the multitude, the outstretched finger of scorn, and the whispered mockery of pity, standing up for the lowest of the low."¹⁰²

Conclusion

Before leaving this discussion on Angelina Grimké, it is important to lift up two other events that speak volumes for her moral character and that of her sister. First, several years after the Civil War, the sisters made a profound discovery, although they were not entirely surprised. In the February 1868 issue of the *National Anti-Slavery Standard*, Angelina read that at the all-black Lincoln University in Pennsylvania, a student with the last name of Grimké gave a phenomenal speech. Feeling strongly that this was a person who was from Charleston, and possibly related to her family, Grimké wrote to the student, who responded that he was Archibald Henry Grimké and that he was indeed from Charleston. He and his brothers, Francis and John, were the sons of Henry Grimké (brother of Angelina and Sarah). Their mother was the enslaved woman Nancy Weston, a deeply religious woman of "enormous intellectual capacity" and a strong believer in education.¹⁰³ Grimké biographer Mark Perry contends that Weston was not only Henry's slave and nurse but also his wife.¹⁰⁴ Having moved away from Charleston's white community, they "lived as man and wife or as near to that ideal as they could manage."¹⁰⁵ Historian Mary Bushkovitch writes that Angelina was "ashamed, mortified, fearing that her beloved brother had not provided for Nancy and her sons in a substantial and safe way before his death."¹⁰⁶ Angelina took the initiative to write to Archibald and Francis, and from this

---

101. Bushkovitch, *Grimkés of Charleston*, 584.
102. Quoted in Weld, *In Memory*, 11.
103. Perry, *Lift Up Thy Voice*, 237.
104. Perry, introduction to *On Slavery and Abolitionism*, xiv.
105. Perry, *Lift Up Thy Voice*, 237.
106. Bushkovitch, *Grimkés of Charleston*, 682. Mark Perry questions the validity of Bushkovitch's claim, saying, "It is hard to imagine that Henry and Nancy's relationship could really have been kept from Angelina and Sarah, for though the two would express surprise on learning of the three children in 1868, Sarah's worries about Henry's slaves after his death must have been founded on at least a suspicion of a more personal bond. They had corresponded with their brother often and known him well" (*Lift Up Thy Voice*, 238–39).

and other letters and the actions that followed, we get an even clearer sense of the depth and genuineness of her commitment to Christian principles and what she perceived to be God's expectation of her.

> Dear young friends, I cannot express the mingled emotions with which I perused your deeply interesting and touching letter. The facts disclosed were *no* surprise to me. Indeed had I not suspected that you might be my nephews, I should probably not have addressed you. . . . I will not dwell on the past—let that all go—it cannot be altered—our work is in the present. I am glad you have taken the name of Grimké—it was *once*, one of the noblest names of Carolina. . . .[107]

Grimké knew that she was not responsible for her brother's failure, but she felt entirely responsible for how she responded to it.

After exchanging several letters with her nephews, Grimké decided to visit them at Lincoln. She went to the graduation ceremony and stayed a week, getting to know Archibald and Francis. She assured them that they were welcome in her home. The sisters accepted their nephews fully as members of the family and "offered more than dutiful recognition and support—they offered their love."[108] This included advice of all kinds, particularly regarding their continued education. The sisters assured their nephews that they could count on financial assistance until they completed their degree programs, "even when it meant [the sisters] denying themselves."[109]

A second important event was the sisters' decision to part ways with the Quakers. Both sisters experienced the Orthodox Friends of the Arch Street Meeting in Philadelphia as more rigid and conservative in their views than either could abide. These Friends disapproved of the sisters' abolition and women's rights work, and even disapproved of Angelina's marriage to Theodore Weld, a non-Quaker. Moreover, when Sarah was disrespectfully and abruptly asked to stop talking at the annual Meeting by presiding Elder Jonathan Evans (she having been rebuffed and silenced on another occasion for trying to speak), something that was "unheard of in Quaker Meetings,"[110] she was deeply embarrassed and sat down immediately. She was so embittered that she wrote an angry letter in response, but it remained unpublished.[111] The silencing of Sarah did much to cause the sisters to leave the Society of Friends. Not long after the incident Sarah received a letter

---

107. Quoted in Bushkovitch, *Grimkés of Charleston*, 682–83.
108. Lerner, *Grimké Sisters*, 362.
109. Todras, *Angelina Grimké*, 143. See also Birney, *Grimké Sisters*, 294, 295.
110. Bushkovitch, *Grimkés of Charleston*, 585.
111. Lerner, *Feminist Thought*, 165.

from Angelina in which she conveyed some of her own concerns about the group. This only reinforced Sarah's waning sense of loyalty, leading finally to their separation from the Friends. On an earlier occasion Angelina told her sister that she felt "no openness among Friends" and that being in the group made her spirit "oppressed and heavy-laden, and shut up in prison."[112] She had come to see many in the group as "a bigoted, sanctimonious lot," and told her husband, "I'll never join an organized religious group again. With you to help me, I'll rely only on God for guidance."[113] She did, however, worship in a Unitarian church in her last years,[114] but there is no evidence that she joined that group.

The important lesson I see in the Grimkés' experiences with the religious groups with which they affiliated was their unwillingness to be permanently and uncritically wedded to a denomination such that no matter what stances it took they would feel compelled to remain members even when it made clear its unwillingness to change. Rather, they understood that all religious institutions are humanly contrived, and therefore one's loyalty should be, not to these, but to the God of the Hebrew prophets and Jesus. This is where the sisters' allegiance lay, not with an institution. The object, as Angelina Grimké realized, was to retain one's prophetic edge in order to do what God requires. This was more important than being uncritically attached to a denomination. The ethical prophet may surely choose to remain within a given denomination and to make her witness from there, even if the denomination is known to be on the wrong side of justice, freedom, and history. It so happens that Angelina Grimké was an ethical prophet who chose to relinquish her denominational ties, desiring instead to answer only to God.

That Angelina Grimké was a white person is no small matter to this writer, who has personally known so very few white people, even among the most liberal and progressive, who really get it regarding the matter of race. That Grimké lived and worked to abolish slavery and to establish the rights of women is a reminder that the God of the Hebrew prophets did not create white people as racists or to be racists—that white people are not *born* racists but learn through socialization to be racially prejudiced and bigoted. Because this is learned behavior, it can be unlearned, albeit not easily. The witness of Angelina Grimké against racism is the test for the white liberal and progressive.

---

112. Quoted in Bushkovitch, *Grimkés of Charleston*, 581.
113. Quoted in Bushkovitch, *Grimkés of Charleston*, 648, 649.
114. Weld, *In Memory*, 9.

Our next hall of fame candidate was a contemporary of the sisters' nephews, Archibald and Francis Grimké, who were intellectuals and activists who fought for equality for blacks. The brothers were inspired and influenced by the example of their famous aunts, and their activism anticipated the civil rights movement of the 1950s and 1960s. They were also passionate, outspoken critics of racism and the lynching of blacks. This did not go unnoticed by our next candidate, Ida B. Wells-Barnett, who launched a one-woman crusade for justice and against the lynching of her people.

3

Ida B. Wells-Barnett as Ethical Prophet[1]

Ida B. Wells-Barnett (1862–1931) stressed the dignity of her people, but she was always mindful that the God of the Hebrew prophets infused *all* people with the image of God and with inestimable worth. All were invaluable to God, but Wells-Barnett emphasized the dignity of her people because whites treated them like objects to be used for their comfort and pleasure. They believed that blacks possessed instrumental value only, thus having no value in themselves. Despite this, Wells-Barnett insisted on the essential humanity and sacredness of persons—*every* person, regardless of race-ethnicity, class, or gender. She believed that each possesses absolute dignity because of their relatedness to God. This is what Wells-Barnett had in mind during her sheroic[2] one-woman campaign against lynching—when, for example, she declared, "We plead not for the colored people alone, but for all victims of the terrible injustice which puts men and women to death without form of law."[3] Wells-Barnett knew that whites also lynched whites, which was evidence of their disrespect and disregard even for their own inherent dignity. She understood that human beings as human beings ought to be treated as sacred just because they are human beings. Moreover, as a devoutly religious person

---

1. Throughout this chapter I use Wells' name after her marriage to Ferdinand L. Barnett of Chicago in 1895, viz., Wells-Barnett.

2. The late literary artist Maya Angelou introduced the term *shero*, preferring this to calling women heroes. See Elliot, *Conversations with Maya Angelou*, 112, 197.

3. Wells, *Red Record*, 82.

she believed God to be the source of human dignity—that each and every human being is immeasurably valuable to God.

Wells-Barnett's strong, abiding religious faith was grounded in her belief in a personal, loving creator-God, whom she considered to be the source of her deep religious faith—a faith that was instilled in her by her devoutly religious mother. She was also a fervent believer in the relevance of the Christian religion for addressing social evils that undermined the humanity and dignity of her people. The Christian faith was nothing if not applicable to the predicament of her people. Rightly understood, Christianity rejects injustice and human oppression of all kinds. For Wells-Barnett the basic positive principles of Christianity—the goodness of created existence, the equality of all people under God, the fundamental value and sacredness of all human beings, the unity of the entire human family in God, and the requirement to do love-justice in the world—required that proponents lead lives consistent with these principles.

According to Wells-Barnett Christianity was totally relevant to solving social problems that demeaned the humanity and dignity of her people. The message could not be Christian if it did not seek to address and eradicate problems that created in blacks a lost sense of humanity and dignity. Therefore, Wells-Barnett maintained that it was the task of blacks to live the true meaning of the Christian message—most especially its emphasis on the sacredness of persons and establishing justice. In light of this, it should be understandable why she unequivocally and unapologetically rejected the unjust and racist treatment of her people, frequently appealed to the Bible and the best in the Christian tradition for support of her stance, and used every available resource to resist such treatment and to demand its eradication.

Before identifying and discussing specific elements of ethical prophecy that were prevalent in Wells-Barnett's life and witness, I briefly examine her family background. This will provide some of the foundation on which she waged her relentless campaign against the lynching of her people from roughly the last decade of the nineteenth century to the third decade of the twentieth. I will then set the stage for the discussion of the elements of ethical prophecy by first examining the phenomenon of lynching as it pertained to her people.

Taking Charge at an Early Age

Ida B. Wells-Barnett was born on July 16, 1862, about six months before President Abraham Lincoln issued the Emancipation Proclamation. She grew up in Holly Springs, Mississippi, and was the oldest of eight children born to Jim and Elizabeth Warrenton Wells. Her father was the son of his enslaved mother and their white enslaver. Like most (if not all) mulatto children of the period Jim Wells was essentially a child of rape, inasmuch as his white father had absolute power over his enslaved mother, who could not refuse his sexual advances had she wanted to, and did not have the protection of civil law.

Jim Wells grew up on his father's plantation where he trained as an apprenticed carpenter. He was fortunate that his father did not allow him to be abused by overseers and other enslavers or be put on the auction block. Although enslaved, Jim did not suffer the cruel hand dealt to most of his people. Notwithstanding this, and to his credit, in his adult years he was known as a "race man"[4] who early became interested in the plight of his people and was determined to do what he could to remedy it. He refused to pretend that he was better than they, or that his own privileged situation was based solely on his efforts alone. Instead, he attended secret political meetings that aimed to make things better for his people. Understandably, his interest in politics was a real concern for his wife, who fretted and worried about his safety whenever he attended those meetings.

Wells-Barnett's mother was born one of ten children in Virginia, but lost contact with her parents and siblings when she was sold in Mississippi. Unlike Jim Wells, she knew firsthand the cruel brutalities of slavery and its devastating effects on black families. Elizabeth Wells told her children that she was beaten by those who presumed to own her. In addition to being an excellent cook, she was a woman of strong, devout religious faith, which helped her negotiate the tough times.

In 1878 a yellow fever epidemic took the lives of Wells-Barnett's parents and youngest brother. Early exhibiting phenomenal strength of will and character, she refused the advice to let her siblings be split up. Instead, she took charge and kept them together. Taking charge became one of her most characteristic and enduring traits. In addition, she exhibited a strong sense of self-determination and the importance of voice, that is, of talking back,[5] and this at a time when children (as well as blacks in the presence of whites) were expected to be seen but not heard.[6] Her insistence on keeping her family together said much about the person Wells-Barnett was becoming and how much she was influenced by her strong-willed, deeply religious mother and politically active father. The values instilled in her were evident early in

---

4. McMurry, *To Keep the Waters Troubled*, 11.

5. These traits, *self-determination* and *talking back*, served Wells-Barnett well throughout her life. These are also key elements in present-day womanist thought.

6. Duster, *Crusade for Justice*, 10.

her life. She developed a strong sense of self, self-love, and self-esteem, coupled with the strength of character gained from both parents.[7] She learned to depend first and foremost upon her own resolve and resourcefulness, which served her well for the rest of her life.

Wells-Barnett spent a significant portion of her adult life crusading against whites' lynching of blacks. Therefore, a good way to gather a sense of her conviction about the humanity and dignity of her people and her belief in a personal, loving, and compassionate God is to examine her role and struggles against lynching. Her fearless and unrelenting efforts to protect and save her people from white lynch mobs speak volumes for her sense of their humanity and value before the God of the Hebrew prophets. Moreover, from this we also get a good indication of a number of other elements of ethical prophecy that were present in her activism and witness, thus lending support to my decision to include her as a candidate for the ethical prophet hall of fame.

In addition to her strong belief in a personal and loving creator-God and her focus on the inherent worth of persons—two key elements of ethical prophecy—Wells-Barnett also believed herself to be called by God, another important criterion for the type of prophecy under discussion. Still another prominent feature of ethical prophecy in her work is the importance of speaking the truth—to white racists, the powers, and to her own people. In addition, Wells-Barnett stressed the need to do justice. Furthermore, few exploited the use of the sweeping allegation as fully and powerfully as she did, and few were more vocal, passionate, and critical of the silence of the pulpit and the press regarding the frequent lynching of blacks. Wells-Barnett refused to soft-pedal the truth about this. In addition, her leadership style was one of "imperious impatience." Both her passion and impatience made it difficult for Wells-Barnett to function well in committees. But we will see that although some of her contemporaries, as well as more recent admirers and critics, viewed this as a flaw, it is not deemed so in ethical prophecy. The ethical prophet is not called to be a good committee member who has perfected the art of compromise and working well with others. That is the role of other people on the committee. The ethical prophet is called to convey God's perspective to the people and the powers, and this requires a razor-sharp prophetic edge that does not easily lend itself to compromise. The prophet's job is to keep the ideal alive. I return to this important point later. In the meantime, what of the tragedy of lynching and Wells-Barnett's courageous and persistent solo crusade against it? It is primarily through

---

7. Royster, *Southern Horrors*, 15.

her labors in this regard that we see clear evidence of elements of ethical prophecy.

The Making of an Anti-lynching Crusader

Ida B. Wells-Barnett did not plan on a life of vigorous social activism. It was the lynching of three black friends in Memphis, Tennessee—Thomas Moss, Calvin McDowell, and Henry Stewart[8]—that changed the course of her life. Later she would learn that neither of the major political parties included anti-lynching in their political platform. This explained why neither Congress nor the president did anything about this form of terrorism; why major newspapers, including the *New York Times*, failed to support blacks in their struggle for equal rights and protection of the laws; and why they more often sensationalized the mob lynching of blacks.[9] Although Wells-Barnett knew the danger it posed for blacks to criticize lynching, this did not deter her from speaking and remonstrating against it.

As a leader, Wells-Barnett was courageous, devoted to principle, and always concerned about the plight of her people.[10] In addition, she was persistent and generally exhibited self-control, and was convinced that the most important quality of leadership was "a deep abiding love for humanity,"[11] a characteristic she believed was most perfectly revealed in Jesus. "We cannot hope to equal the infinite love, tenderness and patience with which He taught and served fallen humanity," she said, "but we can approximate it."[12] This calls for perseverance. One cannot read Wells-Barnett's anti-lynching tracts and her autobiography and not conclude that she considered all people to be sacred and of inestimable worth, because all were equally invested with the image of God. At a time when whites' respect and appreciation for Afrikan Americans was diminishing, Wells-Barnett risked reputation, limb, and life defending her people's right to a life of wholeness, justice, and empowerment.

The brutality of American slavery and the ongoing systemic racial discrimination that followed emancipation was evidence of whites' refusal to acknowledge, let alone respect, the humanity and dignity of blacks. But as if this were not sufficient degradation of blacks' humanity and dignity, whites resorted to the indiscriminate lynching of black men, women, and children,

---

8. Duster, *Crusade for Justice*, 47.
9. Logan, *Betrayal of the Negro*, 392; also 382–92.
10. Riggs, *Can I Get a Witness?*, 64–65.
11. Riggs, *Can I Get a Witness?*, 66.
12. Riggs, *Can I Get a Witness?*, 66.

especially after the Reconstruction era (roughly 1866–77). The claim of whites was that black men had to be lynched in order to curb their alleged lust for white women. We will see that this was—more often than whites would admit—a pretense, for it in no way explained why black women and black children were also lynched.

Ralph Ginzburg made a partial listing of approximately five thousand blacks lynched in the United States from 1859 to 1962.[13] Of course, the lynching of blacks has not ceased. Rather, lynchings are frequently unreported or ignored, or else they are reported as suicides or as crimes other than hate crimes.[14] Police brutality against black boys, men, and women is one of the most blatant contemporary examples of blacks facing the lynching mob. The severe police beating of Rodney King by white Los Angeles police officers on March 3, 1991, captured on videocam, was more than a brutal beating. It was a near-lynching. Tragically, but not surprisingly, not even the video was deemed sufficient evidence to convict even one of the white policemen. Indeed, in the minds of many blacks (including this writer), much white-sanctioned violence—including but not limited to police brutality—that leads to the deaths of blacks is the equivalent of lynching. White non-police perpetrators often commit these crimes with virtual impunity as well. The shooting death of unarmed seventeen-year-old Trayvon Martin by neighborhood watchman George Zimmerman on February 26, 2012, in Sanford, Florida, is a case in point. Zimmerman was eventually arrested, charged, given his day in court, and deemed not guilty. Indeed, as I was writing an early draft of this chapter the country was reeling from yet another shooting (dare I say lynching!) of an unarmed teenage black male by a white policeman. On August 9, 2014, eighteen-year-old Michael Brown was fatally shot by a white policeman in Ferguson, Missouri. Brown was but *one* in a long, seemingly unending string of suspicious police shootings of unarmed young black males all over the United States of America.

Most of those lynched in the United States after the Reconstruction years and through the first two decades of the twentieth century were black men. Of 846 lynchings committed from 1901 to 1910, 92 victims were white and 754 were black. As intimated earlier, black women and children were also victims of brutal lynching. One[15] of the most graphic, gruesome, and

---

13. See Ginzburg, *100 Years of Lynchings*, 253–70.

14. Marable, *How Capitalism Underdeveloped Black America*, 233–34.

15. There were in fact many gruesome lynchings of blacks. Frequently it was not enough for the mob to merely hang them—they were often viciously violated in other ways, such as chopping off fingers; using large corkscrews to bore into the flesh, then pulling out large pieces of it; tarring and feathering; pouring oil or gasoline over their clothing and setting fire to it; cutting out the genitals and beating the burning body,

heartrending of these was the lynching of Mary Turner and the brutal murder of her unborn child (who was near full term) in Valdosta, Georgia, on May 19, 1918. Because Turner threatened to file charges against the white men who lynched her husband, the local good white people decided that they needed to "teach the damn nigger wench some sense."[16] Walter White recorded the incident in *Rope and Faggot: A Biography of Judge Lynch*:

> Securely they bound her ankles together and, by then, hanged her to a tree. Gasoline and motor oil were thrown upon her dangling clothes; a match wrapped her in sudden flames. Mocking ribald laughter from her tormentors answered the helpless woman's screams of pain and terror. The clothes burned from her crisply toasted body, in which, unfortunately, life still lingered, a man stepped towards the woman and, with his knife, ripped open the abdomen in a crude Caesarian operation. Out tumbled the prematurely born child. Two feeble cries it gave— and received for answer the heel of a stalwart man, as life was ground out of the tiny form.[17]

White women had not been raped by Mary Turner or by her unborn child. The claim that black men raped white women was, more often than not, merely an excuse to lynch them. Indeed, between 1889 and 1941, less than 17 percent of black men lynched were accused of raping white women,[18] and many of those were in fact innocent. While most never touched a white woman, nor wanted to, a few did in fact engage in consensual sex with them. In some instances the women voluntarily confessed to this, but their black lovers were lynched anyway. Let us also remember that many who were lynchers or who were among the onlookers claimed also to be Christians. Indeed, some even attended lynchings before or after Sunday church services. Imagine! In one case, the mob held a prayer service prior to the lynching of two men, which, as Leon Litwack observes, "spoke quite eloquently to the degree to which lynchings took place in some of the most churchified communities of the South. If white churches showed a relative indifference to

---

and riddling it with bullets, often five hundred or more. Frequently the mobsters were among the most ignorant, uneducated, uncultured people. A white author who lived in the South described them as "wholly ignorant, absolutely without culture, apparently without even the capacity to appreciate the nicer feelings or higher sense, yet conceited on account of their white skin." Quoted in Terrell, "Fundamental Cause of Lynching," 131.

16. Quoted in Marable, *How Capitalism Underdeveloped Black America*, 120.

17. White, *Rope and Faggot*, 27–29. Quoted in Marable, *How Capitalism Underdeveloped Black America*, 120.

18. Gossett, *Race*, 270.

lynching violence"—and they did!—"there were some compelling reasons. The lynch mobs often included their parishioners."[19] Moreover, it was not unusual for these to return to the lynching scene to search for bones to give away as souvenirs.[20]

There were a number of times when Wells-Barnett herself could have been lynched because of her courage, outspokenness, and refusal to compromise principle. Nothing, she maintained, was more important than the humanity and dignity of herself and her people. It is important to acknowledge that during her crusade against lynching there were also a few black male leaders who spoke forcefully against lynching. These included, but were not limited to, Archibald H. Grimké, Francis J. Grimké, and Frederick Douglass. But without question, Wells-Barnett was chief among these.

Lynching as Political Terrorism against Blacks

Wells-Barnett,[21] Frederick Douglass,[22] and many other blacks at one time uncritically and wrongly believed that presumed lasciviousness among black men led them to rape white women and that this was the true underlying cause of lynching. But when Wells-Barnett's friend Thomas Moss and his two grocery store business associates were snatched from the local jail, put on a train, and lynched just outside the city of Memphis, for the "crime" of defending their person and property from their racist grocery store competitors, she gave no thought to where she was (the Deep South!) and what could be the consequence of her actions. This was unquestionably an instance in which the men had not raped white women. In fact, they had committed no crime at all.

Not long after the lynching, Wells-Barnett began to suspect that it was very likely the case that most lynchings of black men had nothing to do with raping white women but that rape was a pretext for beating the entire black race back into antebellum submission as slaves to white Southerners.[23] The basic causes of lynching were racism and lawlessness of the whites. To justify their atrocities whites branded blacks "as a race of rapists, who were especially mad after white women."[24] Black men were labeled rapists by the very men who raped thousands of black women with impunity. While

---

19. Litwack, *Trouble in Mind*, 297.
20. Terrell, "Fundamental Cause of Lynching," 126.
21. Duster, *Crusade for Justice*, 64.
22. See Duster, *Crusade for Justice*, 72.
23. Duster, *Crusade for Justice*, 70–71.
24. Duster, *Crusade for Justice*, 70.

committing this heinous crime against black women and girls without fear of consequences, white men tortured and lynched black men, "even when the white women were willing victims"[25]—and Wells-Barnett was certain that many of them were in fact willing. The lynchings of blacks, she came to believe, were little more than acts of political, psychological, and physical terrorism intended to keep blacks in a place of subservience and to totally destroy them mentally, physically, and spiritually. Columbia University professor and sociopolitical theorist Manning Marable had this in mind when he said, "Lynching was the ultimate weapon used by whites to 'keep the nigger in his place.'"[26] The primary aim, Marable said, was to "insure white supremacy."

In Tunica County, Mississippi, the accusation was made that a black man, who was described in the white media as "a big burly brute," viciously raped a seven-year-old white girl. The man was summarily lynched. When Wells-Barnett investigated she found that the alleged seven-year-old girl was actually "a grown woman more than seventeen years old."[27] The fact of the matter was that the girl's father found her in the man's cabin, which indicated that it was likely a case of consensual sex. The man worked on the father's farm.[28] The charge of rape was made solely for the purpose of "saving his daughter's reputation." Wells-Barnett documented many such cases. There were so many that she wrote an editorial in which she argued that no one who was honest and in his right mind could believe that black men were so eager to rape white women that they were willing to risk being lynched. Moreover, she quoted approvingly J. C. Duke's statement in a Montgomery, Alabama, newspaper that there was strong evidence of "the growing appreciation of white Juliets for colored Romeos."[29] In any event, Wells-Barnett's editorial, written on May 21, 1892, led to her banishment from the South (and she would not return there for thirty years).[30]

Four days after Wells-Barnett's editorial appeared, the *Daily Commercial* spoke for much of the white South in its response, saying,

> The fact that a black scoundrel is allowed to live and utter such loathsome and repulsive calumnies is a volume of evidence as to the wonderful patience of Southern whites. But we have had enough of it. There are some things that the Southern white man

25. Duster, *Crusade for Justice*, 70.
26. Marable, *How Capitalism Underdeveloped Black America*, 115; also 115–21.
27. Duster, *Crusade for Justice*, 65.
28. Duster, *Crusade for Justice*, 65.
29. Quoted in Royster, *Southern Horrors*, 53.
30. Duster, *Crusade for Justice*, 65–66.

will not tolerate, and the obscene intimations of the foregoing have brought the writer to the very outermost limit of public patience. We hope we have said enough.[31]

Wells-Barnett was not a pacifist but a staunch advocate of self-defense. Although she rejected random, unprovoked violence, she believed wholeheartedly in defense of self and one's dignity, especially when legal authorities refused to provide such protection. In fact, she went so far as to say that "a Winchester rifle should have a place of honor in every black home, and it should be used for that protection which the law refuses to give."[32] If black lives truly mattered, she reasoned, if blacks respected their own humanity and dignity, then *they* must be willing to defend their lives—by violence, if necessary. Indeed, the late historian Herbert Aptheker once said that as editor of the *Memphis Free Press*, Wells-Barnett "walked the streets with two pistols on her hips (to keep her press free, as she put it)."[33]

To the extent that Wells-Barnett believed that truth would prevail in the cause of lynching and other social injustices that crushed her people she was naive. History and experience have shown repeatedly that simply being made aware of the truth and the facts is seldom a guarantee that human beings—particularly if they are privileged and powerful—will do the right thing. Theological social ethicist Reinhold Niebuhr made this point in 1932 when he wrote, "Men will not cease to be dishonest, merely because their dishonesties have been revealed or because they have discovered their own deceptions. Wherever men hold unequal power in society, they will strive to maintain it. They will use whatever means are most convenient to that end and will seek to justify them by the most plausible arguments they are able to devise."[34] And when there are no tenable arguments, when the arguments are seen to be implausible and dishonorable, they will persist in fighting to maintain their power and privilege. They will fight on without honor and truth, a point confirmed every single day in the Trump administration and among sycophantic Republicans in Congress.

Wells-Barnett was sorely disappointed that the white pulpit, especially that of evangelist Dwight L. Moody, was virtually silent regarding the lynching of blacks. She recalled that when Moody came South to preach he said nothing about the newspaper advertisement that blacks who wanted to hear him preach must sit in the balcony or attend a service for blacks only.[35] In

---

31. Quoted in Royster, *Southern Horrors*, 52.
32. Royster, *Southern Horrors*, 70.
33. Aptheker, "Negro Woman," 125.
34. Niebuhr, *Moral Man*, 34.
35. Duster, *Crusade for Justice*, 112.

addition, when Wells-Barnett lectured in London she expressed her deep disappointment in the stance of Frances Willard, president of the National Women's Christian Temperance Union. On a visit to the South, Willard had had ample opportunity to criticize racism and lynching. Instead, according to Wells-Barnett, "she practically condoned lynchings" when she returned to the North.[36] Wells-Barnett felt compelled "to tell the truth" about this.[37] In the case of both Willard and Moody, she said that when asked in England about their stance regarding the rights of blacks, she was obligated "in the interest of truth to say that they have given the weight of their influence to the southern white man's prejudices."[38] As for herself, Wells-Barnett would speak the truth, regardless of the cost.

Wells-Barnett had married (in 1895) and settled down in Chicago with a family of her own when word came about a lynching in the state. When "a shiftless, penniless colored man known as 'Frog' James" was accused of murdering a white woman in Cairo, Illinois, he was placed in the custody of Sheriff Frank Davis.[39] Claiming to fear for the man's safety, Davis and one of his deputies took him to a presumed secure place out in the woods. The mob located them and put James on a train—he was taken back to town and lynched. Afterward—and as a means of instilling even more terror into blacks—five hundred bullets were fired into his lifeless body, which was then burned beyond recognition.

Prominent black leaders demanded that the governor remove Sheriff Davis from office, but they needed someone to go to Cairo to get the facts to present to the governor. None was better at fact gathering than Wells-Barnett. However, when her husband volunteered her she "objected very strongly" because she had already been accused by some of the men of her race "of jumping in ahead of them and doing work without giving them a chance."[40] When her ten-year-old son (who had heard the conversation about the "Frog" James case at the dinner table) awakened her the next morning to say it was time for her to leave for the train station to go to Cairo, she responded that she had told his father that she was not going. Seemingly waiting for her to change her mind, the child finally said, "Mother if you don't go nobody else will."[41] Wells-Barnett did go to Cairo, but only to find

---

36. Duster, *Crusade for Justice*, 112.
37. Duster, *Crusade for Justice*, 113.
38. Duster, *Crusade for Justice*, 151.
39. Duster, *Crusade for Justice*, 309.
40. Duster, *Crusade for Justice*, 311.
41. Quoted in Duster, *Crusade for Justice*, 311.

that she had also to verbally present the case to the Governor. She did so and won the day, and Davis was not reinstated.

Wells-Barnett had strong "regard for the sacredness of human life."[42] Persons, she believed, were simply priceless to God. In addition to the sacredness of human beings, a number of other elements of ethical prophecy have been hinted at in the foregoing discussion. I now consider more explicitly those other factors that support my selection of Wells-Barnett as a candidate for the ethical prophet hall of fame. How were these manifested in her life and work? The elements to be discussed include sense of divine call, belief in a personal God, emphasis on the sacredness of persons, speaking the truth to individuals and the powers, making sweeping allegations, and demanding that justice be done. All of these, when seen together, place Ida B. Wells-Barnett in the camp of ethical prophecy.

Sense of Divine Call

Like Micah and, to a lesser degree, Amos, there is no evidence of an explicit call narrative in Wells-Barnett's writings. However, there is solid evidence that she was sorely troubled by the injustices done to her people, possessed a burning desire to do something about it, and had a strong sense of God's displeasure regarding the treatment of blacks. Taken together, these criteria may be viewed as a means of determining whether God called her to the work of ethical prophecy.

Wells-Barnett named God as the source of all she tried to do and whatever she was able to accomplish.[43] She felt called to address the problem of lynching. Indeed, she was once offered a contract by the head of the Slayton Lyceum Bureau to go on the lecture circuit (for which she would have been well compensated), but with the understanding that she not speak on lynching. She rejected the offer, saying, "I told [Mr. Slayton] that there was no other excuse for my being before the public except to tell about the outrages upon my people, that I regarded myself an instrument that had been *chosen* to do this and that I could not accept his offer."[44] This is the closest thing one sees regarding call language in Wells-Barnett's writings. Because she saw herself as an instrument, a microphone, chosen by God to be the voice of her voiceless, unjustly treated people, she chose to be faithful to her calling to expose the injustice and inhumanity of lynching. Looking back, Wells-Barnett said that she "was too inexperienced and unappreciative of the great

---

42. Royster, *Southern Horrors*, 107.
43. See Duster, *Crusade for Justice*, 225.
44. Duster, *Crusade for Justice*, 226 (my italics).

opportunity [Mr. Slayton] was offering me with which to make some money for myself, and therefore positively refused to consider the proposition for a moment."[45] Because she was committed to that for which she had been chosen, she concluded that it would be nothing short of sacrilege to succumb to turning her speaking ability into a moneymaking enterprise. Her true calling was to convey God's point of view on lynching. Historian Paula Giddings rightly observes that Wells-Barnett "had made up her mind that her campaign, wherever it took her, was her calling and that she would see it through. It was the determination of a woman who was indeed 'dauntless,' as the black press characterized her."[46]

It was important to Wells-Barnett that blacks be defended on moral and religious grounds—that it be shown definitively that they were more often victimized, particularly in the matter of alleged rapes of white women. "It is with no pleasure I have dipped my hands in the corruption here exposed," she wrote. "Somebody must show that the Afro-American race is more sinned against than sinning, and it seems to have fallen upon me to do so."[47] She clearly implies that some higher power summoned her to that work.

Without question, Wells-Barnett believed that God was the authority behind her call to seek justice for her people. This is evident from the exchange she had with several African Methodist Episcopal (AME) ministers ("ministers of my own race," she said) who urged her to soften her language about the relation between white women and black men, and who refused to give her unqualified support in her campaign against lynching. "Why gentlemen," she declared, "I cannot see why I need your endorsement. *Under God I have done work without any assistance from my own people.* And when I think that I have been able to do the work with his assistance that you could not do, if you would, and you would not do if you could, I think I have a right to a feeling of strong indignation."[48] *Under God* she did her work. Like the nineteenth-century enslaved preacher "Old Elizabeth," whose ordination was questioned by men of her day, Wells-Barnett did the work because she believed that God chose her to do it. That made all the difference. *God* chose her. Men had nothing to do with it. Old Elizabeth told her critics that she had not been commissioned by the hands of men, but that "if the Lord had ordained me, I needed nothing better."[49] Similarly,

45. Duster, *Crusade for Justice*, 226–27.
46. Giddings, *Ida*, 229.
47. Wells, "Preface," in Royster, *Southern Horrors*, 50.
48. Duster, *Crusade for Justice*, 222 (my italics). See also 225.
49. Gates, "Memoir of Old Elizabeth," 17.

the work that Ida B. Wells-Barnett was called to do had primarily to do with speaking God's truth to the people and to power, for which she answered not to men but to God only.

As I see it, the call is the benchmark of ethical prophecy. Along with the commission from God the call gives ethical prophecy a strong theological foundation and is a reminder that God is its source, authority, and sustainer. The call is also a constant reminder that the prophet is not in the struggle alone, since the One who calls promises to go with him and to provide what he will need in order to do the work he is called to do. Although there is no explicit call narrative in her writings, Wells-Barnett's fearless and relentless crusade against lynching and other forms of dehumanizing treatment of her people is strong evidence that she was called to do her work. In addition, she acknowledged that her liberation work was done in the name of the One who called her.

Dependence on a Personal God

Wells-Barnett grew up in a home that instilled strong family, religious, and educational values. Entries in *The Memphis Diary of Ida B. Wells* reveal that she was deeply religious and for a variety of reasons attended a number of different denominational churches along the way, including the Christian Church (in Memphis),[50] African Methodist Episcopal, Episcopalian, Baptist, and, later in her career, a Presbyterian church. Similar to the Grimké sisters she was not bound by any church that was not true to the teachings of the prophets and Jesus. In any event, she was, by all accounts, a regular church attendee, a point verified by her daughter.[51] Furthermore, Wells-Barnett appreciated only that religion that cost believers something.[52]

Wells-Barnett's diary depicts her as a praying woman. The practice of prayer is among the strongest indicators that she believed the God of her faith to be personal and loving, for only a personal being is intelligent and is able and desirous of receiving and answering petitions in the form of prayers. When Wells-Barnett received word that the Tennessee Supreme Court ruled against her suit against the Chesapeake and Ohio Railroad Company, she reflected in her diary, "I have firmly believed all along that the law was on our side and would, when we appealed to it, give us justice. I feel shorn of that belief and utterly discouraged, and just now if it were

---

50. McMurry, *To Keep the Waters Troubled*, 69. The author notes that "Vance Street Christian Church became her spiritual home" in Memphis.

51. Sterling, "Afterword," in DeCosta-Willis, *Memphis Diary*, 193.

52. DeCosta-Willis, *Memphis Diary*, 138.

possible would gather my race in my arms and fly far away with them."[53] This further diminished her belief or trust in the rule of law. Reminiscent of the prophets of old she took her concern to God in one of her numerous prayers, saying, "O God is there no redress, no peace, no justice in this land for us? Thou hast always fought the battles of the weak & oppressed. Come to my aid at this moment & teach me what to do, for I am sorely, bitterly disappointed. Show us the way, even as Thou led the children of Israel out of bondage into the promised land."[54] She not only believed that God understood her petitions but expected that God would respond. In an earlier diary entry Wells-Barnett decried the lynching of Eliza Woods, a black woman falsely accused of poisoning a white woman in Jackson, Tennessee, with rat poison. The woman was taken from the jail, stripped of all clothing, hung on the grounds of the courthouse, and, as was so often the case, her body was riddled with bullets and left hanging in the street. Her innocence was determined posthumously: the murdered woman's husband confessed to the killing.[55] This was also an occasion for Wells-Barnett to publicly criticize black men in Jackson "for allowing 'white men to outrage all decency and law by stripping one of our women and hanging her merely on suspicion.'"[56] She insisted that black men should be outraged and vocal about such acts of terrorism. Like the Hebrew prophets she did not hesitate to speak hard truths, even to her people. The lynching of Eliza Woods caused Wells-Barnett to again cry out to her God, "O my God! can such things be and no justice for it?"[57]

Wells-Barnett believed that as an intelligent being whose nature is love and justice, God understood her supplications and prayers. In addition, God, she was convinced, was not only a just God, but expected that justice would be done in the world. No one knew this better than Wells-Barnett, and few sought more persistently to be a coworker with God in efforts to achieve justice. Like the prophets she believed that God privileges the weak and downtrodden over the strong and wealthy: "O thou Help of the weak & helpless!" she prayed, "help me be firm and strong for the right & watchful

---

53. DeCosta-Willis, *Memphis Diary*, 141. See *Crusade for Justice* (18–20) for the account of the train incident that led to her suit, the lower court's favorable ruling, and its reversal by the state's supreme court.

54. DeCosta-Willis, *Memphis Diary*, 141.

55. Giddings, *Ida*, 152.

56. Giddings, *Ida*, 152.

57. DeCosta-Willis, *Memphis Diary*, 102.

for my own conduct."[58] She prayed that God's assurance would be with her in all her struggles.[59]

Without question, Wells-Barnett was convinced that as personal, God was a constant presence, companion, and help in times of struggle, especially when one did one's part to help oneself and one's people. She had absolute trust in and dependence on God,[60] believing that God always helps those who help themselves. Moreover, she was certain that every person, without doubt, was absolutely precious to God, who most assuredly was not pleased about the lynching of black men, women, and children. Each was priceless to God.

Emphasis on the Sacredness of Persons

When Wells-Barnett began her crusade against lynching her primary concern was the safety and protection of her people. However, it soon became clear that at bottom her concern was for the well-being of all people—that the dignity of all people must be respected. This is why she insisted that her concern was not for her people only but for all victims of injustice and lynching.[61] The plea was for the safety and well-being of the entire human race. She saw the behavior of many Southern whites as nothing short of disregard for the rule of law.[62] But such disregard also implied a low estimate of the worth of human beings, since the law was not applied to protect blacks. Indeed, Wells-Barnett declared, "Lawbreakers must be made to know that human life is sacred."[63] Lynch law, she maintained, was nothing but "growing disregard of human life,"[64] most especially black life. While circumstances necessitated her emphasis on the worth of her own people, Wells-Barnett was convinced that by virtue of human beings' relationship to God, *all* are infinitely precious to God and should be treated accordingly. Failure to challenge the existence and proliferation of lynch law and lynching implied a disregard not only for human law but also for the dignity and sacredness of human beings. In addition, Wells-Barnett agreed with Colonel A. S. Colyar

---

58. DeCosta-Willis, *Memphis Diary*, 134.
59. DeCosta-Willis, *Memphis Diary*, 128.
60. Duster, *Crusade for Justice*, 50.
61. Royster, *Southern Horrors*, 82.
62. Royster, *Southern Horrors*, 66.
63. Wells-Barnett, "Lynching, Our National Crime," 149.
64. Royster, *Southern Horrors*, 66.

of Nashville, Tennessee, that the disregard for human life was also evidence among Southern whites of a deterioration of their own sense of humanity.[65]

Standing squarely in the tradition of ethical prophecy, Wells-Barnett acknowledged both her own sense of humanity and sacredness and that of human beings in general. On the one hand, she argued for the need to defend and preserve one's own life even through violent self-defense. Such emphasis on the importance of preserving one's life implies a high estimate of one's own humanity and dignity. Clearly not one to advocate the indiscriminate use of violence, Wells-Barnett was just as firm about the need for self-defense when one's life is threatened. In fact, when Tom Moss and his two companions were lynched, she bought a pistol in order to defend herself from those who might come after her because of her outspokenness against lynching. She frequently had the pistol on her desk as she wrote articles on lynching. Her strong sense of her own dignity and sacredness convinced Wells-Barnett that her life was just as valuable and precious as any and that it was better to die fighting against injustice and trying to preserve one's life than to passively allow oneself to be taken by the mob and lynched.[66] Aware of her own fundamental dignity, she would simply not give up her life without a fight to preserve it. In this she anticipated Malcolm X, whom we will meet in chapter 5. Wells-Barnett knew that among whites it was not considered a crime to kill blacks, which is why she counseled that the Winchester rifle should have a place of honor in every black home. In addition, she declared that "God expects us to defend ourselves."[67]

Wells-Barnett proclaimed that any persons who are interested in the welfare of humanity as such, as well as "the good name of our country," will resist lynch law with all their might, including their life. She was also eager to point to the common features of the whole of humanity.[68] In addition, she was openly and highly critical of white Southerners' failure to acknowledge the common humanity of blacks with white people.[69] Furthermore, she rightly observed that baseness is not confined to any one race or class of people and that people of questionable character exist in every group. No group of people has a monopoly on stupidity, incivility, and immorality, although every group has individuals in it that exhibit one or more of these traits.

---

65. McMurry, *To Keep the Waters Troubled*, 163.
66. Duster, *Crusade for Justice*, 62.
67. Quoted in Giddings, *Ida*, 153.
68. Duster, *Crusade for Justice*, 199.
69. Duster, *Crusade for Justice*, 98.

Speaking the Truth

Ida B. Wells-Barnett was adamant that educated and privileged blacks had social responsibilities and obligations to the less fortunate in their community. Therefore, she did not hesitate to voice strong opposition to black ministers and other leaders who turned a deaf ear to the cries of the weak and exploited or were at best indifferent toward them. There was no excuse for educated and privileged blacks to shirk their moral and social responsibility toward those who were treated worse than they were.[70] As one who was better educated and more privileged than many in her community, Wells-Barnett courageously claimed responsibility for speaking truth to her people and to power. In virtually all of her writings one sees evidence of this trait. She did not hold her tongue and pen when she believed there was truth to be told.

When the group of A. M. E. ministers questioned whether to endorse her, Wells-Barnett retorted that God called her to the work she was doing and that she had, to that point, not received support from any of them, but only from God. Having set the record straight, she abruptly left the room full of stunned ministers. She also excoriated black ministers for failing to use their power to influence church members toward the greater good. In this she spoke truth to denominational leaders and pastors of black churches.[71] Treated harshly by black men when she criticized them, she later recalled that she received the same type of treatment from black women. This was a disappointment to Wells-Barnett and earned her many criticisms, even posthumously, a point to be discussed below. For now, suffice to say that as a prophet in the tradition of Amos and Micah, Wells-Barnett's action regarding the A. M. E. ministers and others was both intelligible and appropriate.

Wells-Barnett told Frederick Douglass that she understood herself to be a "mouthpiece through which to tell the story of lynching."[72] She conceded that she was not the eloquent orator that Douglass was, but said that she sought only to be obedient to God's requirement that she speak the truth about the lynching of her people. This is what drove her to speak truth in the face of danger, but there is strong evidence that even before she began her crusade against lynching she had already developed a consistent track record of speaking truth to power. While teaching in Memphis as a young woman, for example, she found it necessary to criticize the board of education in the *Free Speech*. Members of the board had seen that issue of the newspaper, and when the time came to re-employ teachers for the

---

70. DeCosta-Willis, *Memphis Diary*, 178.
71. Giddings, *Ida*, 131.
72. Duster, *Crusade for Justice*, 231.

next school year Wells-Barnett was not offered a contract, even though she had been retained for seven years. Because she believed that black children deserved better from the school board, she spoke out against both the poor conditions in the school and the practice of sending poorly trained teachers to the black school. Apparently neither board members nor some black parents agreed with her criticisms.[73] She was, for all intents and purposes, fired.

Wells-Barnett courageously spoke truth to a white attorney general in Tennessee who issued a "rare, if backhanded, declaration of moral equivalency between black and white women." He said that "black women were no longer the 'harlots' they had been in the past; they could be as 'decent or disgraceful' as white women."[74] Agreeing with him to a point, Wells-Barnett decided that some clarification was needed. "Black women, she said, were not 'consoled by the knowledge that . . . aristocratic circles . . . furnish parallel examples of immorality.' The most 'disheartening' aspect of race relations was the 'wholesale contemptuous defamation' of black women and the 'refusal to believe there are among us mothers, wives, and maidens who have attained a true, noble, and refining womanhood.'"[75]

When black sharecroppers in Elaine, Arkansas, formed a union and refused to sell their cotton below market price, they were attacked by armed white men who killed a number of them. The remaining twelve sharecroppers were arrested, and a trial lasting for only a few minutes led to death sentences for each of them. When Wells-Barnett heard about this she wrote a letter of protest to the *Chicago Defender*, arguing that the riot that led to the deaths of union members and the death sentences of the remaining twelve was actually instigated by whites who resented the fact that the men had formed a union and refused to sell their crop for less than market value. She continued to talk up the incident and to make her protest known. Her efforts and those of other concerned people forced the governor of Arkansas to look into the matter and to guarantee another trial.[76]

By posing as the cousin of one of the condemned men, Wells-Barnett was able to visit with the twelve men in prison and retrieve enough information to write several articles and a pamphlet titled *The Arkansas Race Riot* (1920). During her visit with the men she heard them talk and pray about their situation but noticed that they focused only on dying, forgiving their enemies, and how God would give them their due in the hereafter. She told the men that if they believed God was all they said God was, they should

---

73. Duster, *Crusade for Justice*, 35–37.
74. Giddings, *Ida*, 131.
75. Giddings, *Ida*, 131.
76. Duster, *Crusade for Justice*, 399–400.

be praying for life, justice, and liberation. Even though they were on death row, she did not hesitate to admonish them to express a more positive faith and belief in what God and human beings could accomplish cooperatively.[77] She spoke truth not only to the authorities but also to the condemned men.

None was more courageous than Ida B. Wells-Barnett when it came to speaking the truth to the people and to power. Indeed, we have seen that she spoke the truth about lynching and injustice even when she knew in advance that it was not popular, politically feasible, or safe to do so. On more than one occasion she was shunned by the leadership of white and black-led organizations because of her proclivity and courage to speak painful and hard truths. Closely connected to this tendency was her uncanny ability to use sweeping generalizations to call attention to the issues that adversely affected her people.

Sweeping Allegations

Sweeping allegations are intended to encompass an entire group of people without considering that there might be exceptions.[78] It does not matter whether the statement is true or false. This is a rhetorical device intended to get the attention of individuals and the powers in order to alert them that a serious problem exists that warrants immediate attention and resolution. The language can be as jarring and unpleasant as deemed necessary by the speaker. Indeed, the words of the prophet are often harsh and shocking.

Addressing the issue of injustice against her people, Wells-Barnett invoked the sweeping allegation early and often. Even before beginning her crusade against lynching she revealed familiarity with prophetic exaggeration. She knew how to draw attention to what she perceived to be unjust. When she sued the railroad company for denying her first-class passage she expressed disappointment that her people did not see the incident as being racially motivated. "*None of my people* had ever seemed to feel that it was a race matter and that they should help me with the fight,"[79] she lamented. Not *some* of my people, or *a few* of my people, but *none* of my people. That her statement was not factually accurate, since there were surely exceptions,

---

77. Sterling, "Afterword," in DeCosta-Willis, *Memphis Diary*, 193.

78. As used in the literature of the Hebrew prophets the sweeping allegation pointed to the existence of a serious social problem. The *Israelites* or the *nation* was guilty of injustice against the poor. It is quite possible that a sweeping generalization could reference something positive about an entire group that may not be supported by fact: "Americans are people of character." However, in ethical prophecy the sweeping allegation refers to that which is negative and needs to be corrected.

79. Duster, *Crusade for Justice*, 21 (my italics).

is not at issue. Her intention was to bring attention to the matter. Similarly, when she lectured in England she told of lynchings not only in the South but also in the North. Just as there was no redress in the South, there was none in the North. Neither was there protest among white Christians: "The Christian bodies North and South remain inactive in the face of these great outrages which all know are taking place,"[80] she said. Even though she uncovered the real facts about lynching and presented them to U.S. politicians, those facts were received in silence, and it was the "moral cowardice shown by the Christian bodies" in her country that led to her decision to take the battle to Britain. *The white Christian bodies* in the United States—not *some* white Christian bodies—were guilty of silence and neglect. "Our American Christians are too busy saving the souls of white Christians from burning in hell-fire to save the lives of black ones from present burning in fires kindled by white Christians,"[81] she said in Bristol. One gets the impression that *all* white Christians in the United States were guilty of ignoring the tragic lynching of blacks. Such sweeping allegations generally capture the attention of people and the nation, and this is precisely the effect that Wells-Barnett hoped for. "*Nobody* is moving a finger to stay outrages upon the Negroes,"[82] she declared.

As previously observed, Wells-Barnett was most disheartened that neither the pulpit nor the press treated the problem of lynching. Instead, voices from both tended to side with the lynch mobs. While hundreds of blacks were being lynched, "the rest of America has remained silent,"[83] she lamented. The nation did not raise the voice of protest. Wells-Barnett was most disappointed that members of the Christian community were generally silent, or at best indifferent, to lynching. She knew that many were Christian in name only and that there was no substance to their claim of being Christian. Moreover, she knew that true Christians were not racists and did not lynch people or condone lynching. She liked the preaching of Dwight Moody but was highly critical of his silence on the question of race and lynching. She was certain that "no Negroes had ever heard of Rev. Moody's refusal to accept . . . Jim Crow arrangements, or knew of any protest of his against lynchings."[84]

Wells-Barnett expended no energy to determine whether there might be an exception here or there among white Christians, the press corps, or

---

80. Duster, *Crusade for Justice*, 197.
81. Duster, *Crusade for Justice*, 154–55.
82. Duster, *Crusade for Justice*, 157 (my italics).
83. Duster, *Crusade for Justice*, 100 (my italics).
84. Duster, *Crusade for Justice*, 112.

politicians regarding the lynching of blacks. She was too smart and aware of current events to not know that there were exceptions. Indeed, she surely knew of the efforts of Jessie Daniel Ames, a white feminist who sought to establish a link between the rights of women and the civil rights of blacks, and other white women in the Association of Southern Women for the Prevention of Lynching, founded in 1930,[85] not long before Wells-Barnett died. She very likely knew of the Commission on Interracial Cooperation (CIC), founded in Atlanta in 1919 and comprised of anti-lynching activists (including Ames).

Demanding Justice

Beginning with her suit against the railroad company, Wells-Barnett effectively served notice that she would not suffer injustice without a fight. Before long, it was evident that silence and passivity were not options when her people were being subjected to racial discrimination and lynching. She would fight fiercely and incessantly for her own justice and that of her people. She would not be stymied by the refusal of others to support and join her and would seek the truth. In addition, she would listen only to conscience and her sense of what God required of her. When justice was at stake, Wells-Barnett insisted that absolutely no one is released from moral responsibility. She expected her people to resist wrongs done to them and not feel that forgiving the perpetrators should be their first and primary concern and responsibility. Rather, they were to protest the injustice being done to them. Because she believed in the absolute sacredness of black lives, she had no patience with blacks who would not do all in their power to defend their own lives.

Similar to the Hebrew prophets and others in the ethical prophet hall of fame, Ida B. Wells-Barnett fought constantly for justice. Although the specific problems of racial injustice and lynching caused her to focus primarily on her people, she was fully aware that because persons are sacred, they are precious beyond measure. She no more wanted whites to be treated unjustly and lynched than her own people.

Conclusion

I do not know whether the Hebrew Bible scholar Charles Foster Kent was aware of the anti-lynching crusade of his contemporary Ida B. Wells-Barnett,

---

85. See Hall, *Revolt against Chivalry*.

but what he said about the prophet Micah could just as easily be said about Wells-Barnett and her time:

> He was stern, uncompromising, and fearless. Almost alone he faced the princes, courtiers, and royal priests and prophets of the nation. On the simple authority of justice and his own inspired convictions, he pointed his finger in turn at each of these classes and, in a few pregnant sentences full of burning zeal and indignation, held up before them their crimes in all their heinousness, and then pointed out the inevitable consequences. Undoubtedly he was the most unpopular man of the hour; but in the light of history he shares with Isaiah the honor of being one of Judah's most effective citizens. The simple directness of his appeal perhaps also explains why he was one of the few prophets whose words were heeded by the men to whom they were first addressed.[86]

As Micah and other Hebrew prophets refused to compromise God's requirement to do justice, and would have had difficulty working with committees and organizations, so too did Ida B. Wells-Barnett. She herself wrote of her difficulty working with black pastors and bishops,[87] the NAACP,[88] and even with black women's groups.[89] Moreover, in a letter to Albion Tourgée, Temperance Movement leader Frances Willard criticized Wells-Barnett, saying that she lacked "the balance and steadiness that are requisite in a successful reformer."[90] Willard's criticism was perhaps appropriate for a common, ordinary reformer, but Wells-Barnett did not fall into that category. Rather, as one who was in the tradition of the ethical prophet, her aim was not to be balanced, or a successful reformer. She did not prophesy by committee. Instead, her aim was to be faithful to God's call to speak truth to the people and the nation about what God required of them, namely, to do justice, love

---

86. Kent, *Kings and Prophets*, 167–68.
87. Duster, *Crusade for Justice*, 221–23, ch. 35.
88. Duster, *Crusade for Justice*, ch. 37.
89. Duster, *Crusade for Justice*, chs. 31, 33. See also Giddings, *Ida*, 411, 415–16, 478, 533, 534, 589, 603, 608. Not long after Wells-Barnett moved to Chicago she had the support of a leading member of the black elite in that city, Fannie Barrier Williams. Williams was president of the Illinois Federation of Colored Women's Clubs. As she and her attorney husband, S. Laing Williams, grew more and more affiliated with Booker T. Washington, and as Wells-Barnett's relationship with Williams and other Negro club women in Chicago grew more volatile, the distance between them grew. It is therefore not surprising that Wells-Barnett did not mention Fannie Barrier Williams in her autobiography, *Crusade for Justice*. However, she did name Williams's husband (279).
90. Quoted in Giddings, *Ida*, 337–38.

mercy, and walk humbly with God. Her job was to keep the ideal alive, and that cannot be done by seeking compromise in committees.

Womanist Christian ethicist Emilie M. Townes is among the contemporary scholars who have been critical of Wells-Barnett's difficulty working in committees and other groups. Townes observes, rightly, that a key element of the prophetic voice is that it is confrontational. However, she implies that although Wells-Barnett—who once characterized her own temper as a limitation at times[91]—exhibited this trait to a greater degree than many, she needed to soften her approach in order to work communally with others who sought to address issues of injustice. "Wells-Barnett was excellent at addressing unjust structures," Townes writes, "but she did not always remember that people are the ones who help create, maintain, and even tear down those structures. In confronting, the prophetic voice must always keep in mind that a root meaning of confrontation is to face together. The emphasis must be on together. If one thrives in a power dynamic which places one over and against rather than with, all prophetic voice is lost."[92]

There is no question that the ethical prophet, in attempts to be faithful to what God requires of him, especially in the face of injustice and dehumanization, must be unequivocally and fearlessly confrontational. I do not take issue with Townes' view that the prophet should be mindful that he lives out his vocation in community—that when he confronts he stands face to face with another human being. However, in light of the view of the ethical prophet conveyed in this book, the voice of prophecy is generally placed in an individual rather than a group.

In any case, one is hard-pressed to produce examples of groups that uncompromisingly and persistently engage in ethical prophecy. Generally speaking, groups tend to water down or compromise the highest ethical ideals, and compromise generally dulls the prophetic edge. This may be acceptable for some types of prophecy but not the type under consideration. Indeed, according to Heschel, "The prophet hates the approximate, he shuns the middle of the road."[93] He does not compromise God's requirement to do justice. He never settles for less than full justice, and he always knows that anything less than justice is short of what God requires. He never compromises the ideal. This was the stance of Ida B. Wells-Barnett, who was praised by black women at the First National Conference of Colored Women of

---

91. Berry, *From Bondage to Liberation*, 445. Women's Christian Temperance Union president Frances Willard once characterized Wells-Barnett's character as "percussive" and charged that she "lacked 'the balance and steadiness that are requisite in a successful reformer.'" Quoted in Schechter, *Ida B. Wells-Barnett*, 111.

92. Townes, *Womanist Justice*, 211.

93. Heschel, *Prophets*, 16.

America, which met in Boston in 1895, as "our noble 'Joanna of Arc.'"[94] The prophet's call is to convey God's point of view and requirement to do justice—period. It is the work of committees, clubs, and other groups to figure out the best possible means of eradicating injustice and establishing justice. In 1930 personalist Methodist bishop Francis J. McConnell well said, "One of the surest ways for the prophet to lose his power as a prophet is to consent to attempt to work out his own insights into social machinery. It is too often true that the quickest path by which a radical can be transformed into a conservative is to shoulder him with an official responsibility."[95] The latter is the responsibility of others, of committees and other groups. The prophet's responsibility is to remind the group that God demands adherence to the ideal and that any compromise made should favor the oppressed and unjustly treated.

The communal voice of prophecy that Townes prefers tends not to be prophetic at all, especially when it engages in compromise, frequently to the disadvantage of the forgotten. The ethical prophetic voice is an uncompromising, passionate voice and a reminder that God's perspective is radically different from and transcends ours—that God always requires more than is put forth in compromises. The prophetic voice is needed as a reminder to committee members that no matter how good they are at working together to arrive at compromises, God expects more. Every group that is sincere about working for justice needs a prophetic voice that holds the moral line.

Townes is right to point to Wells-Barnett's humanity, and thus her lack of perfection. Indeed, no human being is perfect. Townes intended it as a criticism when she wrote that Wells-Barnett repeatedly "forged ahead with her own agenda and methods. Oftentimes this was at the expense of relationships with her peers. She alienated herself among black club-women and with black and white leaders of her day."[96] To reiterate, Townes is not entirely wrong in her criticism of Wells-Barnett. We have seen that Wells-Barnett understood herself to be called by God (and her good friend Susan B. Anthony surely believed she was called[97]) and therefore believed that her agenda was given by God. Her intention was to enact not her own but God's program, and she intended to bear any and all consequences, knowing that the work she was called to do would be costly. She decided that wherever her crusade against lynching took her, it "was her calling and . . . she would

---

94. Bay, *To Tell the Truth Freely*, 222.
95. McConnell, *Prophetic Ministry*, 245.
96. Quoted in Trimiew, *Voices of the Silenced*, 45.
97. Berry, *From Bondage to Liberation*, 443.

see it through. . . . Ida's crusade to tell the truth about lynching gave her means to reorder the world and her and the race's place within it."[98]

What Townes sees as a weakness in Wells-Barnett I see as consistent with what ethical prophecy requires. She was unquestionably "a person who suffers from profound maladjustment to the spirit of society, with its conventional lies, with its concessions to man's weakness."[99] She was in the best sense a disturber of the peace—a perpetual disturber of the waters. Biographer Linda O. McMurry rightly observes that although her anger and militancy made it difficult for her to work with others, which often caused her to be alienated and discredited for her audacious and indefatigable labors, Wells-Barnett "played a very important role in history by being, in her own words, the 'disturbing element which kept the waters troubled.'"[100] She was not called to be an "organizational leader," social engineer, or one who could work well with committees. She was called to be a voice of the voiceless and to stand up for justice. Her witness is a reminder that every era of history needs its "disturbing elements" in order to stir and "keep the waters troubled."[101] We will see in the next chapter that James Baldwin followed this path as well. In addition, and not at all unlike Wells-Barnett, Baldwin gave strong voice to the tragedy and horror of lynching. One senses his rage when he wrote, in "Alas, Poor Richard," of "blood dripping down through leaves, gouged-out eyeballs, the sex torn from its socket and severed with a knife."[102]

---

98. Giddings, *Ida*, 229.
99. Heschel, *Prophets*, 408.
100. McMurry, *To Keep the Waters Troubled*, xvi.
101. McMurry, *To Keep the Waters Troubled*, 339.
102. Baldwin, *Nobody Knows My Name*, 213.

4

James Baldwin as Ethical Prophet

Literary artist James Arthur Baldwin (1924–87) was the author of many books, including novels, nonfiction, essays, plays, and investigative reporting. His books, plays, and essays primarily address problems of the self, which he saw as the basis of the race problem in the United States. So much of what he wrote was about what it means to be a person, how human beings treat each other, and how they ought to treat each other.[1] He sometimes referred to the race problem as the raging "plague" of race, which, left unchecked, has "the power to destroy every human relationship."[2] The problem of race—so prominent in the U.S. and in Baldwin's writings—is related to the deeper issue of the unwillingness of human beings to relate to others as human beings who also possess absolute dignity. It is also related to the difficulty of seeing one's self and one's own fundamental sacredness in the other. How human beings are related to each other, how they treat each other, and how they ought to treat each other is a recurring theme in Baldwin's writings.

In this chapter we will see that God-language is pervasive in James Baldwin's writings. This is not surprising since he not only grew up in the church but also was a boy preacher for three years. Although Baldwin left the institutional church in his late teens, God and God-language remained central throughout his life and work. He had a strong impression that human beings are not alone in the world, although he believed just as strongly

---

1. Weatherby, *James Baldwin*, 265.
2. Baldwin, *Blues*, 7.

that they are responsible for what happens in it, or for how they respond to what happens.

Baldwin admitted that the first Christian he knew was his mother, Emma Berdis Jones Baldwin, who came to New York from Deal Island, Maryland, in the early 1920s. It was she who taught him and his siblings that love for each other and for other people, regardless of race-ethnicity and other social identities, was more important than anything else—that, in the words of Baldwin biographer David Leeming, "people must not be put on pedestals or scaffolds, that people have to be loved for their faults as well as their virtues, their ugliness as well as their beauty."[3] Baldwin was careful to clarify that he did not learn this from some preacher or the church.[4] He learned such important things—including what it means to be a human being and how to treat other human beings—from his mother, and he was proud of this fact. His stepfather, David Baldwin, was a laborer and Pentecostal preacher who moved to New York from New Orleans in the early 1920s. He was a bitter, enraged, and frustrated man who subjected all in his house to a puritanical discipline.

James Baldwin was critical of the church and its leaders for their failure to behave in accordance with the Christian principles they espoused. He was a boy preacher from ages 14 to 17, but said that he was finally compelled to leave the institutional church in order to discover what it truly meant to be a Christian and also to save his soul.[5] He wondered whether one could learn anything at all about authentic Christianity and the Christian ethic by attending church every Sunday. One had to get such an education elsewhere. Indeed, years later, having been out of the church for twenty years and no longer adhering to "Christianity as an organized religion," Baldwin reflected, "The church is the worst place to learn about Christianity. I have rejected it because the Christians have rejected Christianity. It is too pious, too hypocritical."[6] In Baldwin's mind and experience the church and its members did not believe and abide by their own ethical teachings and principles, let alone practice them, especially in the area of race. So in order to be a Christian or a "moral human being," Baldwin told anthropologist Margaret Mead that he found it necessary to "hang out with the publicans and sinners, whores and junkies, and stay out of the temple where they told us nothing but lies anyway."[7] One who sought to be a "truly moral hu-

3. Leeming, *James Baldwin*, 9.
4. Mead and Baldwin, *Rap on Race*, 88.
5. Leeming, *James Baldwin*, 31.
6. Quoted in Weatherby, *James Baldwin*, 228.
7. Mead and Baldwin, *Rap on Race*, 89.

man being" had to "divorce himself from all the prohibitions, crimes, and hypocrisies of the Christian church."[8] Baldwin saw that the church preached and taught one ethic on Sunday morning, while its preachers and members lived by another ethic throughout the week. He would not naively trust white Christians, and he most assuredly had no reason to trust the institutional church.[9]

Baldwin did not hesitate to proclaim that neither he nor his ancestors were ever under the illusion that the U.S. was a Christian country. Instead, in "A Talk to Teachers" in 1963, he said, "We understood very early that this was not a Christian nation. It didn't matter what you said or how often you went to church. My father and my mother and my grandfather and my grandmother knew that Christians didn't act this way. It was simple as that. And if that was so there was no point in dealing with white people in terms of their own moral professions, for they were not going to honor them."[10] White Christians were not going to honor either their promises or what they taught as the requirements of the Christian faith. Many did not even seem to know what basic Christian principles were, let alone strive to live by them. Baldwin learned that there was no need to listen to their words. Rather, unknowingly anticipating black liberation theology, he asserted that all that he and his people had to do was observe whites' behavior toward them. Deeds, not words, he announced, tell us what we need to know about white people.

According to Baldwin, it was necessary for the truly moral or Christian person to completely separate the self "from all the prohibitions, crimes, and hypocrisies of the Christian church."[11] One who persistently and uncritically engages in such things can be Christian in name only. Baldwin believed himself and his people to have been betrayed many times by white people and the white church.[12] In addition, insofar as he was ever a Christian, he said, he became one "by not imitating white people."[13] He rejected whites' theology and morality and had no use for their God. Why, he wondered, would one believe in what whites themselves claim to believe but do not practice? He knew how whites treated him and his people; as professed Christians they consistently said one thing and did the complete opposite in matters of race. Baldwin put it this way to white people: "I reject

8. Baldwin, *Fire Next Time*, 46.
9. Baldwin, *Not Your Negro*, 88–89.
10. Baldwin, *Price of the Ticket*, 330.
11. Baldwin, *Fire Next Time*, 46.
12. Baldwin, *Price of the Ticket*, 435.
13. Mead and Baldwin, *Rap on Race*, 88.

your theology, your history, your morality by which you don't live, your Gods and your standards and in total all of it, lock stock and barrel, because you don't live by them and I know that you don't live by them by the way that you treat me."[14] This was a powerful truth that Baldwin spoke to white Christians and their leaders. He believed that had he imitated white Christians, he would either be a monster or dead. Accordingly, the Christianity of whites was seen as synonymous with death, and its proponents behaved devilishly. It was critical for Baldwin that both whites and blacks hear and respond to this critique. He was unquestionably a witness in the tradition of the Hebrew prophets.

Raised in the church and "obsessed with religion," James Baldwin never could understand whites who professed to be Christians. He did not understand, for example, how white, presumably Christian women could stand with their babies in their arms while simultaneously cursing and spitting on young black children entering desegregated schools in the late 1960s and 1970s. What Baldwin did understand, however, was what white people's religion did to him and his people, and he did not hesitate to speak about it in sweeping generalizations in order to make his point in the strongest terms. "And so," he said, "I could—can—accuse *the white Christian world* of being nothing but a tissue of lies, nothing but an excuse for power, as being as removed as anything can possibly be from any sense of worship and, still more, from any sense of love."[15] Truly, blacks would have to be crazy to trust anything at all that white people say,[16] or to believe that they will keep their promises.[17] Consequently, Baldwin absolutely refused to see whites as models for how to live in the world, or as people whose values should be emulated by his people. "How can one respect, or even adopt, the values of a people who do not, on any level whatever, live the way they say they do, or the way they should?"[18]

Unashamedly homosexual, James Baldwin did in fact consider himself to be religious, declaring that "every artist is fundamentally religious."[19] But he did not think of himself as religious in the way that most churchgoers would approve or understand. His faith was deep, and he believed in God, but not as whites understood God. *His* faith required that people be treated differently than whites treated blacks, Native Americans, Latinos/as, other

---

14. Standley and Pratt, *Conversations with James Baldwin*, 116.
15. Mead and Baldwin, *Rap on Race*, 86 (my italics).
16. Baldwin, *Tell Me How Long*, 475.
17. Baldwin, *Tell Me How Long*, 182.
18. Baldwin, *Fire Next Time*, 95.
19. Quoted in Weatherby, *James Baldwin*, 228.

people of color, and the poor. Indeed, Baldwin had no doubt that blacks were a religious people and had been from the time they were ripped from their Afrikan homeland and forced into dehumanizing slavery in the Western world. "It is axiomatic," he said, "that the Negro is religious, which is to say that he stands in fear of the God our ancestors gave us and before whom we all tremble yet."[20]

Baldwin did not always use explicit God-language when affirming his faith and conviction that human beings are created and sustained by a much larger, broader being, or when he declared that they have been created such that they can be better than they are, and therefore need not treat each other inhumanely or like impersonal cogs. This point was well illustrated near the end of Baldwin's life when he was teaching at Bowling Green University. One day a student inquired whether he believed in God. He responded, "My dear, I believe that nothing happens by accident. I believe that my coming to Bowling Green was not an accident. If for a moment I give in to the belief that life is an accident, then for me life becomes intolerable. *There is and always has been a purpose and meaning to life.*"[21] He did not name God but clearly implied belief in a Supreme, self-aware Intelligence. Although much influenced by the existentialist philosopher and literary artist Jean-Paul Sartre and his emphasis on human freedom and responsibility, Baldwin was not, like Sartre, an atheist. Because God was so important to him it will be instructive to examine his God-concept. Although he admittedly was not a formally trained theologian,[22] nevertheless God was a central figure in the way he saw and did things, particularly regarding the making of better human beings and a better world in pursuit of what he frequently referred to as the New Jerusalem. Indeed, Baldwin's concept of God seems to ground all that he believed about human dignity, human freedom, and how human beings should relate to each other and the world. One cannot adequately talk about James Baldwin as ethical prophet and the way he witnessed to the U.S. and the world without also examining his God-concept and what he believed God requires of human beings and the world.

God of Love and Liberation

One cannot miss the numerous references to God in Baldwin's writings, despite the fact that he had some real struggles with the meaning of God, God's responsibility to human beings generally, and to downtrodden blacks

---

20. Baldwin, *Notes of a Native Son*, 65.
21. Quoted in Hardy, *James Baldwin's God*, 48 (my italics)
22. Baldwin, *Price of the Ticket*, 435.

and other historically dispossessed peoples more especially. Reflecting on a time when he believed God was white he said, "And if His love was so great, and if He loved all His children, why were we, the blacks, cast down so far?"[23] Why were blacks, who suffered so much degradation, treated so cruelly? Why, Baldwin seemed to ask, did God permit such treatment of presumably sacred and precious beings? Through characters in his novels he reflected that God was omnipresent,[24] but assuming that God was also omnipotent, he could not help wondering why the lives of black parents, other adults, and even children were so troubled by hardship.[25] For if God is everywhere present, is all-powerful and all-loving, as many Christians believe, how can one reasonably explain black suffering? Without question, Baldwin struggled with the problem of evil.

And make no mistake: James Baldwin was also (like the philosopher Spinoza) a "God-intoxicated man,"[26] so frequently did he grapple with the meaning of God for his people. "If the concept of God has any validity or any use," he said, "it can only be to make us larger, freer, and more loving. If God cannot do this, then it is time we got rid of Him."[27] A God who unduly restricts human freedom and does not require that human beings love each other and God to the utmost should not be accepted as the true God of black ancestors, for the latter unquestionably believed that God is love and required that justice and righteousness be done in the world. God's compassion was such that God was concerned about human beings and all that happened to them in the world. God was most especially concerned about the "least of these." Therefore God, as such, was not the *problem* for Baldwin. The problem was how one thinks of God and the mutual, ongoing interactive relationship between God, human beings, and the world. In this sense, Baldwin rejected the idea of God that far too many blacks uncritically received from whites. According to Baldwin, this is the white God who cares nothing about blacks and seems not to be troubled that whites treat them like nonpersons.

From the time of the writing and publication of his first book and novel, *Go Tell It on the Mountain*, Baldwin rejected the white God—the God who was not the God of black liberation. The white God permitted the systematic

---

23. Baldwin, *Fire Next Time*, 30.
24. Baldwin, *Go Tell It on the Mountain*, 87, 199.
25. Baldwin, *Go Tell It on the Mountain*, 164.
26. The poet-philosopher Friedrich von Hardenberg (1772–1801), whose pseudonym was Novalis, eulogized the philosopher Spinoza by characterizing him as "the god-intoxicated man." See Tsanoff, *Moral Ideals*, 350. See also Tsanoff, *Great Philosophers*, 296.
27. Baldwin, *Fire Next Time*, 46.

oppression and destruction of blacks. Many blacks saw themselves as cursed by this God. When the character Elizabeth "timidly" mentioned the love of Jesus to her lover, Richard—who, along with his friends, never attended church and made a habit of cursing God—he angrily told her what Jesus could do for him: "You can tell that puking bastard to kiss my big black ass."[28] Where was the evidence that Jesus or the God that white people worship actually cares about black people and what happens to them? This God "don't care what happens to nobody, unless, of course, they're white,"[29] an angry, defiant Lorenzo declares in Baldwin's play *Blues for Mister Charlie*. This God, the God of the white man, has meant nothing but death to black people. "It's that damn white God that's been lynching us and burning us and castrating us and raping our women and robbing us of everything that makes a man a man for all these hundreds of years," Lorenzo shouts. "If I could get my hands on Him, I'd pull Him out of heaven and drag Him through this town at the end of a rope."[30] *This* God—not the God of liberation, the God who, as Love, is "the Amen of the universe"[31]—is the enemy of black people from which they must distance themselves absolutely, once and for all. This is the God that the protagonist Leo Proudhammer (who is representative of Baldwin's voice and stance) comes to despise in *Tell Me How Long the Train's Been Gone*. In a heated dispute with his fundamentalist, "holy roller" preacher brother, Caleb, Leo shouts, "'That God you talk about . . . ,—look at His handiwork, look!' And I looked around the avenue, but he didn't. He looked at me. 'I curse your God, Caleb, I curse Him, from the bottom of my heart I *curse* Him.'"[32] This God did nothing about the conditions that blacks endured in Harlem and similar places and was unresponsive to the cries of blacks for deliverance. Leo had had enough and would not pretend that Caleb's God had even an ounce of compassion, concern, and love for his people. This was the God that James Baldwin rejected.

Increasingly, Baldwin came to see that the only God that made sense to him was much bigger and broader than the God of his white counterparts. His God, like Heschel's, was the God of all people or no people—the God of justice, righteousness, and love, who expected that every human being would be treated like the precious one that she is. For Baldwin, as for the Hebrew prophets, God is always compassionate and concerned about all that happens to human beings and the world. Baldwin's God-concept

28. Baldwin, *Go Tell It on the Mountain*, 186.
29. Baldwin, *Blues*, 15.
30. Baldwin, *Blues*, 15.
31. Novalis, as quoted in Tsanoff, *Moral Ideals*, 350.
32. Baldwin, *Tell Me How Long*, 421.

is strikingly similar to that of the eighth-century prophets. As further evidence of this he expressed the idea of the God of pathos—the God who is overwhelmingly and unfailingly concerned about human beings. We find him expressing this view in a number of places, but nowhere more cogently than in his essay "In Search of a Majority":

> I suggest that the role of the Negro in American life has something to do with our concept of what God is, and from my point of view, this concept is not big enough. It has got to be made much bigger than it is because God is, after all, not anybody's toy. To be with God is really to be involved with some enormous, overwhelming desire, and joy, and power which you cannot control, which controls you. I conceive of my own life as a journey toward something I do not understand, which in the going toward, makes me better. I conceive of God, in fact, as a means of liberation, and not a means to control others. Love does not begin and end the way we seem to think it does. Love is a battle, love is a war; love is a growing up.[33]

Love in action, the type of love that Baldwin advocated, is that "harsh and dreadful thing" that Fyodor Dostoyevsky referenced through the protagonist Father Zosima in *The Brothers Karamazov*.[34] It is a thoroughly active love that requires that human beings put forth their best efforts to make life and society better than they are. Baldwin described this love further, saying, "I don't mean anything passive. I mean something active, something more like a fire, like the wind, something which can change you. I mean energy. I mean a passionate belief, a passionate knowledge of what a human being can do, and become, what a human being can do to change the world in which he finds himself."[35] A love that builds up, that pushes us toward establishing the New Jerusalem, is what Baldwin desired. Like Alice Walker, our hall of fame candidate in chapter 8, Baldwin was convinced that those who claim to be educated are charged with the responsibility of changing society and the world,[36] making them and people better than they are.

James Baldwin was an artist, or poet. Further discussion of him as ethical prophet necessitates a consideration of the relationship between artist and prophet in his work, much of which will also be applicable to Alice Walker. Baldwin's conception of the artist and her role is very similar to my

---

33. Baldwin, *Nobody Knows My Name*, 136.
34. Dostoyevsky, *Brothers Karamazov*, 66.
35. Standley and Pratt, *Conversations with James Baldwin*, 48.
36. Baldwin, *Price of the Ticket*, 331.

understanding of the ethical prophet. Consequently, I do not hesitate to use the terms "artist" and "prophet" interchangeably.

Artist as Prophet

During a return trip to the U.S. from France in March 1974, Baldwin was honored at the Cathedral of St. John the Divine in New York City with its centennial medal in recognition of "the artist as prophet." None was more qualified than Baldwin to receive such an award. During his acceptance speech before friends, family members (including his mother), other guests, and church officials he let loose "a rousing condemnation of his nation's betrayal," expressing his disdain for President Richard Nixon and the war in Vietnam. Baldwin went on to remind those gathered what was the true role of the artist as prophet, namely, to be "disruptive of the peace." And furthermore, he said, "It's time to think about the Messiah in a new way ... time to learn to love each other. The love of God means responsibility to each other."[37]

James Baldwin was certain that to be an artist is to be political, which also means that one is to do everything in one's power to change people and the world for the betterment of all—and to believe, truly believe, that they *can*, with persistent effort, be better than they are. Often this will mean having to ruffle feathers and upset the powers that resist change with all their might. The writer in this camp leaves no room for the reader to guess at her stance, for she makes it unequivocally clear that she is not on the side of oppression of any kind, that she will never be caught on the wrong side of racism, anti-Semitism, sexism, heterosexism, militarism, rape, homophobia, child abuse, and other forms of human degradation. This is similar to the ethical prophet, and in this regard to be a poet, an artist, is to be in the camp of ethical prophecy.

For James Baldwin, being a poet or artist did not primarily have to do with his talent or the mechanics of his art. Rather, he expressed his true view of the artist to Margaret Mead when he said, "I'm talking about a certain kind of responsibility."[38] What is important is a commitment to the future and to young people. "It has to do with what we know human beings have been and can become, and that is so subversive that it is called poetry."[39] Baldwin would have agreed with his friend, blues-jazz singer Nina Simone, who replied to a question about the relationship between art and politics

---

37. Quoted in Leeming, *James Baldwin*, 322.
38. Mead and Baldwin, *Rap on Race*, 201.
39. Mead and Baldwin, *Rap on Race*, 201.

by saying, "How are you gonna be an artist and not reflect the times?"[40] Accordingly, what the artist says, paints, sings, or writes should reflect that she is aware of the injustices and inhumanity all around her and that she protests them with all her might. To be an artist or poet, much like the ethical prophet, is to be an "incorrigible disturber of the peace,"[41] to be nothing short of subversive.[42] James Baldwin, like the Hebrew prophets, was nothing if not revolutionary, or a transformed nonconformist. The poet-artist was, for Baldwin, that "breed of men and women historically despised while living and acclaimed when safely dead."[43] The responsibility of the poet-artist, like the ethical prophet, is that under no circumstance is she to stop doing battle with society as long as injustice and oppression abound.

In the face of injustice and oppression, the artist calls out the culprits and tries to change their consciousness[44] and their way of being, relating, and behaving in the world. Consistent with many other Afrikan American and Afrikan artists, not least his good friend Lorraine Hansberry,[45] Baldwin saw no radical distinction or contradiction between art and protest.[46] Accordingly, it is the responsibility of the artist to challenge people and the world to live by a higher standard. Moreover, to talk about being better means that one has entered the realm of politics,[47] so the artist cannot avoid being political. If this is a given, then the real issue has to do with *how* the artist will be political—by siding with the oppressors or with the oppressed. Does the artist seek to pacify the oppressed and urge them to accept their socioeconomic status, or does she challenge them to take their destiny into their own hands and to fight for their total liberation and empowerment? Either way, the artist is engaged in politics. She must simply decide whether hers is a politics of the status quo or of empowerment and liberation.

If society is sick, the artist, like the ethical prophet, is obligated to sound the alarm. Her role is precisely what Baldwin said when reflecting on his *Blues for Mister Charlie*, namely, "to shock the people and make them think."[48] In every case the artist is responsible for telling society the truth

---

40. Garbus, *What Happened, Miss Simone?*
41. Baldwin, *Price of the Ticket*, 316.
42. Standley and Pratt, *Conversations with James Baldwin*, 178.
43. Baldwin, *Price of the Ticket*, 316–17.
44. Standley and Pratt, *Conversations with James Baldwin*, 154.
45. Hansberry, "Challenge to Artists," 134, 135, 137.
46. Standley and Pratt, *Conversations with James Baldwin*, 241.
47. Achebe, *There Was a Country*, 58.
48. Quoted in Weatherby, *James Baldwin*, 252.

about itself.[49] Some artists do their work as if it has nothing to do with what's going on in the world around them. They believe that the artist has no role in the social disturbances of her day. Baldwin, Hansberry, Chinua Achebe, Alice Walker, Toni Morrison, and artists like them reject this approach. If art and community are linked, as Baldwin and others believe,[50] then art must be a protest against injustice. Achebe argued, and Baldwin would have wholeheartedly agreed, "that decency and civilization would insist that the writer take sides with the powerless. An artist, in my definition of the word, would not be someone who takes sides with the emperor against his powerless subjects."[51] This is precisely the stance of the ethical prophet. She does not find herself on the side of unjust rulers against powerless citizens—does not find herself on the side of Donald Trump and present-day Congressional Republicans.

The Baldwin type of artist cannot live in the face of injustice and human degradation and pretend to do her work in the closet, entirely oblivious to what is happening around her. To be an artist, Baldwin said in "The Creative Dilemma," is to be an "incorrigible disturber of the peace," whose presence has been felt in all societies.[52] Because the artist sees so clearly and feels the pain of the injustices and inequities in society she is almost constantly warring against it, for society's sake, hers,[53] and the beaten and crushed people around her. Much like the Hebrew prophets, the artist's war with her society is "a lover's war," in which she does her best to make freedom a reality for all.[54] Although deeply disturbed by the unjust and oppressive conditions of her country, the artist, like the ethical prophet, refuses to divorce herself from her country or leave it to its own self-destructive devices. Still, angered by the wrongdoings of the people and the nation, the artist's love for them will not allow her to desert them.

Further elaborating on what it means to be an artist, Baldwin said, "The poet and the people get on generally very badly, and yet they need each other.... The poet or the revolutionary is there to articulate the necessity, but until the people themselves apprehend it, nothing happens.... An artist is here not to give you answers, but to ask you questions."[55] The work of the artist is neither easy nor popular. "The hardest thing [the artist] has to do

49. Baldwin, *Price of the Ticket*, 396.
50. Achebe, *There Was a Country*, 56.
51. Achebe, *There Was a Country*, 58–59.
52. Baldwin, "Creative Dilemma," 15.
53. Baldwin, "Creative Dilemma," 15.
54. Baldwin, "Creative Dilemma," 58.
55. Quoted in Sylvander, *James Baldwin*, 13.

is to remain an artist," Baldwin said. "I have to do what I can do and bear witness to something that has to be there when the battle is over."[56]

The artist, like the prophets of old, knows that she is not called to be popular. She has only to do the work to which she is called. She must find or make ways to get the work done, to persist in the face of all adversity, criticism, and rejection. This is the extent to which one should be committed to ethical prophecy, to art. Baldwin expressed this very idea in an interview with *The Black Scholar* in 1973. Tenacity and fortitude are necessary for the artist, much like the prophet. Reflecting on himself as a literary artist and his sense of what was required of him, Baldwin said, "I am a writer and . . . there are no excuses. I must get my work done. It is not up to the world to tell me how to do it, it is up to me. The important thing is the work. The world's judgment is something I have to live with."[57] This is all connected to what it means to be called to one's vocation. Pure and simple, the artist, the prophet, must continue the work. She must perform her prophetic duties, no matter how unpopular they or she may be. Her calling is to do a certain work, to warn the people that there is need for change and to somehow make them see that they can make the world better than it was before they were born into it—that this is indeed their responsibility.

As literary artist, then, James Baldwin was an excellent example of what it means to be prophetic in an ethical sense—of what it means to call people back to covenant relation with God and each other and to insist that justice should be done in ways that are consistent with love and respect for the dignity of human beings. The poet-prophet speaks through Baldwin when he likens the vision of the artist to that of the revolutionary. Both are possessed by the vision and find themselves not so much following it as being driven by it.

Unquestionably, James Baldwin was in the ethical prophet camp. To what extent did he possess other traits of ethical prophecy—for example, sense of call, emphasis on the sacredness of persons, courage to speak truth to the people and to power, declaration of God's judgment against injustice, awareness of the cost of prophecy, and expressing words of hope—a sense that things can be better than they are? So important is the call that I begin by considering whether this element was present in Baldwin's work and witness.

---

56. Quoted in Sylvander, *James Baldwin*, 21.

57. Standley and Pratt, *Conversations with James Baldwin*, 154.

The Call

The ethical prophet is called by God. The call is critical, since it could mean the difference between a professional or "official" prophet and an *ethical* prophet. There is no question that Baldwin at times saw himself in the role of the Hebrew prophet. For example, he opened his address "The American Dream and the American Negro" in 1965 by saying, "I find myself, not for the first time, in the position of a kind of Jeremiah."[58] As such, he *must* address social issues through his art, not run away from them or relegate them to the sideline. He told M. S. Handler of the *New York Times*, "Writers are running away from social commitments. In some strange way I don't understand they seem to have the idea that one can be an artist and be safe, too. That is the American idea of success."[59] But Baldwin rejected this. The prophet is not called to be successful but to be faithful. "Success" is not one of the ingredients in the recipe for ethical prophecy, but speaking God's truth about the need to do justice is indeed a main ingredient. Like Jeremiah, Baldwin also warned the people and the nation of impending judgment if they did not awaken to the existing injustices and do something about them. This is what he meant when he said, "Unless we can establish some kind of dialogue between those people who enjoy the American dream and those people who have not achieved it, we will be in terrible trouble."[60] Unfortunately, the people and the nation did not heed his warning, and the so-called riots of the mid- to late 1960s erupted in Detroit, Watts, and other urban centers.

James Baldwin did not have to guess at what it means to be black in the United States. He had grown up in the horrid conditions of Harlem and experienced firsthand what it meant to have his personhood and that of his family members and neighbors undermined and denied by whites and the system from which they benefited in so many ways. He could speak with authority about the horrible conditions because he was a member of the community. He too had been the victim of racism and other life-threatening practices.

Baldwin had virtually no patience with blacks who seemed to think that racism was not a serious issue—that it was a mere figment of blacks' imagination or that they were somehow making it all up. "Only a really shattered, scotch- or martini-guzzling, upward-mobility-struck house nigger could possibly deny the relentless tension of the black condition," Baldwin asserted. "Being black affected one's life span, insurance rates, blood

---

58. Baldwin, *Price of the Ticket*, 403.
59. Quoted in Weatherby, *James Baldwin*, 229.
60. Baldwin, *Price of the Ticket*, 406.

pressure, lovers, children, every dangerous hour of every dangerous day. There was absolutely no way *not* to be black without ceasing to exist. But it frequently seemed that there was no way to be black, either, without ceasing to exist."[61] Baldwin was convinced that his calling as an artist was to speak and witness against racism, economic exploitation, and all other injustices done to his people—indeed to any people. He knew that every human being was precious beyond words, and he did not hesitate to champion this view.

Sacredness and Interrelatedness of Persons

As seen earlier, much of Baldwin's writing is devoted to unraveling the meaning of the self or person, especially the black self or person, in a nation that continues to systematically undermine their *sense* of worth. Baldwin always knew that in the deepest sense blacks are as valuable and sacred to God as any group of human beings; that the value of a human being has nothing to do with her skin color, class, gender, or religion; that the value of a human being was all that Baldwin held to be sacred; and that one does not become more valuable or better by mistreating and devaluing others.[62] However, his experience growing up in Harlem, his understanding of his nation's history, and his awareness of current events convinced him that in light of the way they were being treated, blacks were being systematically taught to devalue and hate everything about themselves and their culture. Calculated efforts were being made to undermine their sense of self-worth, if not destroy it entirely. This is not to say that Baldwin believed that blacks' actual self-worth could be taken away or destroyed by the powers. This was not possible in his view, since he believed that God is the source of human dignity. In order to destroy human self-worth the source has to be destroyed. Human beings are capable only of undermining or destroying the *sense* of self-worth, but this is not the same as destroying human dignity itself. Furthermore, if the *sense* of self-worth is destroyed, it can be regained by one who is determined to reclaim it. None knew this better than James Baldwin, who was committed to convincing his people that they are inestimably valuable beings and that they themselves needed to take the lead in proclaiming and defending their dignity.

However, Baldwin also knew that one who has had everything taken away, and who lacks a sense of self-worth, is dangerous beyond words, both to self and to society. He was certain that human beings cannot live productively without a sense of their own worth; they cannot lead quality lives and

---

61. Baldwin, *Price of the Ticket*, 643.
62. Baldwin, *Cross of Redemption*, 205.

lives that are respectful of other human beings. Such persons are desperate beyond all measure and therefore have nothing to lose. They are, Baldwin concluded, among "the most dangerous creation of any society."[63] They may be prone to do anything necessary to regain their sense of dignity. Furthermore, Baldwin was aware that whenever one group of people presumes to be superior to another by virtue of race, it is a blueprint for murder. This has been borne out countless times in this country. For example, on June 17, 2015, Dylann Roof, a young, crazed white supremacist, walked into a prayer meeting at the Emanuel AME Church in Charleston, South Carolina, sat down among congregants for about an hour, and then opened fire on members, killing nine, including the pastor. "The glorification of one race and the consequent debasement of another—or others—always has been and always will be a recipe for murder," Baldwin declared. "If one is permitted to treat any group of people with special disfavor because of their race or the color of their skin, there is no limit to what one will force them to endure, and, since the entire race has been mysteriously indicted, no reason not to attempt to destroy it root and branch."[64] This is what comes to mind when I think about police shooting after police shooting of unarmed black boys and men throughout the U.S.—sometimes in the back, and sometimes by other means while in police custody, such as the mortal wounding of Freddie Gray while being transported in a police van in Baltimore, Maryland, and the suspicious hanging death of Sandra Bland in a Waller County jail cell in Hempstead, Texas, in 2015.

Unlike many whites, James Baldwin *assumed* the humanity and sacredness of black people, insisting that they are just like everybody else, capable of doing all the things that other human beings are capable of doing, both good and bad. "We are also mercenaries, dictators, murderers, liars,"[65] Baldwin told his people. Morally, blacks are not necessarily better than whites. "We treat each other just the way the rest of the human race treats itself," he told Julius Lester. "Abominably."[66] It was never Baldwin's intention or desire to put blacks on a moral pedestal or to claim that they were somehow fundamentally more moral than white people. His aim was to show that their humanity and dignity should be acknowledged by white people in word and deed. Although individuals of every race sometimes behave in ways that fail to honor the human race and the Creator—a fact that led Baldwin to conclude that "most people are not, in action, worth very much"—still

63. Baldwin, *Fire Next Time*, 75.
64. Baldwin, *Fire Next Time*, 82.
65. Baldwin, *Price of the Ticket*, 406.
66. Standley and Pratt, *Conversations with James Baldwin*, 227.

he firmly believed that "every human being is an unprecedented miracle."[67] He went on to say, "One tries to treat them as the miracles they are, while trying to protect oneself against the disasters they've become."[68] Moreover, Baldwin believed that black lives are as sacred and precious as white lives.[69]

The Hebrew prophets had no doubt about the sacredness of human beings and their interrelatedness with each other and with God. Regardless of how mean and cruel whites are to blacks, Baldwin unhesitatingly proclaimed through one of his characters that he "was part of these people, no matter how bitterly I judged them."[70] Whites were as much his "countrymen" as blacks—that was a historical and biological fact. He acknowledged that his ancestors were both black and white and that blacks and whites need each other—and must live and behave as if they do if this is ever to be a great nation.[71]

When Baldwin acknowledged that his countrymen, his ancestors, were both black and white, and that they needed each other, he made more than a biologico-socio-historical statement of fact. Biologically, blacks and whites in the U.S. are unquestionably related to each other as a result of the rapes of numerous black women by white men during and beyond American slavery. But Baldwin also knew that there is a much deeper sense in which it is true to say that blacks and whites—indeed all people—are integrally interrelated and interdependent and thus part of each other. Human beings are inextricably connected by something greater than themselves, he admonished. "Whether I like it or not, or whether you like it or not, we are bound together forever," he told white people. "We are part of each other. What is happening to every Negro in the country at any time is also happening to you. There is no way around this."[72] This must mean that the source of this fundamental connection is beyond human beings.

We find numerous statements like this in Baldwin's writings, which should leave no doubt about his ethical personalism, that is, his strong belief in the humanity and sacredness of human beings and his conviction that we are kin on the deepest level. In "Fifth Avenue, Uptown," he wrote, "It is a terrible, an inexorable, law that one cannot deny the humanity of another without diminishing one's own: in the face of one's victim, one sees

---

67. Baldwin, *No Name in the Street*, 10.
68. Baldwin, *No Name in the Street*, 10.
69. Baldwin, *Cross of Redemption*, 210.
70. Baldwin, *Tell Me How Long*, 329.
71. Baldwin, *Price of the Ticket*, 407.
72. Baldwin, *Nobody Knows My Name*, 136.

oneself."[73] There are few more profound theological statements than this. The humanity of every human being is inextricably bound up in the humanity of every other, and there is absolutely nothing that any of us can do about it. Insisting on taking the higher moral ground, Baldwin staunchly opposed any attempt on the part of blacks to do to whites what they have done (and do) to them. "I think I know—we see it around us every day—the spiritual wasteland to which that road leads," Baldwin said. "It is so simple a fact and one that is so hard, apparently, to grasp: *Whoever debases others is debasing himself.*"[74] We are, all of us, inextricably bound together with God and each other. Consequently, what happens to any one or a group of us happens to the rest of us and to God as well.

James Baldwin refused to deny what he knew to be true about human beings and how supremely valuable and integrally interrelated he believed them to be. Failure in this regard would be self-destructive, since one cannot deny the humanity and dignity of another without also denying her own. "If I deny what I know to be true," Baldwin asserted, "if I deny that that white child next to me is simply another child, and if I pretend that that child, because its color is white, deserves destruction, I have begun the destruction of my own personality and I am beginning the destruction of my own children."[75] No one worked more persistently than Baldwin to help white people understand that human beings have been created such that all are part of each other and need each other for their very survival. What affects one affects all others, directly or indirectly. Human beings belong to each other and are invariably affected by what happens to each. They are part of each other. Nowhere did Baldwin articulate this idea more poignantly than in "Here Be Dragons." One is left with absolutely no doubt as to Baldwin's view of the fundamental interrelatedness of human beings, and his conviction that they need each other in order to be all that God intends for them to be.

> But we are all androgynous, not only because we are all born of a woman impregnated by the seed of a man but because each of us, helplessly and forever, contains the other—male in female, female in male, white in black and black in white. We are a part of each other. Many of my countrymen appear to find this fact exceedingly inconvenient and even unfair, and so, very often, do I. But none of us can do anything about it.[76]

73. Baldwin, *Nobody Knows My Name*, 71.
74. Baldwin, *Fire Next Time*, 82 (Baldwin's italics).
75. Baldwin, *Price of the Ticket*, 440–41.
76. Baldwin, *Price of the Ticket*, 690.

Like Alice Walker, Baldwin clearly saw the feminine in the masculine, a point I revisit in chapter 8. For now, suffice to say that *my* people, *your* people, are, in the deepest way imaginable, *all* people. Now, Baldwin did not explicitly name God's role in all this, but as in other places in his writing and speeches it is implied. Baldwin was certain that each of us is a part of the rest of us. This is *given*, indeed, is instilled in each person by God.

Because of the relational nature of human beings Baldwin saw all too clearly that what happens to black youth ultimately puts white youth at risk as well. His message to white people was simple: "As long as my children face the future that they face, and come to the ruin that they come to, your children are very greatly in danger, too."[77] For in the final analysis, all children belong to every adult, regardless of race-ethnicity.[78] The destiny of every person is mutually and inextricably tied to the destiny of every other person.

The ways of thinking and writing about the sacredness and interrelatedness of human beings found in Baldwin's work are in perfect alignment with ethical prophecy. Just like the Hebrew prophets, James Baldwin saw the tremendous value of human beings to God generally, and that of oppressed and broken human beings more especially. Human beings have value in themselves, of course, but because God imbues each with the image of God and loves each and every one, the value and sacredness of each is all the more significant. Because so many human beings, not least Baldwin's own people, were systematically treated as nonpersons, Baldwin was compelled to speak, protest, and witness against such treatment. In this he, like the Hebrew prophets, courageously spoke truth to power.

Witnessing and Speaking the Truth about Race and Persons

James Baldwin did not want to be a spokesman for his people, insisting instead that they can speak for themselves. He preferred to think of himself as a *witness*—a witness to the truth about what it means to be black in the United States, and what blacks needed to do to contribute toward their total liberation. Reading Baldwin's writings, one discovers that a precondition for speaking truth is cleansing one's entire being. A person does this by doing her first works over. This requires "vomiting up all the filth" and rejecting all the lies she has been taught about herself and her people.[79]

---

77. Baldwin, *Price of the Ticket*, 400.
78. Baldwin, *Price of the Ticket*, 643, 667.
79. Baldwin, *Price of the Ticket*, 227.

According to Baldwin it was critical to do one's first works over if liberation was even to be a possibility. Doing one's first works over requires going back to the beginning—as far back as one can go—and reexamining everything about oneself: one's family, beliefs, history, and culture. "Go back to where you started," Baldwin instructed, "examine all of it, travel your road again and tell the truth about it. Sing or shout or testify or keep it to yourself: but *know whence you came*."[80] That's what it means to do one's first works over—knowing without doubt where one came from and how one got to where one is. A person knows that she is doing her first works over when she looks at her whole experience with critical mind and eyes, sees it for what it really is, and then tells the truth about it. This is how she frees her mind for liberation and freedom. In effect, it is how a people who have been as deprived as blacks cleanse and reinvent themselves. Baldwin recognized this as being critical. In an interview with Studs Terkel in 1961 he said, "All you are ever told in this country about being black is that it is a terrible, terrible thing to be. Now, in order to survive this, you have to really dig down into yourself and re-create yourself, really, according to no image which yet exists in America. . . . You have to decide who you are, and force the world to deal with you, not with its idea of you."[81] This is part of the cleansing process for doing one's first works over.

As a witness one not only sees but also experiences what the people see and experience. A witness writes it all down and then endeavors to tell the truth about it so that the world will know about it—and in this case will know that blacks did not approve of being treated inhumanely. As witness, then, Baldwin could speak for himself, while also authenticating the experiences of his people. When asked what he meant to convey when he used the term "witness," Baldwin replied, "Witness to whence I came, where I am. Witness to what I've seen and the possibilities that I think I see."[82] But in order to tell the world what he had seen and what he believed was possible to achieve (e.g., the New Jerusalem), he acknowledged that he would likely have to offend many, "but that also comes with the territory."[83] People are seldom as interested and eager to hear the truth about race and related matters as they claim. Baldwin knew this. As witness, he was more than a messenger who is sent only to deliver the words of another. "As a messenger,

---

80. Baldwin, *Price of the Ticket*, xix.
81. Standley and Pratt, *Conversations with James Baldwin*, 5-6.
82. Standley and Pratt, *Conversations with James Baldwin*, 225.
83. Standley and Pratt, *Conversations with James Baldwin*, 225.

his task is to deliver the word; as a witness, he must bear testimony that the word is divine."[84]

Although Baldwin did not explicitly bear testimony that the words he spoke were divine or from God, he was aware that those words were consistent with the only concept of God that was reasonable to him. His words were about human dignity, justice, and liberation and the only God worth believing in. After all, to be a witness in the black church tradition and that of the Hebrew prophets means also to be subversive and a disturber of the peace. Baldwin never denied that as artist it was his responsibility to disturb the peace when massive numbers of people were subjected to malicious treatment by the powers and by the wealthy. It was not about his art or his talent as such. It was about speaking truth to the people and to the powers. Experience taught Baldwin that when one speaks truth one disturbs the way things are. In fact, one cannot be a witness to truth and not also be a disturber of the peace.

The way the term "witness" is used in this discussion also implies something significant about the witness herself. Depending on what was witnessed, she would have to possess both courage and integrity in order to tell what was seen, heard, or otherwise experienced. She would have to be faithful to her highest moral code relative to speaking truth. The witness must be faithful to the God of her faith. In addition, as noted previously, the witness—more often than not—lives in the conditions witnessed, that is, she experiences those very things herself. In this way she lives and feels what the people experience. So when she testifies to what she has seen, heard, or experienced there can be no doubt that she knows what she is talking about.

But there is something else. The witness brings her faith and the Word of God to bear on the social, political, and other circumstances that adversely affect the people. She does not hesitate to testify forthrightly. Womanist Christian ethicist Marcia Riggs points to this as one of three characteristics of what it means to be prophetic in the religious and ethical sense.

> Like biblical prophets, the women [in *Can I Get a Witness?*] relate faith and history; they were individuals who brought "faith out of the temple or sanctuary to the marketplace of human affairs where history was in process; history—the present and immediate future viewed in light of the past." Also, these women, like biblical prophets, were "sensitive to evil, felt fiercely, recognized that any injustice has major consequences, agonized,

---

84. Heschel, *Prophets*, 22.

evoked responsibility, were impatient with excuses, disdained pretense and self-pity, and envisioned a transformative end."[85]

When such a person testifies she does it on the basis of what she knows. If she is a proponent of the Jewish or Christian faith, she does so in the name of the God of the Hebrew prophets.

In 1964, James Baldwin courageously spoke the truth about what happens when a nation loses all human feeling, noting that when it does, as it surely did in the U.S., "you can do anything to anybody and justify it."[86] Thanks to Donald Trump and his bootlicking minions we are living and witnessing just such a tragedy on a scale seldom if ever experienced in this nation. Furthermore, Baldwin could see that when a nation is "ruled by the least able and the most abject among us,"[87] we may expect to be anything but a great nation. Because he saw the leadership in this country as "represented by so stunning a pantheon of the relentlessly mediocre,"[88] Baldwin rightly concluded that the nation was experiencing a crisis in leadership. That was in 1984, and it is much worse in the era of Trump.

The prophet's duty is to speak the truth, but she has no control over who will hear and receive it, how it will be received, or how they will respond. Later we will see that the witness that one makes is not merely to what is but to what can and ought to be in light of a higher ideal. In Baldwin's case that higher ideal is the New Jerusalem. For now, it is important to examine the theme of judgment in his work and witness.

God's Judgment

James Baldwin believed that the universe, created by the God of Jeremiah, is a moral universe, that is, one that recognizes and seeks moral ends—one in which justice and good will ultimately triumph, or have the last word.[89] This must be the case for one who believed so fervently that people and the world can be better than they are. A just God requires that justice should be done in the world. Even so, because God is relentlessly compassionate and fair, God does not strike even oppressors without giving ample warnings. In *Go Tell It on the Mountain*, Baldwin had Bathsheba, the elderly cook, tell her children, "God gave men time, but all the times were in His hand, and one day the time to forsake evil and do good would all be finished: then only

---

85. Riggs, *Can I Get a Witness?*, xii.
86. Baldwin, *Cross of Redemption*, 71.
87. Baldwin, *Cross of Redemption*, 71.
88. Baldwin, *Cross of Redemption*, 137.
89. Wright, *Student's Philosophy of Religion*, 336, 337.

the whirlwind, death riding on the whirlwind, awaited those people who had forgotten God."[90] God forewarns about impending judgment. Baldwin seemed to be aware that in a moral universe there would be a day of reckoning for those who continued to ignore God's warnings and requirement that all human beings be treated like the precious, sacred ones they are. Old Bathsheba knew that God had a plan and she trusted God's promise to deliver her and her people from racist oppression: "She had only to endure and trust in God."[91] There was a bill due for the nation's racism and refusal to face what whites had done and were doing to blacks.[92]

Baldwin's way of thinking about religion, then, included a strong element of divine judgment that was at times seen as a way of balancing things out. This seems to be the idea behind his statement that "white people own the earth and commit all manner of abomination and injustice on it; the bad will be punished and the good rewarded, for God is not sleeping, the judgment is not far off."[93] Baldwin was certain that black preachers, especially fundamentalist ones like his father, frequently preached divine judgment which also "assures the chosen of their place in Zion."[94] Judgment could be avoided if oppressors liberated their captives, but Baldwin, knowing his white countrymen as he did, was not at all certain that they would comply, or could even be saved.[95] Nevertheless, the judgment that follows can be stopped by no human power. Its occurrence is the equivalent of a law of nature.[96] To the extent that human beings refuse to hear and comply with the prophet's truth, God's judgment will come crashing down. Looking at history, Baldwin wrote of his belief that the United States was in the direct path of divine judgment:

> Time catches up with kingdoms and crushes them, gets its teeth into doctrines and rends them; time reveals the foundations on which any kingdom rests, and eats at those foundations, and it destroys doctrines by proving them to be untrue. In those days, not so very long ago, when the priests of that church which stands in Rome gave God's blessing to Italian boys being sent out to ravage a defenseless black country—which until that event, incidentally, had not considered itself to be black—it was

90. Baldwin, *Go Tell It on the Mountain*, 77.
91. Baldwin, *Go Tell It on the Mountain*, 77.
92. Leeming, *James Baldwin*, 216, 220.
93. Baldwin, *Notes of a Native Son*, 66.
94. Baldwin, *Notes of a Native Son*, 67.
95. Baldwin, *Cross of Redemption*, 87.
96. Baldwin, *Fire Next Time*, 104.

not possible to believe in a black God. To entertain such a belief would have been to entertain madness. But time has passed, and in that time the Christian world has revealed itself as morally bankrupt and politically unstable.[97]

He was aware that divine wrath as taught in the Old Testament is based on an *if-then* relation. There was therefore no reason to be entirely pessimistic and without hope. For *if* the people and the nations hear and obey God's truth, *then* they will be spared God's vengeance. As Baldwin warned on the last pages of *The Fire Next Time*, "If . . . the relatively conscious whites and the relatively conscious blacks . . . do not falter in our duty now, we may be able, handful that we are, to end the racial nightmare, and achieve our country, and change the history of the world."[98] But *if* the small number of committed whites and blacks will stand for truth and justice, *then* they may be able to end the racial nightmare. In order to avoid God's judgment, however, there must be a willingness to comply with God's expectations and to risk everything. Otherwise "the fire next time!"[99]

According to the Hebrew prophets nothing is fated to be and cannot be otherwise (Jer 18:7–8). In ethical prophecy words of judgment are not God's final words. Judgment is always conditional. Heschel reminds us that "the word of God never comes to an end," which means that "prophetic predictions are seldom final."[100] The fact that human beings are free to comply with God's requirements is also and necessarily a part of the equation. That Baldwin believed that the realization of the New Jerusalem was possible and that he was committed to working for it—and his insistence that he knew people who proved to him that human beings can be better than they are[101]—is evidence enough that he did not believe judgment to be the last word for human beings and the world. But it also meant that a certain type of behavior was expected if the New Jerusalem was to have a real chance of being actualized. Baldwin did not believe he would live to see the New Jerusalem, but he was working towards it, because he was confident that "we're going to be better than we are."[102]

---

97. Baldwin, *Fire Next Time*, 50–51. The reference here is to the Second Italo-Ethiopian War during the seven-month period of October 1935 to May 1936. Ethiopia was defeated and annexed by Italy (notorious for its use of mustard gas during the war).

98. Baldwin, *Fire Next Time*, 104–5.

99. Baldwin, *Fire Next Time*, 105.

100. Heschel, *Prophets*, 194.

101. Leeming, *James Baldwin*, 225.

102. Goldstein, "Go the Way Your Blood Beats," 184.

Cost of Prophecy

One pays for what one does in the world. In Baldwin's case, he missed out on professional opportunities to further advance his art because of his outspokenness during the civil rights and antiwar movements. He was angry about what was happening to his people and to the Vietnamese, and he did not care who knew it. He did not care that Attorney General Robert Kennedy was deeply angered by his insistence that he would have problems trying to convince his nephew or other young black males to fight for the United States, a nation that had total disregard for their humanity and dignity and that of the people of Vietnam.[103]

Baldwin lost out on potential opportunities to make movies because of his outspokenness and disregard for authority. According to one of his biographers it was "the loss of what might have been if he had kept his mouth shut and maintained a low profile. It was a price he was apparently willing to pay."[104] The prophet calls for the necessity of change in the face of a higher reality and does not focus on the cost to the extent that she loses sight of what that reality requires. What Baldwin suffered was part of the price for witnessing to a higher truth, and there is no evidence that he ever regretted it.

Every candidate for the ethical prophet hall of fame pays for her witness and her faithfulness to God. Without question, the ethical prophet bears scorn and reproach, is despised and hated. We saw in an earlier chapter that the prophet Amos was convinced that the one who criticizes and speaks truth at the gate is hated (Amos 5:10). Likewise, Jeremiah appealed to God to punish those who persecuted him and implored God to "know that on your account I suffer insult" (Jer 15:15). He desired that God deal with his enemies even in God's anger and that God not overlook or forgive their sin (Jer 18:23). In truth, the witness of this type of prophet tends, unwittingly, to alienate both the wicked and the pious, which means that she generally knows much about loneliness and sadness.

One who truly knows what an ethical prophet is does not grow up aspiring and wishing to be one. Far from it! "The prophet . . . is not moved by a will to experience prophecy. What he achieves comes against his will. He does not pant for illumination. He does not call for it; he is called upon. God comes upon the prophet before the prophet seeks the coming of God."[105] She does not strive to be an ethical prophet but does all she can to avoid it,

---

103. Weatherby, *James Baldwin*, 221–27. See also Hansberry, *To Be Young*, 229; and Standley and Pratt, *Conversations with James Baldwin*, 35, 41–42, 69.

104. Weatherby, *James Baldwin*, 270.

105. Heschel, *Prophets*, 358.

as Jeremiah resisted God's call, saying that he was too young. The prophet understands that her duty is to speak truth to the people and to power, for whether they hear or not, "they will know that there has been a prophet among them" (Ezek 2:5). She is called to speak the truth, not to be successful or popular. Few understood and modeled this better than James Baldwin.

As prophet, Baldwin was a consistent disturber of the peace,[106] refusing to allow racists, the powers, and the privileged to be comfortable in their wrongdoing. He incessantly reminded the U.S. of its downward fall from truth.[107] Chinua Achebe reflected on the cost of Baldwin's role as prophet, saying, "Principalities and powers do not tolerate those who interrupt the sleep of their consciences. That Baldwin got away with it for forty years was a miracle. Except of course that he didn't get away; he paid dearly every single day of those years, every single hour of those days. What was his crime that we should turn him into a man of sadness, this man inhabited by a soul so eager to be loved and to smile?"[108] And yet, as long as injustice and oppression prevailed, Baldwin's words and witness remained to challenge the powers and the oppressors.

For one who loved his country as much as Baldwin did, it saddened him that there seemed to be little evidence that the conscience of the U.S. could be reached and altered. By the publication of *No Name in the Street* in 1972, he seemed utterly distraught and pessimistic regarding black-white relations. This is nowhere more evident than in the following passage:

> It is not necessary for a black man to hate a white man, or to have any particular feeling about him at all, in order to realize that he must kill him. Yes, we have come, or are coming to this, and there is no point in flinching before the prospect of this exceedingly cool species of fratricide—which prospect white people, after all, have brought on themselves. Of course, whenever a black man discusses violence he is said to be "advocating" it. This is very far indeed from my intentions, if only because I have no desire whatever to see a generation perish in the streets. But the shape and extent of whatever violence may come is not in the hands of people like myself, but in the hands of the American people, who are at present among the most dishonorable and violent people in the world. I am merely trying to face certain blunt, human facts. I do not carry a gun and do not consider myself to be a violent man: but my life has more than once depended on the gun in a brother's holster. I know

---

106. Leeming, *James Baldwin*, 338.
107. Leeming, *James Baldwin*, 52.
108. Quoted in Weatherby, *James Baldwin*, 346–47.

that when certain powerful and blatant enemies of black people are shoveled, at last, into the ground I may feel a certain pity that they spent their lives so badly, but I certainly do not mourn their passing, nor, when I hear that they are ailing, do I pray for their recovery. I know what I would do if I had a gun and someone had a gun pointed at my brother, and I would not count ten to do it and there would be no hatred in it, nor any remorse. People who treat other people as less than human must not be surprised when the bread they have cast on the waters comes floating back to them, poisoned.[109]

Baldwin was angry and unapologetic. He was devastated by the assassinations of Medgar Evers, Malcolm X, and Martin Luther King Jr., admitting that when King was assassinated something left him, and he feared he would never be able to regain it.[110] In fact, the assassination of King "devastated" his world.[111] Some even believed that with King's death Baldwin lost much of his hope.[112] And yet, something deep within would not allow him to forego belief in the possibility of achieving the New Jerusalem. Because human beings made the world what it is, they can remake it into something better.

Vision of Hope, and the New Jerusalem

James Baldwin argued that one who truly believes in the sacredness of human beings will immediately cease doing those things that only undermine and devalue them. This would most especially be the case for one who claimed to be Christian or of some other religious persuasion, and who claimed to believe that we are—all of us—sisters and brothers. "If one believes in the Prince of Peace," Baldwin (a stand-in for the recently assassinated Martin Luther King Jr.) told attendees at the World Council of Churches in 1968, "one must stop committing crimes in the name of the Prince of Peace. The Christian Church still rules this world, it still has the power to change the structure of South Africa. It has the power, if it will, to prevent the death of another Martin Luther King, Jr. It has the power, if it will, to force my government to cease dropping bombs in Southeast Asia."[113] Baldwin was challenging the church to bring its practices in line with its teachings. He

---

109. Baldwin, *No Name in the Street*, 191–92.
110. Baldwin, *No Name in the Street*, 9.
111. Weatherby, *James Baldwin*, 303.
112. Weatherby, *James Baldwin*, 297.
113. Baldwin, *Price of the Ticket*, 441.

wanted the church to know that if it had the will as it had the power, it could absolutely change the world.

Like each of the hall of fame candidates, James Baldwin felt compelled to speak and write words of judgment to an otherwise disobedient, rebellious, unjust nation. But one does not get the sense that this was his most important—and certainly not his final—message. Rather, time and again we see him uttering or writing words of hope, even when others cannot see reason for it. In an interview with Joe Walker in 1972, Baldwin acknowledged that the world—not only the U.S.—was in serious trouble. However, he admitted that he had "too much faith in people to be hopeless,"[114] and even believed that some whites were changing for the better. Remember, the prophet Jeremiah prophesied doom and destruction, but he was also compelled to prophesy renewal and building up (Jer 1:10; also 31:28). Similarly, Baldwin was not merely a prophet of doom. He was also a prophet of hope. Asked by an interviewer for *Penthouse* in the early 1970s if he had hope for this country's future, he replied that he was "a lover and therefore an optimist . . . the trick is to love somebody. . . . If you love one person, you see everybody else differently."[115]

The theme of the New Jerusalem appears often in Baldwin's writings, especially in his later years. He had seen with his own eyes that human beings could be better than they were. He said that he would "go to [his] grave believing that we can build Jerusalem, if we will."[116] What was lacking was not the know-how but the will. Baldwin's was an unending hope. He saw no reason to live without hope, for hope gives reason to go on living and to seek to live life to the fullest. His was a hope not only for the individual but for the community, the nation, indeed, the world. Truly, Baldwin was not confident of this in every moment, for he wrote of how he trembled at times when wondering whether "there is left in the Christian civilizations . . . the moral energy, the spiritual daring, to atone, to repent, to be born again; if it is possible, if there is enough leaven in the loaf, to cause us to discard our actual and historical habits, to cause us to take our places with that criminal Jew, for He was a criminal, who was put to death by Rome between two thieves, because He claimed to be the Son of God."[117] But as with the Hebrew prophets, such sentiments lasted only for a moment.

Ethical prophecy begins with words of doom but ends with words of hope or a vision of hope, although Baldwin realized, as did other hall of

---

114. Standley and Pratt, *Conversations with James Baldwin*, 140.
115. Quoted in Leeming, *James Baldwin*, 329.
116. Quoted in McBride, *James Baldwin Now*, 352.
117. Baldwin, *Price of the Ticket*, 441.

fame candidates, that merely espousing words is not enough to prompt the privileged and powerful to begin working toward actualizing the vision. And yet, for Baldwin there was no place for enduring pessimism, even when it seems that human beings do not know how to undo the devastation they cause. Baldwin refused to believe that all is permanently lost, even when we cannot see how a brighter future is possible. The hope must remain, and blacks must look to themselves and to no other, besides God, to insure the salvation of their children. For this to happen it is necessary to work toward "a new society." Clarence Hardy rightly contends that "even with his continued intimations that a frightful end was surely coming for a society addicted to whiteness, violence, and domination, Baldwin still believed in a New Jerusalem"[118]—a community that will be free of oppression, inequality, inequity, and injustice.

James Baldwin was not a pessimist. However, he was not optimistic about society in its present form. Barely two years after Martin Luther King Jr. was assassinated, he said to John Hall, "I'm optimistic about the civilization which will replace this one."[119] A lot of hard questions and hard work must go into the creation of this new society, but Baldwin was convinced that the people were up to the task. As for himself, he was committed to working to achieve the New Jerusalem even though he did not believe he would live to see it, just as Malcolm X and Martin Luther King Jr. did not believe they would live to see the society they envisioned.

Conclusion

The poet-prophet is part of her culture and society and much of the truth she speaks is directed there. It is true that in 1948, at the age of twenty-four, James Arthur Baldwin found that in order to survive and to make constructive contributions to the U.S. and the world he had to leave the country of his birth. So he moved to Paris (his European home base), and for many years he lived in various parts of Europe, returning to the U.S. only occasionally. As badly as he and his people were treated in his native country, and as much as he was distraught over it, he retained a love-hate relationship with it. In any event, Paris is where he completed his first novel, *Go Tell It on the Mountain*. Initially he had not intended to return to the U.S. But at bottom he always knew that he was "an American writer"—that the U.S. was actually his chief subject. He was "just a displaced black boy . . . driven

---

118. Hardy, *James Baldwin's God*, 97.

119. Standley and Pratt, *Conversations with James Baldwin*, 102.

to Europe . . . , who learned things about France while I was there, but what I mainly learned was about my own country, my own past."[120]

James Baldwin had a sense of calling as artist-prophet. He saw the injustices done to his people and others in the U.S. and throughout the world and could not hold his peace about it. He was convinced that it was his responsibility to find ways to live out his call, even if it meant becoming an exile. With great risk to his reputation and (at times) his life, he courageously and persistently spoke truth to power. Not interested in using his platform for personal gain, he was true to the promise to his people that he would not sell out. This trait was found in other hall of fame candidates as well. Baldwin knew he would have to face strong headwinds for being the type of artist he was—the type who refused to be found on the wrong side of justice, on the side of those who oppress and demean human beings.

Malcolm X is our next contender for the ethical prophet hall of fame. Malcolm was neither Jewish nor Christian. He was a Muslim. He learned fundamentalist Christian teachings from his Baptist-Garveyite father and later came to believe that Islam was the religion taught by all of the prophets, including Jesus. Moreover, to him, Islam was "the true name of the religion God gave to the prophets . . . to cure their people of whatever moral or spiritual ailments that were afflicting them in that day."[121] Malcolm X is, arguably, the most militant of the hall of fame candidates discussed in this book. Baldwin saw that Malcolm was a danger and a threat to white people not because of what they perceived as his hatred for them during the pre-Mecca years but because of his deep love for his own people.[122]

---

120. Standley and Pratt, *Conversations with James Baldwin*, 106.
121. Lomax, *When the Word Is Given*, 161.
122. Weatherby, *James Baldwin*, 262.

5

Malcolm X as Ethical Prophet

As with the other candidates for the ethical prophet hall of fame it is important to situate Malcolm X and his work. At bottom, Malcolm was a human being with the strengths and limitations of human beings generally. He was not perfect and did not pretend to be. What set Malcolm apart from most was the consistency with which he both acknowledged and sought to learn from his mistakes, rather than allow them to hinder his role in the black struggle for survival, liberation, and justice. He always tried to retain an open mind and to be willing to change his views in light of new evidence and experiences.[1] We will see that at no time was this more evident than after his pilgrimage to Mecca and subsequent travels internationally.

Malcolm never wanted to be anybody's leader. He was but one witness, one spokesman for Allah and for the liberation of his people. He was adamant about voicing the need for the total recognition of the humanity, dignity, and rights of his people as full-fledged human beings. Were he alive today he would be the first to say that we have no need for messiahs, nor should we passively await the arrival of one. What Afrikan Americans need, he would say, is each other, and to love, respect, and acknowledge—in word and deed—the absolute dignity of each other. Malcolm tried to impress upon his people that having been taught by the white man to hate everything about themselves and their Afrikan heritage, blacks must find ways to love and respect themselves and their culture. This was critical to virtually

1. Malcolm X, *Autobiography*, 371.

all that Malcolm tried to do. All blacks needed to contribute toward their total liberation and empowerment. Every member of the black community could contribute something meaningful to the struggle, for human beings are endowed with moral agency, that is, the capacity to act on the basis of moral principles.

When discussing and criticizing Malcolm one must be careful to note *which* Malcolm or which period of his life is being discussed, analyzed, and criticized: *Malcolm Little* (and the several Malcolms of the pre-Muslim years, e.g., "Homeboy," "Detroit Red," "Satan"); *Malcolm X* (during his twelve years as a Muslim minister under Elijah Muhammad and prior to the *hajj* or pilgrimage to Mecca); or *El-Hajj Malik El-Shabazz* (during the brief period he was on his own after the pilgrimage and after leaving the Nation of Islam). Which Malcolm was a racist and a separatist: pre- or post-Mecca Malcolm? It is critical that we be clear about the distinction when discussing Malcolm, since failure to do so will make it unnecessarily difficult to see him as ethical prophet.

For our purpose, the discussion on Malcolm X as ethical prophet must focus more on post-Mecca Malcolm. That was the period of his conversion to what he came to know as true Islam. Prior to then he was the uncritical servant and voice not of God (Allah) but of Elijah Muhammad, whom, at the time, he naively viewed as a god. When Malcolm left the Nation of Islam, he reflected that his behavior toward Muhammad had been idolatrous,[2] and he did not hesitate to repent.

We will see that even pre-Mecca Malcolm exhibited a few of the elements of ethical prophecy—for example, his powerful, convincing use of sweeping exaggerations; his emphasis on the dignity and sacredness of his people; his insistence that justice should be done to them; and his strong focus on the impending judgment of Allah. But as long as he placed uncritical faith in a man (i.e., Elijah Muhammad) instead of Allah, he fell short of what it truly means to be an ethical prophet. The pilgrimage to Mecca opened the way for Malcolm to more nearly approach the type of prophecy that is the subject of this book. After Mecca, for example, his emphasis was on Allah, not Elijah Muhammad's interpretation of Allah. His new focus was on God's expectations, a central trait of ethical prophecy. It was also during this period that Malcolm saw more clearly the fundamental sacredness of white people. We have seen that this type of prophecy is all about God's program, and therefore about what God requires—first, foremost, and last.

Less than two months after Malcolm was assassinated, noted sociologist and author of *The Black Muslims in America* (1961), C. Eric Lincoln,

---

2. Malcolm X, *Autobiography*, 400.

made the following accurate prediction: "His spirit will rise again, phoenix-like, because he is worthy to be remembered, and because the perpetuation of the ghetto which spawned him will not let us forget."[3] In light of Malcolm X paraphernalia, film director Spike Lee's movie *Malcolm X*, and numerous other indicators of a resurgence of interest in Malcolm during the 1990s, it is quite evident that Lincoln's prediction was accurate. Nevertheless, none of those indicators produced a real genuine *spirit* of Malcolm X. For it is important to ask whether this "resurgence of interest" in Malcolm went beyond lining the pockets of a few greedy, selfish capitalists. Certainly whoever mass-produced and distributed the Malcolm X paraphernalia enjoyed a financial boon.

Much like the Hebrew prophets, Malcolm was not concerned with being popular but only with speaking the truth to the people and the powers. The prophet Ezekiel was told at the beginning of his ministry that he was not to concern himself with success or popularity: "And you, O mortal, do not be afraid of them, and do not be afraid of their words, though briers and thorns surround you and you live among scorpions; do not be afraid of their words, and do not be dismayed at their looks, for they are a rebellious house. You shall speak my words to them, whether they hear or refuse to hear" (Ezek 2:6–7). Malcolm knew that the gravity of the problems in his community was such that there was no time to worry about who was popular and who was not. And he surely was not concerned about white assessments of his level of acceptance among either blacks or whites.

Malcolm carried the day primarily with black youth in the urban ghettos of the North. Biographer Peter Goldman even wrote in 1973 of signs of an emerging "Malcolm cult."[4] Just as there was a recurrence of this in the 1990s, we will likely see it again. What cannot be predicted, however, is how positive will be its influence upon young Afrikan Americans and other youths. Indeed, the father of contemporary black liberation theology, the late James H. Cone, observed that a 1992 *Newsweek* poll revealed that 57 percent of all Afrikan Americans regarded Malcolm as a "hero." This included 84 percent of blacks 15–24 years of age. To these, Cone asserted, Malcolm "is an inner city cultural icon who often receives as much devotion from the hip-hop generation as Christians give to Jesus. 'Saint Malcolm' is what they sometimes call him."[5] Although this was strong evidence of a resurgence of interest in Malcolm, it unfortunately did not translate into

---

3. Lincoln, "Meaning of Malcolm X," 12. Malcolm considered Lincoln to be a friend and much appreciated his book *The Black Muslims in America*. See *Autobiography*, 438.

4. Goldman, *Death and Life of Malcolm X*, 384–85.

5. Cone, *Risks of Faith*, 98.

strong sociopolitical activism to make blacks and the nation better than they were. It did not radicalize a large number of people. Essentially all it did—through the marketing and selling of Malcolm X accoutrements—was line the pockets of a few greedy entrepreneurs. Nevertheless, young blacks needed someone to look up to, and there was no better person in this regard than Malcolm X. Cone said instructively,

> Malcolm represents an abrasive, "in-your-face" assertion of blackness, a "don't mess with me" attitude. Young blacks love Malcolm's courage to speak the truth that whites did not want to hear. . . . Malcolm said in public what most blacks felt but were afraid to say except in private among themselves. He was able to talk defiantly to white people because he did not want anything from them.[6]

Before examining some of the elements of ethical prophecy in Malcolm's ministry and his witness I briefly examine his background and how he came to be associated with what C. Eric Lincoln called the "Black Muslims."[7]

Background

Malcolm X was born Malcolm Little on May 19, 1925, in Omaha, Nebraska, to Earl Little and Louise Langdon Norton Little. Mrs. Little grew up on the Caribbean island of Grenada, the daughter of a Grenadan woman and her rapist Scottish father, whom she never met or knew. Malcolm's father was a Baptist preacher and a committed follower of Marcus Garvey, leader of the Universal Negro Improvement Association (UNIA). Reverend Little and three of his brothers were—in separate instances—brutally murdered by white men. When Malcolm's father was murdered the insurance company refused to pay the life insurance policy, claiming that he committed suicide. Malcolm's family was broken up by welfare authorities, who also had his mother institutionalized in a mental health facility. Moreover, he recalled that the white family in Mason, Michigan, with whom the state placed him treated him like a "mascot"—a pet or nonperson. In addition, his white eighth-grade English teacher (whom Malcolm had considered to be his favorite teacher), Mr. Ostroski, told him that he had "to be realistic

---

6. Cone, *Risks of Faith*, 98–99.

7. Although members of the Nation of Islam referred to themselves only as Muslims, "they did not object to the term employed by [C. Eric] Lincoln." See Lomax, *Negro Revolt*, 164n. Malcolm himself believed that the catalyst to his popularity on college campuses was Lincoln's popular book *The Black Muslims in America*. See Malcolm X, *Autobiography*, 307.

about being a nigger"—that he should give up the idea of being a lawyer and consider being a carpenter,[8] since blacks were so good with their hands. Malcolm was given this advice even though he was the class president and one of the smartest students in the predominantly white school.

By the time he was thirteen, Malcolm had already experienced enough racism and discrimination to cause him to want to literally hate all white people for the rest of his life. Hatred is not necessarily a bad thing, nor can it be said to be an abnormal expression. Indeed, the *abnormal* practice may be the withholding of hatred in situations that seem to warrant it. Alice Walker, literary artist par excellence, saw the positive value in hatred, pointing out that some people, some institutions, *ought* to be hated—particularly when they are unrepentant—for the horrific crimes they commit against humanity. Walker's important caution is that we should "exercise our noblest impulses with our hate" and not allow it to fester and destroy us.[9] I return to this theme in chapter 8. Malcolm had good reason to hate white people, not only for what they did to him and his family, but to blacks generally.

Malcolm left school after the eighth grade and moved to Boston to live with his sister Ella.[10] When he got a job on a train that ran from Boston to New York City he discovered Harlem and became fascinated, even intoxicated, with the Harlem experience. When he got to Harlem he knew almost instinctively that this was where he wanted to be—where he needed to be. For the first time in his life he was among a critical mass of his own people. He became a hustler, drug dealer and user, and burglar, and he steered men—white and black—to houses of sex pleasure. He chronicled all of these activities in his *Autobiography*, as told to Alex Haley.

When Malcolm and his newfound best friend, Shorty, and their white girlfriends were caught and arrested during a burglary in Boston, he once again faced the cruelty and racism of white men and the system they controlled and benefited from at blacks' expense. According to Malcolm, both his court-appointed attorney and the judge were more interested in his and Shorty's relationship with their white girlfriends than the actual burglaries.[11] The women were sentenced to one to five years, while Malcolm, not yet twenty-one, was sentenced to ten years in February 1946.

While in Charlestown State Prison in Massachusetts, Malcolm reportedly displayed such strong "antireligious" sentiments that fellow inmates

8. Malcolm X, *Autobiography*, 41–42.
9. See Walker, *Our Mothers' Gardens*, 136–37.
10. Ella was actually one of three children born to Malcolm's father in a previous marriage. I prefer not to use the term "half sister" to refer to her, as it is inconsistent with my personal experience as an Afrikan American.
11. Malcolm X, *Autobiography*, 163.

nicknamed him "Satan."[12] Although the religion that he knew best during this time was Christianity, we may surmise that he had no use for it. Christianity was surely not the "true" religion for him since he did not believe it spoke to the condition of his people. Malcolm simply had no use for Christianity, which seemed to counsel his people to endure their socioeconomic condition in this world, while putting their faith and hope in a blond-haired, blue-eyed Jesus and a heaven beyond the grave. He said that Christianity taught blacks that their skin color was a curse and taught them to hate everything about themselves.[13] Accordingly, he believed that Christianity for blacks was little more than an opiate that kept their minds on the riches of heaven, rather than changing their earthly condition.

During his incarceration Malcolm aggressively self-educated by reading books from the prison library. Unknown to him at the time this helped prepare him to excel during future debates, lectures, and question-answer periods at major universities in the U.S., England, and other places. He later reflected that nobody ever got as much out of going to prison as he did.[14] He taught himself about the nineteenth-century enslaved revolutionary Nat Turner and read W. E. B. DuBois's classic book *The Souls of Black Folk*. In addition, he said that he read Carter G. Woodson's important, masterful work *Negro History*.[15] All of this was part of Malcolm's self-education.

Interestingly enough, Malcolm never explicitly distinguished between the radical version of Christianity espoused by Nat Turner that led to his efforts to liberate his enslaved people and the more fundamentalist, conservative type that Malcolm experienced as a boy. He did not clearly distinguish between conservative and more progressive and radical strands of Christianity. This is quite interesting since he thought so highly of Nat Turner, who was not opposed to taking up arms against white enslavers. The truth is that as long as blacks have been Christians in this country they have been influenced by conservative and radical strands[16] of Christianity. However, Malcolm was silent on the point.

Not long after Malcolm was transferred to Concord Prison in Massachusetts, his brother Philbert introduced him to the Nation of Islam.[17] He later converted to Islam after being transferred to the Norfolk Prison

---

12. Malcolm X, *Autobiography*, 167.
13. Malcolm X, *Autobiography*, 178.
14. Malcolm X, *Autobiography*, 196.
15. Malcolm X, *Autobiography*, 190.
16. See Wilmore, *Black Religion*, and Marable, *How Capitalism Underdeveloped Black America*, ch. 7. See also Marable, *Blackwater*, ch. 3.
17. Malcolm X, *Autobiography*, 169.

Colony,[18] where his brother Reginald visited and taught him the basic principles of the Muslim faith based on Elijah Muhammad's interpretation. Although he had learned of the Nation of Islam in a letter from Philbert, it was Reginald who first told Malcolm that Elijah Muhammad taught that "the white man is the devil"[19] and that there were no exceptions. When Malcolm reflected on his life and experience, including his relationship with his white girlfriend Sophia, he was convinced that Muhammad's interpretation was accurate. *All* whites were devils! Furthermore, Malcolm believed that the white man was the cause not only of the predicament of blacks in this country, but of people of color throughout the world.[20] Once he converted to Islam he began corresponding with Elijah Muhammad.

When Malcolm was released from prison he was strongly advised by his sister Hilda to go to Detroit and join a Muslim temple in order to learn more about the teachings of Elijah Muhammad.[21] Ella also supported the move to Detroit, not to join a Muslim temple, but because the police would not know him.[22] In any case, Malcolm moved to Detroit, where he lived with Wilfred and his family and worked in a used furniture store with him. Wilfred modeled for him what it meant to be a Muslim family man.

By his own admission, it had never occurred to Malcolm that he might become a minister. He had "never felt remotely qualified to directly represent Mr. Muhammad."[23] Indeed, this is how Malcolm responded as a minister in the Nation of Islam, not as one who had a sense of being called by Allah but as one called or appointed by Elijah Muhammad. For nearly a dozen years he spoke Muhammad's truth to Muhammad's people, *not* Allah's. He told them about "the true teachings of . . . Elijah Muhammad,"[24] not those of Allah. This is one reason it is important to distinguish between pre- and post-Mecca Malcolm when trying to determine whether he was in the camp of ethical prophecy. The ethical prophet seeks to convey God's point of view, not that of a human being.

On December 4, 1963, Elijah Muhammad, self-avowed Messenger of Allah and leader of the Nation of Islam, silenced Malcolm for ninety days, ostensibly for the infamous "chickens coming home to roost" comment he made to a reporter in the aftermath of the assassination of President John

---

18. Malcolm X. *Autobiography*, 171.
19. Quoted in Malcolm X, *Autobiography*, 173.
20. Malcolm X, *Autobiography*, 192.
21. Malcolm X, *Autobiography*, 208.
22. Malcolm X, *Autobiography*, 209.
23. Malcolm X, *Autobiography*, 218.
24. Malcolm X, *Autobiography*, 228.

F. Kennedy. Muhammad had previously instructed Nation of Islam ministers to say nothing about the president's assassination. But other—probably more important—things were at play as well. For example, Malcolm had heard from Nation of Islam women that Muhammad fathered children with some of them. He interviewed the women in question and was not at all pleased with what they told him. He was no longer willing to uncritically support Muhammad. Those who were closest to Malcolm knew that it was only a matter of time before he would put Muhammad and the Nation of Islam behind him. On March 8, 1964, Malcolm announced that he was leaving the Nation and that he would be forming a new organization, the Muslim Mosque, Inc., based on orthodox Islam. He also announced the formation of a nonreligious, more broadly politically based organization, the Organization of Afro-American Unity (OAAU), "which all black Americans could become a part of and play an active part in striking out at the political, economic, and social evils that all of us are confronted by."[25] Whites could not join, although Malcolm had strong affinity for the nineteenth-century radical abolitionist John Brown,[26] who was willing to kill and be killed for black liberation.

Deepening of His Conversion

According to Malcolm, it was in the holy city of Mecca that he witnessed a spirit and practice of brotherhood among people of all races and nationalities that he had never experienced. He was taken by what he described as "the color-blindness" of the Muslim world's religion and society.[27] He also wrote of "the overwhelming spirit of true brotherhood as is practiced by people of all colors and races . . . in this ancient holy land . . . that erases the race problem from its society."[28] Malcolm was convinced that he went through a major conversion experience during the pilgrimage, especially pertaining to race. While still in Mecca he began reappraising his stance on the white man. On reflection he said, "It was when I first began to perceive that 'white man,' as commonly used, means complexion only secondarily; primarily it described attitudes and actions. In America, 'white man' meant specific attitudes and actions toward the black man, and toward all other non-white men. But in the Muslim world, I had seen that men with white complexions were more genuinely brotherly than anyone else had

---

25. Malcolm X, "Whatever Is Necessary," 183.
26. Breitman, *Malcolm X Speaks*, 225.
27. Malcolm X, *Autobiography*, 370.
28. Breitman, *Malcolm X Speaks*, 59.

ever been."²⁹ The hajj opened his eyes regarding race and caused him to declare, "I no longer subscribe to racism. I have adjusted my thinking to the point where I believe that whites are human beings . . . as long as this is borne out by their humane attitude toward Negroes. I'm *not* a racist. I'm not condemning whites for being whites, but for their deeds. I condemn what whites collectively have done to our people collectively."³⁰

One cannot take issue with Malcolm's claim that he met Muslims of all races in Mecca for whom racism was not an issue because of their belief in the unity and oneness of all people under Allah. Nor can one reject his claim that "true Islam removes racism" and that it showed him that "a blanket indictment of all white people is as wrong as when whites make blanket indictments against blacks."³¹ Without question, there were non-racist Muslims on the pilgrimage with Malcolm. However, it would be naïve and not based in fact to claim that one is necessarily non-racist solely because he is Muslim. There are proponents of orthodox Islam who are also racists, just as there are proponents of the Christian faith and Judaism who are racists. True Islam, like true Christianity and true Judaism, rejects racism. Those who accept and live by the highest principles of these religions recognize that racism has no place in them. Malcolm surely met some true believers in Mecca, but not all who professed Islam were true believers, nor were all Islamic countries free of racism,³² a point that Malcolm seemed to have missed when he characterized the Muslim world as color-blind. It is the same in Christianity, Judaism, and other religions.

In any event, as late as January 18, 1965 (approximately one month before he was assassinated), Malcolm was still insisting that he was *not* a racist and that he was against racism and discrimination in any form. He went on to specify that he simply believed in human beings and that every person "should be respected as such," regardless of their color.³³ Malcolm convinced himself that what he relished most about the experience in Mecca was, as he told Alex Haley, "the *brotherhood*! The people of all races, colors, from all over the world coming together as *one*! It has proved to me the power of the One God."³⁴

Malcolm concluded that "whiteness," or the term "the white man," had more to do with an attitude, a way of thinking, or the white man's actions

29. Malcolm X, *Autobiography*, 364.
30. Malcolm X, *Autobiography*, 450.
31. Malcolm, *Autobiography*, 395.
32. Turner, *Islam*, 215–16.
33. Clark, *Malcolm X Talks to Young People*, 83.
34. Malcolm X, *Autobiography*, 369.

toward blacks. It had less to do with skin color alone. In Malcolm's view white complexioned men in Mecca had been the most brotherly he had ever met. The brotherliness of American whites, however, would have to be tested by the nature of their treatment of blacks on a day-to-day basis. "The *problem* here in America," said Malcolm, "is that we meet such a small minority of individual so-called 'good,' or 'brotherly' white people."[35]

As we saw before, Malcolm conceded that only the John Brown type of white liberal would be allowed to join the OAAU.[36] Such a one puts *everything* on the line, as Brown and two of his sons did during the assault on the armory at Harpers Ferry, Virginia, in 1859, in the failed attempt to free the enslaved blacks. However, the truth—then and now—is that the history of white racism in the U.S. and Malcolm's own experience of it prevented him from fully trusting even the most radical, seemingly sincere, whites. He therefore settled for what Peter Goldman described as "arms-length alliances with the right kind of whites"[37] (i.e., John Brown types).

After Mecca, Malcolm declared that his friends now included representatives from virtually every group. "I have friends who are called Capitalists, Socialists, and Communists," he told Alex Haley. "Some of my friends are moderates, conservatives, extremists—some are even Uncle Toms! My friends today are black, brown, red, yellow, and *white*."[38] Post-Mecca Malcolm insisted that he was not a racist and that he did not "subscribe to any of the tenets of racism."[39] Indeed, in the *Autobiography*, we find Malcolm saying (*after* Mecca) that the white man is not inherently evil.[40] He not only denied being a racist but went further, claiming, "*I've never been a racist*."[41] Nevertheless, *this* is the Malcolm X who is an excellent candidate for the ethical prophet hall of fame. I now turn to a more direct consideration of some important elements of ethical prophecy detected in the mature Malcolm's teaching and witness, including, but not limited to, sense of call, staunch belief in the sacredness of persons, use of sweeping allegations, warnings of divine judgment, and recognition of the cost of prophecy.

35. Malcolm X, *Autobiography*, 395.
36. Malcolm X, *Autobiography*, 454.
37. Goldman, *Death and Life of Malcolm X*, 226.
38. Malcolm X, *Autobiography*, 410.
39. Malcolm X, "Racism," 302.
40. Malcolm X, *Autobiography*, 406.
41. Malcolm X, *Two Speeches*, 26 (my italics).

Sense of Call

As with several of the hall of fame candidates there is no obvious call narrative for Malcolm X, although he like the others had a sense of being called by a higher purpose, or the one God of the universe. As observed previously, when there is no call narrative the thing to look for is the person's awareness that injustice exists and must be fought and eradicated. Called to a higher purpose, he devotes his life to trying to achieve justice. Malcolm did not talk or write directly about a call, but it is not difficult to see that he met the criteria for one who is called. Indeed, one is hard-pressed to find a person who was more troubled by the injustice done to his people on a massive scale, and more determined and committed to fighting against it and establishing justice, than Malcolm.

While still in prison, Malcolm had a vision of what he later believed was "Master Wallace D. Fard, the Messiah." It happened one night as he lay in his bed. "I suddenly . . . became aware of a man sitting beside me in my chair. . . . I remember. I could see him as plainly as I see anyone I look at. He wasn't black, and he wasn't white. He was light-brown-skinned, an Asiatic cast of countenance, and he had oily black hair."[42] Malcolm reported that he was transfixed—could neither move nor speak. This incident is the closest thing to a call narrative we find in Malcolm's iterations. He would speak truth to his people, to power, and to the white man, what he characterized as the "raw, naked truth between blacks and whites."[43] He would demand justice for his people, insist that blacks recapture their lost sense of self and dignity, and take the initiative in their struggle for liberation.

Consistent with what he understood to be his call, Malcolm, during a debate with James Farmer at Cornell University on March 7, 1962, said that he would even consider going the integration route *if* he could be assured that the results would be "freedom, justice, equality, and human dignity" for his people.[44] For Malcolm, however, the goal was not integration with white people. Like James Baldwin he had no desire to be integrated into a burning house.[45] Instead, he desired human dignity for all, most especially his people, as well as the right to be fully human and all that that entails. Malcolm declared that what blacks wanted was recognition and respect as

---

42. Malcolm X, *Autobiography*, 203.

43. Malcolm X, *Autobiography*, 298.

44. Farmer and Malcolm X, "Separation vs. Integration." Malcolm came to respect Farmer, Bayard Rustin, and Louis Lomax, if for no other reason than they had the courage to debate him in public.

45. Baldwin, *Fire Next Time*, 93.

human beings. For him, integration and separation are only *means* to this end.[46]

Without question, Malcolm was deemed believable and trustworthy by inner-city blacks because he had been where they were, had suffered what they suffered, had lived among the drug addicts and pushers. In this, he too was similar to the prophets. Jeremiah suffered deeply with his people (Jer 8:18–22; 9:1),[47] as Malcolm did with his. Micah was impoverished and lived among the poor, and "his whole nature revolted against the unnatural excesses of the capital city and the grinding oppression of its poor."[48] Like Jeremiah, like Micah, Malcolm X suffered right along with those whose cause he championed. But even had he not suffered what they suffered and endured, he, like other hall of famers, would most likely have been well received by the people, precisely because he was God's representative speaking the truth about their condition and warning the powers of God's impending judgment if they did not cease their unjust, unrighteous practices.[49]

Malcolm's sense of call is what gave him much of what he needed to stay the course and not sell out or give up in the struggle. He loved his people beyond words and was absolutely committed to their total liberation. He was indeed their champion. And yet, his faith and trust in Allah was even deeper. There was also a deepening of his conviction that blacks are people of unlimited dignity and sacredness, and thus worthy of efforts to liberate them.

Sacredness of Persons

Pre-Mecca Malcolm believed uncritically with Elijah Muhammad that Allah was the God of black people only and that blacks only were divine by nature.[50] The white man was by nature evil,[51] and was believed to be the devil. As such, the terms "sacred" and "precious" did not apply to whites but only to blacks. At least that was the view of Malcolm during the period when he did little more than parrot Muhammad's teachings.

Post-Mecca Malcolm conceded that Elijah Muhammad's version of Islam was not the true form, especially in what it had to say about race. True Islam, he came to see, requires that one be totally "against racism"—that

46. Malcolm X, *Two Speeches*, 13.
47. See Brueggemann, *Like Fire in the Bones*, 148–53.
48. Kent and Smith, *Earlier Prophets*, 79.
49. See Kent and Smith, *Earlier Prophets*, 15.
50. Lomax, *Negro Revolt*, 170–71.
51. Lomax, *Negro Revolt*, 171.

people be judged not by physical attributes but by their deeds and their practice.[52] True Islam teaches that all people are sisters and brothers. "I have been traveling and my scope has broadened," Malcolm told Harry Ring a few weeks before he was assassinated. He went on to say, "For one thing, I believe in the religion of Islam which automatically teaches us the brotherhood of man. Whereas as a follower of Elijah Muhammad, I said that I believed in the religion of Islam, but his teaching or version of it was not based upon the brotherhood of man. It was against people just on the basis of their color. But my beliefs now are 100 percent against racism and against segregation in any form."[53] Malcolm now believed that true Islam was against judging a person or group by their race-ethnicity. Rather, it requires that people be judged on the basis of their behavior or practice. In addition, Islam requires the recognition that Allah is the God of all people. Human beings are all one under Allah. Every human being, regardless of race-ethnicity, is infinitely valuable to Allah. This was one of Malcolm's most significant takeaways from true Islam.

Virtually all that Minister Malcolm did—both before and after Mecca—was intended to reestablish in blacks their lost sense of dignity. He was convinced that this spirit needed to be reignited and restored in his people, that they needed to acknowledge and respect their own inherent worth, individually and collectively. Although many whites, and some blacks, wrongly believed that Malcolm was a hatemonger, the more accurate view is that he was less interested in expending energy hating whites, and admonishing blacks to do the same, than doing all in his power to reawaken, uplift, and enhance his people's sense of self-worth.

Malcolm knew that black liberation and empowerment would come only when his people learned to love and respect themselves and their cultural heritage. He therefore spent countless hours speaking and lecturing about the importance of self-worth, pride, and love of self, people, and culture. Malcolm knew—as all honest blacks did—that black people were not respected as human beings by vast numbers of whites in the U.S.[54] and were not even considered to be human beings. He knew that the key to reversing this lay with blacks themselves, who needed to essentially disregard what whites thought about them and to begin working to enhance their own self-image and sense of worth.

I know of no place where Malcolm made explicit reference to the phrase "sacredness of persons," but he was always criticizing whites and his

---

52. Malcolm X, *Two Speeches*, 40.
53. Malcolm X, *Two Speeches*, 40.
54. Malcolm X, *Two Speeches*, 42.

own people for their low estimation of the humanity and dignity of blacks. When he criticized black self-hate and whites' hatred and mistreatment of blacks, this was essentially a negative way of stressing the preciousness and dignity of his people. Malcolm was convinced that his people were not born hating themselves but were taught by white Christians during American slavery to hate everything about themselves and their Afrikan culture.[55] The result was deeply embedded self-hatred.[56] For Malcolm, few crimes committed by the white man were as tragic as this.

> When you teach a man to hate his lips, the lips that God gave him, the shape of his nose that God gave him, the texture of the hair that God gave him, the color of the skin that God gave him, you've committed the worst crime that a race of people can commit. And this is the crime that you've committed.[57]

Before blacks could progress at all in a nation in which they had been systematically taught to hate everything about themselves, they had first to undergo a radical transformation of how they feel about themselves and each other. It was not necessary or important to change whites' minds about blacks. Instead, Malcolm argued, "We've got to change our own minds about each other. We have to see each other with new eyes. We have to see each other as brothers and sisters."[58]

Blacks will gain respect as human beings when—and only when—they learn to respect and love themselves and let it be known that they will do *anything* to defend their humanity and dignity.[59] Malcolm was certain that Allah infuses all people with dignity. His people must be awakened to their humanity, dignity, and heritage.[60] Using extreme measures to gain one's rights as a human being is not a vice and thus is not to be avoided. One sins, however, when one uses only ordinary means to achieve such an end. "And when one is moderate in pursuit of justice for human beings, I say he's a sinner,"[61] Malcolm told students at Oxford University.

Post-Mecca Malcolm's view of the dignity of human beings is similar to the best in Jewish and Christian thought. At bottom, he too believed that human worth lies in relatedness to God. This had much to do with

---

55. Malcolm X, *Autobiography*, 277.
56. Malcolm X, *Malcolm X on Afro-American History*, 73.
57. Perry, *Last Speeches*, 166–67.
58. Breitman, *Malcolm X Speaks*, 40.
59. Clark, *Malcolm X Talks to Young People*, 67.
60. Clark, *Malcolm X Talks to Young People*, 99.
61. Clark, *Malcolm X Talks to Young People*, 25.

Malcolm's later stance against black separatism. Just weeks before he was assassinated, he told interviewer Pierre Berton that he no longer believed in the viability of a separate black state, but rather he believed in a society in which all people can live together on the basis of equality.[62] Contrary to what many whites seemed to think, Malcolm had come to believe that God so orchestrated the world that human beings are actually interdependent.[63]

Malcolm believed that human beings were so valuable to Allah that they were Allah's most important concern. Like the Hebrew prophets, Malcolm's was not the Aristotelian god who created human beings and the world and then went off into a far corner of the universe to think its own thoughts, oblivious to human beings. Neither was Malcolm's god that of Epicurus and Epictetus, who taught that god is not concerned about small matters that adversely affect human beings. Malcolm understood Allah not as the Wholly Other or the Indifferent One but as the God of Pathos—the God who is involved, is near, and is unceasingly concerned about human beings and everything that happens to them because each and every one is infinitely sacred and important to God.[64] This was the message Malcolm sought to convey to his people; they were imbued with infinite worth. This is why James Cone said that Malcolm was—arguably—"the greatest defender of black dignity in the modern world."[65]

Sweeping Allegations

Few matters are more important to the ethical prophet than the condition of human beings in the world, and most especially the condition of the left-outs, whom God privileges above all others. The Hebrew prophets seemed to declare in one voice that these are special and dear to the heart of God and that God is forever concerned about their day-to-day welfare in the world. God's focus is ever and always on the plight of human beings. Heschel reminds us that God "is preoccupied with man, with the concrete actualities of history rather than with the timeless issues of thought."[66] Whatever happens to human beings is of great concern to God. It is therefore understandable that the prophets' words to the people and the powers were often sharp and stinging. It is important that all know the importance of the plight of human beings to God—and that they know, too, God's expectations—and therefore

---

62. Breitman, *Malcolm X Speaks*, 197.
63. Malcolm X, *Autobiography*, 311.
64. See Heschel, *Prophets*, 227.
65. Cone, *Said I Wasn't Gonna Tell Nobody*, 87.
66. Heschel, *Prophets*, 5.

the words of the prophet were calculated to get the undivided attention of the people and the powers. Although a human being, and susceptible to the same fears and uncertainties as other human beings, the prophet is more concerned about being faithful in speaking God's truth regarding justice and righteousness than how he may be perceived by his contemporaries. What he says is calculated to force the people to think and to burn into their conscience a sense of responsibility to what God requires. Therefore, the prophet "is impatient of excuse, contemptuous of pretense and self-pity."[67] His words are not intended to make wrongdoers feel good in their wrongdoing. If anything, the prophet's words are designed to jolt. Few people in the history of the U.S. fit this description better than Malcolm X. Indeed, having learned as a child that one sure way of getting what he wanted was to protest and make a lot of noise,[68] Malcolm remembered this and made it into an art form when he began the fight for justice for his people. He used everything at his disposal to get the message across, even if it meant making sweeping indictments of whites as well as blacks.

When Malcolm spoke about injustice done to black people and the source of that injustice, he spared no one. His indictments were such that there were no exceptions. Not *some* white people are blond-haired, blue-eyed devils, but "the white man"—*all* white people. Obviously this was not literally true, for not all white people even had blond hair and blue eyes. In addition, white people were not literally the devil, although very many behaved in devilish fashion. Malcolm knew this, but this was not his primary concern. His first priority was the welfare of his people, and he was prepared to do whatever he deemed necessary to remove the feet of oppression from their necks. To this end, no language was too strong or too harsh, and it mattered not whether one was a liberal, a moderate, a diehard racist, or a member of the black community.

The language of the ethical prophet is abrasive and intended to shock rather than to encourage, appease, or bring comfort. In addition, as we have seen regarding other hall of fame candidates, accuracy is not the aim of the sweeping allegation. The purpose is to awaken the people and the powers to a sense of responsibility for existing injustices. In this regard, Heschel reminds us, "What seems to be exaggeration is often only a deeper penetration, for the prophets see the world from the point of view of God, as transcendent, not immanent truth."[69]

---

67. Heschel, *Prophets*, 7.
68. Malcolm X, *Autobiography*, 10.
69. Heschel, *Prophets*, 14.

C. Eric Lincoln offered a helpful observation about Malcolm's penchant for making sweeping indictments: "Malcolm said what he felt—he was outspoken—and sometimes he overstated his case for emphasis. The rhetoric was intended to produce certain kinds of responses both in his black constituency—Malcolm wanted them to understand that the white man was human and that being human he was vulnerable—and among the 'blue-eyed devils' he loved so much to annoy."[70] Pre-Mecca Malcolm did not hesitate to indict *all* white people (and the practice did not end entirely after Mecca). In 1963, he told Louis Lomax,

> *The white man is by nature a devil* and must be destroyed. The black man will inherit the earth; he will resume control, taking back the position he held centuries ago when the white devil was crawling around the caves of Europe on his all fours. Before the white devil came into our lives we had a civilization, we had a culture, we were living in silks and satins. Then he put us in chains and placed us aboard the "Good Ship Jesus," and we have lived in hell ever since.[71]

Even post-Mecca Malcolm often spoke of "the collective white man" as having "*acted* like a devil."[72]

As Malcolm matured and began doing more of his own thinking, he became increasingly uncomfortable with what he referred to as his "sweeping indictments" against the white race. He knew that to say that white men are inherently devils implied that every single individual white person is a devil, a view that was not supported by what he learned about orthodox Islam in Mecca, his later travels in the Middle East, and his many interactions and conversations with white university students in England and the U.S. On reflection, Malcolm said that his uncritical views about the white man were a result of the teachings of Elijah Muhammad. "In the past I permitted myself to be used by Elijah Muhammad . . . to make sweeping indictments of all white people, the entire white race, and these generalizations have caused injuries to some whites who perhaps did not deserve to be hurt."[73] After Mecca, Malcolm vowed no longer to make such indictments. However, that did not mean that he would soften his prophetic critique—only that he would not indict an entire race of people. He worked at this but did not always succeed.

---

70. Quoted in Goldman, *Death and Life of Malcom X*, 68.
71. Quoted in Lomax, *When the Word Is Given*, 180 (my italics).
72. Malcolm X, *Autobiography*, 193, 192, 199 (my italics).
73. Malcolm X, "Racism," 302.

As we have seen regarding other hall of fame candidates, Malcolm X used the sweeping allegation as a rhetorical device to shock the conscience of the people and the powers, to get their attention, to force them to think. His sweeping indictments of white people caused a national and international media frenzy. Malcolm could be just as abrasive in his indictments of members of the black intelligentsia. Nowhere was this more evident than during a question-and-answer period after one of his university speeches. He recounted the incident to Alex Haley:

> One particular university's "token-integrated" black Ph.D. associate professor I never will forget; he got me so mad I couldn't see straight. As badly as our twenty-two millions of educationally deprived black people need the help of any brains he has, there he was looking like some fly in the buttermilk among white "colleagues"—and he was trying to *eat me up*! He was ranting about what a "divisive demagogue" and what a "reverse racist" I was. I was racking my head, to spear that fool; finally I held up my hand, and he stopped. "Do you know what white racists call black Ph.D.'s?" He said something like, "I believe that I happen not to be aware of that"—you know, one of these ultra-proper-talking Negroes. And I laid the word down on him, loud: "*Nigger!*"[74]

Not what white racists call *some* blacks with PhDs, but *all* black recipients of that degree.

That Malcolm X desired to speak more conditionally about whites and those members of his own race who seemed not to get the point of his remonstrations says much about his own humanity and his courage to change. Because of the nature of the sweeping generalization and its purpose, however, Malcolm need not have softened his views. As we saw in the discussion on Ida B. Wells-Barnett, the strength of the ethical prophet is not found in being able to work effectively within organizations in order to arrive at compromises. Rather, she is called to convey to the people and the powers God's point of view and requirement that justice and righteousness should be done, if judgment is to be avoided. Her responsibility is to keep the ideal alive.

Divine Judgment

In chapter 1 we saw that the new and shocking element in eighth-century Hebrew prophecy was that the sentence of judgment had already been

74. Malcolm X, *Autobiography*, 310.

pronounced on Israel. Salvation would come, but only in the "shadow" of God's judgment. The Hebrew prophets did not pretend that all was well in the nation but insisted that God had summoned it to the judgment seat. They were just as convinced that salvation would come, but only on the other side of judgment and "by means of fresh acts" of God.[75] Unlike the false prophet Hananiah, the Hebrew prophets did not seek to appease the people and the nation by preaching hope at a time when the nation was actually in dire trouble. The prophet Jeremiah was certain that God had not called and sent Hananiah, who had made the people believe the lie that all was well in the nation. Jeremiah warned that Hananiah would be punished by God (Jer 28:15–16). Since God is love the point was not that the prophets' last word to the people was one of judgment, but it was a word that God required to be spoken as a means of awakening them to their disobedience and unfaithfulness and the impending judgment. God said to the prophet Jeremiah, "I am about to pluck them up from their land, and I will pluck up the house of Judah from among them." But this was not the end of the story, for God also told Jeremiah that after the destruction, "I will again have compassion on them, and I will bring them to their heritage and to their land, every one of them" (Jer 12:14–15). God's last word was one of hope, but that hope lay on the other side of judgment.

Malcolm X was convinced that there was going to be a day of reckoning—that God would judge the cruel behavior of the white man. In 1962, he told Richard Elman that Allah would "execute judgment and justice in whatever way He sees fit, against the people who are guilty of this crime against our people in this country."[76] God was summoning the United States of America to the bar of judgment for its failure to do justice to black people. In what was his last speech while still a member of the Nation of Islam (December 4, 1964), Malcolm said that the U.S. was living in the day of judgment and that only Allah was the judge. "White America is doomed," he announced. "Death and devastating destruction hang at this very moment in the skies over America."[77] White America was facing divine judgment because of its mistreatment of blacks and its seeds of hypocrisy. Allah alone, Malcolm proclaimed, would issue justice regarding the treatment of blacks. In this, Malcolm accepted the Hebrew Bible tenet of "an eye for an eye." In the *Playboy* interview he told Alex Haley that "as I see the law of justice, it says as you sow, so shall you reap. . . . We Muslims believe that the white race, which is guilty of having oppressed and exploited and enslaved

---

75. Rad, *Message of the Prophets*, 154.
76. Gallen, *Malcolm X*, 106.
77. Malcolm X, "God's Judgment," 131.

our people here in America, should and will be the victims of God's divine wrath."[78] Not long before he was assassinated, Malcolm recalled that Elijah Muhammad taught black Muslims "that 'doomsday' refers to the 'doom of the white race.'"[79]

America must be punished for her sins against black humanity. White America *could* be saved, Malcolm believed, but the white man is too arrogant to repent and seek forgiveness for his sins: "He tries, characteristically, to cover up his past record. He does not possess the humility to admit his guilt, to try and atone for his crimes."[80] But even though judgment was surely coming, Malcolm was just as certain that a good and loving Allah would establish a new world, one based on the brotherhood and sisterhood of all people. Not unlike the Hebrew prophets, he believed that before this could happen, the old world must first be destroyed. Judgment and destruction were looming. Hope lay on the other side of the plucking up, breaking down, overthrowing, and destroying (Jer 18:7–10; 31:28). Pre-Mecca Malcolm declared that "before God can set up his new world, the Muslim world, or world of Islam, which will be established on the principles of truth, peace, and brotherhood, God himself must first destroy this evil Western world, the white world . . . a wicked world, ruled by a race of devils, that preaches falsehood, practices slavery, and thrives on indecency and immorality."[81] There would be a new world, but only on the other side of judgment.

Cost of Prophecy

Malcolm X knew that speaking Allah's truth as it pertained to justice and liberation for his people would be costly—that he himself likely would not live to experience such liberation. He told Alex Haley that he would not even live to see the publication of his autobiography, that he most likely would die a violent death.[82] Consequently, post-Mecca Malcolm lived each day with a sense of extreme urgency, knowing that it could be his last. He said that "each day I live as if I am already dead. . . . When I *am* dead—I say it that way because from the things I *know*, I do not expect to live long enough to read this book in its finished form."[83] Haley reflected on Malcolm's last days, saying, "His old total ease was no longer with him. As if it was the most

---

78. Malcolm X, "*Playboy* Interview," 115.
79. Clark, *Final Speeches*, 248.
80. Malcolm X, *Autobiography*, 311.
81. Malcolm X, "God's Judgment," 124.
82. Malcolm X, *Autobiography*, 150.
83. Malcolm X, *Autobiography*, 417.

natural thing in the world to do, at sudden intervals he would stride to the door; pulling it open, he would look up and down the corridor, then shut the door again. 'If I'm alive when this book comes out, it will be a miracle,' he said by way of explanation."[84]

Although the human in Malcolm caused him to naturally exhibit fear and anxiety about what he believed to be his impending death, he, like James Baldwin (whom he much admired[85]), had early vowed to his people that he would never sell out, and he never did. Indeed, the ethical prophet never uses his office for personal gain.[86] Since Malcolm had a good idea of what daring to speak in the name of Allah would cost, he simply accepted it, refusing to hide or to soften his prophetic critique. With courage, boldness, and devotion he criticized the sins of the powers and the people. Moreover, Malcolm was convinced that true peace and justice would come about only when all people submit to the will of the one God.[87] His realism told him that most people would not do so, at least in his lifetime.

As far as we know Malcolm and Martin Luther King Jr. met only once, and there was talk of a second, more formal meeting between them. However, while addressing his supporters at the Audubon Ballroom in New York City on February 21, 1965, Malcolm X was assassinated by followers of Elijah Muhammad as his wife and young daughters watched in horror. Although Malcolm and King did not get the chance to work together, they were close observers and critics of each other's leadership and contributions. They respected and admired each other. Indeed, upon hearing the tragic news of Malcolm's assassination, King sent a telegram to his wife, Betty Shabazz, saying in part, "While we did not always see eye to eye on methods to solve the race problem, I always had a deep affection for Malcolm and felt that he had the great ability to put his finger on the existence and root of the problem. He was an eloquent spokesman for his point of view and no one can honestly doubt that Malcolm had a great concern for the problems that we face as a race."[88] What might have been had Malcolm and King been able to work together as ethical prophets?

---

84. Malcolm X, *Autobiography*, 447.
85. Malcolm X, *Autobiography*, 438.
86. Zollars, *Hebrew Prophecy*, 76.
87. Malcolm X, *Autobiography*, 411.
88. King, "Letter to Mrs. Betty Shabazz."

Conclusion

When Malcolm X returned from Mecca he felt much freer than he had been. Much of his thinking about race and God had been stifled during his time in the Nation of Islam. He thought differently about the white race after Mecca. His ideas about race were transformed during the hajj, but he knew there was no corresponding change in the attitudes and behavior of most whites in the U.S. He knew upon his return to the States that he dare not soften or cease his criticisms of white racism. So, although there was a shift in his earlier position that the white man was by nature the devil, it would not be correct to say that post-Mecca Malcolm uncritically turned to integration. He did not. Instead, he seemed to be more open to the idea of integration, but not on the terms of white liberals.

As ethical prophet, Malcolm's best, most mature, uninhibited thinking about race had more to do with teaching his own people to love themselves and their Afrikan heritage than with teaching them to hate white people. Neither was he interested to expend much energy teaching white people to be free of their racism. He wanted primarily to address the state of emergency in the black community, that is, the historical tendency of blacks to internalize whites' negative perceptions of them. We have seen that there was no truth in the charge that the driving force behind Malcolm X was a desire to teach blacks to hate whites. In light of Malcolm's deep love for his people and his desire that they awaken to their own sense of humanity and dignity, it may be said that he was not even concerned about the white man. Like Martin Luther King Jr., Malcolm was adamant that despite all that had happened to them, blacks themselves had to recapture and boldly assert their sense of humanity and dignity, a point that King would also drive home.

Called by Allah, there was no question in Malcolm's mind that he was obligated to speak truth to his people and to the powers that demeaned and dehumanized them, both outside and inside the black community. He frequently told his people that he was going to tell them the truth whether they like it or not. This stance is clearly reminiscent of the Hebrew prophets, who felt morally obligated to speak the truth of God's understanding of human existence. Furthermore, prophets speak God's hard truths in season and out, whether or not the people or the powers want to hear those truths. This is precisely what Heschel meant when he asserted, "The prophet's duty is to speak to the people, 'whether they hear or refuse to hear' [Ezek 2:5]."[89] In this regard, religious persons should understand the significance of *the burden of prophecy* becomes more than something one bears psychologically.

---

89. Heschel, *Prophets*, 19.

The prophet is charged with a truly heavy burden and responsibility, namely, opening self to God's truth and then conveying that truth to the people and the nations. Our next candidate for the ethical prophet hall of fame took this to a whole new level.

6

Martin Luther King Jr. as Ethical Prophet

Martin Luther King Jr. was a fourth-generation southern Baptist minister who exceeded all others in the area of social justice activism. Throughout his thirteen-year ministry he was literally on the front lines of nonviolent demonstrations for civil rights and peace. He was also daily in the crosshairs of would-be assassins and was violently attacked a number of times. For example, he was stabbed while autographing his first book in 1958; punched in the face not long before the Birmingham, Alabama, campaign began in 1963; sucker punched in the back of the head while checking in at a Selma, Alabama, hotel in 1965; and hit and knocked down by a rock while marching in a Chicago suburb in 1966. Also during the Chicago march a knife was thrown that missed him and stuck in the shoulder of a white bystander. King saw such attacks as part of the cost of being faithful to God's call on his life.

He was born "Michael" King Jr.[1] in the home of his maternal grandparents in Atlanta, Georgia, on January 15, 1929. His maternal grandfather, Adam Daniel Williams, was pastor of the Ebenezer Baptist Church in Atlanta. The church was co-pastored by King's father, who became senior pastor when Williams died. The family enjoyed a comfortable middle-class

---

1. Since in those days the firstborn son was typically named after his father, the delivering doctor assumed this would be the case with King, and because Daddy King was known and referred to as "Mike," the doctor wrote "Michael" on the child's birth certificate. The elder King later changed his name to "Martin Luther" and did the same for his son. See Burrow, *Extremist for Love*, 58–59, for a fuller discussion of this. See also Branch's discussion in *Parting the Waters*, 44, 46–47, and King Sr.'s discussion in *Daddy King*, 88.

status, which later prompted King to reflect that while growing up he never needed or wanted for any material things. He earned the BA, BD, and PhD degrees at Morehouse College, Crozer Theological Seminary, and Boston University, respectively.

King met and married Coretta Scott of Marion, Alabama, during his doctoral studies at Boston University. Scott was a gifted singer who was studying at the New England Conservatory of Music. She had not wanted to marry a minister because she believed they tended to have narrow, conservative views about male-female relations. In addition, she believed they tended to be overly pious and not well educated. To her delight she found King to be different in these respects, although they would later have many discussions about the role of women in and beyond the home. With some initial reluctance on Scott's part, the couple decided to return to the South to work on racial injustice. King was called to be pastor of the Dexter Avenue Baptist Church in Montgomery, Alabama, in 1954. Barely a year later, Rosa Parks, a black seamstress in Montgomery, refused to relinquish her bus seat to a white patron. That decision led to the yearlong Montgomery bus boycott.

King, Heschel, and Benjamin E. Mays

King, much like his friend, civil rights and antiwar activist Abraham Joshua Heschel, had much to say about the Hebrew prophets. Through his writings, sermons, and speeches he did much to clarify the important contributions and meaning of the prophets for his day.[2] Unlike most, King and Heschel did not simply mention prophecy or an eighth-century Hebrew prophet in passing. Instead, they tried to make it crystal clear who those most peculiar and unusual personalities were, what they stood for, and what they tried to convey to human beings and the powers. When one reads what King and Heschel had to say about the prophets, one should have clarity about the meaning of the type of prophecy discussed in this book. Both men were convinced that God's primary concern is the welfare of human beings. Consequently, they believed that God is incessantly searching for human beings to return to covenant relation with God and each other.

In the chapter on Heschel we saw that King praised and admired him as leader and prophet. There was in fact mutual admiration between them. Heschel characterized King as that rare combination of an "inspired man

---

2. At this writing the best and most systematic treatment of King as prophet is found in the work of Lewis V. Baldwin: "The Minister as Preacher, Pastor, and Prophet"; *There Is a Balm in Gilead*, 322–30, and the entirety of ch. 5; and "The Attuning of the Spirit," 150–62.

and a sophisticated man."[3] Barely a week before King was assassinated on April 4, 1968, Heschel introduced him to a gathering of Jewish rabbis, saying, "Martin Luther King is a voice, a vision, and a way. I call upon every Jew to harken to his voice, to share his vision, to follow in his way. The whole future of America will depend upon the impact and influence of Dr. King."[4] Clearly placing King in the tradition of the Hebrew prophets, he asked, "Where in America today do we hear a voice like the voice of the prophets of Israel? Martin Luther King is a sign that God has not forsaken the United States of America. God has sent him to us. His presence is the hope of America. His mission is sacred, his leadership of supreme importance to every one of us."[5] Honoring King in the ABC televised special "The Heritage of Martin Luther King Jr.," in January 1972, along with two Afrikan American discussants, the Rev. Jesse Jackson and Father George Clements, Heschel praised King for his nonviolence, keen intelligence, powerful presence, and grasp of complex sociological factors.[6] Having first met at the Conference on Religion and Race in Chicago in 1963, the two men quickly became good friends and mutual supporters in the civil rights and antiwar movements. They marched together for voting rights from Selma to Montgomery in 1965. Heschel sat on the speakers' platform at Riverside Church as King delivered his powerful address on the Vietnam War on April 4, 1967. In addition, the two men prayed together for peace and the end of the Vietnam War at Arlington National Cemetery in 1967. Moreover, Heschel recommended King for an honorary degree from the Jewish Theological Seminary, the first non-Jew to receive that accolade.[7] Both men were deeply influenced by the Hebrew prophetic tradition,[8] and each referred to the other as a prophet (but did not often refer to himself as one).

Benjamin E. Mays, late president of Morehouse College and mentor to King, rightly characterized him as "a prophet in the line of duty."[9]

---

3. Quoted in Kaplan, *Spiritual Radical*, 359.
4. King, "Conversation," 657–58.
5. King, "Conversation," 657.
6. Kaplan, *Spiritual Radical*, 359.
7. Branch, *Pillar of Fire*, 327.
8. Interestingly enough, a number of King's lieutenants (e.g., Andrew Young, James Lawson, Vincent Harding, C. T. Vivian, and Bayard Rustin) were familiar with Heschel and were much influenced by his outstanding book *The Prophets*. See Kaplan, *Spiritual Radical*, 222. Young apparently was introduced to the book while in seminary. Furthermore, Heschel's only child, Susannah Heschel, reports that in later years some of King's surviving lieutenants told her that they used to carry around a copy of *The Prophets* for "inspiration and consolation." S. Heschel, "Two Friends, Two Prophets."
9. Quoted in Raines, *My Soul Is Rested*, 460.

When Mays eulogized King he praised him for having been a prophet in the tradition of Amos, Micah, and Isaiah. God, Mays told the mourners, called King to that role. He proceeded to say,

> Surely this man was called of God to do this work. If Amos and Micah were prophets in the eighth century B.C., Martin Luther King, Jr., was a prophet in the twentieth century. If Isaiah was called of God to prophesy in his day, Martin Luther King, Jr., was called to prophesy in his day. If Hosea was sent to preach love and forgiveness centuries ago, Martin Luther was sent to expound the doctrine of nonviolence and forgiveness in the third quarter of the twentieth century. If Jesus was called to preach the Gospel to the poor, Martin Luther King, Jr. fits that designation. If a prophet is one who does not seek popular causes to espouse, but rather the causes he thinks are right, Martin Luther qualifies on that score.[10]

During a speech on the occasion of the fifty-first birthday celebration of King at the University of Maryland on January 15, 1980, Mays again linked King to the prophetic tradition, saying that the prophet "speaks about the conditions of evil, discrimination and racism whenever he finds it—throughout the length and breadth of the world."[11] This is why he defended King's stance against the war in Vietnam. In any case, others told King that "the mantle of the prophets rests well upon your shoulders."[12]

King himself did not hesitate to say that the ethical prophet always speaks what she perceives to be God's truth.[13] Describing himself as both priest and prophet at a staff retreat,[14] King was certain that he had responsibilities in each of these roles, and he consistently did what each required. He said that the priest takes the people to God; the prophet takes God to the people and reminds them of what God says and requires.[15] Moses took the people to God and pleaded on their behalf; Micah took God to the people and pleaded for God.

King insisted that the ethical prophet always asks the moral question: Is it right? It was this question that King, unlike the vast majority of

---

10. Mays, "Eulogy," 359.
11. Mays, "Martin Luther King Jr.," 238.
12. Carson et al., *Papers*, 3:143.
13. King, "To Charter Our Course," 20, 24.
14. King, "To Charter Our Course," 29, 30. Lewis Baldwin has written definitively about King as pastor, priest, and prophet. See his *There Is a Balm in Gilead*, 310–30; and Baldwin and Anderson, *Revives My Soul Again*, ch. 6.
15. King, "To Charter Our Course," 30.

Republicans in both houses of the U.S. Congress today, persistently asked. The question was not, Is this consistent with what the party, the Freedom Caucus, or the base thinks? The question was, Is this consistent with the highest principles and what God requires? This is why King was in the ethical prophet camp and why he was an ethical leader.[16] He was not a consensus leader, and clearly did not think of himself as such.[17] Rather, he was guided by his highest moral ideals. The moral question is not (but should be!) the question that politicians and others ask. There is no more glaring illustration of this today than when Donald Trump and Republican members of Congress sought (successfully) to get Brett Kavanaugh appointed to the Supreme Court, despite his disingenuousness, his lack of appropriate temperament and integrity, and his propensity to lie under oath. Morality was conspicuously absent from virtually all that Kavanaugh, congressional supporters, and Trump said and did. We are living in one of the most damning periods of leadership deprivation in the history of the United States and therefore need to hear and be guided by King's declaration of the need for ethical prophets and ethical leaders.[18]

Renowned King scholar Lewis V. Baldwin has argued convincingly that King's strong spirituality and prayer ethic,[19] as well as his ethic of play, laughter, and his strong sense of humor,[20] enabled him to press forward in the civil rights and antiwar movements, in which his life was frequently pressure-filled and under threat of death. In addition, his faith in God and his staunch belief in the fundamental morality of the universe gave him hope and revived his soul again and again. He expressed this sentiment many times, not least in a London interview in early 1968 (which was not aired until April 4, 1968, the day he was assassinated). To the question, "What nourishes this faith?" King replied that "ultimately what nourishes it is the faith in a kind of undergirding moral structure in the universe. I believe firmly that all reality hinges on moral foundations, and that somehow unarmed truth is the most powerful thing in the universe, and that truth crushed to earth will rise again. If I didn't believe that I wouldn't have a faith to carry me on in the future, but it's the faith in the ultimate triumph of good over evil."[21] Hope, not judgment, must be the last word for one with such faith.

16. King, "To Charter Our Course," 31.
17. King, *Autobiography*, 331.
18. See Burrow, "Martin Luther King Jr., and Ethical Leadership," 11–28.
19. See Baldwin, "Attuning of the Spirit," ch. 6.
20. See Baldwin, *Behind the Public Veil*, ch. 6.
21. King, "Doubts and Certainties," 3.

King and the Prophets

Many, although not all, of King's statements about the Hebrew prophets were made before Jewish audiences. As previously observed, he, like Heschel, said many things about the Hebrew prophets, their moral boldness, meaning, vision, sense of dependence on God, and their influence on King's life and his way of seeing and doing things in the world. King and Heschel gave the prophets center stage, which prompted them to focus frequently on what they sought to accomplish in the name of the God who called and commissioned them. King branded the Hebrew prophets as those "ethical giants" who had the courage to speak boldly and loudly God's truth to power, as well as to the people. We need the prophets because it is they who, in the face of racial injustice, will declare the urgency of eradicating it now rather than later.[22] In an address to the Synagogue Council of America, in December 1965, King described the prophets as "those most extraordinary men of history"[23] and further commended them by saying,

> They did not believe that conscience is a still small voice. They believed that conscience thunders or it does not speak at all. They were articulate, passionate, and fearless, attacking injustice and corruption whether the guilty be kings or their own unrepentant people. Without physical protection, scornful of risks evoked by their unpopular messages, they went among the people with no shield other than truth.[24]

The prophets were courageous, audacious, and forceful in their attacks on injustice and corruption. They spared neither the powers nor their own people if they were out of harmony with God's expectations. In his prophetic function King sought to consistently apply the highest principles of the Jewish and Christian faiths to a trilogy of social evils of his day—racism, militarism, and economic injustice. But that was not all. King believed that the prophets belong to us all and that all—individuals and the powers—need them. In the aforementioned address he spoke cogently about why we need the prophets. In addition, and similar to Heschel's stance, he reminded his audience that not only the prophets but every human being is responsible for denouncing injustice and contributing to the establishment of justice.

> The Hebrew prophets belong to all people because their concepts of justice and equality have become ideals for all races and civilizations. Today we particularly need the Hebrew prophets

---

22. King, "Beyond Discovery, Love," 7.
23. King, "Address at the Synagogue Council," 9, 7.
24. King, "Address at the Synagogue Council," 8.

because they taught that to love God was to love justice: that each human being has an inescapable obligation to denounce evil where he sees it and to defy a ruler who commands him to break the covenant.

The Hebrew prophets are needed today because decent people must be imbued with the courage to speak the truth, to realize that silence may temporarily preserve status or security. But to live with a lie is a gross affront to God. It is scarcely a secret that many congressmen, educators, clergymen, and leaders of national affairs are gravely disturbed by our foreign policy .... Yet, important leaders keep their silence ....

The Hebrew prophets are needed today because we need their flaming courage; we need them because the thunder of their fearless voices is the only sound stronger than the blasts of bombs and the clamour of war hysteria.

The Hebrew prophets are needed today because Amos said in words that echo across the centuries: "Let justice roll down like the waters, and righteousness as a mighty stream"; because Micah said in words lifted to cosmic proportions: "They shall beat their swords into plowshares and their spears into pruning hooks. Nations shall not lift up sword against nation, neither shall they learn war anymore"; because Isaiah said: "Yea when ye make many prayers, I will not hear; your hands are full of blood. Wash you, make you clean; put away the evil of your doings from before mine eyes. Cease to do evil" ...

I think the Hebrew prophets are among us today because although there are many pulpits that are empty while ministers physically occupy them there are others from which the passion for justice and compassion for man is still heard. In the days to come as the voices of sanity multiply we will know that across thousands of years of time the prophets' message of truth and decency, brotherhood and peace survives; that they are living in our time to give hope to a tortured world that their promise of the Kingdom of God has not been lost to mankind.[25]

This proclamation on why we need ethical prophecy, its meaning and importance, and the belief that the prophets are still among us is perhaps King's longest, most definitive statement on the subject. We need to remember, however, that King was already thoroughly committed to ethical prophecy when he met and befriended Heschel in 1963. Indeed, he was so committed while in seminary and during his doctoral studies. Furthermore, we will see below that he even referenced the importance of the prophets in his first

---

25. King, "Address at the Synagogue Council," 8–9.

sermon as senior pastor of the Dexter Avenue Baptist Church. At any rate, his elevation of the importance of the prophets endeared him to Heschel and other Jewish leaders.

Without question, the Hebrew prophets influenced King's life and ministry in profound ways. He expressed this very sentiment in a letter to Sam Wyler in 1967, writing, "I have been strongly influenced by the prophets of old and those who place the truth above expediency."[26] King was answering a question that Wyler raised about the war in Vietnam. King said much more about the prophets in general and about specific prophets (e.g., Amos, Micah, Jeremiah, and Isaiah). For now, however, I turn to an examination of elements of ethical prophecy that were prominent in King's work and witness: belief in a personal God; call to ministry; sacredness of persons; call for justice; speaking truth to power; divine judgment; cost of prophecy; and hope and the beloved community. Because of the importance of *courage* for King and other hall of famers, I also discuss this virtue and its importance in ethical prophecy. What is the foundation of this type of prophecy?

Belief in a Personal God

While growing up, King was wholly infused with two basic ideas: God as personal and loving creator, and the absolute sacredness of human beings. Although these are Jewish[27] and Christian ideas, he later learned that they are also fundamental tenets of the philosophy of personalism. At Crozer Theological Seminary he studied the philosophy of religion of the premier personalist, Edgar S. Brightman of Boston University. He therefore decided to study personalism systematically as a doctoral student under Brightman, which he was fortunate to do during his first year. When Brightman died unexpectedly, L. Harold DeWolf, a personalist protégé of his, was assigned as King's academic and dissertation advisor. King studied personalism

---

26. King to Mr. Sam Wyler, July 20, 1967, 3.

27. At this writing I know of no place where Heschel cites the term "personalism" or describes himself as a personalist. However, in reading his work I have discovered that five elements of the philosophy of personalism that strongly influenced Martin Luther King are also prominent in Heschel's writings: God as personal, freedom, the dignity and worth of human beings, self-consciousness, and unity. These personalist ideas are present in numerous longer and shorter writings of Heschel. We may therefore conclude that he was fundamentally influenced by the long-standing tradition of personalism in Judaism. There is no more systematic and instructive treatment of the centrality of personalism's organic relation to Judaism than Stitskin, *Jewish Philosophy: A Study in Personalism*. Stitskin exhibits strong familiarity with the work of several Boston University personalists who influenced King directly or indirectly (*Jewish Philosophy*, 139). Heschel's personalism is another topic that begs for exploration in Heschel studies.

systematically under DeWolf. He wrote and defended his dissertation on the doctrine of God in the thinking of Paul Tillich and Henry Nelson Wieman, essentially using them as foils to further clarify for himself the personalist doctrine of God. He concluded for the doctrine of God as personal, creator, omnipotent, omnibenevolent, and omniscient as advocated by DeWolf, and consistent with the black religious tradition.

For King, as for Heschel, the personal God of the Hebrew prophets is central to ethical prophecy. God is the source and authority of ethical prophecy, and also where one gets one's charge to speak God's truth.[28] King himself proclaimed on many occasions, "At the center of the Christian faith is the affirmation that there is a God in the universe who is the essence and ground of all reality. A Being of infinite love and boundless power, God is the creator, sustainer, and conserver of values."[29] Here King was right in step with Brightman, who staunchly and persuasively argued that God is *axiogenesis* (the Source of values) and *axiosoteria* (the Conserver and Continuer of values).[30] This God is at the center of the moral universe. One who believes this must see tragedy of all kinds for what it is but also that in tragedy there may be potential for meaning in the world. In addition, one must see the cross of Good Friday but also the promise of Easter, a reminder that Good Friday is not God's last word; see the murderous behavior of an Adolph Hitler but the resistance to that behavior by an Abraham Joshua Heschel as well; and see that evil and wrongdoing are not all there is in a universe founded on morality. This is precisely the stance of ethical prophecy. The last word in a moral universe must be one of hope.

King was frequently thinking, speaking, and writing about the importance and centrality of a personal God in his own life and that of the church. This was the God his maternal grandmother, parents, and Southern black preachers taught him about while growing up in the black church. In seminary and during his doctoral studies he learned about the metaphysics behind this God. But during the dangerous civil rights movement he found that he needed something more than a philosophical understanding of a personal God. Indeed, looking back and reflecting on what it means to have faith in a personal God when one is living under the constant threat of death, he said,

> More than ever before I am convinced of the reality of a personal God. True, I have always believed in the personality of

---

28. King, "Be Not Conformed to This World," 3.

29. King, *Strength to Love*, 94.

30. Brightman, *Philosophy of Religion*, 203, 209. Brightman was here influenced by the Danish philosopher Harald Höffding, *Philosophy of Religion*, 7–13.

God. But in the past the idea of a personal God was little more than a metaphysical category that I found theologically and philosophically satisfying. Now it is a living reality that has been validated in the experiences of everyday life. God has been profoundly real to me in recent years. In the midst of outer dangers I have felt an inner calm. In the midst of lonely days and dreary nights I have heard an inner voice saying, "Lo, I will be with you." When the chains of fear and the manacles of frustration have all but stymied my efforts, I have felt the power of God transforming the fatigue of despair into the buoyancy of hope.[31]

The God who sustained King during the difficult and dangerous struggle for human and civil rights was not the god of the philosophers—and some theologians—but the God of the Hebrew prophets, his parents, maternal grandmother, and other black ancestors. Like most black Christians who have nothing to depend on but self and God, he knew that a more personal characterization of God was needed. This led King to portray God in more down-to-earth terms that he and his people could relate to. For example, in his sermon "The Three Dimensions of a Complete Life," he told the congregation, "One day you ought to rise up and say, 'I know him because he's a lily of the valley.' He's a bright and morning star. He's a rose of Sharon. He's a battle-ax in the time of Babylon. And then somewhere you ought to just reach out and say, 'He's my everything. He's my mother and my father. He's my sister and my brother. He's a friend to the friendless.' This is the God of the universe."[32] This is the God of Martin Luther King Jr. and of the Hebrew prophets, who is always a relentless and compassionate help in times of trouble. This is the personal God who called King to civil rights ministry and to whom King vowed to be faithful to the end of his days. King was not at all troubled by the fact that different people throughout the world call the One God of the universe by different names, including Allah, Elohim, Jehovah, Brahma, the Unmoved Mover, and the Architectonic Good.[33]

Call to Ministry

There is no single right way for one to receive a call from God. Some have described their call as a dramatic, even miraculous event, similar to that experienced by Saul of Tarsus and many years later by Protestant reformer

---

31. King, *Strength to Love*, 141.

32. Carson and Holloran, *Knock at Midnight*, 139; see also 163.

33. Carson et al., *Papers*, 5:157. King included these names for God in the closing prayer of his Palm Sunday sermon on Mohandas K. Gandhi, delivered at Dexter Avenue Baptist Church, March 22, 1959.

Martin Luther. However, the call experience of most people is not linked to a dramatic event but is experienced as a gradual process. This was King's experience. He reflected on this by saying, "My call to the ministry was not a miraculous or supernatural something. On the contrary it was an inner urge calling me to serve humanity."[34] It was an "undying urge to serve God and humanity," and the more he tried to avoid it the more frustrated he became.[35] King also said that his call was "neither dramatic nor spectacular. It came neither by some miraculous vision nor by some blinding light experience on the road of life."[36] His call did not happen all of a sudden. He reflected that his first feeling of being called was experienced in the summer of 1944 after graduating from high school, as "an inescapable urge to serve society."[37]

Confident that he had been called by God to preach the gospel, King, in his first sermon as their pastor, told the members of the Dexter Avenue Baptist Church,

> I come with a feeling that I have been called to preach and to lead God's people. I have felt like Jeremiah, "The word of God is in my heart like burning fire shut up in my bones." I have felt with Amos that when God speaks who can but prophesy? I have felt with Jesus that the spirit of the Lord is upon me, because he hath anointed me to preach the gospel to the poor, to heal the brokenhearted, to preach deliverance to the captives and to set at liberty those that are bruised.[38]

In King's mind nothing greater could happen to a person than to be called, indeed to be favored by God to be a spokesperson and witness for God and to be the voice of the voiceless. For King the one called must possess courage and character, especially in the face of fear and danger. Furthermore, we will see in the discussion on speaking the truth that he did not shy away from criticizing his fellow clergy when they fell into apathy and silence and when they behaved contrary to the ethics of maladjustment.[39]

34. Carson et al., *Papers*, 1:363.
35. King, "Statement on His Call to Ministry," 1.
36. King, "Statement on His Call to Ministry," 1.
37. Carson et al., *Papers*, 1:144.
38. King, *Autobiography*, 46.
39. Interestingly enough, both King and Heschel used the language of "maladjustment." Heschel used the term in *The Prophets* (408) and in other of his writings. King used the term in 1963, in his sermon "Transformed Nonconformist" (*Papers*, 6:475), and also in a 1957 address, "The Christian Way of Life in Human Relations" (*Papers*, 6:327). According to Clayborne Carson and his coeditors, King was influenced by Harry Emerson Fosdick's use of the term "maladjustment." Fosdick "wrote of a prisoner

The call to ministry was significant for King because he regarded ministry as the greatest vocation in the world. Despite the numerous accolades he received for his leadership in the civil rights movement, King was proudest to proclaim, "But before I was a civil rights leader, I was a preacher of the gospel. This was my first calling and it still remains my greatest commitment. You know, actually all that I do in civil rights I do because I consider it a part of my ministry. I have no other ambitions in life but to achieve excellence in the Christian ministry. I don't plan to run for any political office. I don't plan to do anything but remain a preacher."[40] Ministry was King's vocation, and he was honored that the God of the Hebrew prophets and Jesus called him to it. Accordingly, there was no greater vocation, and when Benjamin Spock, William Pepper, Norman Thomas, and others urged him to run for president in 1968, he declined, saying that he had no desire to be a politician but preferred instead to remain faithful to the call to ministry.[41] That was where he believed he could do the most good for his people and other oppressed people, including Mexican Americans and poor whites in Appalachia.[42]

King also maintained that there needed to be clarity around the issue of who anoints the minister to carry out her ministerial responsibilities. Speaking of his own experience as co-pastor with his father and brother at Ebenezer, and reacting to a ministerial colleague who came to him for advice on how to respond to being criticized for being involved in the civil rights movement, King said,

> For the guidelines made it very clear that God anointed. No member of Ebenezer Baptist Church called me to the ministry. You called me to Ebenezer, and you may turn me out of here, but you can't turn me out of the ministry, because I got my guidelines and my anointment from God Almighty.... The word of

---

of conscience who refused to be 'well-adjusted to a state of society that denied such elemental rights as religious liberty.'" Fosdick, *On Being a Real Person*, 205, quoted in *Papers*, 6:327n18. Elsewhere Fosdick wrote, "The deepest obligation of a Christian . . . is to be maladjusted to the status quo." Fosdick, *Hope of the World*, 112, quoted in *Papers*, 6:327n18.

40. "Why Jesus Called a Man a Fool," in Carson and Holloran, *Knock at Midnight*, 146.

41. See Garrow, *Bearing the Cross*, 557, 558, 562.

42. Garrow, *Bearing the Cross*, 559. It is really quite amazing, although not at all surprising, that King frequently conveyed his concern not merely for the poor in general or for blacks and Hispanics who were poor, but also for poor whites in Appalachia and other parts of the country. King did not leave the white poor behind. See King, *Why We Can't Wait*, 151–52; "Playboy Interview," in Washington, *Testament of Hope*, 367–68; *Where Do We Go from Here*, 132.

God is upon me like *fire* shut up in my bones, and when God's word gets upon me, I've got to say it, I've got to tell it all over everywhere. And God has called me to deliver those that are in captivity.[43]

Ebenezer Baptist Church called him to that particular local church, but God alone anointed and called him to ministry. King saw this as a significant distinction. Because God called and commissioned him he had only to answer to God. To King, when a person is called to prophetic ministry she basically takes an oath, makes a firm vow, to be faithful to the call and more importantly to the One who calls her. The call is for a lifetime. When he and Mrs. King were honored by the Dexter Avenue Baptist congregation on January 31, 1960, on his final day as Dexter's pastor, King said that he was called to serve the movement for social justice and that he would be faithful to that call: "I do not intend to desert that call to that movement," he said. "I intend to stay with it until victory is won."[44] He understood himself to be a champion of voiceless and unjustly treated people who, like all human beings, are incalculably precious and sacred to God.

Sacredness of Persons

As a Christian personalist, Martin Luther King Jr. had much to say about the dignity and sacredness of persons and seemed to address this topic as often as he reflected on God as supremely personal and loving. Believing human beings to be God's beloved by virtue of the image of God in them and their relatedness to God and each other, King knew that they possess intrinsic worth and freedom to choose. He was convinced that "the highest expression of the image of God in man is freedom. Man is man because he's free."[45] Moreover, the freedom of human beings is inextricably tied to their sacredness. They are free because sacred and sacred because they are fundamentally free.

King reasoned that if sacredness and dignity are bestowed by God they must be indestructible and cannot be either given or taken away. "The basic thing about a man," he said, "is his dignity and his worth to the Almighty God."[46] Human dignity can be attacked in all sorts of ways; it can be undermined or suppressed, but—and this is critical—it cannot be denied or

---

43. "Guidelines for a Constructive Church," in Carson and Holloran, *Knock at Midnight*, 110-11.
44. Carson et al., *Papers*, 5:354-55.
45. King, "Who Are We?," 7.
46. Carson et al., *Papers*, 6:162.

taken away, since it is constitutive of what it means to be a human being. No matter how badly and inhumanely a person is treated she retains her essential dignity because its source is the God of the prophets, and what God gives no mortal can take away. King asserted that three hundred years of history has proven that no social evil done to blacks has succeeded in destroying their dignity.[47]

Looking to the Bible King saw that the parable of the Lost Sheep "teaches the preciousness of the individual to God" and that "the Christian gospel is committed, once and for all, to the worth of the individual. By his cross, Christ has bound all men into an inextricably [sic] band of brotherhood, and stamped on all men the indelible imprint of preciousness."[48] So the idea of the sacredness of persons was not just a philosophical concept for King but one supported by the Bible and his understanding of the Jewish and Christian faiths. During his student days in seminary King was much influenced by the 72nd Psalm, where the psalmist points to the preciousness of the blood of the poor and the oppressed to God (v. 14). It is therefore not surprising that King liked to say "that God loves all of His children, and that all men are made in His image, and that figuratively speaking, every man from a bass black to a treble white is significant on God's keyboard."[49] This meant that there was "no graded scale of essential worth. . . . Every man must be respected because God loves him. The worth of an individual does not lie in the measure of his intellect, his racial origin, or his social position. Human worth lies in relatedness to God. An individual has value because he has value to God."[50] Like Heschel and Benjamin E. Mays, King was certain that *every* person is sacred before God, or no person is.

In addition, King stressed the interrelatedness or social nature of persons and saw this emphasis not only in personalism but also in the Bible, not least in the prophets. He declared that "all humanity is so interwoven in a single process"[51] that what affects one must affect all—another way of saying that human beings "are caught in an inescapable network of mutuality."[52] To be a human being is to be in relationship with other human beings and with God. Whether we like it or not, whether we wish to admit it, this is our fundamental nature.

---

47. King, "True Dignity," n.d., 9.

48. Carson et al., *Papers*, 6:410.

49. "Address at the Freedom Rally in Cobo Hall," in Carson and Shepard, *Call to Conscience*, 64.

50. King, "Challenge to the Churches," 158.

51. Carson et al., *Papers*, 6:112.

52. Carson et al., *Papers*, 6:339, 417.

King also had much to say about the image of God in human beings. Like Heschel, he urged that we somehow find ways to acknowledge that even white supremacists and the Adolph Hitlers have within them the image of God. Heschel was certain that the criminal as well as the saint possesses the image of God.[53] In any event, King asserted that the whole person, including the body, is sacred.[54] He believed that this was the stance of the prophets as well. God is infinitely concerned about the well-being of the whole person, who is sacred before God, as evidenced by the divine command to do justice. The image of God in human beings means that every person has something in her that was divinely imbued, therefore making it possible to fellowship with God. In this sense, every person carries God within. Accordingly, it is the image of God in persons that is the source of their dignity and capacity for fellowship with each other and with God. Because every person is precious it should not be surprising that like Malcolm X, King insisted that blacks' freedom must necessarily begin with themselves, "by freeing our own psyche, our own souls."[55] Blacks alone can, indeed must, initiate the process to gain freedom by first freeing their own minds. This will necessitate reaching "down into the inner depths of our being and sign with a pen in ink of assertive manhood our own Emancipation Proclamation."[56]

Martin Luther King took seriously the Hebrew prophets' insistence that God demanded that justice be done in ways that respect the importance and sacredness of human beings. He expressed this idea while reflecting on Jewish and Christian teachings. "Deeply rooted in our religious heritage is the conviction that every man is an heir to a legacy of dignity and worth. Our Judeo-Christian tradition refers to this inherent dignity of man in the Biblical term 'the image of God.' 'The image of God' is universally shared in equal portions by all men."[57] Anyone who thinks of human beings in this way cannot disagree with Micah's emphatic reminder that God demands that we do justice, love mercy, and walk humbly with God. Each of our candidates for the ethical prophet hall of fame stands firmly in this tradition.

---

53. Heschel, "Religious Basis of Equality," 66.
54. King, *Strength to Love*, 89.
55. King, "Transforming a Neighborhood," 12.
56. King, "Transforming a Neighborhood," 12.
57. King, *Where Do We Go from Here*, 97.

Call for Justice

King acknowledged the centrality of justice for the Hebrew prophets. The recipient of the Judaism and World Peace Award given by the Synagogue Council of America in 1965, King expressed gratitude for the support of various Jewish groups and individuals in the civil rights movement, and told Rabbi Seymour Cohen, "I must say that *of all the ethnic groups that have supported our struggle, I find none more consistent and unswerving in that support than the Jewish community.* I am sure that a large part of this grows out of the deep sense of justice that stands at the center of the prophetic tradition of Judaism."[58] Heschel and other Jewish rabbis had much appreciation for King's insistence on lifting up the significance of the prophets' emphasis on the obligation and responsibility to do justice.

Martin Luther King was frequently accused of being an extremist. However, he quickly saw the positive value in this when he remembered that the Hebrew prophets were extremists for justice and righteousness and that Jesus was an extremist for love, truth, and goodness. There was nothing wrong with being an extremist as such. The type of extremist was what mattered.[59] This stance led King to posit that Hebrew prophecy is based on the ethics of maladjustment. He in fact called for the creation of an organization, to be called The International Association for the Advancement of Creative Maladjustment, that would be comprised of people with the courage to express their maladjustment to devastating social evils such as injustice, racism, anti-Semitism, militarism, and economic exploitation. Such men and women would be as disagreeable and maladjusted as the Hebrew prophets in the face of dehumanization. King also included among the maladjusted the likes of Jesus and Abraham Lincoln, who exhibited profound courage in their day by standing alone and pressing forward when faced with difficult social issues.[60]

Looking back on the Montgomery bus boycott, King expressed his strong conviction that the universe is on the side of justice. In this regard, he said that "there is something unfolding in the universe whether one speaks of it as an unconscious process, . . . as some unmoved mover, or . . . as a personal God. There is something in the universe that unfolds for justice and so in Montgomery we felt somehow that as we struggled we had cosmic companionship."[61] King did not simply *believe* with Theodore Parker and John Haynes Holmes (whom he never named) that in the deepest sense,

---

58. King to Rabbi Seymour J. Cohen, December 28, 1965, 1 (my italics).
59. King, *Autobiography*, 198.
60. King, "Address before a Dinner," 8.
61. "The Power of Nonviolence," in Washington, *Testament of Hope*, 13–14.

"the arc of the moral universe is long, but it bends toward justice,"[62] as if to imply that such belief alone guarantees the actualization of justice. Instead, he rightly believed just as firmly that because God has created human beings as fundamentally free and therefore as moral agents who can choose, persistent human effort and action are needed to insure that justice will actually materialize in such a universe—that the arc of the universe will, through human endeavor, be bent toward justice. In the absence of justice and righteousness it is incumbent upon all, especially those called by God, to be the voice of the voiceless and to do all they can to establish justice.

Speaking Truth to the People and to Power

Just as Heschel did not hesitate to criticize the Jewish community, Martin Luther King Jr. uttered sharp criticisms against his ministerial colleagues and the church[63] for their apathy and tendency to support and defend the status quo.

> So often the contemporary Church is a weak, ineffectual voice with an uncertain sound. So often it is an arch-defender of the status quo. Far from being disturbed by the presence of the Church, the power structure of the average community is consoled by the Church's silent—and often even vocal—sanction of things as they are.
>
> But the judgment of God is upon the Church as never before. If today's Church does not recapture the sacrificial spirit of the early Church, it will lose its authenticity, forfeit the loyalty of millions, and be dismissed as an irrelevant social club with no meaning for the twentieth century. Every day I meet young people whose disappointment with the Church has turned into outright disgust.[64]

Seldom did one hear such internal criticisms within the ranks of ministry itself (or any profession!), in King's day or since. But King was not averse to being self-critical. He was much influenced by what he described as Gandhi's "amazing capacity for internal criticism."[65] Gandhi criticized the British, his own people, *and* himself. "And whenever he made a mistake,"

---

62. Burrow, *God and Human Dignity*, 190.

63. There is no more powerful and instructive treatment of King's view of the church and his courage to criticize it, as well as his ministerial colleagues, than Baldwin, *The Voice of Conscience*.

64. King, *Autobiography*, 201.

65. Clayborn et al., *Papers*, 5:152.

King said, "he confessed it publicly."[66] So King was not only critical of the church and members of the clergy when they were silent in the face of social evils, or when they lacked courage to be transformed nonconformists. He was also strongly inclined to self-criticism. Not only could he see others' limitations, but he saw his own as well.

Some of King's strongest and most courageous criticisms were directed at his ministerial colleagues. We do not often hear politicians, clergy, police officers, professors, and other professionals criticize themselves and their colleagues for failing to stand courageously against moral wrongdoing. In the "Palm Sunday Sermon on Mohandas K. Gandhi," preached at Dexter Avenue Baptist Church on March 22, 1959, King revealed how prophetic critique should work, and that none should be spared when those who are called shirk their moral responsibility.[67] In an even sharper criticism of his ministerial colleagues for their tendency to be conformists, he declared,

> We preachers have also been tempted by the enticing cult of conformity. Seduced by the success symbols of the world, we have measured our achievements by the size of our parsonage. We have become showmen to please the whims and caprices of the people. We preach comforting sermons and avoid saying anything from our pulpits which might disturb the respectable views of the comfortable members of our congregations. Have we ministers of Jesus Christ sacrificed truth on the altar of self-interest and, like Pilate, yielded our convictions to the demands of the crowd?[68]

King criticized his colleagues in ministry for their silence and complicity regarding the war in Vietnam and other social injustices. He told them that "we preachers can't be totally excused. We too often conform"—and judge ministerial success on the basis of material possessions.[69] It was inexcusable that ministers reduced the gospel to "showmanship," entertainment, and possession of things. The minister of Jesus "has a mandate to stand up courageously for righteousness, to proclaim the eternal verities of the gospel, and to lead men from the darkness of falsehood and fear to the light of truth and love."[70] It is no wonder that King was critical of ministers who "preach nice little comforting, soothing sermons because some deacon out there or deaconess or head of some auxiliary or other members . . . may be

---

66. Clayborn et al., *Papers*, 5:153.
67. Clayborn et al., *Papers*, 5:152–53.
68. "Transformed Nonconformist," in King, *Strength to Love*, 12.
69. King, "Be Not Conformed to This World," 9.
70. King, *Stride Toward Freedom*, 208.

hurt in the process."⁷¹ It is both alarming and embarrassing that even today one can name only a few ministers who are openly and honestly self-critical and critical of their cowardly colleagues and religious institutions when they behave contrary to what God requires of them—when they remain silent amid clergy-involved child molestations; when they remain silent and thus complicit in unjust, virtually unprovoked and suspicious police shootings of black boys and men; when they bow down to the National Rifle Association, refusing even to take a public stand for common-sense gun control; when they choose to remain silent when the Trump administration and obsequious Republican legislators tell lies so frequently that they have successfully duped most members of the Republican base, but especially those who are white, poor, uneducated, and racially and culturally myopic. How is it possible that in such times as these the trumpet of the conscience of religious people and their institutions makes an uncertain sound or no sound at all? King was adamant that the people and the nation must hear the truth and that "if we are going to survive as a nation, somebody has got to have vision, somebody must be willing to stand up and be criticized and called every bad name, out of love for this country."⁷² In the absence of this stance the prophets of old boldly announced God's displeasure and spoke unequivocal words of judgment.

Divine Judgment

Couched in King's criticisms of society and the church are powerful reminders of God's impending judgment when there is persistent failure to see others as God sees us all and to treat human beings lovingly and justly. Unlike many of his ministerial colleagues King was not hesitant to link potential divine judgment to the church's failure to address social evils. In this regard he asserted, "But the church as a whole has been all too negligent on the question of civil rights. It has too often blessed a status quo that needed to be blasted and reassured a social order that needed to be reformed. So the church must acknowledge its guilt, its weak and vacillating witness, its all too frequent failure to obey the call to servanthood. Today the judgment of God is upon the church for its failure to be true to its mission."⁷³ King wanted the church and societal institutions to know that there were consequences for their behavior—that they could not disregard the divine mandate to do justice with impunity. Because human beings are inestimably

71. King, "Be Not Conformed to This World," 9.
72. King, "Be Not Conformed to This World," 8.
73. King, *Where Do We Go from Here*, 96.

loved and valued by a God who cares unceasingly about their well-being and insists that justice should be done, those institutions dare not engage in practices that demean and crush persons to the earth.

King was certain that a basic responsibility of the church to society is prophetic critique or judgment. He told his Dexter Avenue congregation, "The church must forever stand in judgement upon every political, social and economic system condemning evil wherever they exist."[74] In "The Drum Major Instinct," preached at Ebenezer on February 4, 1968, precisely two months before he was assassinated, King spoke powerfully about God's impending judgment on any nation—including the U.S.—that persists in arrogant, selfish behavior on a massive scale, saying, "But God has a way of even putting nations in their place. The God that I worship has a way of saying, 'Don't play with me.' He has a way of saying, as the God of the Old Testament used to say to the Hebrews, 'Don't play with me, Israel. Don't play with me, Babylon. Be still and know that I'm God. And if you don't stop your reckless course, I'll rise up and break the backbone of your power.'"[75] King warned the nation of God's impending judgment if it continued on its wayward path. Like other ethical prophets he was always careful to point out that judgment could be avoided *if* nations ceased to do evil. King was also very much aware that payment would be required of individuals like him who lived out the call to speak truth to the people and to power. It was not the case that he had a death wish, as some have claimed. He simply knew that historically when one speaks truth to power and fearlessly and persistently organizes to fight against injustice, a high price, including death, is the likely outcome. And further, it is not the case that God willed King's death. Instead, as Benjamin Mays rightly argued, it was simply the inevitable outcome of King's persistence in telling the nation and the world about his dream.[76] It was part of the price that one invariably pays when insisting on speaking truth to power, and even more so when one fights to actualize the rights and freedom of the poor and oppressed.

Cost of Prophecy

In 1958 Martin Luther King Jr. was stabbed by a demented woman named Izola Curry as he autographed his first book at Blumstein's department store in Harlem. He later reflected on that incident and on the pattern of violence against him and his family and the cost to be borne by them. He was not

---

74. Carson et al., *Papers*, 6:199.

75. "The Drum Major Instinct," in Carson and Holloran, *Knock at Midnight*, 181.

76. Raines, *My Soul Is Rested*, 460.

surprised by the attacks, he said, because he had "counted the cost early in the struggle."[77] So of course, King did not retaliate against Curry or others who later physically attacked him. The work that he and others had to do "had to be done regardless of the cost."[78] The ethical prophet is always a target when she faithfully does her work. By his own admission, King understood this early. He also understood that it was incumbent on him not to allow such knowledge to force him into apathy and silence. He was still responsible for doing what his call required of him.

Like other hall of famers, and to his credit, King did not devote much time and energy to worrying about his personal safety. When asked about it he replied, "Naturally, I'm concerned about my personal safety and it is true that every day I live under the threat of death. I get numerous letters of a threatening nature and numerous threatening calls, but I think ultimately one has to be philosophical about this."[79] He did not think he could function if he allowed threats to get under his skin. None of this is to say that King did not experience fear at times. As a human being, he most certainly did. What was most important was that he mustered the courage to persevere regardless of his fear. This is what ethical prophets do; as transformed nonconformists who adhere to the ethics of maladjustment, their faith is in the God who calls them and who promises to provide them with what they will need to carry out their call.

King told white people who dared to speak truth to power, "Honesty impels me to admit that such a stand will require willingness to suffer and sacrifice. So don't despair if you are condemned and persecuted for righteousness' sake. Whenever you take a stand for truth and justice, you are liable to scorn."[80] In another place King said that he wanted transformed nonconformists to know that they would likely have to "stand amid the chilly winds of adversity" and "face crowded and agonizing jail cells," not knowing whether they will see their families again because they were "living each day under the threat of death." He went on to say that "sometimes your home will get bombed, sometimes you may be stabbed, sometimes people will misunderstand you. If you're going to be a transformed nonconformist, people are going to lie on you, spread false rumors on you, write bad and ugly editorials about you."[81] All of these things happened to King,

77. King, *Autobiography*, 119.
78. King, *Autobiography*, 120.
79. King, "Transcript of Channel 2, KNXT-TV," 9.
80. "Paul's Letter to American Christians," in Carson and Holloran, *Knock at Midnight*, 33.
81. King, "Be Not Conformed to This World," 12.

who was, nevertheless, encouraged by the fact that there were a few white people who were genuinely committed to paying the price for being transformed nonconformists.

In July 1964, a month after Freedom Summer began, King traveled to Mississippi. His visit came after the disappearance of three young civil rights workers, one black (James Chaney) and two Jewish (Michael Schwerner and Andrew Goodman); later, their remains were discovered in an earthen dam—they had been murdered by local white supremacists. Reflecting on his trip, King told interviewer Alex Haley, "And not long ago, when I was about to visit in Mississippi, I received some very urgent calls from Negro leaders in Mobile [Alabama], who had been told by a very reliable source that a sort of guerrilla group led by a retired major in the area of Lucyville, Mississippi, was plotting to take my life during the visit. I was strongly urged to cancel the trip, but when I thought about it, I decided that I had no alternative but to go on into Mississippi."[82] When asked why, King replied, "Because I have a job to do. If I were constantly worried about death, I couldn't function.... I must face the fact, as all others in positions of leadership must do, that America today is an extremely sick nation, and that something could well happen to me at any time."[83] Interestingly enough, during his first term in seminary in 1948, King wrote a paper on the prophet Jeremiah in which he concluded that societies always destroy the Jeremiah type of prophet.[84] Consequently, early on King had a sense of the risks and cost involved in ethical prophecy.

King came to see threats as part of the cost of prophecy. But as sure as he understood this he was determined to remain hopeful. We have seen throughout that the Hebrew prophets began their prophecy with words of impending judgment but ended with words of hope. This was consistent with their belief—shared by King—that the universe is founded on morality and that human beings are of utmost concern and importance to God. King was convinced that love is the highest ideal and is the heartbeat of the universe.[85] If this is the case, it must also be true that God's final words must

---

82. King, "*Playboy* Interview," in Washington, *Testament of Hope*, 355. Two years after the disappearance and murders of Chaney, Schwerner, and Goodwin, King went to Philadelphia, Mississippi, where the three were initially held in jail. Mississippi was still a most dangerous place for civil rights workers. King told a reporter that his experience on that particular afternoon was "one of the most frightening of his life. 'This is a terrible town, the worst I've seen. There is a complete reign of terror here.'" Quoted in Cagin and Dray, *We Are Not Afraid*, 382.

83. King, "*Playboy* Interview," in Washington, *Testament of Hope*, 355–56.

84. Carson et al., *Papers*, 1:195.

85. Carson et al., *Papers*, 6:303, 345; 6:290, 292.

be words of hope, not judgment and damnation. Even if circumstances are such that judgment in fact occurs, hope must lie beyond it. Without question, this was the view of Martin Luther King Jr.

Hope and the Beloved Community

Because of his personalism and his understanding and acceptance of Jewish and Christian principles, King stood firm in his conviction that human beings were created such that they can be better than they are, and therefore society and the world can be better because human beings can make it so. The inherent freedom of human beings means that they can always choose among their better angels to apply toward radically transforming the world so that their behavior is more in line with what God requires. King knew that when we appeal to our better selves, hope for a better world remains. "When you hope," he proclaimed, "you are really saying that you have faith in something. When you hope, you are really saying that you have faith in the ultimate meaning of life in history. When you hope, you are really saying that you have faith in the fact that the contradictions of life are not ultimate or permanent. This is what you are saying when you hope. You are saying that you have faith in the fact that all reality hinges on moral foundations."[86] Indeed, this may be interpreted to mean that one may have hope precisely because of one's strong belief that the universe is grounded in morality. Such a belief must mean that no matter how bad things are in the world, human beings have reason to believe that their mutual cooperation with each other and with God can lead to the emergence of the "new world," or what King referred to as the new Jerusalem, the new New York, the new Atlanta, the new Birmingham, the new Memphis,[87] or the beloved community. This, according to King, is a community in which the dignity of every person will be acknowledged and respected. Every person will be treated like the sacred one she is, just because she is a person. The beloved community is one in which the basic needs of every person will be met before others may have extras. Furthermore, King characterized this community by saying that it is a world "in which men will live together as brothers; as [sic] world in which men will beat their swords into ploughshares and their spears into pruning hooks; a world in which men will no longer take necessities from the masses to give luxuries to the classes; a world in which all men will respect the dignity and worth of all human personality."[88] This, King concluded, is

---

86. King, "Meaning of Hope," 15.
87. Carson and Shepard, *Call to Conscience*, 214.
88. "Facing the Challenge of a New Age," in Washington, *Testament of Hope*, 144.

what "ultimate community"[89] looks like and is what God requires. Belief in the fundamental morality of the universe means that the establishment of such a community is a real possibility, which is why the prophetic hope, or what Walter Brueggemann calls "hope-telling," *must* remain alive. Hope liberates us from the abyss and from despair.[90] The contradictions of life are not God's last words, and therefore human beings must never give up.[91] This was King's stance and that of his black ancestors and the prophets. From these he learned about the need to develop courage in order to press onward in the face of uncertainty and danger.

Meaning and Significance of Courage

The candidates for the ethical prophet hall of fame are all "profiles in courage" and possess the best qualities of ethical leadership: character, courage, honesty, and devotion and loyalty to the highest ideals.[92] In addition, even the most cursory reading of the Hebrew prophets reveals that these qualities are also reflected in them. Since Martin Luther King Jr. spoke frequently about moral courage, and because it is a virtue found in all ethical prophets, including our hall of fame candidates, it will be instructive to discuss its meaning and importance.

King placed courage among the "supreme virtues,"[93] for without courage it is doubtful that one can consistently live by the other virtues. Maya Angelou made this important point in interviews with Judith Rich and Claudia Tate in 1977 and 1983, respectively, when she told them that without courage one "can't say against a murderous society, I oppose your murdering."[94] No group and its leader illustrate the truth of this point today better than Republican politicians and Donald Trump. No matter how serious the wrongdoing of Trump and other White House officials, Republicans in Congress generally remain silent, or kowtow to them.

For one who possesses it, courage emerges when, in the face of difficult and life-threatening situations, one has the strength of mind to hold in abeyance the fear associated with these and to do what one believes to be best regardless of—and perhaps even without thinking about—the possible consequences. Courage does not necessarily eradicate fear, nor is that its

89. King, *Stride Toward Freedom*, 214.
90. Brueggemann, *Disruptive Grace*, 145–53.
91. King, "Meaning of Hope," 12.
92. See Burrow, "King and Ethical Leadership," 11–28.
93. "Antidotes for Fear," in King, *Strength to Love*, 110–11.
94. Elliot, *Conversations with Maya Angelou*, 85, 156.

purpose. Instead, King characterized courage as "an inner resolution to go forward in spite of obstacles and frightening situations. . . . Courage breeds creative self-affirmation. . . . Courage faces fear and thereby masters it."[95] Similarly, Archbishop Desmond Tutu observes that courage means "acting as you know you must even though you are undeniably afraid."[96] Therefore, a person can be afraid and still do what is morally right if she has chosen to make courage a virtue.

My late teacher and mentor at Boston University, Peter A. Bertocci, taught that from an ethical standpoint, "Only those traits are virtues (or vices) that are deemed to be the product of choice. Why? An action is moral or immoral . . . to the extent that it is the product of choice or will-agency."[97] One might well possess the trait of courage, but it becomes a virtue only when one wills or chooses it. When courage is made a virtue it means that one can summon it when confronted with the most horrific circumstances, thus enabling one to stand firm on principle and to do what one believes to be right.

Bertocci defined courage as "the willingness to face insecurity and to make the sacrifices needed to achieve the goal deemed worthwhile but dangerous."[98] Courage means that one has the capacity *and* the will to stare down one's fear(s) and to press onward toward the goal. The fear might remain, but one stands resolute in its presence and forges ahead anyway. This is what Rabbi Marshall T. Meyer meant when he reflected on the tragedy of so many who were disappeared in Argentina in the 1970s. Fear had been planted in the people in the hope that they would be so overwhelmed and terrified by it that they would do nothing to liberate themselves. But there were those who faced down the fear and resisted it. Meyer put it this way: "What differentiates the activist from the coward is not the presence or absence of fear, but rather that the activist forces him or herself to action in spite of fear, while the coward allows fear to paralyze him or herself."[99]

As part of the human condition, fear is one of our many emotions. One can possess courage and experience fear at the same time. This was the case with Abraham Joshua Heschel, Angelina Grimké, Ida B. Wells-Barnett, and James Baldwin. In addition, Malcolm X experienced fear when it became clear to him that his name was on an assassin's hit list. Martin Luther King Jr. faced down fear and threats of death more times than he could

95. "Antidotes for Fear," in King, *Strength to Love*, 111.
96. Tutu, *God Has a Dream*, 88.
97. Bertocci and Millard, *Personality and the Good*, 363.
98. Bertocci and Millard, *Personality and the Good*, 385.
99. Meyer, *You Are My Witness*, 160.

remember. We will see in the next chapter that Archbishop Óscar Romero also experienced fear caused by almost constant threats of death. Even so, he persisted in his prophetic ministry. Alice Walker also experienced fear, but like other hall of fame candidates she was saved by her courage and commitment to right. What all of these shared in common is that they did not allow fear to deter them from carrying out their call. Because they believed they were called by God, and because they were courageous and believed that God was with them, they worked through the fear. Each of them faced insecurity and fear; each of them made the necessary sacrifices to do what they believed God required. Courage was the inner resolution that made it possible for them to faithfully advance despite their fears. Without question, courage is a fundamental virtue for the ethical prophet, and without it one will not likely speak truth to power—will not consistently stand up for righteousness and the highest ideals.

Conclusion

In seminary and during his doctoral studies Martin Luther King Jr. wrote papers on the prophets. In a course with L. Harold DeWolf at Boston University, Religious Teachings of the Old Testament,[100] King's notes reveal the clear and strong influence of Amos, Jeremiah, and the 72nd Psalm (which depicts God as privileging the needy and the poor over the powerful and the rich, and reveals God as the liberator of the oppressed[101]). The influence of these sources is consistent with King's understanding of ministry from the time he accepted his call. The prophets were influential to him throughout his entire ministry. He frequently rehearsed their legacy and reminded audiences of their importance. In this regard, too, King was very similar to Heschel.

King vowed to be faithful to his call no matter the cost. In "Some Things We Must Do," a presidential address given on December 5, 1957, he spoke passionately about his rationale for believing in the South and the future: "I believe in the future because I believe in God. And I believe that there is a personal power in this universe that works to bring the disconnected aspects of reality into a harmonious whole. I believe that there is a force, a creative force that works at every moment to bring low prodigious hill-tops of evil and to bring down gigantic mountains of injustice."[102]

---

100. The second-generation Boston University personalist Albert C. Knudson wrote *Religious Teaching of the Old Testament* in 1918. DeWolf used the book in his course. King referenced this book in a set of sermon notes (*Papers*, 6:570).

101. Carson et al., *Papers*, 2:165–67.

102. King, "Some Things We Must Do," 3.

The next chapter explores the ethical prophetic witness of Óscar Romero, late archbishop of San Salvador, a reminder that God has ethical prophetic witnesses in every part of the world and among every people, for indeed the whole world and all people belong to God. Romero's is a very interesting and instructive story inasmuch as the people and most of the clergy, especially those affiliated with the prophetic church, initially rejected him as archbishop when he was appointed by the Vatican. The people did not believe Romero to be the one needed in such a tragic situation, in which they were frequently disappeared through systematic acts of terrorism and murder; they saw him as too conservative, critical of the prophetic church, and overwhelmingly supported by the powers, the oligarchs, and the military. And yet, to the surprise of all, including Romero, not long after his appointment, God called him to be prophet to the people and to the powers in El Salvador.

7

Óscar Romero as Ethical Prophet

According to ethical prophecy God is thoroughly and unrelentingly involved in the lives and affairs of human beings. God is not indifferent to human beings but rather is concerned about even the smallest things that happen to them. This suggests that to be a Christian or other religious person, one must be concerned about the well-being of persons both because they are human beings and because they belong to and are loved by God. The Jew or the Christian who knows what it means to be truly Jewish or truly Christian is utterly concerned about the welfare of other human beings. Heschel reminds us that "a person cannot be religious *and* indifferent to other human beings' plight and suffering."[1] One cannot honestly claim to love and to revere the God of the prophets while treating God's children like nonpersons. To be religious is to be determined to do all one can to acknowledge, defend, and otherwise uphold the dignity and preciousness of human beings.

The prophet's primary concern and the theme of his speeches is human conduct, both interpersonal and collective. He is concerned less with issues of private or personal morality, such as drinking, than with issues of public or social morality, such as war and economic injustice. He is concerned about righteousness and nothing but righteousness. This was the fundamental business of the Hebrew prophets.[2] They strove to see the world as God sees it and to convey that perspective to the people and the

---

1. Heschel, "Speech at the Ceremonies," 14.
2. Rauschenbusch, *Christianity and the Social Crisis*, 3.

world. Heschel reminds us that "the prophet does not see the world from the point of view of a political theory; he is a person who sees the world from the point of view of God; he sees the world through the eyes of God."[3] The prophet wants us to see what God sees, to know that what God sees is what we can be and do if we will proceed with courage and do it.

So thoroughly does God love and so involved is God in the affairs of human beings that it is never a matter solely of God *or* human beings to the prophet, but of God *and* human beings simultaneously. The prophet's eye is always on the contemporary scene, even as his ear is always turned toward God. He "is a person struck by the glory and presence of God, overpowered by the hand of God."[4] We saw in chapter 1 that this led Heschel to suggest that the prophet's "true greatness is his ability to hold God and man in a single thought."[5] He cannot think about God without thinking simultaneously about human beings. Neither can the prophet think about human beings without also thinking about God. To be a Christian must mean something much more substantial than merely joining and showing up at a church building on Sunday morning. One cannot, on this view, preach or talk about God and not at the same time exhibit outrage about the tragedy that is intra-community violence and murder among young Afrikan American males. What a profound statement uttered by Heschel—that the greatness of the ethical prophet is his ability to hold God and human beings in a single thought. Very few have done this better than Óscar Romero.

Óscar Arnulfo Romero

Óscar Arnulfo Romero (1917–80) was canonized by Pope Francis on October 14, 2018. After being appointed archbishop in El Salvador Romero had only three years to do the work of prophetic ministry. After his conversion to the poor his level of faithfulness and commitment to God were exemplary. To the chagrin of the powers he fell in love with the poor and the systematically left-outs and became their most forceful, dependable voice and champion.

Óscar Romero was a theologian in the best sense of the word. He understood what many academics and clergy did not (and do not), namely, that although crushing people and denying their basic humanity and dignity is a sociological, political, and economic problem, it is in the deepest, most fundamental sense a moral and theological problem. For such mistreatment

---

3. Heschel, *Prophets*, 138.
4. Heschel, *Prophets*, 21.
5. Heschel, *Prophets*, 21.

of human beings is nothing short of total disrespect and disregard for the image of God in them, as well as God, since whatever is done to human beings, especially the least of our sisters and brothers, is done also to God. More than anything else, it is the business of the church, the clergy, and theologians to speak God's truth about such misconduct and to speak it unremittingly with passion, courage, love, and an insistence on the need to do justice.

For those who knew him, it was not surprising that Óscar Romero was not an advocate of the prophetic church in Central America when he was initially appointed archbishop of El Salvador on February 22, 1977. Prior to his appointment, many of his priests considered him to be "reactionary" at best.[6] They did not trust him and did not want him as their leader. He had been "a traditional cleric, a conservative theologian, a generous but reserved pastor, a man given to regular solitary times of prayer."[7] Salvadoran priests knew that the Vatican had been in consultation with various groups—especially the wealthy upper class—in the search for a new archbishop. The wealthy class heartily gave its support to Romero's appointment, since they believed him to be "one of theirs."[8]

Looking back, Nidia Díaz reflected on the reaction to the news of Romero's appointment, saying, "I worked with several progressive priests in a campesino [peasant] organization. We were in a meeting when the news arrived about Romero's appointment. Although we hadn't talked about it, we'd all been afraid it would happen. And it did. We saw it as a great triumph for the ruling class, and we prepared to confront it."[9] Even the seminarians who had become radicalized did not feel that they could support their new archbishop. The priests and the seminarians were resentful of Romero's appointment because they were aware of his disdain for the prophetic church.

Prior to being appointed archbishop, Romero had little that was positive to say about the prophetic activities of the church. "At that time," recalled Father Rogelio Ponseele, a Belgian Catholic missionary priest, "he appeared to be not just a conservative but even an evil man."[10] Ponseele said that after the government occupation of the National University in 1972, the bishops, including then-bishop Romero, sided with the government and condemned what they called the subversive behavior of the priests and the people. Ponseele recalled that when Romero was invited to address them he

6. Vigil, *Death and Life in Morazàn*, 22.
7. Dennis, Golden, and Wright, *Oscar Romero*, 12.
8. This was the view of Francisco Estrada. See Vigil, *Oscar Romero*, 81.
9. Vigil, *Oscar Romero*, 83.
10. Vigil, *Death and Life in Morazàn*, 22.

harshly criticized their actions and accused them of being, not Christians, but political. Most of those who were present, including Romero, left the meeting filled with rage. Approximately six years later Romero, now archbishop, returned to that community and on his own initiative apologized for his earlier behavior. He admitted that he had been wrong and the people right, and then asked their forgiveness. For now, suffice to say that by the time Romero was assassinated he had won the respect of most priests who had not wanted him to be appointed archbishop. Father Ponseele was one of these. After Romero's death Ponseele gladly said, "He was a unique occurrence in the history of the church. He is a miracle."[11]

Ironically, after his conversion to the poor, Romero himself was frequently accused of teaching politics and leftist ideas, and therefore he felt compelled to clarify the position of the church. It was not so much that his stance of accompanying the poor was political, though he knew full well that in the world of his day it was not possible to be apolitical. The only question was, *How* would one be political, and on whose side would one stand—on the side of God and the poor, or the powerful and the wealthy? To be faithful to God necessarily means that one must be political in a certain way. Romero came to see that one cannot be authentically Christian and not be unconditionally on the side of the poor and the oppressed, which is as political as it gets. But it is also fundamentally theological inasmuch as the God of the Hebrew prophets requires such a stance. For Romero, like the prophets, God stands unconditionally on the side of the poor, the oppressed, and the left-outs.

Óscar Romero might well have followed the script written by the powers and the ruling class were it not for the murder of his longtime friend, Father Rutilio Grande, less than one month after Romero was appointed archbishop.[12] Two others were murdered along with Father Grande: Mr. Manuel Soloranzo, "an old man who was the priest's faithful companion and who tried to protect him from the bullets by covering him with his own body," and Nelson Rutilio Lemus, a young epileptic boy and occasional bell ringer in the Aguilares church. In a September 7, 1979, entry in his diary (published in 1993 as *A Shepherd's Diary*), Romero referred to Father Grande as "the first to fall in this series of crimes against clergy."[13] At the funeral mass for Father Grande, Romero told the congregation,

> True love is what brings Rutilio to his death taking two farmers
> by the hand. In this way he loves the Church, he dies with them,

---

11. Quoted in Sobrino, "Archbishop Romero: Some Personal Recollections," 36.
12. Vigil, *Oscar Romero*, 100.
13. Romero, *Shepherd's Diary*, 322.

and with them he presents himself for the transcendence to heaven. He loves them, and it is significant that while Fr. Grande walked forward for his people to take the message of the Mass and of salvation, this is where he fell pierced with many holes. The love of the Lord inspires the action of Rutilio Grande. Dear priests, let us take up this precious inheritance.[14]

Jon Sobrino and other Latin American liberation theologians rightly contend that the tragic murders of Father Grande and the two compesinos was the occasion for Romero's radical conversion to the poor and for his becoming a prophet to the Salvadoran government, military, and oligarchy.[15] Carolyn Forché observes that the murder of Rutilio Grande was Romero's "moment of truth, his 'Saul to Damascus' conversion; in the myth, he arises from his mournful vigil transformed."[16]

Romero was converted to the poor and the forgotten of history, having allowed them to change his heart, indeed his entire being. "That was his message—that the poor are a sacrament who can transform our lives if we are willing to open ourselves to them, to accompany them."[17] This transformation also said something about how Romero had come to think about God, a God he now knew to be everywhere present—right in the thick of it, in the muck and mire—with the poor and forgotten. "Though a person of scrupulous self-criticism and asceticism, he discovered a God who was enmeshed in the ordinary, messy, conflictive struggle of the Salvadoran people. For Romero, the people were a source of grace."[18] He came to see the poor as the good news of God. Little did anyone know at the time that in barely three years the poor in El Salvador would come to think so proudly of Romero, as "the bishop of the world."[19] Indeed, Sobrino characterized Romero as a gospel, as good news, from God to the poor.[20]

Like the eighth-century prophets and Jesus, Óscar Romero was an ethical prophet who courageously conveyed God's demand that justice and love should be done to the poor and the oppressed in El Salvador. He was willing to give his life in response to God's call, especially during his final three years. This is a reminder that what God requires in ministry is depth of commitment and sincerity, not mere longevity. By considering Romero's

14. Quoted in García, "Monsignor Oscar A. Romero," 75.
15. Sobrino, *Archbishop Romero*, 1.
16. Forché, "Oscar Romero," 61.
17. Dennis, Golden, and Wright, *Oscar Romero*, 14.
18. Dennis, Golden, and Wright, *Oscar Romero*, 12.
19. Vigil, *Oscar Romero*, 415.
20. Sobrino, "Archbishop Romero: Some Personal Recollections," 42.

brief time in prophetic ministry, we learn much about the true nature and character of the ethical prophet and the role of Christians and the church amid massive, systemic violence against the poor. In addition, we learn a great deal about God's expectation that injustice should be denounced and that justice should be established, sustained, and increased by righteous means. For whenever and wherever we do justice, justice expands throughout the universe.[21]

In addition to the all-important divine call, one can identify nearly a dozen traits of ethical prophecy that characterized Romero's ministry and greatly impacted his work in church and society. We have seen throughout that one of the great insights in the theology of prophecy is the idea of God's profound preoccupation, care and involvement with human beings in the world. Like the prophets of old, Óscar Romero came to see that nothing is so important to God as human beings. Heschel reminds us that God's pathos "in all its forms reveals the extreme pertinence of man to God, His world-directness, attentiveness, and concern. God 'looks at' the world and is affected by what happens in it; man is the object of His care and judgment."[22] The God of the Bible is overwhelmingly concerned about human beings and what happens to them. *This* is the meaning of divine pathos. Indeed, we have seen that even when the prophet announces divine judgment, this too reflects his awareness of God's infinite concern and attentiveness to human beings. It is divine concern and compassion for human beings that is at the root of the prophet's effort to save the people. Human beings are indescribably relevant and important to God. "God's presence in the world is, in essence, His concern for the world. . . . The theme of prophetic understanding is not the mystery of God's essence, but rather the mystery of his relation to man."[23]

In what follows I discuss five elements of Romero's ethical prophecy: prophecy grounded in God, sacredness of persons, call to conversion and concern for the poor, speaking truth to power, and his sense of the cost of prophecy. The more these elements are present in the context of one's religious life the more likely it is that one will meet the test for ethical prophet. We may take it as a given that by definition such a person possesses a profound sense of the need to do and increase justice and righteousness. In any case, for one to be considered an ethical prophet in the tradition of Jeremiah, Amos, Micah, Isaiah, and Jesus, most of the characteristics discussed

---

21. I am indebted to Professor Mary Alice Mulligan for this instructive insight. Mulligan is Affiliate Professor of Homiletics and Ethics at Christian Theological Seminary in Indianapolis, Indiana.

22. Heschel, *Prophets*, 483.

23. Heschel, *Prophets*, 484.

must be present to some degree. These are *some* of the criteria by which we can test the presence or absence of ethical prophecy. In addition, I believe that the only real hope for those forced into the margins of the world is to be found in the witness of the ethical prophet.

Prophecy Grounded in God

According to Romero, the prophet is the presence of God in the world. This is a reminder that "the initiative always comes from God."[24] It is God's show, and we need to remember that. Consequently, the work of the ethical prophet is really God's work in the world, since it is God who initiates, sustains, and enhances it. The prophet is the conduit. And yet, he is so overwhelmingly in sympathy with God that the word of God seems to be his own. All of this points to the idea that God is central in ethical prophecy. "God is the Good News," Romero declared. "His presence in the world has brought a seed of renewal to history."[25] It therefore follows that we should once again devote attention to the conception of God, for ethical prophecy is grounded in God, which is to say, with Heschel, that it has a clear-cut theological foundation. Ethical prophecy is not the human-centered prophetic pragmatism of Cornel West.[26] Rather, it is God-centered prophecy. As we saw in the discussion on Heschel in chapter 1, ethical prophecy differs from prophetic pragmatism in that it includes the emphasis on human initiative but goes way beyond that by seeing God as the center of the project. At the very least this means that one has to develop a reasonable God-concept.

We have seen that one's doctrine of God has much to do with his stance regarding the role of individual Christians and the church community in society. For example, if one does not believe that God is a relational God who is integrally related to all of creation (most especially to human beings) and shares power with human beings and the rest of creation, but rather believes in a God who is totally transcendent and out of touch with human beings and the world, it would be difficult at best to conclude that such a God somehow requires that Christians and the church should side with the poor and the oppressed.

The interpretation of prophecy in this book is based precisely on the conception of a God who so loves and cares for human beings that they "and God have business with each other,"[27] and thus they and God need each oth-

---

24. Romero, *Shepherd's Diary*, 280.
25. Romero, *Shepherd's Diary*, 424.
26. See West, "On Prophetic Pragmatism," 149–73.
27. James, *Varieties of Religious Experience*, 507.

er, albeit in different ways. In previous chapters we saw that in ancient Greek and Roman thought God was believed to need nothing beyond God's self; God was entirely self-sufficient, needing no friends or coworkers, and had none. The Hebrew prophets, on the other hand, saw God as fundamentally relational by nature and as God of a relational creation.[28] This God was seen as fundamentally social. "In other words, relationship is integral to the identity of God, prior to and independent of God's relationship to the world. The witness that God is one (Deut 6:4) is not compromised by this recognition of the sociality of God."[29] Such a God cannot have merely created human beings to be in relationship with each other. They are in relationship with each other, the rest of creation, and with God. As is so clearly illustrated in Heschel's theology of prophecy, not only do human beings need God, but God needs human beings. This was an important teaching of the Hebrew prophets.

There is no question that Óscar Romero's prophecy was well grounded in his doctrine of and faith in God.[30] Whatever else he did or did not believe about God, everything that Romero did after his first month as archbishop points to his belief in a God who is fundamentally relational, and love; who cares immensely about the weakest and the poor within the human family; and whose power surpasses all other power and extends to all beings—human and nonhuman—in the world[31] (which is not the same as saying with classical theism that God possesses *all* power). It was Romero's faith that ultimately led to his option for life, and more especially for the life of the poor and the oppressed. He placed nothing in this world above life, and most especially the poor, insisting that it is in life that we find God. Therefore, Romero's faith in God was best exemplified in his defense of life in the world. The glory of God, he said (paraphrasing St. Irenaeus), is the living poor man, woman, and child.[32] After his conversion to the poor, Romero's faith in God enabled him to be fearless in his denunciation of injustice and persecution.

Truly, it was through the poor that Romero himself found "the pathway to belief in God." He came to believe (with Latin American liberation theologians) that God has a preferential option for the poor, the ones most in need, and in this sense a special relationship existed between them and

28. See Freitheim, *God and World*, 13–22.

29. Fretheim, *God and World*, 17.

30. Sobrino, *Archbishop Romero*, 153.

31. This is Charles Hartshorne's characterization of God's power. See his *Omnipotence and Other Theological Mistakes*, 26.

32. Sobrino, *Archbishop Romero*, 63.

God. Because the poor in El Salvador changed his heart and his way of seeing reality, Óscar Romero learned and evolved to the point of approaching God from the perspective of the poor and was soon able to see God in the worn, mangled faces of the poor and the forgotten. Sobrino tells us that "through his partiality for the poor, Romero could be impartial—and find God everywhere."[33] In fact, there is a sense in which the poor actually preached the gospel to him, and he heard them and responded prophetically. One of Romero's basic contributions as ethical prophet is that "he taught theology to speak of God and the poor in one breath. He taught [theology] to speak *of* the God of the poor, and he taught it *how* to speak of God and the poor."[34] We saw a similar emphasis in Heschel and King.

Romero's faith in the God of the poor was at the root of his actions once he himself was converted to the poor. His actions in solidarity with the poor and the oppressed, that is, his insistence on the need to accompany and to be *with* the people in the struggle,[35] concretized his faith and strengthened his belief in their dignity. This was just what the poor needed as they sought to assert the *image of God* in themselves and their sense of being somebody, because of the realization that they were loved and cared for by God.

The Sacredness of Persons

The Hebrew prophets *assumed* the centrality of the sacredness of persons: every person is *the image of God* because created, loved, and sustained by God. For the prophets, every person was sacred by virtue of being invested with the image of God. The prophets took the rights and dignity of human beings in the presence of God as a matter of course and demanded not that human beings, in general, but that each individual human being in particular be respected for the precious one he is. Human beings have supreme worth because they are created by a Personal God who is Love and who loves and cares about each of them. This is quite different from the Greek god Zeus, who was believed to loathe human beings and left them to fend for themselves. This was the stance of Orestes in Jean-Paul Sartre's play *The Flies*. At one point Orestes tells Zeus that human beings are essentially alone in the world and must make their own way—that they dare not count on being rescued by some superior force. "Nature abhors man," he laments, "and you too, god of gods, abhor mankind."[36] Clearly this was not the God of the

---

33. Sobrino, *Archbishop Romero*, 69.
34. Sobrino, *Archbishop Romero*, 175.
35. Romero, *Voice of the Voiceless*, 174.
36. Sartre, *The Flies*, 122. In the play *The Devil and the Good Lord*, Sartre has the

Hebrew prophets, for did not YHWH speak through the prophet Ezekiel to declare that "all persons are mine" (Ezek 18:4)?[37] Because created and loved by God each person has infinite, indescribable, and indestructible worth. Every individual person is precious in God's sight, is honored and loved by God.

Early in his tenure as archbishop, Romero asserted that in all that he did as a leader in the church, he intended to promote the idea of the sacredness of human beings—most especially the weakest, poorest, voiceless ones in Salvadoran society. He challenged the church itself to persistently and bravely bear this same responsibility. In a September 4, 1977, sermon he told the congregation,

> God would not be our author if we were something worthless. You and I and all of us are worth very much, because we are creatures of God, and God has prodigally given his wonderful gifts to every person. And so the church values human beings and contends for their rights, for their freedom, for their dignity. That is an authentic church endeavor. While human rights are violated, while there are arbitrary arrests, while there are tortures, the church considers itself persecuted, it feels troubled, because the church values human beings and cannot tolerate that an image of God be trampled by persons that become brutalized by trampling on others. The church wants to make that image beautiful.[38]

Romero frequently returned to this personalistic theme, insisting that *"there is no dichotomy between human beings and God's image. Whoever tortures a human being, whoever abuses a human being, whoever outrages a human being abuses God's image,* and the church takes as its own that cross, that martyrdom."[39]

Human beings are of incalculable worth to God, and because they are Romero could say, "Nothing is so important to the church as human life, as the human person, above all, the person of the poor and the oppressed, who,

---

protagonist Goetz express the certainty that God is completely silent and absent, and therefore does not hear or see him. He was compelled to say that he "sent messages to Heaven, no reply. Heaven ignored my very name" (141).

37. I am here influenced by Julius Bewer, who believed "persons" and "person" to be truer to the text than "lives" and "life." See his comment on Ezekiel 18:4 in his *Prophets*, 375. Here Bewer writes, "All persons belong to the LORD and each is immediately related to Him and belongs to Him as an individual, not as a member of a family or clan or of the nation; and He deals with everyone directly."

38. Romero, *Violence of Love*, 8.

39. Quoted in Swedish, *Archbishop Oscar Arnulfo Romero*, 30 (my italics).

besides being human beings, are also divine beings, since Jesus said that whatever is done to them he takes as done to him."[40] In the same sermon (preached on March 16, 1980, eight days before he was assassinated), Romero repeatedly spoke of the inherent supreme value of the human being and the obligation of Christians and the church to preserve and defend human life. "This is the fundamental thought of my preaching," he said. "Nothing is so important to me as human life. Taking life is something so serious, so grave—more than the violating of any other human right—because it is the life of God's children."[41] Persons, according to Romero, are not just human beings, but divine beings.[42] Human beings are not made for the Sabbath or the church (Mark 2:27), and most assuredly they are not made for the state.[43] Rather, these things are made for human beings, who have intrinsic worth. The Sabbath, the church, and the state possess only extrinsic or instrumental value. For Romero the person has the right of way, and therefore "takes precedence over all our ways of thought and must be respected."[44]

After Óscar Romero was converted to the poor, he knew in a way he had not previously known that human beings are more important to God than anything else. When Democratic congressman Tom Harkin passed through El Salvador and went to Mass one Sunday at the San Salvador Cathedral, the church was packed to overflowing. One of the people remembered the event and reported that the congressman "was moved by the piety of all the poor people and by the archbishop's homily. But what really made an impression on that gringo's heart was the lousy shape the Cathedral was in."[45] The building was in disrepair, needed painting and a host of other improvements. The man remembered the congressman commenting that the *building* did not leave him with a good impression. Then in broken Spanish the congressman asked, "Doesn't Monseñor Romero take care of his most important church?"[46] The response given truly set Romero apart from all others: "Monseñor Romero spends his energy taking care of others."[47] Romero himself could not have said it better, for when he was appointed archbishop his intention was to remodel the Cathedral, but he soon

---

40. Romero, *Violence of Love*, 236.

41. Romero, *Violence of Love*, 241. This sermon, given just eight days before he was murdered, was one of the longest he ever preached—nearly two hours. See Brockman, *Romero: A Life*, 238.

42. Romero, *Violence of Love*, 236.

43. Romero, *Violence of Love*, 34.

44. Quoted in Brockman, *Romero: A Life*, 240.

45. Vigil, *Oscar Romero*, 217.

46. Vigil, *Oscar Romero*, 217.

47. Vigil, *Oscar Romero*, 217.

relinquished that goal because of the needs of the people and his recognition that they, more than any building, were important to God. "For Monseñor, people came first. And that's why he said the Cathedral would remain that way: halfway done, as a monument to the people who don't have a roof over their heads or land to plant on, people who have neither bread nor peace."[48] In his March 23, 1980, sermon—preached the day before he was assassinated—Romero told of how he and other bishops at the Puebla Conference in Mexico in 1979 signed a document that committed them to doing all they could to promote and enhance the infinite dignity of human beings.[49] By this time, Romero was convinced that the mission of the church was to defend the image of God,[50] and everything he did as archbishop reflected that stance.

Once Romero was converted to the poor he did not hesitate to boldly declare, "I will not abandon my people, but *together with them I will run all the risks that my ministry demands*."[51] Indeed, he pleaded with the poor to pray for him that he would stay the course. He did not allow fear to incapacitate him. Instead, his increasing faith and trust in God, and his deepening love for and solidarity with the poor, enabled him to manage the fear such that the evangelization work of the church would continue. Romero not only learned to love and respect the person of the poor but insisted on the need for them to love and respect themselves as people who are deeply loved by God. In one sermon he pleaded,

> Dear poor people, dispossessed people, you who lack house and food, your very dignity demands your advancement.
> It is a pity that you, the poor, should not respect yourselves as you ought and that you try to drown in drink, in bad habits, in excess, a dignity that could be God's delight, God's presence on earth....
> A sacrament must be respected, because it is a sign of God. The poor must respect themselves....[52]

It was crystal clear to Romero that the poor had suffered so much degradation for so long that it was necessary that they recapture their lost sense of dignity. Inalienable dignity is what it means to be a human being. Romero sought, as Malcolm X and Martin Luther King Jr. did, to awaken the poor and oppressed to their inherent dignity.

48. Vigil, *Oscar Romero*, 217.
49. Romero, "Church and Human Liberation," 8.
50. Brockman, *Romero: A Life*, 157.
51. Romero, *Violence of Love*, 207 (my italics).
52. Romero, *Violence of Love*, 41.

After the murder of Father Grande, Óscar Romero understood that he too must travel the road to Calvary—that he too would likely end up on the cross. Asked by one of his priests why he changed, Romero said, among other things, "And everything that happened to us when I got to the archdiocese, what happened to Father Grande and all . . . it was a lot. You know how much I admired him. When I saw Rutilio dead, I thought, 'If they killed him for what he was doing, it's my job to go down that same road . . .' So yes, I changed. But I also came back home again."[53] Romero discovered anew why God called him to ministry. So he returned home to be with the poor *in* the margins and to take their suffering and persecution as his own.

Father Ponseele reflected how Romero fell in love with the poor and frequently "told jokes and created an atmosphere of great warmth between himself and the people."[54] He also exhibited an amazing sense of humor, as Martin Luther King Jr. did,[55] which helped him manage his fears and lighten the moment for himself and any other who might be present. Here is a case in point.

On one occasion Romero and Salvador Barraza were relaxing in the sun on the beach. Both men had eaten too much food to give serious thought to getting into the water. Quite unexpectedly, Romero asked Barraza if he was afraid to die. He responded that he was not. "Well I am," said Romero. "I really am."[56] Barraza saw his opening and replied, "You're just afraid because you won't be able to preach up there in heaven. You won't be able to find anyone who needs to hear your sermons."[57] Romero quipped, as a comedian might have done, "Be serious man! Do you know what I'm going to miss most in heaven? Beans and avocados. Going without them will be awful."[58] Again, such humor helped him manage his fears arising from the daily threats against his life. The humor could not eradicate the fears, but it was a sure help in managing them so that he could persevere in doing the work.

Through humor, prayer, and meditation, Romero had staying power, insisting in the face of his own imminent demise that not only would he denounce injustice and oppression, but he would stand his ground with his people. Accordingly, Romero declared that it was not difficult to love the poor. "With this people," he announced, "it is not hard to be a good

---

53. Vigil, *Oscar Romero*, 159.
54. Vigil, *Death and Life in Morazán*, 24.
55. See Baldwin, *Behind the Public Veil*, ch. 6.
56. Quoted in Vigil, *Oscar Romero*, 226.
57. Quoted in Vigil, *Oscar Romero*, 226.
58. Quoted in Vigil, *Oscar Romero*, 226.

shepherd. They are a people that impel to their service us who have been called to defend their rights and to be their voice."[59] He just loved hanging out with the folk, often leaving his car and walking along the hot, dusty road as multitudes of the poor left their houses to joyously greet him, while others called to him from their houses.

Call to Conversion

Ethical prophecy requires that those who take the Christian faith seriously must be converted to the poor and others among the systematically oppressed. There is no more admirable example of this than Archbishop Romero's own conversion. He was a humble man and was rather naïve before and during the early days of his appointment as archbishop. However, it is significant that he did not forget the terrible encounter with his priests and the people after the government occupation of the National University in 1972. Romero did not forget the horrible things he said to them. He returned to that church at Zacamil in 1977 and addressed the people, most of whom had been present five years earlier. Father Ponseele recalled the experience, saying, "I remember his first words: he said he remembered everything that had happened and he asked us to forgive him for what he had said that day. He asked for our forgiveness! And he told us that he was determined to accompany his flock like a shepherd and that previously he hadn't understood what was going on."[60] Noemí Ortiz recalled that while everyone remembered the encounter, no one wanted to bring it up. However, she remembered Romero saying, "I was here years ago in this community and in this very place, with many of you who are now gathered. Do you remember? . . . We couldn't even celebrate the Eucharist that afternoon because of the run-in we had between me and all of you. . . . We were insulting each other. . . . Do you remember? . . . I remember it well," he said, "and today, as your pastor, I want to say that I now understand what happened on that day, and here before you I recognize my error. . . . I was wrong, and you were right. That day you taught me about faith and about the Church. Please forgive me for everything that happened then."[61] The entire gathering broke into crying and rejoicing. One of Romero's favorite songs, "Quincho Barrilete," was playing. "All was forgiven," said Ortiz.[62] Whether they are pastors, church executives, judicatories, or laity, believers must not become so high

---

59. Romero, *Violence of Love*, 207.
60. Vigil, *Death and Life in Morazán*, 23.
61. Vigil, *Oscar Romero*, 267.
62. Vigil, *Oscar Romero*, 268.

and mighty that they consider themselves to be above reproach, or that it is acceptable that they offend even one human being and not apologize, repent, and ask forgiveness. Romero modeled this for the people when he apologized and asked their forgiveness. This too was part of his conversion.

Jon Sobrino contends that the most decisive element in Romero's conversion, "the one that kept him faithful to God's will to the end—was his people, a people of the poor. The poor very promptly showed him their acceptance, support, affection, and love."[63] It was as if the poor were just waiting for the arrival of the good shepherd, and they recognized Romero as such almost immediately. In a way, they drew the shepherd to themselves and there was immediate mutual love and affection between them. "The suffering of the poor must have shaken Archbishop Romero to his depths as he watched their oppression swell to such intolerable proportions. The poor were effectively calling for his conversion."[64] Theologically, Óscar Romero's conversion to the poor gave him a new starting point—the poor. From that point forward all would be judged or evaluated in light of its contribution to the liberation and well-being of the poor.

According to Romero, the church that does not join and side with the poor against the injustices committed against them is not the church of Jesus Christ.[65] He came to believe that siding with the poor is a basic requirement of the church and individual Christians. *Being converted to the poor means making their cause the church's,* in addition to acknowledging that "the church's good name is a matter of knowing that the poor regard the church as their own."[66] Romero loved it when poor people who had suffered in jail told him of "the hope they have in the Church when it defends those who are suffering."[67] Indeed, for Óscar Romero, "the Christian who does not want to live this commitment of solidarity with the poor is not worthy to be called Christian."[68]

Like the eighth-century prophets, Romero began his prophecy with words of denunciation and judgment. But these words were conditional, pending the response of the powerful and privileged to the call to conversion and faithfulness to God. Furthermore, and also like the prophets, Romero always ended with words of hope—hope that authentic conversion would in fact occur and that all would live according to God's plan. This was his faith.

63. Sobrino, *Archbishop Romero*, 12.
64. Sobrino, *Archbishop Romero*, 13.
65. Romero, *Violence of Love*, 224.
66. Romero, *Violence of Love*, 227.
67. Romero, *Shepherd's Diary*, 159.
68. Romero, *Violence of Love*, 227.

This was the good news. It is not the aim of the church to seek revenge on those who subject the people to structural violence—that violence whereby the majority of the people are denied the basic necessities of life. The aim of the church is to denounce such heinous crimes against human dignity, offer redemption, and call to conversion those who are guilty.[69]

Romero was resolute in his stance that the church cannot call for the conversion of others while failing to call for its own conversion. The church too, and not individuals alone, must undergo conversion, "a fundamental turning back to Christ—whose mission we should be—and to the radical demands of the Sermon on the Mount."[70] After Medellín (the Second Episcopal Conference of Latin American Bishops, held at Medellín, Colombia, in 1968[71]), Romero came to believe that the church had begun moving toward regaining "the basic attitude for conversion, which is to turn toward 'those who are especially lowly, poor, and weak.'"[72]

After his conversion Romero distinguished himself from all others by using his sermons to "denounce cases of injustice."[73] It was the duty of Christians, he said, "to point out facts that show how the plan of God is being reflected or distorted in our midst."[74] Many among the wealthy and privileged claimed that all was well in El Salvador. Reminiscent of the Hebrew prophets, Romero retorted, "What good are beautiful highways and airports, all these beautiful skyscrapers, if they are all fashioned of the clotted blood of the poor who will never enjoy them?"[75] A week before he was assassinated, Romero thundered, "This blood, these deaths, touch the very heart of God. No land reform, no bank nationalizations, no other promised measures can be fruitful if it is awash in blood."[76] All was not well in El Salvador, and Romero—like the prophets—would not pretend otherwise. This was evident in sermon after sermon where he itemized the terror and abuse of government troops against the people. Many of these soldiers were also poor, thus prompting Romero to make a bold plea, saying, "Brothers: you are part of our own people. You kill your own campesino brothers and sisters. And before an order to kill that a man may give, God's law must prevail

---

69. Romero, *Voice of the Voiceless*, 166.
70. Romero, *Voice of the Voiceless*, 60–61.
71. Gustavo Gutiérrez contends that 1968 is the birthdate of Latin American liberation theology. See Ferm, *Third World Liberation Theologies*, 11.
72. Romero, *Voice of the Voiceless*, 69.
73. Romero, *Shepherd's Diary*, 166.
74. Romero, "Church and Human Liberation," 3.
75. Quoted in Sobrino, *Archbishop Romero*, 111.
76. Quoted in Sobrino, *Archbishop Romero*, 111.

that says: Thou shalt not kill! No soldier is obliged to obey an order against the law of God. No one has to fulfill an immoral law. It is time to take back your consciences and to obey your consciences rather than the orders of sin. . . . In the name of God, and in the name of this suffering people, whose laments rise to heaven each day more tumultuous, I beg you, I beseech you, I order you in the name of God: Stop the repression!"[77] Romero called out the evildoers and declared that God was not pleased with the terrorization and disappearance of the people. He also made it clear that it was not only the archbishop who was responsible for conveying God's truth. It was a shared responsibility with every baptized Christian.[78]

Salvation is not a mere verbal acceptance of Jesus Christ and God's grace without corresponding changes in the way one lives and treats others. Salvation is not cheap grace. This has always been a tough truth for most Christians. Too often they have believed that all that is needed to insure God's favor is to give verbal acceptance of God's love and grace, even as they continue to behave like the devil and to mistreat others or ignore the injustice done to them because of their class, race, gender, religion, sexual orientation, ability, or health.

One undergoes authentic conversion only when one concretizes and lives the meaning of conversion each and every day. One who is truly converted or is becoming converted must, as Romero did, accompany the poor and the oppressed into the margin and pray with them, suffer with them, and fight with them for their right to humanity, dignity, liberation, and empowerment. One must take on all debilities of the poor. And if all else fails, he must be ready to do as Romero did—die with the poor. Romero came to see that the primary reason for the persecution of priests and the church was that a segment of the church had sided with the poor and was doing everything they could to defend them from attack. "The persecution comes about," Romero declared, "because of the Church's defense of the poor, for assuming the destiny of the poor."[79]

Although Romero did not hesitate to denounce the unacceptable practices of the poor and the oppressed and even their would-be liberators, it should be remembered that for him the fundamental sin was the persecution of the masses by the few who "owned" and controlled all of the wealth and resources which alone could make it possible for the people to emerge from poverty. This is why, in a homily preached on the day he was

---

77. Quoted in Brockman, *Romero: A Life*, 241–42.
78. Romero, *Violence of Love*, 173, 177.
79. Quoted in Manuel, *El Salvador's Decade of Terror*, 33.

assassinated, he courageously called the oligarchs to conversion and to an ethic of sharing, spiritually and materially:

> I hope that this call of the church will not further harden the hearts of the oligarchs but will move them to conversion. Let them share what they are and have. Let them not keep on silencing with violence the voice of those of us who offer this invitation. Let them not keep on killing those of us who are trying to achieve a more just sharing of the power and wealth of our country. I speak in the first person, because this week I received notice that I am on the list of those who are to be eliminated next week. But let it be known that no one can any longer kill the voice of justice.[80]

And, of course, Romero did not hesitate to denounce the sins of the church, its leaders, and its members. "We bishops, popes, priests, nuns, Catholic educators, we are human," he said, "and as humans we are sinful and we need someone to be a prophet for us too and call us to conversion and not let us set up religion as something untouchable."[81] Religion and the church also need the voice and witness of the ethical prophet.[82] Even more, the church needs to be reminded why, and for whom, it exists. Only one who has been converted and is faithful and courageous enough to speak God's truth can do this.

Speaking the Truth

As previously implied, once Óscar Romero was converted to the poor his sermons took on a much different tone and purpose. They were as nourishment for the people, that which they looked forward to each and every day. Ernestina Rivera remembered being drawn to the archbishop's sermons. "I loved to go and hear him," she said. "He preached so beautifully that I never tired of it. . . . I was willing to walk any distance or ride any bus just to hear him."[83] Mario Kaplún said that in some of the villages the people seemed to literally hang on every word of his sermons. "He was becoming the only voice in El Salvador that could put forth any kind of alternative position. And the people understood that."[84] Martina Guzmán reflected,

---

80. Quoted in Brockman, *Romero: A Life*, 232–33.
81. Romero, *Violence of Love*, 173.
82. Romero, *Violence of Love*, 173.
83. Vigil, *Oscar Romero*, 206.
84. Vigil, *Oscar Romero*, 209.

> Every day, what he said was what gave us life. His sermons were the most eagerly anticipated event of the week. I was working in the communities of San Ramón, and on Sundays I would leave my house and walk to the Cathedral. I didn't have to carry a radio with me to hear his homily, because I could hear it the whole way there: there wasn't a single house that didn't have its radio on listening to him. My entire route was a homily! It was a chain of radios with a broadcast as uninterrupted as if it were a single transmission.[85]

The people needed to hear both Romero's voice and the words of his sermons, for he spoke the truth about what they were experiencing, and he courageously criticized the powers and challenged the people. Those sermons helped the people bear the atrocities they were subjected to and provided them with an assurance that God demands that things be better for them. Romero's voice and his sermons gave the people the courage and determination to press onward.

Óscar Romero himself personified the willingness and the courage to convey the unadulterated word of God, regardless of the cost. Unlike most ministers, his first concern was not to find ways to make God's truth palatable and acceptable to the powerful and privileged. He preached and spoke with holy boldness. The great preacher William Augustus Jones characterized this stance of speaking God's word very well when he wrote, "The prophet fears no one, except the God He serves. He tells it anywhere and wherever—in the congregation, in royal palaces, in city streets, when the road is rough, when the going is tough, and even when friends forsake. He tells the story until his day is done."[86] The prophet is not called to be the "soothing conscience" of the powers; rather, he condemns "every kind of abuse, every form of keeping the poor in poverty or of creating new poor."[87] He knows that when he persists in speaking God's truth to power, persecution is a real possibility for him, indeed, a virtual inevitability. He is certain of God's faithfulness, and certain that there will be tough consequences for relentlessly speaking God's truth.

After his conversion, none was more exemplary than Romero when it came to speaking the truth about sin in the sociopolitical and economic orders, and also in the church. He knew that the prophet's only obligation is to proclaim God's point of view. God requires not success and popularity in ministry but commitment, obedience, and faithfulness. *One is required*

---

85. Vigil, *Oscar Romero*, 205.
86. Jones, *God in the Ghetto*, 156.
87. Gutiérrez, *Theology of Liberation*, 167.

to try, no matter how often one fails. God does not require success but only persistent effort. *This* is what makes one a true disciple—that he is vigilant in making the effort to do what God requires of him.[88] Since ethical prophecy is ultimately rooted in God, the prophet speaks directly in the name of God.

Whether people respond obediently and appropriately to God's word is not the concern of the prophet. His responsibility is to prophesy—to sow the seeds, to tell the story, to show the people and the nations what God sees and requires. Óscar Romero did this, far surpassing the hopes and expectations of the poor and the forgotten in El Salvador. "His homilies were full of truths," said María Otilia Núñez. "That's why so many people wanted to listen to them. . . . When you're poor, you feel like you've been forgotten. But with these homilies, that changed. For us, Monseñor was like a father who was always looking out for us."[89] When the church, the prophet, or the people speak God's truth they are persecuted by the powers. Romero recognized that more than anything the truth was being suppressed in El Salvador, and indeed could not even be heard in such a dreadful place. Archbishop Romero knew that in those exceptional instances in which the gospel truth is spoken, "it gives offense, and the voices that speak the truth are put to silence"[90]—often permanently. "When the prophet bothers the consciences of the selfish, or of those who are not building with God's plans," said Romero, "he is a nuisance and must be eliminated, murdered, thrown into a pit, persecuted, not allowed to speak the word that annoys."[91] Romero increasingly came to know much about the *burden and cost of ethical prophecy*, how heavy—and yet how necessary—was the prophetic word. He recalled and paraphrased how often Jeremiah prayed that God would remove the burden of prophecy from him: "Lord, take this cross away from me. I don't want to be a prophet. I feel my insides burning because I have to say things even I don't like."[92]

As we saw before, and similar to the other hall of fame candidates, Romero had no doubt that the individual Christian is tasked with the responsibility of speaking God's truth and being the voice of the voiceless. That is, every Christian must contribute to the prophetic mission—"must develop a prophetic awareness."[93] He was just as insistent that the church

---

88. Romero, *Violence of Love*, 211.
89. Vigil, *Oscar Romero*, 222.
90. Romero, *Violence of Love*, 157.
91. Romero, *Violence of Love*, 7.
92. Romero, *Violence of Love*, 7. See Jer 20:7–10.
93. Romero, *Violence of Love*, 104.

has that responsibility too. In his fourth pastoral letter (August 6, 1979) Romero asserted,

> The church . . . would betray its own love for God and its fidelity to the gospel if it stopped being "the voice of the voiceless," a defender of the rights of the poor, a promoter of every just aspiration for liberation, a guide, an empowerer, a humanizer of every legitimate struggle to achieve a more just society, a society that prepares the way for the true kingdom of God in history. This demands of the church a greater presence among the poor. It ought to be in solidarity with them, running the risks they run, enduring the persecution that is their fate, ready to give the greatest possible testimony to its love by defending and promoting those who were first in Jesus' love.[94]

We need to remember that God does not merely speak God's word through pastors and bishops. Archbishop Romero was always reminding the people that "God's best microphone is Christ, and Christ's best microphone is the church, and the church is all of you."[95] Therefore, no matter one's station in life, one can, indeed must, speak God's truth. In his July 8, 1979, homily, "The Prophet Is the Presence of God in Society,"[96] Romero told the people,

> If some day they take the radio station away from us, if they close down our newspaper, if they don't let us speak, if they kill all the priests and the bishop too, and you are left, a people without priests, each one of you must be God's microphone, each one of you must be a messenger, a prophet. The church will always exist as long as there is one baptized person. And that one baptized person who is left in the world is responsible before the world for holding aloft the banner of the Lord's truth and of his divine justice.[97]

Romero was just as quick to remind the people of the cost of speaking God's truth. When fire was set to the printing plant of *La Crónica del Pueblo* in August 1979, he said that its burning "testifies to the glorious risk that anyone runs who dares to publicize in the people's defense the outrageous injustices of those powers."[98]

---

94. Romero, *Voice of the Voiceless*, 138.
95. Romero, *Violence of Love*, 222.
96. See Romero, *Shepherd's Diary*, 280.
97. Romero, *Violence of Love*, 172.
98. Romero, *Violence of Love*, 186.

One must have courage to convey God's point of view in any setting, but most especially in violent, repressive settings such as El Salvador. The archbishop understood this, declaring in a December 5, 1977, homily, "To be a Christian now means to have the courage to preach the true teaching of Christ and not be afraid of it, not be silent out of fear and preach something easy that won't cause problems. To be a Christian in this hour means to have the courage that the Holy Spirit gives in the sacrament of confirmation, to be valiant soldiers of Christ the King, to make his teaching prevail, to reach hearts and proclaim to them the courage that one must have to defend God's law."[99] Ethical prophecy, prophetic ministry, is costly business. When the church speaks the truth, when it deplores and seeks to eradicate sin, it is invariably made to suffer.[100] Romero came to see that he was called to preach the truth against injustice and all forms of terrorism and oppression. He also understood that such preaching is costly to the preacher.

The Cost of Prophecy

Already converted to the poor in late 1977, Archbishop Romero knew that it was easy to claim adherence to the Christian faith as long as one does not disturb the world or seek to change it. Indeed, Joseph Goebbels, Nazi propaganda minister, told Christians during Hitler's reign of terror, "You are free to seek your salvation, as you understand it, provided you do nothing to change the social order."[101] They were free to worship the God of their faith as long as they said and did nothing to challenge the genocidal actions of the Hitler regime. Romero saw clearly the problem with such counsel, as he indicated in a December 10, 1977, homily:

> What starts conflicts and persecutions, what marks the genuine church, is when the word, burning like the word of the prophets, proclaims to the people and accuses: proclaims God's wonders to be believed and venerated, and accuses of sin those who oppose God's reign, so that they may tear that sin out of their hearts, out of their societies, out of their laws—out of the structures that oppress, that imprison, that violate the rights of God and of humanity.[102]

Romero knew that it was easy to preach against sin and injustice in general. The rub comes when one preaches against specific sins—when one

---

99. Romero, *Violence of Love*, 18.
100. Romero, *Violence of Love*, 35.
101. Quoted in Simán, "Impact of Monsignor Romero," 5.
102. Romero, *Violence of Love*, 20.

names and preaches against concrete injustices.[103] *This* is when one gets into trouble with the powers and the wealthy. When the church speaks the truth, when it names and denounces specific individuals and social sins, it will be persecuted. Nevertheless, once Romero converted to the poor he came to see that it was his duty to speak God's truth to the people and the nation, and without allowing fear to prevent him from doing that dangerous work. One who is devoted to preaching truth and justice is always at cross purposes with the powers. But Romero also knew that even when the prophet's voice is silenced in death it can still be heard in the conscience and soul of those who believed as he did.[104]

That the truly committed will suffer and be persecuted does not mean that they have to possess a martyr complex, for Deuteronomy 30:19 implores the people to choose life. It is, rather, a simple acknowledgment that one who accepts God's call and who is faithful to it will suffer various kinds of persecution. The truly devoted will be persecuted precisely because he carries God's viewpoint to the people and to the powerful and privileged. When the prophet speaks the truth uncompromisingly it generally follows that he will be made to suffer, since he comes into conflict with the powerful and privileged segments of society. Such was the experience of the prophets of old and of Jesus. Those who claim to live by the teachings of Jesus and the prophets must expect no less, and indeed must wonder about the quality of their faith if they are not persecuted in some way. Óscar Romero knew, as all ethical prophets have known, that one who is truly committed to the gospel and who is in solidarity with the least of the sisters and brothers must suffer the same fate as they, and therefore will likely be martyred.[105] On the third anniversary of Rutilio Grande's assassination, Romero told the people that "Christ's messenger will always meet the fate Father Grande met if the messenger is faithful."[106] Romero's sharp denunciations of injustice and of those who perpetrated it, his insistence that the church must denounce "everything which destroys individual dignity, and especially whatever limits our ability to build a country which has love, justice and peace as its foundation,"[107] as well as his refusal to speak in generalities could only mean that he, too, would be persecuted. It was not a question of *whether* but of *when* and *how* it would occur. However, he came to accept it as part of his faithfulness to God and his sense of the cost of prophecy.

103. Romero, *Violence of Love*, 70.
104. Romero, *Shepherd's Diary*, 376.
105. Romero, *Violence of Love*, 228.
106. Romero, "Church and Human Liberation," 17.
107. Romero, *Shepherd's Diary*, 135.

Óscar Romero understood his own fate to be that of the church, that of the little ones who are so dear to the heart of God and who he himself came to love so dearly. He was not standing alone. In the Salvadoran situation the prophetic element in the church was being persecuted precisely because it preached against injustice and the torture of human beings, and "because it refuses to be indifferent to, or in complicity with, the situation of sin and structural violence prevailing in [the] land."[108] Óscar Romero and the church were being persecuted for the same reason Jesus was persecuted—for being a prophet. Indeed, the Salvadoran church was being tormented because of its commitment to following Jesus and to being in strict solidarity with the poor and doing all it could to defend them. The church is persecuted because of its efforts "to become incarnate in the interests of the poor."[109]

In the next-to-last sermon that Romero preached before he was assassinated, he praised the archdiocesan radio station, YSAX, "for being an instrument of truth and justice," even though "the risk [of danger] must be taken, because an entire people depend on it as they strive to uphold this word of truth and justice."[110] Just weeks before this, Romero had preached about the bombing of the radio station and the destruction of the transmitter, declaring that it was an attempt to silence the prophetic voice of the church and its efforts to be the voice of the voiceless.[111] Romero understood the cost of prophetic ministry—for naming and uprooting sin and for defending and being in solidarity with poor, oppressed people.

Romero was ecstatic about the church being persecuted along with the people—for the blood of bishops, priests, and nuns to be mixed, literally, with that of the poor, as when Father Grande was murdered alongside two peasants. In one of his sermons Romero went so far as to say, "I am glad, brothers and sisters, that our church is persecuted precisely for its preferential option for the poor and for trying to become incarnate in the interest of the poor."[112] Accordingly, Romero held that the church that suffers no persecution but enjoys the privileges and favor of the world is not the church of Jesus Christ.[113] "A church that sets itself up only to be well off, to have a lot of money and comfort, but that forgets to protest injustices," said Romero,

---

108. Quoted in Sobrino, *Archbishop Romero*, 160.

109. Sobrino, "Monseñor Romero," 171. This is precisely what was called for at Medellín.

110. Romero, "Church and Human Liberation," 2.

111. Romero, *Violence of Love*, 229.

112. Romero, *Violence of Love*, 177.

113. Romero, *Violence of Love*, 152.

"would not be the true church of our divine Redeemer."[114] It is not the business of the church to make evildoers feel good in their wrongdoing. That would be a betrayal of the gospel. During his address on the occasion of the conferral of an honorary doctorate by the University of Louvain, Óscar Romero poignantly stated the stance he had come to regarding the poor:

> I am a shepherd who, with his people, has begun to learn a beautiful and difficult truth: our Christian faith requires that we submerge ourselves in this world. The course taken by the Church has always had political repercussions. The problem is how to direct that influence so that it will be in accordance with the faith. The world that the Church must serve is the world of the poor, and the poor are the ones that decide what it means for the Church to live really in the world.[115]

Óscar Romero did not have a death wish but only sought to be faithful to God. He simply knew enough about the history of the world, the church, the prophetic tradition, and the fate of prophetic priests and campesinos in El Salvador to understand that if he continued to speak God's truth he would very likely share their fate. However, he believed the strongest word of prophecy to be exemplified in martyrdom, claiming that "the voice of blood is the most eloquent of words."[116] Like all ethical prophets, Óscar Romero was thoroughly human and possessed all of the emotions, joys, and fears that all human beings possess. None need inquire whether he experienced fear. When he received word of the threat against his life by a leftist group in November 1979, Romero wrote in his diary, "It is not that it does not worry me, given the seriousness of the way it was reported . . ."[117] He was an earthen vessel, just as other human beings. We get a sense of Romero's humanity as well as his fear when he reflected upon the report from the papal nuncio of Costa Rica, saying,

> I find it hard to accept a violent death, which in these circumstances is very possible. . . . Father gave me strength by telling me that my disposition should be to give my life for God, whatever might be the end of my life. The circumstances yet unknown will be lived through with God's grace. God assisted the martyrs and, if it is necessary, I will feel him very close when I offer him

---

114. Quoted in Swedish, *Archbishop Oscar Arnulfo Romero*, 24.

115. Quoted in Purcell, *Martyrs of Our Time*, 158. I prefer this translation to that which appears in the text of the speech in Romero, *Voice of the Voiceless*, 178.

116. Quoted in Sobrino, *Archbishop Romero*, 164.

117. Romero, *Shepherd's Diary*, 374.

my last breath. More important than the moment of death is giving him all of life and living for him.[118]

This reflection revealed Romero's awareness of his own mortality and fear, but it also revealed his courage and determination to persist in doing God's will.

Óscar Romero believed that even were he to be martyred the word of God would live on. He referred to this one year after he was appointed archbishop, and again just days before he was assassinated. "The word remains," he said. "And this is the preacher's great comfort. My voice will pass away, but my word, which is Christ, will remain in the hearts of those who have been open to receive it."[119] *The word remains!* And then, we find these chilling but prophetic words written in a Mexican newspaper barely two months before the bell tolled for Óscar Romero the final time. Like Malcolm X and Martin Luther King Jr. before him, Romero knew what was to be his fate. He reflected on this, saying,

> If they kill me, *I will rise again in the Salvadoran people* . . .
> As a shepherd, I am obliged by divine law to give my life for those I love, for the entire Salvadoran people, including those Salvadorans who threaten to assassinate me. If they should go so far as to carry out their threats, I want you to know that I now offer my blood to God for justice and the resurrection of El Salvador.
> Martyrdom is a grace of God that I do not feel worthy of. But if God accepts the sacrifice of my life, my hope is that my blood will be like a seed of liberty and a sign that our hopes will soon become a reality.
> My death will be for the liberation of my people and a testimony of hope for the future.
> A bishop will die, but the church of God, which is the people, will never perish.[120]

The last entry in Romero's published diary was on Thursday, March 16, 1980. Eight days later, on March 24th, he celebrated Mass in the chapel of the Divine Providence Cancer Hospital in San Salvador. The occasion for the Mass was the first anniversary of the death of Sara Meardi de Pinto, mother of Jorge Pinto, publisher and editor of *El Independiente*, a newspaper that consistently stood with the people in El Salvador and supported their struggle for human rights and justice. Romero took as his text John

118. Quoted in Brockman, *Romero: A Life*, 233–34.
119. Quoted in Sobrino, *Archbishop Romero*, 165.
120. Quoted in Erdozaín, *Archbishop Romero*, 75, 76.

12:23–26: "The hour has come for the Son of Man to be glorified. Very truly, I tell you, unless a grain of wheat falls into the earth and dies, it remains just a single grain; but if it dies, it bears much fruit. Those who love their life lose it, and those who hate their life in this world will keep it for eternal life. Whoever serves me must follow me, and where I am, there will my servant be also."

This was Romero's last homily. In it, he interpreted the verses in John to mean that a person must not love either himself or life in this world so much that he avoids "getting involved in the risks of life that history demands of us," for "those who try to fend off the danger will lose their lives, while those who out of love for Christ give themselves to the service of others will live, like the grain of wheat that dies, but only apparently."[121] Romero reminded those present that each one can do something, if only to express understanding and sympathy for those who struggle for liberation; if only—and above all—to pray, as did the one for whom the Mass was being celebrated. Nearing the end of the Mass, Romero said,

> This holy mass, now, this Eucharist, is just such an act of faith. To Christian faith at this moment the voice of diatribe appears changed for the body of the Lord, who offered himself for the redemption of the world, and in this chalice the wine is transformed into the blood that was the price of salvation. May this body immolated and this blood sacrificed for humans nourish us also, so that we may give our body and our blood to suffering and to pain—like Christ, not for self, but to bring about justice and peace for our people.
>
> Let us join together, then, intimately in faith and hope at this moment of prayer for Doña Sarita and ourselves.[122]

And then, during a moment of silence, POW!!! The awful, horrific sound of gunfire filled the chapel, sounding like a bomb exploding, perhaps because the single bullet that pierced his heart hit so close to the microphone. His blood literally splattered onto the table of the Lord as his limp body dropped to the chapel floor. Think about that! He was murdered right there at the table of the Lord—murdered because of his persistence in proclaiming "the message of salvation and the inalienable dignity of the human being made in the image of God," and for fearlessly denouncing injustice. A published statement by the Salvadoran bishops' conference read, "For being faithful to the truth, he fell like the great prophets 'between the sanctuary and the altar'

---

121. Romero, *Voice of the Voiceless*, 191.
122. Romero, *Voice of the Voiceless*, 193.

[Matt 23:35]."[123] Romero was rushed to a nearby hospital where, within minutes, he was pronounced dead.

Óscar Romero's blood was spilled on the table and floor of the chapel because he loved, befriended, stood, and lived with the poor and the oppressed in El Salvador. His was a deep love for the poor, who were his friends. He had agonized over their disappearances and murders. Like Malcolm X and Martin Luther King Jr., he made his peace with the strong possibility that he too would be martyred. As we saw previously, he loved life and tried to live it as fully as he could, even during those three tremendously tumultuous, pressure-filled, dangerous years when he served as "bishop of the world." Those of us who believe in the existence of an objective moral order and thus live by the conviction that the universe is built on a moral foundation also believe that somehow meaning can be elicited from Óscar Romero's martyrdom.

Conclusion

Óscar Romero conveyed words of warning, denunciation, and judgment to the oligarchy, the wealthy, the military junta, and even the church. Still, it is important to remember that these warnings were conditional, since ethical prophecy always ends with words of hope—hope for the conversion of all who are not in step with God's vision for the world, hope that all will be converted to God and the poor. The word of God is, finally, good news for all who hear and respond accordingly. Óscar Romero's hope was first and foremost in the God of the Hebrew prophets and Jesus Christ. However, his was also a hope in the people and their eventual liberation and empowerment in this world. Like literary artists James Baldwin and Alice Walker, Romero never stopped believing that human beings and the world can be better than they are.

We can be sure that the Hebrew prophets were nothing short of rabble-rousers and troublemakers in the minds of the privileged and powerful. In addition, we can be certain that every religious person is morally obligated to be a troublemaker in the face of injustice, oppression, atrocity, and other types of human degradation. Heschel was convinced that the major activity of the Hebrew prophets was remonstrating and interference against injustice. In this regard, the prophets were troublemakers in the best sense. They were both incessant and "remorseless" in exposing moral pretension and the wrongs and injustices committed against the people. Like the Hebrew prophets, Romero did not hesitate to identify and name specific, concrete

123. Quoted in Brockman, *Romero: A Life*, 246.

sociopolitical and economic evils.[124] Once converted to the poor he refused to speak and preach in generalities about existing social evils. He was "repeatedly threatened as a result of his forthright sermons; in the months preceding his assassination, he had become the most outspoken and influential opponent of the military's merciless campaign against its perceived enemies. His homilies were a weekly catalogue of carnage by government troops."[125] He named the atrocities committed against the people.

There is much that the church, the synagogue, and the mosque can learn from the prophetic ministry of Óscar Romero. He exemplified what Heschel believed was needed in a world marked by injustice and oppression. "What is called for is not a silent sigh," said Heschel, "but a voice of moral compassion and indignation, the sublime and inspired screaming of a prophet uttered by a whole community."[126] What greater hope can there be for those who are forcibly kept in the margins and gutters of this world than courageous prophetic voices and a prophetic church, synagogue, or mosque taking its place in the margins, right there in the muck and mire with the forgotten and left-outs? What ethical prophets throughout history dreamed of remains a viable and a possible dream whose actuality will not be realized without a sense of call, determination and courage to speak God's truth, insistence on the sacredness of every person, conversion to the poor, and a willingness to endure persecution, which is the cost of conveying God's point of view on what is happening in the world—all of this, while acknowledging and insisting that human beings and the world can be better than they are. Our next and final hall of fame candidate champions this ideal in her art and practice.

---

124. Heschel, *Prophets*, 204. See also Romero, *Violence of Love*, 142.
125. Manuel, *El Salvador's Decade of Terror*, 34.
126. Heschel, "Speech at the Ceremonies," 27.

8

Alice Walker as Ethical Prophet

Like James Baldwin, Alice Walker is a first-rate and prolific literary artist who sees her writing as a means of making human beings and the world better than they are. This can be best accomplished by insuring "the survival whole" of human beings generally and black women, the elderly, and the black community more particularly. In one way or another she conveys this ideal in all of her writings. She made the point explicitly in a 1973 interview:

> I am preoccupied with the spiritual survival, the survival *whole* of my people. But beyond that, I am committed to exploring the oppressions, the insanities, the loyalties, and the triumphs of black women.... For me, black women are the most fascinating creations in the world.
>
> Next to them, I place the old people—male and female— who persist in their beauty in spite of everything. How do they do this, knowing what they do? Having lived what they have lived? It is a mystery, and so it lures me into their lives.[1]

Walker is also the recipient of the Pulitzer Prize for *The Color Purple* (1982). Her work is a mechanism through which the artist can, indeed must, write and speak truth to power about the condition of those with their backs pressed against the wall,[2] and the need to fully and thoroughly liberate them.

---

1. Walker, *Our Mothers' Gardens*, 250, 251.
2. See Thurman, *Jesus and the Disinherited*, 13.

Fully the poet-prophet-activist that Baldwin was, Alice Walker has felt called to witness against racism, anti-Semitism, sexism, heterosexism, elitism, colorism, classism, exploitation of the environment, and nuclear proliferation, to name a few life-destroying practices. Her writings are not primarily for entertainment but are calculated to make better people and a better world. Therefore, it will be helpful to approach this discussion a bit differently. Not least is it important to discuss Walker's relationship with white feminism and her decision to name black women and their experience *womanist* rather than *feminist*. What does Walker mean by *womanist*? Are there womanist traits that are similar to what we find in the ethical prophet? But first, let's look at Walker's background.

Alice Walker as Person

Born in 1944, Alice Walker is the youngest of eight children born to sharecropper parents, Willie Lee Walker and Minnie Lou Tallulah Grant Walker, in Eatonton, Georgia. She graduated valedictorian of her class at Butler-Baker High School in 1961 and matriculated at Spelman College in Atlanta in the fall of that year. Walker traveled to Helsinki, Finland, as a delegate to the World Festival of Youth and Students, and later attended the famous March on Washington for Jobs and Freedom on August 28, 1963. A few months later she transferred from Spelman to Sarah Lawrence College. Not long thereafter she went to Kenya under the aegis of the Experiment in International Living.

At Sarah Lawrence, Walker was the student of poets Jane Cooper and Muriel Rukeyser. The latter proved a valuable early mentor and was helpful in getting Walker's first book of poems, *Once*, published in 1968. Walker did not hesitate to praise Rukeyser, who taught her that it was possible to live in the world on her own terms.[3] She credits her teacher with helping her find the courage to take the necessary steps to become a writer. Rukeyser spoke in adulatory terms about her student as well.[4]

After graduating from Sarah Lawrence, Walker accepted a position as caseworker at the Department of Welfare in New York City. Before long she became actively involved in the civil rights movement through activities of the Student Nonviolent Coordinating Committee (SNCC). During this period she worked for the NAACP Legal Defense and Educational Fund in Jackson, Mississippi, under the supervision of Marian Wright Edelman. While there she met and married Melvyn Leventhal, a young Jewish civil

---

3. Walker, *Our Mothers' Gardens*, 38.
4. White, *Alice Walker*, 109.

rights attorney. The couple married in 1967, had one child, Rebecca, two years later, and divorced in 1976.

An incredibly prolific writer, Alice Walker became the first black woman to win the Pulitzer Prize for fiction. Writers, she contends—and not unlike ethical prophets—"should care desperately," particularly about morality and questions of right and wrong.[5] She is painfully aware that not all writers fall into this category. Having written more than two dozen books of fiction, nonfiction, and poems, there is no indication that Walker will stop writing anytime soon. It is what she does. Indeed, writing is so much a part of who she is that she vows to continue writing even if no one reads her work.[6] Furthermore, in the spirit of literary artist and Nobel Laureate Toni Morrison, Walker has been intentional about writing books that she wants to read,[7] that is, writing "all the things *I should have been able to read*."[8] In this regard, she unapologetically writes whatever she feels needs to be written,[9] and especially that which lends itself to the survival and liberation of her people, in particular, and all human beings in general. To a large extent writing has been cathartic for Walker, and similar to Baldwin, it is the work she absolutely *must* do, almost as if she has no choice, as if she absolutely must write or be destroyed. Writing does many things for Alice Walker, not least saves her "from the sin and *inconvenience* of violence,"[10] that is, of committing violence against her enemies.

Importance of Black Women Naming Themselves

When a woman names herself she stands a good chance of becoming what she says she is or desires to become. In the mid-1980s, many black feminist theologians and ethicists intentionally sought to name themselves, their experience, and their theologico-ethico project. Essentially, they strove to answer the question, What shall *we* call ourselves? Black women religious scholars such as Jacquelyn Grant (considered by many to be the Mother of Womanist Theology), Katie Cannon, Delores Williams, Karen Baker-Fletcher, Emilie Townes, Diana Hayes, Kelly Brown Douglas, Carroll Watkins Ali, Marcia Riggs, Cheryl Kirk-Duggan, Traci West, Monica Coleman,

---

5. Byrd, *World Has Changed*, 231.

6. In an interview, Elena Featherston asked Walker if she would continue to write if no one read her work, to which she replied, "Yes. It is a very natural way that I've been given to deal with my reality." See Walker, *Same River Twice*, 201.

7. Walker, *Our Mothers' Gardens*, 7.

8. Walker, *Our Mothers' Gardens*, 13 (Walker's italics).

9. White, *Alice Walker*, 293.

10. Walker, *Our Mothers' Gardens*, 369.

and others have all adopted and adapted the term "womanist" as the best way of naming who they are and what they do. The term was coined by Walker in the late 1970s and appropriated by black feminist ethicist Katie Cannon around 1985.[11]

In 1979, Walker was invited by Laura Lederer to write the introduction to the third world women's chapter of a book titled *Take Back the Night: Women on Pornography*.[12] It was there that she introduced the term "womanist."[13] In the body of her contribution, which she described as a "fable," Walker wrote that a womanist is a feminist, "only more common."[14] She included the fable, titled "Coming Apart," in her book *You Can't Keep a Good Woman Down: Stories*, where she identified herself as a womanist.[15] In an extended explanatory footnote she further explicated the meaning of the term, saying,

> "Womanist" encompasses "feminist" as it is defined in Webster's, but also means instinctively pro-woman. It is not in the dictionary at all. Nonetheless, it has a strong root in black women's culture. It comes (to me) from the word "womanish," a word our mothers used to describe, and attempt to inhibit, strong, outrageous or outspoken behavior when we were children: "Your're acting womanish!" A labeling that failed, for the most part, to keep us from acting "womanish" whenever we could, that is to say, like our mothers themselves, and like other women we admired.
>
> An advantage of using "womanist" is that, because it is from my own culture, I needn't preface it with the word "Black" (an awkward necessity and a problem I have with the word "feminist"), since Blackness is implicit in the term; just as for white women there is apparently no felt need to preface "feminist"

---

11. See Cannon, "Emergence of Black Feminist Consciousness," 56.

12. See Walker, *You Can't Keep a Good Woman Down*, 41.

13. Womanist theologian Karen Baker-Fletcher contends that much of Walker's early characterization of "womanist" is "in response to Jean Humez's publication of Rebecca Cox Jackson's (1795–1871) writings in *Gifts of Power*." Baker-Fletcher, "Dusting Off the Texts," 291–92. In a footnote, Baker-Fletcher asserts that to her knowledge Cheryl J. Sanders is the first to note that Walker's earliest definition of womanism "appears in her article on Humez's discussion of Rebecca Cox Jackson" ("Dusting Off the Texts," 292n).

14. Walker, "Coming Apart," 100.

15. "Coming Apart," in Walker, *You Can't Keep a Good Woman Down*, 48. Walker's parenthetical statement that "the author of this piece is a womanist" is not included in the version of the fable that appears in the Lederer collection.

with the word "white," since the word "feminist" is accepted as coming out of white women's culture.[16]

Walker was seeking a means by which black women could name themselves and their experiences regardless of the sexist views of men—all men!—and/or the racist views of white women and white men. She desires that black women name their own experience after their own fashion, while rejecting anything foreign to that experience.[17] Karen Baker-Fletcher contends that in the term "womanist," Walker saw a way "to define the diverse ways in which black women have bonded, sexual or not." She further maintains that Walker "seeks a term that is spiritual, concrete, 'organic and characteristic not simply applied' to describe black women's womanbonding."[18]

Walker stresses the primacy of black humanity and dignity in her writings. Indeed, she affirms the interrelatedness of all life, declaring that "every affront to human dignity necessarily affects me as a human being on the planet, because I know *every single thing on earth is connected*."[19] Truly, for Walker, the defilement or killing of a human being, for any reason at all, is nothing to boast about, even if one is compelled to kill the person who oppresses her. In her poem "Revolutionary Petunias," Walker imagines the protagonist, Sammy Lou, who killed the white oppressor (because he long subjected her to unbearable suffering), as looking up to the heavens as if trying to explain why she did what she did. Sammy Lou had not intended to kill her oppressor. Walker writes that she pictures Sammy Lou "as tall, lean, black, with short, badly straightened hair and crooked teeth. . . . Her reaction, after killing this cracker-person, would be to look up at the sky and not pray or ask forgiveness but to say—as if talking to an old friend—'Lord, you know my heart. I never wanted to have to kill nobody. But I couldn't hold out to the last, like Job. I had done took more than I could stand.'"[20] Sammy Lou felt no sense of sheroism about what she did, because she knew that she had taken a human life, and therefore part of her own self died that day. After all, the womanist holds that all human beings are connected. Walker insists on the importance of seeing people within and outside their immediate group "not as strangers but as kin."[21] This is a theme that will be examined more fully in the subsequent discussion on the degree to which

---

16. Walker, "Coming Apart," 100n.
17. Walker, *Our Mothers' Gardens*, 82.
18. Baker-Fletcher, "Dusting Off the Texts," 292.
19. Walker, *Our Mothers' Gardens*, 353 (my italics).
20. Walker, *Our Mothers' Gardens*, 266.
21. Walker, *Our Mothers' Gardens*, 201.

Walker believes in the fundamental spiritual nature of reality and the innate sacredness of persons.

As is true of James Baldwin's writing, God is important in Walker's work as literary artist. She does not hold traditional ideas about God, but without question, she is much influenced by the idea of a supreme being as the source of all things. Human beings are not left solely to their own devices—although they must depend heavily on these—and ultimately must answer for how they spent their time in this world. What is the significance of God in Walker's work and witness?

Nontraditional View of God

Alice Walker did not have the type of experience in the black church that James Baldwin had. Still, her religious upbringing—she grew up in the Methodist church[22]—had a significant impact on her life, despite the fact that she came to reject her parents' version of Christianity while in college.[23] She has little personal use for the institutional church and the way that many professed Christians live out their faith. Walker does not hesitate to confess that she "wavers" in her convictions about God,[24] and based on her many writings one can only conclude that she continues to work out a conception of God that makes sense to her.

Suffice to say that I applaud Alice Walker's willingness and courage to think beyond traditional ideas and conceptions of God, human beings, nature, and their interrelatedness. I also cheer her insistence that nature and *all* life forms are valuable in themselves. What I question, however, is her view that all life forms are *equally* valuable: "That we [human beings] are no more precious than the rest of the species on Earth."[25] I especially take issue with this stance at a time when certain groups of people, not least Native Americans, Afrikan Americans, and Latinos/as, are treated as nonpersons by Donald Trump and much of white America. The very first order of business, it seems to me, is to acknowledge the absolute worth of *every* human being, most especially those among the historically left-outs. Once that is established—once these are seen to be utterly precious beings in the sight of God—it would be reasonable to then begin focusing on the value of nonhuman life forms and their relation to human beings. I care about all life forms and believe that all life possesses intrinsic value, but I cannot believe

---

22. Walker, *Our Mothers' Gardens*, 252.
23. Walker, *Our Mothers' Gardens*, 17.
24. Walker, *Our Mothers' Gardens*, 265.
25. Byrd, *World Has Changed*, 301.

that all life forms have equal value. Rather, it would seem that some are more valuable than others. An infant is surely infinitely more valuable than a mosquito, a cat, or a dog, for example. Most important for our purpose, the Hebrew prophets and Jesus were unquestionably more concerned about the worth and plight of human beings than nonhuman life forms. Right or wrong, ethical prophecy focuses on the sacredness and welfare of human beings. Interestingly enough, Walker also focuses on this, although she prefers to think of other life forms as equally valuable.

Sacredness and Interrelatedness of Persons

Alice Walker rebelled against many of her childhood religious teachings, including how one should think about Jesus Christ and God. Much of the rebellion occurred while she was in college, where she read, pondered, and was influenced by the ideas of existentialist and other philosophers. This was during a particularly tough period when she was grappling with the problem of suicide—the possibility of her own and that of others. She had returned pregnant from a student study trip to Afrika and did not know what to do about it. She concluded that the two philosophers who helped her most were the atheistic existentialists Friedrich Nietzsche and Albert Camus. These, she believed, "made the most sense, and were neither maudlin nor pious. God's displeasure didn't seem to matter much to them, and I had reached the same conclusion."[26] She found no comfort in Christian religious teachings about suicide at that time, and she was terrified, knowing that her mother believed abortion to be a sin.

Life experiences and the reading and pondering of Nietzsche and Camus led Walker to a different outlook on God, human beings, nature, and the world. Nevertheless, she is comfortable with at least some aspects of the two Genesis accounts of creation. For example, she agrees that all that God created is fundamentally good and therefore possesses intrinsic value. What she takes issue with, however, is the further claim that human beings matter most to God and that because they are invested with God's image, they are superior to all other creatures and have been appointed as stewards over them.

Looking back over history and reexamining her own surroundings, Walker concluded that human beings, especially rich and powerful corporate executives, have consistently behaved destructively toward nature and nonhuman life forms on a massive scale, exhibiting no consideration or respect for their worth. With this in mind, she shuns the idea conveyed in

26. Interview with John O'Brien, in Byrd, *World Has Changed*, 35.

Genesis that God gave human beings dominion over nature and nonhuman life forms (Gen 1:26). Because she believes human beings have seriously undervalued the entire created order, she thinks it would help substantially if all areas of life were thought to have equal value.

Walker believes that human beings are evolving to the point that many more will begin to see that all life forms "have the right to live without fear. And without fear of being eaten, for instance. And that's a real hard one because we have been addicted to meat, to animals as meat.... And I struggle with that myself, and I think most people do. But I do really believe that is where we're headed—that if we do survive as a species, we will get it. That we are no more precious than the rest of the species on Earth."[27] "Existence," she contends, "makes us all equal."[28]

Walker's is a valid point, inasmuch as she does not want life on any level to be disrespected, violated, or unnecessarily destroyed. According to one of the two Genesis accounts of creation, God created all there is and declared it to be not simply good, but *very* good (Gen 1:31), a point Walker agrees with. While she accepts the church's teaching about the absolute dignity and sacredness of human beings, she expands this teaching to include all other life forms, adopting the position that they possess the same value and sacredness as human beings. This provocative stance is not the Christian view, but presently it is Alice Walker's.

Nevertheless, in no way does Walker downplay the idea of the value and sacredness of human beings. Neither does she consider human beings, nonhuman life forms, or nature to be her natural enemies. Instead, she fervently believes in the fundamental goodness of each.[29] Even so, it is important that we be aware of her high estimation of human beings. She believes that human beings exist "to be enjoyed," an idea she conveys when she writes, "When I am in the presence of other human beings I want to revel in their creative and intellectual fullness, their uninhibited social warmth. I want their precious human radiance to wrap me in light. I do not want fear of war or starvation or bodily mutilation to steal both my pleasure in them and their own birthright. Everything I would like other people to be for me, I want to be for them."[30] She rightly insists that if human beings are truly

---

27. Byrd, *World Has Changed*, 301.
28. Byrd, *World Has Changed*, 293.
29. Walker, *Anything We Love*, xxii, xxv.
30. Walker, *Anything We Love*, xxii.

treasures they must "demand to be treasured"[31] and that it might well be that the only real treasure left to human beings is their inherent right to choose.[32]

One cannot love human beings as Alice Walker does without also considering them to be sacred and deserving of the deepest, utmost reverence and respect. "I have learned nothing about human beings that has stopped my loving them," she writes, "and this is especially true of African and African-American human beings, who seem to me unsurpassed inspirers of affection, and love."[33] Even when it comes to the sexism of black men, she resists the impulse not to engage them, saying instead, "No matter in what anger I have written about the black man, I have never let go of his hand."[34] Walker unquestionably loves her people—who ultimately are *all* people, a point she makes over and over again in her writings.

Like James Baldwin (the two deeply admired and respected one another[35]) and other hall of fame candidates, Alice Walker is certain that no person or group stands alone but that human beings are interconnected such that "all people must be our people."[36] This means that there is virtually nothing that happens in the world that does not affect—directly or indirectly—all human beings. This, in part, is why Walker rightly and passionately insists that every bomb ever made and dropped on human beings anywhere in the world falls on every human being.[37] So inextricably interrelated are human beings, she maintains, that by saving the life of another person one also saves one's own life.

Regardless of what we think about Alice Walker's claim that all life forms are of equal value, there is no question that she acknowledges the inestimable worth of human beings and their interdependence with each other and all of nature. Accordingly, all derive from and are sustained by the same source. Walker does not often name God as this source, but gives it other names (e.g., *Mother, Nature, It, Earth, Goddess, the All, Great Spirit, Truth,* and *the Great Mystery*), which are meant to depict a Supreme Being who is also Creator and Sustainer of all life,[38] a stance that places her squarely in the camp of ethical prophecy.

31. Walker, *Anything We Love*, 145.
32. Walker, *Anything We Love*, 146.
33. Walker, *Anything We Love*, 150.
34. Walker, *Living by the Word*, 95.
35. White, *Alice Walker*, 436.
36. Walker, *Living by the Word*, 166.
37. Walker, *Living by the Word*, 160.
38. Walker refers to the Supreme Being in many different ways. Some of these include the following: "the All" (*World Has Changed*, 312); "Great Spirit" (*Living by the Word*, 95, 96); "Mother" (her favorite name for God); "Nature," "All-ness," (*We Are the*

To a large extent Walker's writing has been about declaring and enhancing the sacredness of human beings, most especially those who are among the historically left-outs. She loathes the idea that the U.S. does not honor blacks as human beings.[39] Moreover, she knows the challenge of loving people who have all the advantages and privileges and behave as if Goddess ordained them to have these things, while denying them to others. It is hard to love such people. "Even with much effort," Walker writes, "I still find it difficult to love people who control, who have everything. And it's so sad because no matter what they do, the feeling remains. They can be ever so wonderful, and yet this barrier rises like a ghost."[40] As poet-artist her job, her call, is to work to destroy all instances of disregard for the sacredness of human beings.

Call and Witness

When the people are mercilessly and unjustly treated and trampled upon, it is the duty of the ethical prophet to sound the alarm, to speak the truth about it. Alice Walker is unmistakably clear about this. She speaks and writes out of what happens to her and to the people in her community. "The artist is the voice of the people," she writes, "but she is also The People."[41] We have seen throughout that this too is the stance of the ethical prophet. In addition, and like the prophets of old, Walker is aware that just as the heart of the Great Spirit is on the side of the weak and the downtrodden, and just as the Great Spirit's special concern is not for the strong and the successful but for the lowly and disinherited, the stranger, the poor, the homeless, and the widow, so too must the poet-prophet privilege these over those others. The ethical prophet is incensed by the absence of justice and righteousness and expresses a burning desire to do something about it. This is an apt description of Alice Walker.

One who is called by God is charged with conveying God's outlook regarding human beings and the world. Walker contends that if she cannot do anything else, she can be a witness and tell the story of what happened. Discussing writing and the role of the writer in 1993, she told Jean Shinoda Bolen and Isabel Allende, "Well, I just really feel that if you're in a situation where something horrible is happening, and soul is being destroyed, spirit

---

Ones, 82); "Truth" (*We Are the Ones*, 188); the "Great Void" (*Our Mothers' Gardens*, 246); "It" (*Color Purple*, 190; *Anything We Love*, 25); etc.

39. Walker, *Our Mothers' Gardens*, 91.
40. Byrd, *World Has Changed*, 235.
41. Walker, *Our Mothers' Gardens*, 138.

is being crushed, if you can't do anything else, you can witness it. And that is something that you do in your role as storyteller."[42] It is also what one does in one's role as ethical prophet. As witness and storyteller one learns and develops the courage to tell the story, the truth and nothing but the truth, thereby effectively keeping awareness of the story alive and not allowing us to forget—not allowing innocent, voiceless people to be forgotten. The storyteller is courageous and by no means gullible or easily deceived, for "the duty of the writer is to not be tricked, seduced, or goaded into verifying by imitation or even rebuttal, other people's fantasies. In an oppressive society it may well be that *all* fantasies indulged in by the oppressor are destructive to the oppressed."[43] The artist aims to speak the truth about the condition of the downtrodden.

Alice Walker has long had a sense of being called to the work she does: called to bear witness to the truth, called to be a voice for those whose voices have been silenced. Everything about Walker suggests that she intends to bear witness and speak truth to power until she can no longer hold a pen or utter a word. This is the stuff of ethical prophecy.

Speaking the Truth

In addition to speaking truth about racism, sexism, homophobia, and classism Alice Walker has courageously spoken truth about many things, not least the nature of true feminism; the enormity of the white man's crimes against humanity, nature, and the animal kingdom; and police brutality. She has also protested against the practice of men fathering children and failing to support them financially and otherwise. For example, she did not hesitate to criticize some of her brothers for failure in this regard, but is pleased that her oldest brother was a responsible father to his children.[44]

Our candidate for the ethical prophet hall of fame has not hesitated to write and speak against black male sexism. Looking back on the civil rights and Black Nationalist movements and the relations between black men and black women in both the South and the North, she has expressed dismay that black men saw black women as second-class citizens—as little more than their servants. She quotes Barbara Sizemore approvingly in this regard.

> The nationalist woman cannot create or initiate. Her main life's goal is to inspire and encourage man and his children. Sisters in this movement must beg for permission to speak and function

---

42. Byrd, *World Has Changed*, 115.
43. Walker, *Our Mothers' Gardens*, 312.
44. Walker, *Our Mothers' Gardens*, 330.

as servants to men, their masters and leaders, as teachers and nurses. Their position is similar to that of the sisters in the Nation of Islam. When Baraka is the guiding spirit at national conferences only widows and wives of black martyrs such as Malcolm X and Martin Luther King, Jr. and Queen Mother Moore can participate. Other women are excluded.[45]

This was disheartening to Walker, who declared that "subservience of any kind is death to the spirit."[46] It disappointed her that some black men who read her novels *The Third Life of Grange Copeland* and *Meridian* revealed their "inability to empathize with black women's suffering under sexism, their refusal even to acknowledge our struggles." Furthermore, she said that many black men "appear unaware that sexism exists (or do not even know what it is), or that women are oppressed in virtually all cultures, and if they do recognize there is abuse, their tendency is to minimize it or to deflect attention from it to themselves,"[47] as if to imply that racism is much worse than what black women experience.

Reflecting on what she learned from her mother, Walker has written perceptively about white women feminists and the tendency of many to be less than genuine. While claiming to be feminists many white women seem to be unaware of their racism, elitism, classism, and heterosexism, and too many who are aware give no indication of wanting to divest themselves of these. Consequently, there are far fewer genuine white feminists than there could (or should) be. Walker speaks to this in "One Child of One's Own" saying that "in America white women who are truly feminist—for whom racism is inherently an impossibility—are largely outnumbered by *average* American white women for whom racism, inasmuch as it assures white privilege, is an accepted way of life. Naturally, many of these women, to be trendy, will leap to the feminist banner because it is now the place to be seen."[48] In addition, Walker boldly advises that black women should only expend their time and energy collaborating with white women who are truly feminists and thus are free of racism. Feminism and racism are antithetical, she rightly maintains. One cannot be feminist and racist at the same time.

Alice Walker has also written and witnessed powerfully against the arrogance and destructive tendencies of far too many white men who are

---

45. Sizemore, "Sexism and the Black Male," quoted in Walker, *Our Mothers' Gardens*, 169.
46. Walker, *Our Mothers' Gardens*, 169.
47. Walker, *Living by the Word*, 79.
48. Walker, *Our Mothers' Gardens*, 379.

blind to their sexism, racism, patriarchy, classism, heterosexism, and elitism. She is convinced that one interested to know the cause of global warming and other destructive forces affecting the state of planet Earth need look no further than white men who essentially control everything[49] and are also fast destroying the planet. Walker has courageously spoken and witnessed against this and has not allowed her prophetic voice to be softened or silenced. Indeed, she would rather the planet and all on it be destroyed than to allow white men to continue along their destructive path. In this regard, she lodged a devastating critique against white men in "Only Justice Can Stop a Curse," saying,

> And it would be good, perhaps, to put an end to the species in any case, rather than let white men continue to subjugate it, and continue their lust to dominate, exploit, and despoil not just our planet, but the rest of the universe, which is their clear and oft-stated intention; leaving their arrogance and litter not just on the moon, but on everything else they can reach.
>
> If we have any true love for the stars, planets, the rest of Creation, we must do everything we can to keep white men away from them. They who have appointed themselves our representatives to the rest of the universe. They who have never met any new creature without exploiting, abusing, or destroying it. They who say we poor (white included) and colored and female and elderly blight neighborhoods, while they blight worlds.
>
> What they have done to the Old, they will do to the New.
>
> Under the white man every star would become a South Africa, every planet a Vietnam.[50]

With all that is happening throughout the U.S. regarding police-black community relations it is of interest to note that Alice Walker also speaks powerful truths about police brutality against blacks, as well as the wrongheaded tendency of the police to see themselves solely as "the police" (a view unthinkingly shared by many residents as well), rather than as *the people* and therefore as members of the community. For that is what the police are—members of the community! Although Walker was aware of numerous instances of police brutality when she did civil rights work in Mississippi, she knows U.S. history well enough to know that this phenomenon roots deep in the nation's history, and therefore existed long before the advent of the civil rights movement[51]—and, tragically, continues to this day. In 1973

---

49. White, *Alice Walker*, 448.
50. Walker, *Our Mothers' Gardens*, 341.
51. See the powerful, instructive discussion of police-black community relations in

Walker described police brutality as "the newest form of lynching" and knew that it was "no longer accepted as a matter of course,"[52] that blacks were beginning to publicly challenge the continual occurrence of such despicable behavior.

Close encounters with the police frequently occurred during Walker's participation in civil rights, peace, and nuclear disarmaments protests, but there were also other encounters. When she went to the Houston Astrodome to take books and other items to Hurricane Katrina evacuees, for example, she found herself in dialogue with police officers and some of the people. Both the police and ordinary citizens made it clear that they make a distinction between "the police" and "the community"—that the police are somehow separate and apart from the people. Walker recalled one of the officers saying, "I really would like a book, but I'm not the people. I'm the police." She disagreed with this and told the officers and the people that "*the police are the people*, and we have to remember that the police are the people."[53] Walker knew that as long as police officers feel that they are only the police and not part of the community, there can be little hope of consistently civilized, common-sense, and smart policing in black and other communities of color and communities of the poor. *The police are not merely the police. They are also citizens—the people.* As citizens they are not somehow above or better than the people. Police officers and administrators who think of themselves as police only, rather than citizens too, tend always to be at odds with the people, which is what we see too much of today. This interferes with the potential for sensible, civilized policing. Walker would agree that intelligent and civilized policing is needed in communities in general, and in black, Hispanic, and poor communities in particular, and that this can only be done by well-trained people who possess superior character and integrity. In addition, she would agree wholeheartedly with August Vollmer's criteria for the ideal police officer, put forth in the 1930s:

> The citizen expects police officers to have the wisdom of Solomon, the courage of David, the strength of Samson, the patience of Job, the leadership of Moses, the kindness of the Good Samaritan, the strategical training of Alexander, the faith of Daniel, the diplomacy of Lincoln, the tolerance of the Carpenter of

---

Myrdal, *American Dilemma*, 525, 527, 532, 535–46. See also the informative explanatory footnotes, 1339–43. Myrdal focused on these relations after the Civil War up to the publication of his massive book in 1944.

52. Walker, *Our Mothers' Gardens*, 167.
53. Byrd, *World Has Changed*, 270 (my italics).

Nazareth, and, finally an intimate knowledge of every branch of the natural, biological, and social sciences.[54]

Vollmer concluded that one who meets these criteria *might* be a good police officer. Walker would surely add that in addition to Vollmer's criteria, the good officer must be free of racism, sexism, homophobia, classism, and cultural stereotypes and be committed to serving the people in the community and doing all in her power each and every day to earn their respect. This is truly what is needed today.

Alice Walker knows that so long as police officers are not trained and educated to the extent noted there is need to speak truth to police chiefs, commissioners, mayors, and others who are responsible for police oversight. After all, the pen and voice of writers, Walker maintains, are "capable . . . of changing some horrendous situations. . . . It's within our power to do some really good things just for the health of people."[55] In light of this she has not hesitated to speak truth to the police.

Divine Judgment and the Cost of Prophecy

Like the Hebrew prophets and other hall of fame candidates, Alice Walker has a strong awareness of the presence of injustice on a massive scale. Frankly, much of her writing is intended to alert people to the hardship and injustices in the world and their responsibility to work to end human oppression of all kinds. Having grown up in the South, Walker herself has spoken of having "a very keen sense of injustice" and "a very prompt response to it."[56] Although we do not see explicit "divine judgment" language in her writing, we see many instances in which she makes it unequivocally clear that the Supreme Being is not pleased with injustice and the mistreatment of human beings. In addition, Walker does not hesitate to suggest that it is quite acceptable for the oppressed to call on God to grant their petitions or prayers to punish those who persistently crush their sense of humanity and dignity.

Previously I cited a passage from the "curse prayer," collected by anthropologist, folklorist, and novelist Zora Neale Hurston in the 1920s. Walker included the prayer in *In Search of Our Mothers' Gardens*. The prayer, most likely written by a woman of color, petitions God to grant her

---

54. Vollmer, *Police and Modern Society*, 222. Vollmer was police chief in Berkeley, California, from 1905 to 1932. Afterward he was professor of police administration at the University of Chicago, and then at the University of California. He profoundly influenced a generation of police administrators.

55. Byrd, *World Has Changed*, 258.

56. Quoted in Davis, "Walker's Celebration of Self," 26.

request that her oppressors be punished and made to suffer as ruthlessly as she and her people:

> I ask that their fathers and mothers from their furthest generation will not intercede for them before the great throne, and the wombs of their women shall not bear fruit except for strangers, and that they shall become extinct. I pray that the children who may come shall be weak of mind and paralyzed of limb and that they themselves shall curse them in their turn for ever turning the breath of life into their bodies. I pray that disease and death shall be forever with them and that their worldly goods shall not prosper, and that their crops shall not multiply and that their cows, their sheep, and their hogs and all their living beasts shall die of starvation and thirst. . . . I pray that the sun shall not shed its rays on them in benevolence, but instead it shall beat down on them and burn them and destroy them. . . . O Man God, I ask you for all these things because they have dragged me in the dust and destroyed my good name; broken my heart and caused me to curse the day that I was born.[57]

The petitioner of long ago clearly believed and expected that the Almighty would honor her prayer. Walker herself marveled at the preciseness of the anger, bitterness, and even hatred expressed in the prayer, and did not disagree with any of it. The context of Walker's reflections on the prayer was the antinuclear movement and the white man's massive crimes against humanity generally and black people more especially. In 1982, Walker expressed strong feelings about this, saying,

> When I have considered the enormity of the white man's crimes against humanity. Against women. Against every living person of color. Against the poor. Against my mother and my father. Against me . . . When I consider that at this very moment he wishes to take away what little freedom I have died to achieve, through denial of my right to vote . . . Has already taken away education, medicine, housing, and food . . . That William Shockley is saying at this moment that he will run for the Senate of my country to push his theory that blacks are genetically inferior and should be sterilized . . . When I consider that he is, they are, a real and present threat to my life and the life of my daughter, my people, I think—in perfect harmony with my sister of long ago: Let the earth marinate in poisons. Let the bombs cover the

---

57. Quoted in Walker, *Our Mothers' Gardens*, 339.

ground like rain. For nothing short of total destruction will ever teach them anything.[58]

Without question, Alice Walker believes that those who persist in doing such things will (or should!) face divine judgment, as well as the hatred of other human beings. Very truly, as an artist, she holds, much like Baldwin,[59] that hatred has a place in art and is a normal human response to certain behaviors—that there are even persons and institutions that should be hated. Men like Byron De La Beckwith, who assassinated civil rights leader Medgar Evers in Jackson, Mississippi, and Sheriff Jim Clark, who authorized the use of cattle prods on civil rights demonstrators in Selma, Alabama, deserve to be hated. Furthermore, Walker holds that "some corporations like Dow and General Motors should be hated too. Also the Chase Manhattan Bank and the Governor of Mississippi."[60] This begs the question of whether Trump and politicians who lack moral courage to stand up to him should be hated. This writer thinks they should be. And yet I fully agree with Walker that there are individuals and groups that ought to be loved, "or at least respected on their merits."[61] Because she is a lover and not a hater of humanity, and because she knows full well the damage that hate can do to both the hater and the hated, Walker pushes just as hard for the haters of callous, mean, cowardly, selfish, racist politicians, for example, to exercise their noblest impulses with their hate and not allow it to destroy them or even those who are hated.[62] I agree. But make no mistake. For Alice Walker, "*a little hatred, keenly directed, is a useful thing.*"[63] One who finds it necessary to hate the white nationalist, racist, classist, sexist, anti-Semite, elitist, or heterosexist must be able, at some point, to move beyond the hatred and toward a posture of forgiveness and reconciliation. This is likely what Cornel West had in mind when, eulogizing James Cone, he characterized him as having possessed "charitable Christian hatred."[64] It was the Christian acknowledgment that the sin, not people as such, should be hated.

Another term that Walker uses that conveys her sense that wrongdoers should be punished or even hated is "compassionate wrathfulness."[65] She probably prefers this term to "hatred" since it implies that one should strive

58. Walker, *Our Mothers' Gardens*, 340–41.
59. Baldwin, *Cross of Redemption*, 204.
60. Walker, *Our Mothers' Gardens*, 137.
61. Walker, *Our Mothers' Gardens*, 137.
62. Walker, *Our Mothers' Gardens*, 136–37.
63. Walker, *Our Mothers' Gardens*, 137 (my italics).
64. West, foreword to Cone, *Said I Wasn't Gonna Tell Nobody*, xii.
65. Walker, *Anything We Love*, 109.

to maintain a certain humane disposition even as one subjects an evildoer to her just deserts. The term is a reminder that one is not to go too far in one's hatred toward another, and also that the other, regardless of what she has done, is still a child of God. By virtue of her relation to God and the image of God instilled in her, she is still a being of absolute sacredness.

By this juncture it should be evident to the reader that like the Hebrew prophets, Alice Walker is in complete agreement with the idea of *justified anger*. She unhesitatingly writes and speaks of her own anger being justified when conveying her feelings about brutal injustices committed against her and/or others she knows about. She maintains that if one cannot be angry about such practices as the brutal genital mutilation (clitoridectomy) of thousands of young girls in Kenya and other Afrikan nations, for example, then one must already be dead.[66] One ought to get angry about such injustices and find ways of protesting and eliminating them. But when a person does so she must know that a price will be exacted of her. Walker realizes that all human beings are flawed in one way or another, and this includes even those who strive to right wrongs and to remind the rest of us and the world that we can be better than we are. She knows that every time we insist that people appeal to the best in themselves "we risk disappointment, disillusionment, even despair.... Every time we decide to believe the world can be better. Every time we decide to trust others to be as noble as we think they are."[67] The ethical prophet must know that what she is called to do will cost her. But when she remembers who calls her, it should serve to keep alive her sense of hope and optimism about the future.

Vision of Hope

Alice Walker is convinced that the world cannot survive the way it is going and that to save it we must, at the bare minimum, "Live by the Word and keep walking."[68] In other words, we must get in touch with and live by our highest, noblest values and ideals, most especially the communal values that can potentially save the human race. No one of us, no group, can do it alone. But somehow we must appeal to our better selves, what Abraham Lincoln referred to as our "better angels."[69]

---

66. Byrd, *World Has Changed*, 96. See also Walker and Parmar, *Warrior Marks*.

67. Walker, *Anything We Love*, xxv.

68. Walker, *Living by the Word*, 2.

69. Lincoln used the phrase in the last sentence of his first inaugural address, March 4, 1861. See Lincoln, "First Inaugural Address," 588.

Although Walker is adamant that it is the job of the college graduate to change the world and to do what she can to make the people and the world better than they are, she realizes, like other hall of fame candidates, that time is running out. Notwithstanding this, she reminds us that each of us is obligated to decide what we will do with the time remaining. We all have something to contribute toward making the world a better place for all. Although always aware of the need for structural and institutional changes, Walker insists that there is always something meaningful that each one of us can do. "And the reason that's true," she asserts, "is that you always can work with yourself. You don't have to go out and worry about what other people are doing or how to start this or that out there; you can start ever so much in yourself. And that will evolve outwardly. So if you just hold that thought—that it really is up to each of us, and we're all trying to get to a place where collectively we can effect change. But we can't really do it from being a collective before we are actually self-collected."[70] With Abraham Joshua Heschel, James Baldwin, Malcolm X, and Martin Luther King Jr., she holds that the transformation of the present world order must necessarily begin within each individual. Walker also believes that there is a better angel in each of us—that we have merely to choose to access it and apply it.

Despite Walker's realism about the state of her country and the world, she, like the Hebrew prophets, retains a strong vision of hope, of how things can be if human beings learn how to love and respect self and each other truly. Loving the other is possible only if we first learn to love self. Walker believes that it is both easier and harder to change self. "Because the change begins with each one of us saying to ourselves, and meaning it: *I will not harm anyone or anything in this moment*. Until, like recovering alcoholics, we can look back on an hour, a day, a week, a year, of comparative harmlessness."[71] And as for the poet-prophet, what is her responsibility regarding constructive change in the world? Walker answers, "To work for it, but also *to be* it. If you want a world where people are concerned about life on the planet, then you have to be concerned and work for change. But everyone is responsible for the whole creation and the artist has her or his part to do."[72] Everybody must pay dues by working determinedly to make people and the world better than they are. This, Walker maintains, "pays the rent on being alive and being here on the planet."[73] We are doomed if we continue waiting passively for a messiah to appear to save us. The hope of

70. Byrd, *World Has Changed*, 287.
71. Walker, *Anything We Love*, 214.
72. Byrd, *World Has Changed*, 72 (Walker's italics).
73. Byrd, *World Has Changed*, 80.

saving the world must be in each of us, and we must, each of us, be willing to do our part. In this, Walker agrees with her late friend, poet June Jordan: "We are the ones we have been waiting for."[74] Herein must reside the hope for the New Jerusalem, the beloved community.

Similar to James Baldwin, who believed "we are all androgynous,"[75] Alice Walker maintains that every woman, every man, is infused with both the feminine and the masculine, and that in some cultures, at least, each of these plays a significant role. Nevertheless, Walker sees reason for highlighting the role of the feminine in saving the world and making it a better place for all. To this end she likes how the Swa people of the Amazon have been portrayed. Reflecting on a CD called *Shamanic Navigation* by John Perkins she writes,

> These are indigenous people who've lived in the Amazon rain forest for thousands of years. They tell us that in their society men and women are considered equal but very different. Man, they say, has a destructive nature: it is his job therefore to cut down trees when firewood or canoes are needed. His job [is] also to hunt down and kill animals when there is need for more protein. His job [is] to make war, when that becomes a necessity.[76]

The role of Swa women is just as important, if not more so. "The woman's nature is thought to be nurturing and conserving. Therefore her role is to care for the home and garden, the domesticated animals and the children. She inspires the men. But perhaps her most important duty is to tell the men when to stop."[77] How important for there to be someone whose very nature seems to equip them with the courage and ability to say stop, when it is evident that failure to do so will lead only to self-destruction and the possible destruction of entire communities. "*Stop*. We have enough firewood and canoes, don't cut down any more trees. Stop. We have enough meat; don't kill any more animals. Stop. This war is stupid and using up too many of our resources. *Stop*."[78] Walker believes it is the feminine in women and in men, too, that prompts them to say stop to the epidemic of virtually unprovoked police shootings of black boys and men, and the feminine that will cause

---

74. Jordan, "Poem for South African Women." In 2006 Walker published a book with the title *We Are the Ones*.
75. Baldwin, *Price of the Ticket*, 690.
76. Walker, *We Are the Ones*, 59.
77. Walker, *We Are the Ones*, 59–60.
78. Walker, *We Are the Ones*, 60.

women and men to tell Donald Trump and groveling Republican politicians to stop.

Alice Walker is troubled by the silence of women and the silence of the feminine within women *and* men, and she wants to know when the feminine will rise up and say to the destructive forces all around—stop![79] Nevertheless, she still holds out the hope that the feminine will emerge and that the human race will not only continue to exist but will appeal to the best in persons. She remains optimistic that human beings can live together civilly and as one, and she is not apprehensive about saying that her writings exude "an indomitable belief in the future and in man's capacity for survival."[80] Walker rightly argues that the oppressed owe their oppressors one thing only: "our example to them of how not to be like them."[81] Furthermore, she proclaims that in order to make ourselves and the world better it will be necessary to work as if ours is the last generation capable of work.[82] We must, each of us, begin working like we are humanity's last and only best hope.

Alice Walker believes that at the end of the day, it is all about love—that love is strong, big, and broad enough to hold "anger," "pain," and "hatred."[83] Life is created out of love. And from reading Alice Walker one gets the sense that women (with some exceptions) know more about love, and what it means concretely, than do men—that women in general, and most especially black and other women of color, know a lot about the direction we human beings ought to be going in and how to get us there. Indeed, did Walker not have the protagonist Celie say of God in *The Color Purple*, "If [God] ever listened to poor colored women the world would be a different place"?[84] Celie was also certain that whenever and wherever man appeared on the scene nothing but trouble erupted.[85]

In 1971, Walker did an interview with Coretta Scott King in which Mrs. King made a statement about the incredible and powerful potential of black women for leading the U.S. and the world in the direction of the beloved community. Walker quoted her approvingly as saying,

> Women, in general, are not a part of the corruption of the past, so they can give *a new kind of leadership, a new image for*

---

79. Walker, *We Are the Ones*, 60.
80. Byrd, *World Has Changed*, 40.
81. Walker, *Living by the Word*, 82.
82. Walker, *Our Mothers' Gardens*, 276.
83. White, *Alice Walker*, 463.
84. Walker, *Color Purple*, 187.
85. Walker, *Color Purple*, 203.

> *mankind*. But if they are going to be bitter or vindictive they are not going to be able to do this. But they're capable of tremendous compassion, love, and forgiveness, which, if they use it, can make this a better world. When you think of what some black women have gone through and then look at how beautiful they still are! It is incredible that they still believe in the values of the race, that they have retained a love of justice, that they can still feel the deepest compassion, not only for themselves but for anybody who is oppressed; this is a kind of miracle, something we have that we must preserve and must pass on.[86]

This is a powerful womanist statement, just the type we expect to read or hear about in ethical prophecy. In comparison with how men have led in the world in times past and present, Walker is convinced that "any twelve black women anywhere in the world could do a much better job of running the world than [men] are doing."[87] Because she believes that patriarchy and patriarchal practices have destroyed any chance of the present world being a place where all persons can live life to the fullest, Walker believes that the feminine—in both women and in men—is our only hope.[88] The feminine is our better self.

Conclusion

In this book, we have met eight candidates for the ethical prophet hall of fame: Abraham J. Heschel, Angelina E. Grimké, Ida B. Wells-Barnett, James A. Baldwin, Malcolm X, Martin Luther King Jr., Óscar A. Romero, and Alice Walker. We have seen that each of these more than adequately meets the criteria for the ethical prophet hall of fame. The scheme for determining the eligibility of each candidate is based on Heschel's theology of prophecy with its emphasis on divine pathos, that is, God's total, unrelenting, absolute concern and compassion for human beings. Indeed, according to Heschel, human beings have never been taken as seriously as in ethical prophecy. Human beings are more than the image of God; they are God's fundamental and relentless concern.[89] This is the basis of Heschel's theology of prophecy, which is the type advocated in this book.

We have also seen that the prophets of old exhibited a number of other traits, not least an awareness of the importance of a divine call (reflected

---

86. Quoted in Walker, *Our Mothers' Gardens*, 153 (my italics).
87. Byrd, *World Has Changed*, 82.
88. Byrd, *World Has Changed*, 128.
89. Heschel, *Prophets*, 226.

minimally in an awareness of injustice and a burning desire to eradicate it); stressing the sacredness of persons; insisting on speaking truth to the people and to power; acknowledging that God's dissatisfaction with injustice and human beings' failure to accept God's point of view inevitably lead to divine judgment; highlighting the importance of sweeping allegations; and focusing on the importance of hope that human beings and the world will be better than they are. While inevitable, judgment was not God's last word to Israel or to us today. After all, God not only insisted on the need to do justice (as seen in Amos), but is also in love with the people, as taught by Hosea. God's love was (indeed is!) indestructible, for God is Love. Consequently, God cannot, indeed will not, give up those loved so deeply (Hos 11:8). And yet, God's is not a blind love, forgiving everything wrongfully done by human beings.[90] Although in love with human beings, God nevertheless expects them to do justice and avoid wrongdoing. Failure to do this opens human beings to the possibility of divine judgment, although God generally provides ample opportunity to escape such an end.

I am convinced that in every era of history, and in every place in the world, voices of ethical prophecy have arisen—and will arise—in obedience to God's call and summons. These have always been few in number (rare birds indeed!), but their courage, faithfulness, determination, and accomplishments have generally been phenomenal, and their voices have reached vast numbers of people. Moreover, they have transformed areas of the world in ways that are more commensurate with God's expectations. Such personalities have been constant reminders that human beings and the world can be better than they are.

Ethical prophets need not be celebrities such as those discussed in this book, although celebrity types unquestionably have important roles to play. As Walter Brueggemann helpfully asserts, they "continue to push the edges of thought and imagination to create space for the rest of us in which to maneuver. Celebrity prophets among us say things that sound to some folk to be utterly outrageous, but then the rest of us sound less outrageous."[91] Celebrity prophets generally do not have to contend with difficult and complex issues in local church, synagogue, or mosque. The pastor, rabbi, or imam doing prophetic ministry finds their work to be more difficult in many ways "because of face-to-faceness that makes everything complex, because budgets must be raised and institutions must be nurtured, tasks not so obvious for the celebrities among us."[92] Most ethical prophets, however, are

---

90. Heschel, *Prophets*, 50.
91. Brueggemann, *Disruptive Grace*, 129.
92. Brueggemann, *Disruptive Grace*, 129.

ordinary people who find themselves called to speak God's truth and hope with courage, integrity, the highest respect for the dignity and sacredness of human beings, and with eyes on the highest ideals.

Although the personalities discussed in this book all believed in God and on some level felt called by God, I am not unmindful that the agnostic and/or the atheist may meet all requirements of ethical prophecy except belief in a personal God. I have no doubt that even atheists and agnostics can make important contributions toward efforts to make persons and the world better than they are. My commitment to the best in the Afrikan American religious tradition and the Jewish and Christian Scriptures convinces me of the even deeper significance of the role played by theistic ethical prophets such as those discussed in this book.

Afterword

Through the millennia, we humans have told and retold ourselves our ancestral stories to remind us who we are, to call us to our best selves, to establish our place in the chaos of the universe. The stories were passed down to family members, communities, and whole societies. They told of brave or selfless or sacrificial people who shaped our identity. Religious groups have told and retold their creative narratives, detailing where they came from, how their understanding of holy truth was discovered, and how their foreparents acted to remain faithful.

Hebrew Scripture is full of genealogical accounts of those who gave rise to the Hebrew people, those who blazed trails, those who ruled ill or well, and how LORD Yahweh was made known to them. Ask a religious Jew today about her faith and you may very well hear, "My father was a wandering Aramean . . ." Christian Scripture claims followers of Jesus Christ were grafted into the Jewish people. Christian subgroups continue to chronicle stories of those who shaped them. Just about any Methodist will talk of John Wesley's preaching out in the fields among British workers and the American Methodist circuit riders; any Mennonite will begin not by naming a specific person but by recounting the faithfulness of the Anabaptist "hermeneutical community"[1] in the face of deadly persecution during the Reformation; Disciples of Christ will talk of the Restoration movement, frontier camp meetings, Barton Stone, and Alexander Campbell.

A good place for any Christian to hear early foundational stories is in the eleventh chapter of the biblical book of Hebrews, where the writer

---

1. See Greiser, "What Exactly Is Anabaptist-Mennonite Preaching?," 19–20.

recounts people of faith who moved forward toward God's promise. It is an amazing reminder of the fierce commitment some people had to follow where they believed God was leading them. The book of Hebrews has a sermonic flavor; the writer is clearly eager to encourage listeners to persevere. Scholars believe the hearers were under persecution, or at least a credible threat of persecution. So, when life circumstances threaten to crush us, how do people stay faithful? How do we persevere? In part, we listen to who we are. We tell our foundational stories and find our place in what we realize is God's story.

Obviously, I read Rufus Burrow Jr.'s book as standing in line with others who remind us of who we are in the face of threats, during those times when we could easily wander away from God's guidance, when we feel exhausted and discouraged, and when not rocking the boat seems the safest way to survive in a society where forces seem mightily turned against the characteristics we have been taught to live by.

At such a time as this, we benefit from knowing these candidates Burrow has nominated for the ethical prophet hall of fame. Their stories matter. These people helped shape some of the best parts of our shared history. Although these eight figures are what Burrow calls "celebrity" types, most of us actually do not know them very well. The names may be familiar; we may even know a little something about them—perhaps from an article we read during African American history month or a show on public television. But Burrow adds depth to that knowledge, giving us fuller views of their lives. However, more importantly, he links qualities from their lives with characteristics of the eighth-century ethical prophets described in Rabbi Abraham Joshua Heschel's work. As an important part of that, Burrow continuously reminds us of the profoundly theological ingredients in the thinking of these persons. It is not just behavior that makes these candidates ethical prophets; it is a recognition that God is personally invested in what they are doing.

We are shown that a cluster of characteristics helps identify the ethical prophet: a divine call, the value of speaking truth to power, holding the inestimable sacredness of persons, a tendency to make sweeping allegations, belief in divine judgment, the unavoidable cost of being a prophet, and a confident vision of hope. Fortunately, as we consider the witness of these people, we must not just tick off those traits one by one, as if we were looking for a certain set of qualities like a judge at a dog show. Each of Burrow's candidates is a singular person, whose movement into an ethical prophetic role not only changed their life but often made a difference in the welfare of others around them and showed God's will for justice in the world. Reading about the lives and activities of these persons reveals to us a variety of arenas where ethical prophets have acted in our society, a society that has often neglected and abused them, yet always benefited from them. These candidates acted from a holy vision of the purposes of God.

We might recall a similar trait recounted in the book of Hebrews: "All of these died in faith without having received the promises, but from a distance they saw and greeted them" (11:13). The writer continues, saying of earlier faithful ones, "They were stoned to death, they were sawn in two, they were killed by the sword; they went about in skins of sheep and goats, destitute, persecuted, tormented—of whom the world was not worthy" (11:37–38a). Appropriately we also treasure these more modern ethical prophets Burrow lists, who, like the ancestors in the faith, earnestly sought God's will, caught a vision of the way the world is supposed to be, put up with painful abuse, yet never saw God's purposes fulfilled on earth. Burrow notes, "Like other hall of fame candidates [Angelina] Grimké insisted not on success but on unrelenting faithfulness to God's requirement to actualize justice." In light of their stories, of course, we must acknowledge: the world (that is, each of us) is not worthy of them. Our society fails to live up to deserving them; nevertheless we need to hear their stories. We must know and honor them.

But we must not only know and honor them. Their lives must encourage us to live as ethical prophets, too. Throughout the book, Burrow notes the importance of emulating these hall of famers, who stand in line with the eighth-century Hebrew prophets. For instance, he claims that the witness of Sarah and Angelina Grimké disallowed any excuse for supporting the enslavement of human beings while professing to be "Christian, liberal-minded, and egalitarian . . . The witness of the sisters essentially conveyed the message that one cannot claim to be committed to basic Christian principles while failing to acknowledge and fight for the human and political rights of all persons, regardless of race, gender, and class." These strong words cannot be avoided by the reader. Burrow clarifies that as each person is sacred to the ethical prophet, so must all Christians understand God's intentional creation of each person, who is endowed with the divine image. So as enslavement in the nineteenth century was unjustifiable, so is enslavement or whatever demeans persons in the twenty-first century unjustifiable. That means we need to pay attention to the reports stating that about forty million persons are enslaved around the world today—children as young as six or seven are trapped as domestic workers in homes of strangers; women are lured into sex trafficking and cannot escape; men are kidnapped and beaten until they work. In our world people are chained up or locked in rooms, isolated, far from home, abused. It is telling that in 1809 the average price for a slave was the equivalent of $40,000. Today, the average cost of an enslaved person is $90.[2] Those who claim to be people of God cannot look away. In other words, people of faith need to share the characteristics of the candidates in this book.

Many times, the book quite sharply points a finger in our direction. Note: "According to Romero, the church that does not join and side with the poor against the injustices committed against them is not the church of Jesus Christ." To learn about these candidates challenges us to be like them or admit we are not what we say we are. What the hall of famers say shows the reader how the faithful person is to live. Even as we read about them, they are teaching and testifying. They are calling us to be like them.

In various places in Burrow's book, the reader is reminded of the universal quality of moral responsibility. For instance, of anti-lynching crusader Ida B. Wells-Barnett he writes, "When justice was at stake, Wells-Barnett insisted that absolutely no one is released from moral responsibility." Malcolm X believed that all African Americans could meaningfully contribute to the struggle against the powers that would crush them because, as Burrow states, "human beings are endowed with moral agency." And in discussing Alice Walker he concludes, "Each of us is obligated to decide what we will do. . . . We all have something to contribute toward making the world a better place for all."

As we read these chapters, we are not just gaining information. When speaking of Romero and the Hebrew prophets, Burrow tells us, "We can be certain that every religious person is morally obligated to be a troublemaker in the face of injustice, oppression, atrocity, and other types of human degradation." If we intend to call ourselves Christian, our behavior needs to be closer to that of the hall of fame candidates.

Ethical prophets burn with the desire to get people to see the oppression and injustice in the world, to help us realize the world is not the way God created it to be. So, those of us who read about God's prophets should not remain untouched. We cannot help being drawn into the prophet's commitment. In other words, this entire book is saying, "Reader, these are the characteristics your life should take on." As the ethical prophets profiled here model faithful living in their setting, so do they challenge us to figure out how ethical prophecy might be manifest in our lives. Returning to the eleventh chapter of Hebrews, we learn this: "Yet all these, though they were commended for their faith, did not receive what was promised, since God had provided something better so that they would not, apart from us, be made perfect" (11:39–40). The candidates for the ethical prophet hall of

---

2. Information from the National Underground Railroad Freedom Center in Cincinnati, Ohio: https://freedomcenter.org.

fame model a steadfast commitment to God's purposes for humanity and the entire world. As we learn about their lives, we rightly feel drawn toward the heavenly goals they see, because we are interconnected. But then we are forced to face the startling claim: the prophets' efforts cannot be perfected apart from our participation in the work. Success depends on our joining the struggle.

One final assertion I want to make about what we receive from this book is this: ethical prophets offer us supportive companionship. We might notice that even the title of the book reminds us these people are not isolated in the past; they are ethical prophets "along the way." They can be our companions on the journey. This book reminds any who work to be prophetic: you are not alone.

Once upon a time, the author told me about his dissertation defense. Burrow brought with him to the defense table framed photos of W. E. B. DuBois and Malcolm X, which he set up so he could see them during the conversation. A young African American man, defending his dissertation at a table of old white men, appropriately brought his own support system. DuBois and Malcolm reminded him he was not alone. They had blazed this trail before him and they accompanied him even as he was questioned about his own work that day.

As we read this book, we too are reminded: we are not alone. Ethical prophets often seem called to "go it alone," but in reading about the faithful struggles of these eight candidates, we can sense needed companions for our journey. When we bring the photos, read the stories, get to know the prophets, our own resolve is strengthened.

I think about a white woman, Juliette Hampton Morgan, a librarian in Montgomery, Alabama, in the mid-1950s. She was appalled by the treatment African Americans were receiving and called for people to treat each other fairly. Her letters to the editor during the famous bus boycott compared Dr. King and the campaign to Gandhi's nonviolent civil disobedience in India. The mayor of Montgomery threatened her job, but the library council refused to fire her, so the mayor cut the amount of her salary from the library's budget. When the Ku Klux Klan burned a cross in her yard and broke every window in her house, she finally resigned from the library. The following morning her mother found her, lifeless, a bottle of sleeping pills near her bed.[3] How isolated and alone she must have felt to have resorted to suicide. How tragic it is that ethical prophets frequently do not hear the strong voices around them saying, "You are not alone."

---

3. Material from Southern Poverty Law Center, *SPLC Report*, summer 2019, 7.

Certainly ethical prophets benefit from sensing the presence of other people who affirm their positions. But they also benefit from sensing the divine presence. Burrow quotes King's important claim that he sensed God's real presence, especially during his most trying days. He heard the divine voice within himself saying, "Lo, I will be with you." And Archbishop Romero's claim that God did not create people merely to be in relationship with each other. They need to be relationship with God: "Not only do human beings need God, but God needs human beings."

Malcolm X and several others clearly believed we need each other. Burrow says of Malcolm, "Contrary to what many whites seemed to think, Malcolm had come to believe that God so orchestrated the world that human beings are actually interdependent." Burrow points out in his conversation about James Baldwin that all people are connected—"integrally interrelated and interdependent and thus part of each other. Human beings are inextricably connected." As such, the reader cannot separate herself from the ethical prophet or pretend that what the prophet says does not pertain to her. Alice Walker agrees that we are all interconnected, concluding that "all people must be our people." And of King, Burrow says, "To be a human being is to be in relationship with other human beings and with God." In other words, we are not alone. In fact, we cannot be alone; we are eternally connected to God and each other.

In his conversation about Wells-Barnett, Burrow points out the *seemingly* individual work of ethical prophets, noting they most often do not (perhaps even cannot) work with committees and groups. They often seem to be alone, facing the tremendous reality that groups of people create and enforce injustice. The evils in society are systemic. But Burrow reminds us that organized, committed groups of people are also capable of dismantling unjust systems. As we learn about these candidates, we can connect with them, discovering them as companions for our personal journeys toward ethical prophecy; they become our coworkers in the struggle against injustice.

Of course, there are ethical prophets among us today who can also serve as companions "along the way." Here is one example. As current governmental structures around the world ossify while climate change threatens the survival of the human race, a fifteen-year-old Swedish student begins cutting school on Fridays to make a witness at the Swedish parliament building. All alone, in August 2018, young Greta Thunberg shows up with her cardboard sign reading "School Strike for Climate," calling upon her government to cut greenhouse gases so young people will grow up to live on a habitable planet. One teenage schoolgirl, a lone ethical prophet, she protests by herself, Friday after Friday—but she has now sparked the world's attention to the critical importance of protecting the planet. In fact, she was nominated for the 2019 Nobel Peace Prize. Ms. Thunberg speaks out forcefully, keeping the waters stirred, but she also calls on groups, committees, and governments to act. Certainly her dynamic presence on the world stage is making a difference, but she also makes a difference one on one, sometimes across great distances, in the life of someone she's never met.

A lesser-known climate activist is twenty-four-year-old Arshak Makichyan, who since March 2019 has been the solitary Fridays for Future protester holding his cardboard sign in Pushkin Square in central Moscow, trying to warn his people and the Russian government of the dangers of climate change. After three months of showing up on Fridays, Al Jazeera reported he had earned the nickname of "Moscow's lone climate protester."[4] Local police have questioned him several times, which, he admits, is scary; he also reports that he is encouraged when he receives messages of support. Al Jazeera relates that "he was especially happy to see Greta Thunberg, the Swedish teenager who has spearheaded global climate strike protests, tweeting about his Friday pickets."[5] More recently, the BBC concurred, stating "his inspiration is Swedish climate activist Greta Thunberg."[6] Makichyan started his protests after reading about climate change and hearing about Greta. As of October, he had been in the Square for thirty consecutive Fridays. Knowing that Greta started alone has given him prophetic strength to keep going back, Friday after Friday. He knows he is not alone.

We have seen the power of young people as ethical prophets before. Of course, an ethical prophet can be any age, living in any circumstance. But the witness of young people is particularly effective. When pictures circulated during the civil rights movement of young children facing fire hoses, being put in handcuffs, sitting at lunch counters, joining the protest marches, and filling local jails to overflowing, people knew the back of segregation was about to be broken. In more recent times, students who survived the mass shooting at Marjorie Stoneman Douglas High School in Parkland, Florida, created a public narrative around gun violence and gun control. These young people in such different settings share a steadfastness in the face of strong opposition, no matter what the cost. Although they might not use the language, their dedication bears similarities to having received a divine call. They are committed to speaking truth to power. And they all seem confident that what they are striving for will eventually come

---

4. Jonathan Brown, "Moscow's Lone Climate Protester: 'We Need to Talk about It Now,'" *Al Jazeera*, June 30, 2019.

5. Ibid.

6. Sarah Rainsford, "Climate Strikes: Why Russians Don't Get Greta's Message," *BBC*, October 4, 2019.

to fruition—what Burrow calls "a confident vision of hope." In other words, they show the characteristics of being ethical prophets.

Rufus Burrow Jr. has given us eight candidates for the ethical prophet hall of fame whose lives have helped shape who we are. We need to know their stories to understand better our own communal identity. When we learn about these ethical prophets, we appropriately rise to honor them. And the more we learn about them, the more we realize that despite the chronological distance, they are calling forth the ethical prophet in us. We hear them encouraging us to get bolder in our lives, or to admit we are not who we say we are. They also show us how God is involved in what goes on among us. God seriously loves each one of us and is participating in humanity's efforts to follow sacred purposes for the earth. The ethical prophets in this book tell us our endeavors matter. Our energy toward justice makes a difference; we are not alone. We have strong companions along the way—some of whom are twenty-eight hundred years old, others from the recent past, and still others right among us. We are interconnected, so we can all work together in light of the witness of these candidates for the ethical prophet hall of fame, and in companionship with them, so that the ethical prophets continue in us.

—Mary Alice Mulligan

Bibliography

Achebe, Chinua. *There Was a Country: A Personal History of Biafra*. New York: Penguin, 2012.
Ahlstrom, Sydney E. *A Religious History of the American People*. New Haven: Yale University Press, 1972.
Allen, Leslie C. *Jeremiah: A Commentary*. Louisville: Westminster John Knox, 2008.
Anderson, Bernhard W. *The Eighth Century Prophets: Amos, Hosea, Isaiah, Micah*. Philadelphia: Fortress, 1978.
———. *Understanding the Old Testament*. 4th ed. Englewood Cliffs, NJ: Prentice-Hall, 1986.
Anderson, Bernhard W., with the assistance of Steven Bishop. *Contours of Old Testament Theology*. Minneapolis: Fortress, 1999.
Andolsen, Barbara Hilkert. *"Daughters of Jefferson, Daughters of Bootblacks": Racism and American Feminism*. Macon, GA: Mercer University Press, 1986.
Aptheker, Herbert. "The Negro Woman." In *Herbert Aptheker on Race and Democracy*, edited by Eric Foner and Manning Marable, 121–27. Urbana: University of Illinois Press, 2006.
Baker-Fletcher, Karen. "Dusting Off the Texts: Historical Resources for Womanist Ethics." In *The Annual of the Society of Christian Ethics, 1994*, edited by Harlan Beckley, 291–98. Boston: Society of Christian Ethics, Boston University, 1994.
Baldwin, James. *The Amen Corner*. New York: Dial, 1968.
———. *Blues for Mister Charlie*. New York: Dell, 1964.
———. "The Creative Dilemma—'The War of an Artist with His Society Is a Lover's War.'" *The Saturday Review*, February 8, 1964, 14–15, 58.
———. *The Cross of Redemption: Uncollected Writings*. Edited with introduction by Randall Kenan. New York: Pantheon, 2010.
———. "Disturber of the Peace: James Baldwin." Interview by Eve Auchincloss and Nancy Lynch. In *The Black American Writer*, edited by C. W. E. Bigsby, 1:199–216. Deland, FL: Everett/Edwards, 1969.
———. *The Fire Next Time*. New York: Modern Library, 1995.

———. *Go Tell It on the Mountain*. New York: Dial, 1963.
———. *I Am Not Your Negro*. Compiled and edited by Raoul Peck. New York: Vintage, 2017.
———. *No Name in the Street*. New York: Dial, 1972.
———. *Nobody Knows My Name: More Notes of a Native Son*. New York: Dial, 1961.
———. *Notes of a Native Son*. Boston: Beacon, 1955.
———. *The Price of the Ticket: Collected Nonfiction, 1948-1985*. New York: St. Martin's/Marek, 1985.
———. *Tell Me How Long the Train's Been Gone*. New York: Dial, 1968.
Baldwin, Lewis V. "The Attuning of the Spirit: Martin Luther King Jr. and the Circle of Prayer." In *Revives My Soul Again: The Spirituality of Martin Luther King Jr.*, edited by Lewis V. Baldwin and Victor Anderson, 135-67. Minneapolis: Fortress, 2018.
———. *Behind the Public Veil: The Humanness of Martin Luther King Jr.* Minneapolis: Fortress, 2016.
———. "The Minister as Preacher, Pastor, and Prophet: The Thinking of Martin Luther King Jr." *American Baptist Quarterly* 7 (1988) 79-97.
———. *There Is a Balm in Gilead: The Cultural Roots of Martin Luther King Jr.* Minneapolis: Fortress, 1991.
———. *To Make the Wounded Whole: The Cultural Legacy of Martin Luther King Jr.* Minneapolis: Fortress, 1992.
Baldwin, Lewis V., and Amiri YaSin Al-Hadid. *Between Cross and Crescent: Christian and Muslim Perspectives on Malcolm and Martin*. Gainesville: University Press of Florida, 2002.
Baldwin, Lewis V., and Victor Anderson, eds. *Revives My Soul Again: The Spirituality of Martin Luther King Jr.* Minneapolis: Fortress, 2018.
Barnes, Gilbert H., and Dwight L. Dumond, eds. *Letters of Theodore Dwight Weld, Angelina Grimké and Sarah Grimké, 1822-1844*. 2 vols. Gloucester, MA: Peter Smith, 1965.
Barth, Karl. *Church Dogmatics*. 2/1: *The Doctrine of God*. Translated by T. H. L. Parker et al. Edited by. G. W. Bromiley and T. F. Torrance. Edinburgh: T&T Clark, 1985.
Bay, Mia. *To Tell the Truth Freely: The Life of Ida B. Wells*. New York: Hill & Wang, 2009.
Berry, Faith, ed. *From Bondage to Liberation: Writings by and about Afro-Americans from 1700 to 1918*. New York: Continuum, 2001.
Bertocci, Peter A., and Richard M. Millard. *Personality and the Good: Psychological and Ethical Perspectives*. New York: David McKay, 1963.
Bewer, Julius. *The Prophets in the King James Version*. New York: Harper, 1955.
Birch, Bruce C. *Let Justice Roll Down: The Old Testament, Ethics, and Christian Life*. Louisville: Westminster John Knox, 1991.
Birch, Bruce C., et al. *A Theological Introduction to the Old Testament*. Nashville: Abingdon, 1999.
Birney, Catherine H. *The Grimké Sisters: Sarah and Angelina Grimké; The First American Women Advocates of Abolition and Woman's Rights*. 1885. Reprint, Westport, CT: Greenwood, 1969.
Bowne, Borden P. *Personalism*. Boston: Houghton Mifflin, 1908.
Boydston, Jeanne, Mary Kelley, and Anne Margolis. *The Limits of Sisterhood: The Beecher Sisters on Women's Rights and Woman's Sphere*. Chapel Hill: University of North Carolina Press, 1988.
Bracke, John M. *Jeremiah 1-29*. Louisville: Westminster John Knox, 2000.

Branch, Taylor. *At Canaan's Edge: America in the King Years 1965-68*. New York: Simon & Schuster, 2006.
―――. *Parting the Waters: America in the King Years 1954-63*. New York: Simon & Schuster, 1988.
―――. *Pillar of Fire: America in the King Years 1963-65*. New York: Simon & Schuster, 1998.
Breitman, George, ed. *By Any Means Necessary: Speeches, Interviews and a Letter by Malcolm X*. New York: Pathfinder, 1980.
―――, ed. *Malcolm X Speaks: Selected Speeches and Statements*. New York: Pathfinder, 1965.
Bright, John. *A History of Israel*. Philadelphia: Westminster, 1959.
Brightman, Edgar S. *A Philosophy of Religion*. Englewood Cliffs, NJ: Prentice-Hall, 1940.
Brockman, James R. *Romero: A Life*. Maryknoll, NY: Orbis, 1989.
Brueggemann, Walter. *A Commentary on Jeremiah: Exile & Homecoming*. Grand Rapids: Eerdmans, 1998.
―――. *Disruptive Grace: Reflections on God, Scripture, and the Church*. Minneapolis: Fortress, 2011.
―――. *Like Fire in the Bones: Listening for the Prophetic Word in Jeremiah*. Minneapolis: Fortress, 2006.
―――. *The Practice of Prophetic Imagination: Preaching an Emancipating Word*. Minneapolis: Fortress, 2012.
―――. *The Prophetic Imagination*. Philadelphia: Fortress, 1978.
―――. *Theology of the Old Testament: Testimony, Dispute, Advocacy*. Minneapolis: Fortress, 1997.
Burrow, Rufus, Jr. *Extremist for Love: Martin Luther King Jr., Man of Ideas and Nonviolent Social Action*. Minneapolis: Fortress, 2014.
―――. *God and Human Dignity: The Personalism, Theology, and Ethics of Martin Luther King Jr*. Notre Dame: University of Notre Dame Press, 2006.
―――. "Malcolm X as Racist: The Great Myth." *The Western Journal of Black Studies* 20 (1996) 104-13.
―――. "Martin Luther King Jr., and Ethical Leadership." *Telos* 182 (2018) 11-18.
Bushkovitch, Mary. *The Grimkés of Charleston*. Greenville, SC: Southern Historical Press, 1992.
Byrd, Rudolph P., ed. *The World Has Changed: Conversations with Alice Walker*. New York: New Press, 2010.
Cagin, Seth, and Philip Dray. *We Are Not Afraid: The Story of Goodwin, Schwerner, and Chaney, and the Civil Rights Campaign for Mississippi*. New York: Nation Books, 2006.
Cannon, Katie G. *Black Womanist Ethics*. Atlanta: Scholars, 1988.
―――. "The Emergence of Black Feminist Consciousness." In *Katie's Canon: Womanism and the Soul of the Black Community*, 47-56. New York: Continuum, 1995. First published in *Feminist Interpretation of the Bible*, edited by Letty M. Russell, 30-40. Philadelphia: Westminster, 1985.
Carson, Clayborne, and Peter Holloran, eds. *A Knock at Midnight*. New York: Warner, 1998.
Carson, Clayborne, and Kris Shepard, eds. *A Call to Conscience: The Landmark Speeches of Dr. Martin Luther King Jr*. New York: Warner, 2001.

Carson, Clayborne, et al., eds. *The Papers of Martin Luther King, Jr.* 7 vols. Berkeley: University of California Press, 1992–2014.

Ceplair, Larry, ed. *The Public Years of Sarah and Angelina Grimké: Selected Writings, 1835–1839.* New York: Columbia University Press, 1989.

Champion, Ernest A. *Mr. Baldwin, I Presume: James Baldwin–Chinua Achebe, a Meeting of the Minds.* Lanham, MD: University Press of America, 1995.

Clark, Kenneth B. *The Negro Protest: James Baldwin, Malcolm X, and Martin Luther King Talk with Kenneth B. Clark.* Boston: Beacon, 1963.

Clark, Steve, ed. *February 1965: The Final Speeches.* New York: Pathfinder, 1992.

———, ed. *Malcolm X Talks to Young People: Speeches in the U.S., Britain, and Africa.* New York: Pathfinder, 1991.

Clarke, John Henrik, ed. *Malcolm X: The Man and His Times.* Trenton, NJ: Africa World, 1990.

Collier-Thomas, Bettye. *Daughters of Thunder: Black Women Preachers and Their Sermons, 1850–1979.* San Francisco: Jossey-Bass, 1998.

Cone, James H. *Malcolm & Martin & America: A Dream or a Nightmare?* Maryknoll, NY: Orbis, 1991.

———. *Risks of Faith: The Emergence of a Black Theology of Liberation, 1968–1998.* Boston: Beacon, 1999.

———. *Said I Wasn't Gonna Tell Nobody: The Making of a Black Theologian.* Maryknoll, NY: Orbis, 2018.

Cooper, Anna Julia. *A Voice from the South.* With an Introduction by Mary Helen Washington. 1892. Reprint, New York: Oxford University Press, 1988.

Craigie, Peter C., Page H. Kelley, and Joel F. Drinkard Jr. *Jeremiah 1–25.* Word Biblical Commentary 26. Dallas: Word, 1999.

Davis, Thadious M. "Walker's Celebration of Self in Southern Generations." In *Alice Walker,* edited by Harold Bloom, 25–37. New York: Chelsea House, 1989.

DeCosta-Willis, Miriam, ed. *The Memphis Diary of Ida B. Wells.* Boston: Beacon, 1995.

Demos, Raphael. *The Philosophy of Plato.* New York: Scribner's, 1939.

Dennis, Marie, Renny Golden, and Scott Wright. *Oscar Romero: Reflections on His Life and Writings.* Maryknoll, NY: Orbis, 2000.

Dorr, Rheta Childe. *Susan B. Anthony: The Woman Who Changed the Mind of a Nation.* New York: AMS, 1970.

Dorrien, Gary. *Social Ethics in the Making: Interpreting an American Tradition.* Malden, MA: Wiley-Blackwell, 2009.

Dostoyevsky, Fyodor. *The Brothers Karamazov.* Translated by Constance Garnett, with a new afterword by John Bayley. New York: Signet Classic, 1999.

Dresner, Samuel H., ed. *I Asked for Wonder: A Spiritual Anthology.* New York: Crossroad, 1992.

Duster, Alfreda M., ed. *Crusade for Justice: The Autobiography of Ida B. Wells.* Chicago: University of Chicago Press, 1970.

Eagleson, John, and Philip Scharper, eds. *Puebla and Beyond: Documentation and Commentary.* Translated by John Drury. Maryknoll, NY: Orbis, 1979.

Elliot, Jeffrey M., ed. *Conversations with Maya Angelou.* Jackson: University Press of Mississippi, 1989.

Epictetus. *The Teaching of Epictetus: Being the Encheiridion of Epictetus, with Selections from The Dissertations and Fragments.* Translated by T. W. Rolleston. Chicago: Donohue, 1881.

Epps, Archie, ed. *Malcolm X: Speeches at Harvard*. New York: Paragon House, 1991.
Erdozaín, Plácido. *Archbishop Romero: Martyr of Salvador*. Maryknoll, NY: Orbis, 1984.
Farmer, James, and Malcolm X. "Separation vs. Integration." Debate held at Cornell University, Ithaca, New York, March 7, 1962. *Dialogue* 2 (May 1962) 14–18.
Ferm, Deane William. *Third World Liberation Theologies: An Introductory Survey*. Maryknoll, NY: Orbis, 1986.
Forché, Carolyn. "Oscar Romero: Seed of Liberty/Sign of Hope." In *Martyrs: Contemporary Writers on Modern Lives of Faith*, edited by Susan Bergman, 56–78. San Francisco: HarperSanFrancisco, 1996.
Fretheim, Terence. *God and World in the Old Testament: A Relational Theology of Creation*. Nashville: Abingdon, 2005.
Friedman, Murray, with Peter Binzen. *What Went Wrong? The Creation and Collapse of the Black-Jewish Alliance*. New York: Free Press, 1995.
Gallen, David, ed. *Malcolm X: As They Knew Him*. New York: Carroll & Graf, 1992.
Garbus, Liz, dir. *What Happened, Miss Simone?* 2015. Netflix.
García, Samuel Ruiz. "Monsignor Oscar A. Romero: Martyr of the Option for the Poor." In *Monsignor Romero: A Bishop for the Third Millennium*, edited by Robert S. Pelton, Robert L. Ball, and Kyle Markham, 65–77. Notre Dame: University of Notre Dame Press, 2004.
Garrow, David J. *Bearing the Cross: Martin Luther King, Jr., and the Southern Christian Leadership Conference*. New York: William Morrow, 1986.
Gates, Henry Louis, ed. "Memoir of Old Elizabeth." In *Six Women's Slave Narratives*, with an Introduction by William L. Andrews, 1–19. New York: Oxford University Press, 1988.
Giddings, Paula J. *Ida: A Sword among Lions; Ida B. Wells and the Campaign against Lynching*. New York: Amistad, 2008.
Gilson, Étienne. *God and Philosophy*. New Haven: Yale University Press, 1944.
Ginzburg, Ralph. *100 Years of Lynchings: A Shocking Documentary of Race Violence in America*. New York: Lancer, 1962.
Goldman, Peter. *The Death and Life of Malcolm X*. New York: Harper, 1973.
Goldstein, Richard. "'Go the Way Your Blood Beats': An Interview with James Baldwin." In *James Baldwin: The Legacy*, edited by Quincy Troupe, 173–85. New York: Simon & Schuster, 1989.
Gossett, Thomas F. *Race: The History of an Idea in America*. Dallas: Southern Methodist University Press, 1963.
Greiser, David. "What Exactly Is Anabaptist-Mennonite Preaching? A Nod to the Ancestors." In *Anabaptist Preaching: A Conversation between Pulpit, Pew, and Bible*, edited by David B. Greiser and Michael A. King, 17–29. Telford, PA: Cascadia, 2003.
Grimké, Angelina E. "Appeal to the Christian Women of the South." In *The Public Years of Sarah and Angelina Grimké: Selected Writings, 1835–1839*, edited by Larry Ceplair, 36–79. New York: Columbia University Press, 1989.
———. "An Appeal to the Women of the Nominally Free States." In *Root of Bitterness: Documents of the Social History of American Women*, edited by Nancy F. Cott, 194–99. Boston: Northeastern University Press, 1986.
———. Letter XIII. In *The Public Years of Sarah and Angelina Grimké: Selected Writings, 1835–1839*, edited by Larry Ceplair, 199–204. New York: Columbia University Press, 1989.

———. Letter to Jane Smith. In *The Public Years of Sarah and Angelina Grimké: Selected Writings, 1835–1839*, edited by Larry Ceplair. New York: Columbia University Press, 1989.

———. *Letters to Catherine E. Beecher, in Reply to an Essay on Slavery and Abolitionism, Addressed to A. E. Grimké*. Boston: Isaac Knapp, 1838.

Grimké, Sarah. *Letters on the Equality of the Sexes and Other Essays*. Edited by Elizabeth Ann Bartlett. New Haven: Yale University Press, 1988.

Grimké, Sarah, and Angelina Grimké. *On Slavery and Abolitionism: Essays and Letters*. Introduction by Mark Perry. New York: Penguin, 2014.

Gurko, Miriam. *The Ladies of Seneca Falls: The Birth of the Woman's Rights Movement*. New York: Schocken, 1974.

Gutiérrez, Gustavo. "Liberation and the Poor: The Puebla Perspective." In *Third World Liberation Theologies: A Reader*, edited by Deane William Ferm, 22–63. Maryknoll, NY: Orbis, 1986.

———. *A Theology of Liberation: History, Politics, and Salvation*. Rev. ed. Maryknoll, NY: Orbis, 1988.

Hall, Jacquelyn Dowd. *Revolt against Chivalry: Jessie Daniel Ames and the Women's Campaign against Lynching*. Rev. ed. New York: Columbia University Press, 1993.

Hansberry, Lorraine. "A Challenge to Artists." In *Harlem U.S.A.*, edited with an introduction by John Henrik Clarke, 132–37. Berlin: Seven Seas, 1964.

———. *To Be Young, Gifted, and Black: Lorraine Hansberry in Her Own Words*. Adapted by Robert Nemiroff. New York: Signet, 1970.

Hardy, Clarence E. *James Baldwin's God: Sex, Hope, and Crisis in Black Holiness Culture*. Knoxville: University of Tennessee Press, 2003.

Hartshorne, Charles. *Omnipotence and Other Theological Mistakes*. Albany: State University of New York Press, 1984.

Heschel, Abraham J. *Abraham Joshua Heschel: Essential Writings*. Edited by Susannah Heschel. Maryknoll, NY: Orbis, 2011.

———. *God in Search of Man*. Foreword by Susannah Heschel. Northvale, NJ: Jason Aronson, 1987.

———. *Heavenly Torah as Refracted through the Generations*. Edited and translated by Gordon Tucker with Leonard Levin. New York: Continuum, 2007.

———. *In This Hour: Heschel's Writings in Nazi Germany and London Exile*. Edited and annotated by Helen Plotkin. Translated by Stephen Lehmann and Marion Faber. Lincoln: University of Nebraska Press and The Jewish Publication Society, 2019.

———. *The Insecurity of Freedom: Essays on Human Existence*. New York: Jewish Publication Society of America, 1966.

———. *Israel: An Echo of Eternity*. New York: Farrar, Straus & Giroux, 1967.

———. *Man Is Not Alone: A Philosophy of Religion*. New York: Farrar, Straus & Young, 1951.

———. *Moral Grandeur and Spiritual Audacity: Essays*. Edited by Susannah Heschel. New York: Farrar, Straus & Giroux, 1996.

———. "The Moral Outrage of Vietnam." In *Vietnam: Crisis of Conscience*, by Robert McAfee Brown, Abraham J. Heschel, and Michael Novak, 48–61. New York: Association Press, 1967.

———. *The Prophets*. New York: Harper & Row, 1962.

———. "The Religious Basis of Equality of Opportunity." In *Race: Challenge to Religion*, edited by Mathew Ahmann, 55–71. Chicago: Henry Regnery, 1963.

---. "Speech at the Ceremonies Commemorating the Centenary of the Emancipation Proclamation." *United Synagogue Review* 16 (1964) 14, 26–27.

---. "What We Might Do Together." *Religious Education* (March–April 1967) 133–40.

Heschel, Susannah. "Following in My Father's Footsteps: Selma 40 Years Later." *Vox of Dartmouth*, April 4, 2005, 1–3. http://www.dartmouth.edu/~vox/0405/0404/heschel.html.

---. "A Friendship in the Prophetic Tradition: Abraham Joshua Heschel and Martin Luther King Jr." *Telos* 182 (2018) 67–84.

---. "Heschel as *Mensch*: Testimony of His Daughter." In *To Grow in Wisdom: An Anthology of Abraham Joshua Heschel*, edited by Jacob Neusner with Noam M. M. Neusner, 195–211. New York: Madison, 1990.

---. "Introduction to the Perennial Classics Edition." In *The Prophets*, xiii–xx. New York: HarperCollins, 2001.

---. "Theological Affinities in the Writings of Abraham Joshua Heschel and Martin Luther King Jr." *Conservative Judaism* 50:2–3 (1998) 126–43. Reprinted in *Black Zion: African American Religious Encounters with Judaism*, edited by Yvonne Chireau and Nathaniel Deutsch, 168–86. New York: Oxford University Press, 2000.

---. "Two Friends, Two Prophets: Abraham Joshua Heschel and Martin Luther King Jr." *Plough Quarterly* 16 (Spring 2018). https://www.plough.com/en/topics/community/leadership/two-friends-two-prophets.

Höffding, Harald. *The Philosophy of Religion*. Translated by B. E. Meyer. New York: Macmillan, 1906.

James, William. *The Varieties of Religious Experience: A Study in Human Nature*. New York: Modern Library, 1936.

Jefferson, Thomas. *Autobiography of Thomas Jefferson*. In *The Life and Selected Writings of Thomas Jefferson*, edited by Adrienne Koch and William Peden, 3–114. New York: Modern Library, 1972.

---. *Notes on Virginia*. In *The Life and Selected Writings of Thomas Jefferson*, edited by Adrienne Koch and William Peden, 187–288. New York: Modern Library, 1972.

Jeyifo, Biodun. "Interview with Chinua Achebe." In *Conversations with Chinua Achebe*, edited by Bernth Lindfors, 110–23. Jackson: University Press of Mississippi, 1997.

Jones, W. T. *A History of Western Philosophy: The Classical Mind*. 2nd ed. New York: Harcourt Brace Jovanovich, 1970.

Jones, William Augustus. *God in the Ghetto*. Elgin, IL: Progressive Baptist, 1979.

Jordan, June. "Poem for South African Women." http://www.junejordan.net/poem-for-south-african-women.html.

Junker, Tercio B. *Prophetic Liturgy: Toward a Transforming Christian Praxis*. Eugene, OR: Pickwick, 2014.

Kaplan, Edward K. *Holiness in Words: Abraham Joshua Heschel's Poetics of Piety*. Albany: State University of New York Press, 1996.

---. *Spiritual Radical: Abraham Joshua Heschel in America, 1940–1972*. New Haven: Yale University Press, 2007.

Kaplan, Edward K., and Samuel H. Dresner. *Abraham Joshua Heschel: Prophetic Witness*. New Haven: Yale University Press, 1998.

Kaplan, Mordecai M. *The Meaning of God in Modern Jewish Religion*. New York: Behrman's Jewish Book House, 1937.

Karim, Benjamin, ed. *The End of White World Supremacy: Four Speeches by Malcolm X.* New York: Arcade, 1971.

Kasimow, Harold, and Byron L. Sherwin, eds. *No Religion Is an Island: Abraham Joshua Heschel and Interreligious Dialogue.* Maryknoll, NY: Orbis, 1991.

Kaufmann, Yehezkel. *The Religion of Israel: From Its Beginnings to the Babylonian Exile.* Translated and abridged by Moshe Greenberg. Chicago: University of Chicago Press, 1960.

Kent, Charles Foster. *The Kings and Prophets of Israel and Judah.* New York: Scribner's, 1909.

———. *The Social Teachings of the Prophets and Jesus.* New York: Scribner's, 1917.

Kent, Charles Foster, and Robert Seneca Smith. *The Work and Teachings of the Earlier Prophets.* New York: Young Men's Christian Association Press, 1911.

King, Martin Luther, Jr. "An Address at the Synagogue Council of America." December 5, 1965. King Center Library and Archives.

———. "An Address before a Dinner Sponsored by The Episcopal Society for Cultural and Racial Unity." Given at the 61st General Convention, St. Louis, Missouri, October 12, 1964. King Center Library and Archives.

———. *The Autobiography of Martin Luther King Jr.* Edited by Clayborne Carson. New York: Warner, 1998.

———. "Be Not Conformed to This World." Ebenezer Baptist Church, Atlanta, Georgia, January 16, 1966. King Center Library and Archives.

———. "Beyond Discovery, Love." Address at the International Convention of the Christian Church (Disciples of Christ), Dallas, Texas, September 25, 1966. King Center Library and Archives.

———. "A Challenge to the Churches and Synagogues." In *Race: Challenge to Religion*, edited by Mathew Ahmann, 155–69. Chicago: Henry Regnery, 1963.

———. "Conversation with Martin Luther King Jr." In *A Testament of Hope: The Essential Writings and Speeches of Martin Luther King Jr.*, edited by James M. Washington, 657–79. New York: Harper, 1991.

———. "Doubts and Certainties." Interview in London, possibly taped in February 1968. King Center Library and Archives.

———. Letter to Mr. Sam Wyler of San Pedro, CA. July 20, 1967. King Center Library and Archives.

———. Letter to Mrs. Betty Shabazz. February 26, 1965. King Center Library and Archives.

———. Letter to Rabbi Seymour J. Cohen of the Synagogue Council of America. December 28, 1965. King Center Library and Archives.

———. "The Meaning of Hope." Sermon given at Dexter Avenue Baptist Church, December 10, 1967. King Center Library and Archives.

———. "Press Conference, Biltmore Hotel." Los Angeles, April 12, 1967. King Center Library and Archives.

———. "Some Things We Must Do." President's Address, December 5, 1957. King Center Library and Archives.

———. "Statement on His Call to Ministry." August 7, 1959. King Center Library and Archives.

———. *Strength to Love.* New York: Harper, 1963.

———. *Stride Toward Freedom: The Montgomery Story.* New York: Harper, 1958.

———. "Transcript of Channel 2, KNXT-TV Los Angeles Program 'Newsmakers.'" July 10, 1965. King Center Library and Archives.

———. "To Charter Our Course for the Future." Speech given at SCLC staff retreat, Penn Center, Frogmore, South Carolina, May 22, 1967. King Center Library and Archives.

———. "Transforming a Neighborhood." National Association of Radio Announcers Convention, Atlanta, Georgia, August 11, 1967. King Center Library and Archives.

———. "True Dignity." King Center Library and Archives.

———. *Where Do We Go from Here: Chaos or Community?* Boston: Beacon, 1967.

———. "Who Are We?" Sermon given at Ebenezer Baptist Church, Atlanta, February 5, 1966. King Center Library and Archives.

———. *Why We Can't Wait.* New York: Harper, 1964.

King, Martin Luther, Sr., with Clayton Riley. *Daddy King: An Autobiography.* New York: William Morrow, 1980.

Kirkpatrick, A. F. *The Doctrine of the Prophets.* 2nd ed. 1897. Reprint, Grand Rapids: Zondervan, 1958.

Knudson, Albert C. *The Prophetic Movement in Israel.* New York: Methodist Book Concern, 1921.

Leeming, David. *James Baldwin: A Biography.* New York: Knopf, 1994.

Lerner, Gerda, ed. *The Feminist Thought of Sarah Grimké.* New York: Oxford University Press, 1998.

———. "The Grimké Sisters and the Struggle against Race Prejudice." In *The Feminist Thought of Sarah Grimké*, edited by Gerda Lerner, 158–74. New York: Oxford University Press, 1998.

———. *The Grimké Sisters from South Carolina: Rebels against Slavery.* Boston: Houghton Mifflin, 1967.

Lincoln, Abraham. "First Inaugural Address." In *Abraham Lincoln: His Speeches and Writings*, edited by Roy P. Basler, 579–88. Cleveland: World Publishing Group, 1946.

Lincoln, C. Eric. *The Black Muslims in America.* Boston: Beacon, 1961.

———. "The Meaning of Malcolm X." In *Malcolm X: The Man and His Times*, edited by John Henrik Clarke, 7–12. Trenton, NJ: Africa World, 1990.

Lindblom, Johannes. *Prophecy in Ancient Israel.* Philadelphia: Muhlenberg, 1962.

Litwack, Leon F. *Trouble in Mind: Black Southerners in the Age of Jim Crow.* New York: Knopf, 1998.

Logan, Rayford. *The Betrayal of the Negro.* New enl. ed. New York: Collier, 1965.

Lomax, Louis. *The Negro Revolt.* New York: Harper, 1962.

———. *When the Word Is Given: A Report on Elijah Muhammad, Malcolm X, and the Black Muslim World.* New York: New American Library, 1963.

Lumpkin, Katharine Du Pre. *The Emancipation of Angelina Grimké.* Chapel Hill: University of North Carolina Press, 1974.

Lundbom, Jack R. *Jeremiah 1–20.* Anchor Bible 21A. New York: Doubleday, 1999.

Malcolm X. *The Autobiography of Malcolm X.* As told to Alex Haley. New York: Ballantine, 1992.

———. "God's Judgment of White America." In *The End of White World Supremacy: Four Speeches by Malcolm X*, edited by Benjamin Karim, 121–48. New York: Arcade, 1971.

———. *Malcolm X on Afro-American History.* New York: Pathfinder, 1970.

———. "The *Playboy* Interview: Malcolm X Speaks with Alex Haley." In *Malcolm X: As They Knew Him*, edited David Gallen, 109–30. New York: Carroll & Graf, 1992.

———. "Racism: The Cancer That Is Destroying America." In *Malcolm X: The Man and His Times*, edited by John Henrik Clark, 302–6. Trenton, NJ: Africa World, 1990.

———. *Two Speeches by Malcolm X*. New York: Pathfinder, 1990.

———. "Whatever Is Necessary." In *Malcolm X: As They Knew Him*, edited by David Gallen, 179–87. New York: Carroll & Graf, 1992.

Manuel, Anne, ed. *El Salvador's Decade of Terror: Human Rights since the Assassination of Archbishop Romero*. New Haven: Yale University Press, 1991.

Marable, Manning. *Blackwater: Historical Studies in Race, Class Consciousness, and Revolution*. Dayton, OH: Black Praxis, 1981.

———. *How Capitalism Underdeveloped Black America*. Boston: South End, 1983.

———. "The Meaning of Racist Violence in Late Capitalism." In *How Capitalism Underdeveloped Black America*, 231–53. Boston: South End, 1983.

Mays, Benjamin E. "Brotherhood: A Moral Imperative." In *A Long Journey: Dr. Benjamin E. Mays Speaks on the Struggle for Social Justice in America*, edited by Freddie C. Colston, 113–17. Xlibris, 2011.

———. "Eulogy at the Funeral Services of Martin Luther King Jr." In *Born to Rebel: An Autobiography*, 357–60. New York: Scribner's, 1971.

———. "Martin Luther King Jr." In *A Long Journey: Dr. Benjamin E. Mays Speaks on the Struggle for Social Justice in America*, edited by Freddie C. Colston, 232–39. Xlibris, 2011.

Mbiti, John S. *African Religions and Philosophy*. 2nd ed. Ibadan, Nigeria: Heinemann, 1989.

McBride, Dwight A., ed. *James Baldwin Now*. New York: New York University Press, 1999.

McConnell, Francis J. *The Prophetic Ministry*. New York: Abingdon, 1930.

McMickle, Marvin A. *Where Have All the Prophets Gone? Reclaiming Prophetic Preaching in America*. Cleveland: Pilgrim, 2006.

McMillen, Sally G. *Seneca Falls and the Origins of the Women's Rights Movement*. New York: Oxford University Press, 2008.

McMurry, Linda O. *To Keep the Waters Troubled: The Life of Ida B. Wells*. New York: Oxford University Press, 1998.

McNeil, Jesse Jai. *The Preacher-Prophet in Mass Society*. Grand Rapids: Eerdmans, 1961.

Mead, Margaret, and James Baldwin. *A Rap on Race*. New York: J. B. Lippincott, 1971.

Meyer, Marshall T. *You Are My Witness: The Living Words of Rabbi Marshall T. Meyer*. Edited by Jane Isay. New York: St. Martin's, 2004.

Miller, Joshua L. "The Discovery of What It Means to Be a Witness: James Baldwin's Dialectics of Difference." In *James Baldwin Now*, edited by Dwight A. McBride, 331–59. New York: New York University Press, 1999.

Moss, Otis, Jr. "A Prophetic Witness in an Anti-Prophetic Age." In *Preaching with Sacred Fire: An Anthology of African American Sermons, 1750 to the Present*, edited by Martha Simmons and Frank A. Thomas, 777–82. New York: Norton, 2010.

Mueder, Walter G. *Moral Law in Christian Social Ethics*. Richmond: John Knox, 1966.

Mulligan, Mary Alice, and Rufus Burrow Jr. *Daring to Speak in God's Name: Ethical Prophecy in Ministry*. Cleveland: Pilgrim, 2002.

———. *Standing in the Margin: How Your Congregation Can Do Ministry with the Poor (and Perhaps Recover Its Soul in the Process)*. Cleveland: Pilgrim, 2004.

Myrdal, Gunnar. *An American Dilemma: The Negro Problem and Modern Democracy*. New York: Harper, 1944.
Neusner, Jacob, with Noam M. M. Neusner, eds. *To Grow in Wisdom: An Anthology of Abraham Joshua Heschel*. New York: Madison, 1990.
Niebuhr, Reinhold. *Leaves from the Notebook of a Tamed Cynic*. Chicago: Willett, Clark & Colby, 1929.
———. *Moral Man and Immoral Society*. New York: Scribner's, 1932.
Perry, Bruce, ed. *Malcolm X: The Last Speeches*. New York: Pathfinder, 1989.
Perry, Mark. *Lift Up Thy Voice: The Grimké Family's Journey from Slaveholders to Civil Rights Leaders*. New York: Viking, 2001.
Plato. *The Republic of Plato*. Translated by Francis M. Cornford. London: Oxford University Press, 1945.
Prévost, Jean-Pierre. *How to Read the Prophets*. New York: Continuum, 1998.
Purcell, William. *Martyrs of Our Time*. St. Louis: CBP, 1983.
Quarles, Benjamin. *Black Abolitionists*. New York: Da Capo, 1991.
Rad, Gerhard von. *The Message of the Prophets*. Translated by D. M. G. Stalker. New York: Harper & Row, 1967.
———. *Old Testament Theology*. Vol. 2, *The Theology of Israel's Prophetic Traditions*. Translated by D. M. G. Stalker. New York: Harper, 1965.
Raines, Howell, ed. *My Soul Is Rested: Movement Days in the Deep South Remembered*. New York: Putnam's, 1977.
Randall-Tsuruta, Dorothy. "In Dialogue to Define Aesthetics: James Baldwin and Chinua Achebe." In *Conversations with James Baldwin*, edited by Fred L. Standley and Louis H. Pratt, 210–21. Jackson: University Press of Mississippi, 1989.
Rauschenbusch, Walter. *Christianity and the Social Crisis in the 21st Century: The Classic That Woke Up the Church*. New York: HarperOne, 2007.
———. *Christianizing the Social Order*. New York: Macmillan, 1926.
———. *A Theology for the Social Gospel*. New York: Macmillan, 1917.
Riggs, Marcia Y., ed. *Can I Get a Witness? Prophetic Religious Voices of African American Women*. Maryknoll, NY: Orbis, 1997.
Romero, Óscar. "The Church and Human Liberation." In *Romero: Martyr for Liberation*, by Jon Sobrino, 1–32. London: Catholic Institute for International Relations, 1982.
———. *A Shepherd's Diary*. Translated by Irene B. Hodgson. Cincinnati: St. Anthony Messenger Press, 1993.
———. *The Violence of Love*. Compiled and translated by James R. Brockman. New York: Harper, 1988.
———. *Voice of the Voiceless: The Four Pastoral Letters and Other Statements*. Translated by Michael J. Walsh. Maryknoll, NY: Orbis, 1985.
Rothschild, Fritz A., ed. *Between God and Man: An Interpretation of Judaism, from the Writings of Abraham J. Heschel*. New York: Harper, 1959.
Royster, Jacqueline Jones, ed. *Southern Horrors and Other Writings: The Anti-Lynching Campaign of Ida B. Wells, 1892–1900*. Boston: Bedford, 1997.
Sartre, Jean-Paul. *The Age of Reason*. Translated by Eric Sutton. New York: Bantam, 1968.
———. *The Devil and the Good Lord*. In *The Devil and the Good Lord and Two Other Plays*, 3–149. Translated by Kitty Black. New York: Vintage, 1960.
———. "Existentialism." In *Existentialism and Human Emotions*, 9–51. New York: Philosophical Library, 1957.

———. *The Flies*. In *No Exit and Three Other Plays*, 49–127. New York: Vintage, 1955.
Schechter, Patricia A. *Ida B. Wells-Barnett and American Reform, 1880–1930*. Chapel Hill: University of North Carolina Press, 2001.
Schleiermacher, Friedrich. *The Christian Faith*. Edited by H. R. Mackintosh and J. S. Stewart. Edinburgh: T&T Clark, 1948.
Simán, José Jorge. "The Impact of Monsignor Romero on the Churches of El Salvador and the United States." Working Paper of the Latin American Program of the Woodrow Wilson International Center for Scholars. Washington, DC: Wilson Center, 1983.
Skinner, John. *Prophecy and Religion: Studies in the Life of Jeremiah*. Cambridge: Cambridge University Press, 1955.
Snaith, Norman. *The Distinctive Ideas of the Old Testament*. London: Epworth, 1944.
Sobrino, Jon. *Archbishop Romero: Memories and Reflections*. Maryknoll, NY: Orbis, 1990.
———. "Archbishop Romero: Requirement, Judgment and Good News." In *Witnesses to the Kingdom: The Martyrs of El Salvador and the Crucified Peoples*, 179–94. Maryknoll, NY: Orbis, 2003.
———. "Archbishop Romero: Some Personal Recollections." In *Witnesses to the Kingdom: The Martyrs of El Salvador and the Crucified Peoples*, 11–53. Maryknoll, NY: Orbis, 2003.
———. "Monseñor Romero, a Salvadoran and a Christian." In *Witnesses to the Kingdom: The Martyrs of El Salvador and the Crucified Peoples*, 167–78. Maryknoll, NY: Orbis, 2003.
Spender, Dale. *Women of Ideas and What Men Have Done to Them: From Aphra Behn to Adrienne Rich*. London: Ark, 1983.
Spurgeon, C. H. "The Call to the Ministry." In *Lectures to My Students*, 18–39. Lynchburg, VA: Old-Time Gospel Hour, 1894.
Standley, Fred L., and Louis H. Pratt, eds. *Conversations with James Baldwin*. Jackson: University Press of Mississippi, 1989.
Sterling, Dorothy. "Afterword." In *The Memphis Diary of Ida B. Wells*, edited by Miriam Decosta-Willis, 191–99. Boston: Beacon, 1995.
Stinespring, William F. "A Problem of Theological Ethics in Hosea." In *Essays in Old Testament Ethics*, edited by James L. Crenshaw and John T. Willis, 131–44. New York: KTAV, 1974.
Stitskin, Leon D. *Jewish Philosophy: A Study in Personalism*. Brooklyn: Yeshiva University Press, 1976.
Strahan, James. *God in History*. London: James Clarke, 1925.
Swedish, Margaret. *Archbishop Oscar Arnulfo Romero: Prophet to the Americas*. Washington, DC: Religious Taskforce on Central America, 1995.
Sylvander, Carolyn Wedin. *James Baldwin*. New York: Ungar, 1980.
Terrell, Mary Church. "The Fundamental Cause of Lynching Is Racism." In *African Americans: Opposing Viewpoints*, edited by William Dudley, 119–32. San Diego: Greenhaven, 1997.
Thompson, J. A. *The Book of Jeremiah*. Grand Rapids: Eerdmans, 1980.
Thurman, Howard. *Jesus and the Disinherited*. Boston: Beacon, 1976.
Todras, Ellen H. *Angelina Grimké: Voice of Abolition*. North Haven, CT: Linnet, 1999.
Tolnay, Stewart E., and E. M. Beck. *A Festival of Violence: An Analysis of Southern Lynchings, 1882–1930*. Urbana: University of Illinois Press, 1995.

Townes, Emilie M. *Womanist Justice, Womanist Hope*. Atlanta: Scholars, 1993.
Trimiew, Darryl M. *Voices of the Silenced: The Responsible Self in a Marginalized Community*. Cleveland: Pilgrim, 1993.
Tsanoff, Radoslav A. *The Great Philosophers*. 2nd ed. New York: Harper, 1964.
———. *The Moral Ideals of Our Civilization*. New York: Dutton, 1942.
Turner, Richard Brent. *Islam in the African-American Experience*. Bloomington: Indiana University Press, 1997.
Tutu, Desmond. *God Has a Dream: A Vision of Hope for Our Time*. New York: Doubleday, 2004.
Vigil, María López. *Death and Life in Morazán: A Priest's Testimony from a War-Zone in El Salvador*. London: Catholic Institute for International Relations, 1989.
———. *Oscar Romero: Memories in Mosaic*. London: CAFOD, 2000.
Vollmer, August. *The Police and Modern Society*. 1936. Reprint, Montclair, NJ: Patterson Smith, 1971.
Walker, Alice. *Anything We Love Can Be Saved: A Writer's Activism*. New York: Random House, 1997.
———. *The Color Purple*. New York: Harcourt, 1992.
———. "Coming Apart." In *Take Back the Night: Women on Pornography*, edited by Laura Lederer, 95–104. New York: Morrow, 1980.
———. *In Search of Our Mothers' Gardens*. New York: Harcourt Brace Jovanovich, 1983.
———. *Living by the Word*. New York: Harcourt Brace Jovanovich, 1988.
———. *The Same River Twice: Honoring the Difficult*. New York: Scribner's, 1996.
———. *We Are the Ones We Have Been Waiting For: Inner Light in a Time of Darkness*. New York: New Press, 2006.
———. *You Can't Keep a Good Woman Down: Stories*. New York: Harcourt Brace Jovanovich, 1981.
Walker, Alice, and Prathbha Parmar. *Warrior Marks: Female Genital Mutilation and the Sexual Blinding of Women*. New York: Harcourt Brace, 1993.
Ward, James M. *The Prophets*. Nashville: Abingdon, 1982.
———. *Thus Says the Lord: The Message of the Prophets*. Nashville: Abingdon, 1991.
Weatherby, William J. *James Baldwin: Artist on Fire; A Portrait*. New York: D. I. Fine, 1989.
Weems, Renita J. *Battered Love: Marriage, Sex, and Violence in the Hebrew Prophets*. Minneapolis: Fortress, 1995.
Weld, Theodore D. *American Slavery as It Is: Testimony of a Thousand Witnesses*. New York: American Anti-Slavery Society, 1839.
———. *In Memory: Angelina Grimké Weld*. 1880. Reprint, Memphis: General Books, 2010.
Wells, Ida B. *A Red Record: Lynchings in the United States, 1892–1893–1894*. In *Southern Horrors and Other Writings: The Anti-Lynching Campaign of Ida B. Wells, 1892–1900*, edited with introduction by Jacqueline Jones Royster, 73–157. Boston: Bedford, 1997.
Wells-Barnett, Ida B. "Lynching, Our National Crime." In *Can I Get a Witness? Prophetic Religious Voices of African American Women*, edited by Marcia Y. Riggs, 146–50. Maryknoll, NY: Orbis, 1997.

———. "The Requisites of True Leadership." In *Can I Get a Witness? Prophetic Religious Voices of African American Women*, edited by Marcia Y. Riggs, 62–67. Maryknoll, NY: Orbis, 1997.

West, Cornel. Foreword to *Said I Wasn't Gonna Tell Nobody: The Making of a Black Theologian*, by James H. Cone, ix–xiii. Maryknoll, NY: Orbis, 2018.

———. "On Prophetic Pragmatism." In *The Cornel West Reader*, 149–73. New York: Basic Civitas, 1999.

West, Hollie I. "James Baldwin: No Gain for Race Relations." In *Conversations with James Baldwin*, edited by Fred L. Standley and Louis H. Pratt, 172–76. Jackson: University Press of Mississippi, 1989.

Westermann, Claus. *What Does the Old Testament Say about God?* Edited by Friedemann W. Golka. Atlanta: John Knox, 1979.

White, Evelyn C. *Alice Walker: A Life*. New York: Norton, 2004.

White, Walter. *Rope and Faggot: A Biography of Judge Lynch*. New York: Arno, 1969.

Wilbanks, Charles, ed. *Walking by Faith: The Diary of Angelina Grimké*. Columbia: University of South Carolina Press, 2003.

Wilmore, Gayraud. *Black Religion and Black Radicalism: An Interpretation of the Religious History of African Americans*. 3rd ed., rev. and enl. Maryknoll, NY: Orbis, 1998.

Woodson, Carter G., ed. *The Works of Francis J. Grimké*. Vol. 4. Washington, DC: Associated Publishers, 1942.

Wright, William K. *A Student's Philosophy of Religion*. Rev. ed. New York: Macmillan, 1935.

Young, Andrew. *An Easy Burden: The Civil Rights Movement and the Transformation of America*. New York: HarperCollins, 1996.

Zimmerli, Walther. *Old Testament Theology in Outline*. Edinburgh: T&T Clark, 1994.

Zollars, Ely Vaughan. *Hebrew Prophecy*. Cincinnati: Standard Publishing, 1907.

Index

A

Abraham Joshua Heschel: Essential Writings, 29
Achebe, Chinua, 117, 131
"Address at the Synagogue Council of America," 164–65
"Address to the Free Colored People," 68
African Religions and Philosophy, 4n8
Afrika, 4n8
agnostic, x
Ali, Carol Watkins, 217
Allende, Isabel, 224
A.M.E. Church, 93, 94, 98
American Colonization Society, 58, 60
"American Dream and the American Negro, The," 119
American Jewish community, 31
Ames, Jessie Daniel, 102
Amos, 2, 4, 8, 9, 34, 38, 48, 75, 130, 162, 184, 191, 237
Anderson, Bernhard, 9, 49
Andolsen, Barbara, 57, 60
Angelou, Maya, 182
anthropotropism, 14, 15
anti-lynching crusader, 85–88
anti-Semitism, ix, 17, 23, 35, 115, 174, 216

Appeal to the Christian Women of the South, 56, 66, 70, 71
Appeal to the Women of the Nominally Free States, An, 59
Arch Street Meeting, 62, 64, 78
Aristotle, 10, 11
artist as prophet, 115–18
Arkansas Race Riot, The, 99
Arlington National Cemetary, 161
artist, 114–15, 231
Association of Southern Women for the Prevention of Lynching, 102
atheist, x
Audubon Ballroom, 156
authoritarian regimes, ix
axiogenesis, 167
axiosoteria, 167

B

Baker-Fletcher, Karen, 217, 218n13, 219
Baldwin, David, 108
Baldwin, Emma Berdis, 108
Baldwin, James A., ix, xiv, 18, 20, 26, 37, 106, ch. 4, 146, 183, 213, 215, 217, 220, 223, 231, 233, 234
Baldwin, Lewis V., xvi, 163
Barraza, Salvador, 198

Barth, Karl, 37
Basset, William, 64
Bathsheba, 36
Bea, Cardinal Augustin, 23
Beckwith, Byron de la, 231
Beecher, Catherine, 59, 65
beloved community, 49, 181, 234
Bertocci, Peter A., 183
Berton, Pierre, 150
"better angels," 232
Birch, Bruce, xiv
Birney, Catherine, 55
Black Consciousness Movement, 4n8
"Black Muslims," 139
Black Muslims in America, The, 137
Black Scholar, 118
Bland, Sandra, 121
"bloody Sunday," 24, 34
Blues for Mr. Charlie, 113, 116
Bolen, Jean Shinoda, 224
Bowling Green University, 111
Boston University, 160, 166, 183, 184
Bracha, Sarah, 31
Branch, Taylor, 33n30, 159n1
Brightman, Edgar S., 166
Bring, Ellen, 55
Brothers Karamazov, The, 114
Brown, John, 143, 145
Brown, Michael, 86
Brown, Robert McAfee, xiv
Brueggemann, Walter, 41, 182, 237
burden of prophecy, 157, 205
Burrow, Fannie B., xvi
Burrow, Rufus Jr., 159n1, 240, 241, 242, 244
Bushkovitch, Mary, 77
Butler-Baker High School, 216

C

Camus, Albert, 221
Can I Get a Witness, 126
Cannon, Katie G., 217
Chaney, James, 180, 180n82
"charitable Christian hatred," 231
Charlestown State Prison, 140
Chase Manhattan Bank, 231
Chesapeake and Ohio Railroad Company, 94
Chicago Defender, 99
Christian Church, 94
Christian Church (Disciples of Christ), xv
Christian Theological Seminary, xiii, xiv, xv, 16
Christianizing the Social Order, 5
Cicero, 10 11
Clark, Jim (Sheriff), 231
Clements, George, 161
Clergy Concerned about Vietnam, 24
clitoridectomy, 232
Cohen, Seymour (Rabbi), 174
Coleman, Monica, 217
Color Purple, The, 215, 235
Columbia University, 32, 89
Colyar, A. S., 96
"Coming Apart," 218
Commission on Interracial Cooperation (CIC), 102
communal voice of prophecy, 105
"compassionate wrathfulness," 231
Concord Prison, 141
Cone, James H., xiv, 138, 139, 150, 231
Conference on Race, 24, 33, 34, 161
Congress, 85, 163, 17785, 163, 177
congressional republicans, 13, 90, 117, 182
Cooper, Anna Julia, xiv
Cooper, Jane, 216
Cornell University, 146
courage, 166, 182–84
"Creative Dilemma, The," 117
Crónica del Pueblo, La, 206
Crozer Theological Seminary, 160, 166
Curry, Izola, 178, 179
"curse prayer," 229

D

David, 36
Daily Commercial, 89
Daring to Speak in God's Name, xv, 1, 23n1
Dartmouth College, xv, 26

INDEX

Davis, Frank (Sheriff), 91
Day, Dorothy, xiv
Demos, Raphael, 10
"Detroit Red," 137
Deutero-Isaiah, 43
DeWolf, L. Harold, 166, 167, 184
Dexter Avenue Baptist Church, 160, 166, 169, 171, 176, 178
dialectic of divine judgment, 47–49
dialectic of seduction, 40
Díaz, Nidia, 188
Dickinson, Richard D. N., xiii, xiv
dignity, xi, 14, 28–29, 46, 65, 84, 120. 136, 148, 149, 171, 172, 181, 194, 229
Distinctive Ideas of the Old Testament, The, 1, 23n1
"The Drum Major Instinct," 178
divine pathos, x, xiii, 7, 25, 36–37
Divine Providence Cancer Hospital, The, 211
Douglas, Kelly Delaine Brown, 217
Douglass, Frederick, 88, 98
Douglass, Grace, 58, 64
Douglass, Sarah M., 58, 60, 64, 68, 70
Dow Jones, 231
Drew University Theological School, xvi
DuBois, W. E. B., 141, 243
Duke, J. C., 89

E

Ebenezer Baptist Church, 159, 171, 178
Edelman, Marian Wright, 216
Elaw, Zilpha, 2
El-Hajj Malik El-Shabazz. *See* Shabazz, el-Hajj Malik; Malcolm X.
Eli Black Professor (Dartmouth College), xv, 26
Elman, Richard, 154
Independiente, El, 211
Elizabethtown College, xvi
Emancipation Proclamation, 18, 173
Emanuel A.M.E. Church, 121
Epictetus, 10, 11, 150
Epicurus, 10, 150
Episcopalian Church, 56, 94

Esther, 71
ethical leadership, 182
ethical prophecy, xiv, 1, 27
ethics of maladjustment, 2, 169, 179
European Jews, 31
Evans, Jonathan, 78
Evers, Medgar, 132, 231
"everydayness of life," 7, 26, 32
Experiment in International Living, 216
Extremist for Love, 159n1
Ezekiel, 44, 138

F

Fard, Wallace D., 146
Farmer, James, 146
Father Zosima, 114
feminist, 216, 226
"Fifth Avenue, Uptown," 122
Fire Next Time, The, 129
Flies, The, 194
Forché, Carolyn, 190
Forten, Sarah, 68
Francis (Pope), 187
Free Speech, The, 98
Freedom Caucus, 163
Freedom Summer, 180
"Frog" James, 91

G

Gandhi, Mohandas K., 175–76
Garrett-Evangelical Theological Seminary, xvi
Garrison, William Lloyd, 62, 65, 76
Garvey, Marcus, 18, 139
Gendler, Everett, 35
General Motors, 231
Giddings, Paula, 93
Ginsburg, Ralph, 86
God and Human Responsibility, xvi
God in Search of Man, 14n33, 29
"God intoxicated man," 112
God of pathos, 114
Goebbels, Joseph, 207
Goldman, Peter, 138
Goodman, Andrew, 180, 180n82

Go Tell It on the Mountain, 112, 127, 134
Grande, Rutilio, 189, 190, 198, 208
Grant, Jacquelyn, 217
Gray, Freddie, 121
Grimké, Angelina E., ix, xiv, 2, 17, 18, 37, ch. 2, 183
Grimké, Archibald H., 77, 80, 88
Grimké, Francis J., 77, 80, 88
Grimké, Henry, 77
Grimké, John, 77
Grimké, John Faucheraud, 56
Grimké, Mary Smith, 56
Grimké, Sarah, xiv, 17, ch. 2
Guzmán, Martina, 203

H

hajj, 144
Haley, Alex, 154
Hall, John, 134
Hamer, Fannie Lou, xiv
Hananiah, 154
Handler, M. S., 119
Hansberry, Lorraine, 116, 117
Harding, Vincent, 16, 161n8
Hardy, Clarence, 134
Harkin, Tom (congressman), 196
Harper's Ferry, 145
Harrell, Gara Mae, xvi
hate, 140, 231, 235
Hayes, Diana, 217
hazak, 40
Hebrew Union College, 31
"Here Be Dragons," 123
Heschel, Abraham J., x, xiii, xiv, xv, 2, 6, 7, 11, 12, 15, 16, ch. 1, 43, 75, 76, 104, 150, 151, 157, 160, 161, 164, 165, 167, 172, 174, 175, 183, 186, 191, 214, 233
"Heschel and King," 33–36
Heschel, Gittel, 31
Heschel, Jacob, 31
Heschel, Moshe Mordecai, 30
Heschel, Rivka Reizl, 30
Heschel, Susannah, xv, xvi, 16, 25, 26, 29, 31, 32, 34, 35, 44
Heschel, Sylvia, 32

Hebrew Union College, 31
Hitler, Adolph, 27, 173, 207
Holmes, John Haynes, 174
"Homeboy," 137
Hosea, 8, 9, 38, 40, 45, 48, 49, 237
"hope-telling," 182
Houston Astrodome, 228
Huldah, 71
Humboldt University, 30
humor, 198
Hurston, Zora Neale, 229

I

image of God, 45, 173
indifference to evil, 27
"Indifferent One," 150
"In Search of a Majority," 114
In Search of Our Mothers' Gardens, 229
Irenaeus, Saint, 193
Isaiah, 8, 38, 162, 191
Isasi-Díaz, Ada María, xiv
Islam, 135, 147

J

Jackson, Jesse, 161
Jefferson, Thomas, 74
Jeremiah, 8, 9, 12, 38, 40, 43, 48, 59, 75, 127, 130, 131, 133, 147, 154, 180, 184, 191, 205
Jewish Theological Seminary, 23, 32, 33n30, 161
Jews, x, 27, 35
"Joanna of Arc," 105
Jones, William Augustus, 204
Junker, Debora B. A., xvi
justified anger, 232

K

Kaplan, Edward, 16, 33, 161n8
Kaplún, Mario, 203
Kavanaugh, Bret, 163
Kennedy, John F., 142
Kennedy, Robert, 130

Kent, Charles Foster, 39, 61, 102
King, Coretta Scott, 235
King, Martin Luther Jr., ix, xiv, xv, 2, 6, 8, 13, 15, 16, 19, 24, 25, 33n30, 37, 38, 43, 132, 156, 157, ch. 6, 183, 197, 198, 211, 213, 233
and the prophets, 164–66
King, Michael Jr., 159
King, Michael Sr., 159n1
King, Rodney, 86
Kirk-Duggan, Cheryl, 217
Knight, Timothy A., xvi
Knudson, Albert C., 36n45

L

Lady's Anti-Slavery Society, 69
Lawson, James, 161n8
Lederer, Laura, 218
Lee, Spike, 138
Leeming, David, 108
Lemus, Nelson Rutilio, 189
Lerner, Gerda, 58
Lester, Julius, 121
Let Justice Roll Down, xiv
Levanthal, Melvyn, 216
liberation theology, 3
Liberator, The, 62
Lincoln, Abraham, 18, 174, 232
Lincoln, C. Eric, 137, 138, 139, 152
Lincoln University (Pennsylvania), 77, 78
Little, Earl, 139
Little, Ella, 140
Little, Hilda, 142
Little, Louise, 139
Little, Philbert, 141
Little, Reginald, 142
Little, Wilfred, 142
Litwick, Leon, 87
Lomax, Louis, 152
Long, Michael G., xvi
Luther, Martin, 169
lynching, 84, 85–92, 228

M

Makichyan, Arshak, 245
Malachi, 46
Malcolm X, ix, xiv, 18, 19, 37, 50, 97, 132, 135, ch. 5, 173, 183, 197, 211, 213, 233, 243
March on Washington, 216
Marable, Manning, 89
Marjorie Stoneman Douglas High School, 245
Martin, Travon, 86
Martin University, xvi
Mays, Benjamin E., 45, 161, 162, 172, 178
Mbiti, John, 4n8
McConnell, Francis J., 105
McDowell, Calvin, 85
McMickle, Marvin, xiv, 43
McMurry, Linda O., 106
Mead, Margaret, 108, 115
Mecca, 19, 136, 137, 143, 144, 145, 152
Medellín, 201
Memphis Diary of Ida B. Wells, The, 94
Memphis Free Press, 90
Menchú, Rigoberta, xiv
Meridian, 226
Meyer, Marshall T., (Rabbi) 183
Micah, 8, 9, 20, 38, 92, 103, 147, 162, 173, 191
Miriam, 71
Moody, Dwight L., 90, 101
Moral Grandeur and Spiritual Audacity, 29
Mordecai, 71
Mordecai, Moshe, 30
Morehouse College, 160, 161
Morgan, Juliette Hampton, 243
Morgenstern, Julian, 31
Morrison, Toni, 117, 217
Moses, 15, 33, 70
Moss, Otis Jr., ix, 7–8
Moss, Thomas, 85, 88, 97
Muhammad, Elijah, 18, 19, 137, 142, 143, 147, 152, 154, 156
Mulligan, Mary Alice, xv, 1, 2, 23n1
Muslim, x, 135, 144
Muslim Mosque, Inc., 143

N

NAACP, 103, 216
nabi, 8
nabu, 8
Nathan, 36
National Conference of Colored Women, 104
National Enquirer, 61
National Rifle Association, 177
National Anti-Slavery Standard, 77
National University, 188
National Women's Christian Temperance Union, 91
Nation of Islam, 19, 137, 141, 142, 143, 157
Negro History, 141
neo-Nazi groups, ix
New England Conservatory of Music, 160
New Jerusalem, 111, 125, 127, 129, 132–34, 234
Newsweek, 138
New York Times, 85, 119
Niebuhr, Reinhold, 38, 90
Nietzsche, Friedrich, 221
Nixon, Richard, 115
No Name in the Street, 131
Norfolk Prison Colony, 141–42
Núñez, María Otilia, 205

O

Old Bathsheba, 128
"Old" Elizabeth, 93
Once, 216
"One Child of One's Own," 226
"Only Justice Can Stop a Curse," 227
Organization of Afro-American Unity, 143, 145
Ortiz, Noemí, 199
Ostroski (teacher), 139
Oxford University, 149

P

Parker, Margaret, 63

Parker, Theodore, 174
Parks, Rosa, 160
"Pastoral Letter of the General Association," 60
patah, 40
Pennsylvania Hall, 68, 72, 73
Pepper, William, 170
Perkins, John, 234
Perry, Mark, 77
Personalism, 166, 166n27
persons-in-community, 4
persons-in-relationship, 4
persuasive love, 41
Pharaoh, 33, 59
Pinto, Jorge, 211
Pinto, Sara Meardi, 211
Plato, 10, 11
Playboy interview (Malcolm X), 154
poet, 114–15
police, 225, 227, 228–29
Ponseele, Rogelio, 188, 189, 198, 199
post-Mecca Malcolm, 137, 142, 145, 147, 149, 155, 157
pre-Mecca Malcolm, 137, 142, 152, 155
Presbyterian Church, 56, 59, 94
"profiles in courage," 13
Prophētēs, 8
Prophetic and Ethical Witness of the Church (seminary course), xiii, xiv, xv, 16
prophetic drama, x
prophetic pragmatism, 192
Prophetie, Die, 30
The Prophets, x, xiii, xiv, 16, 28, 29, 32
Proudhammer, Leo, 113
Puah, 71
Puebla Conference (1979), 197

Q

Quakers, 56, 62, 69, 78, 79
"Quincho Barrilete," 199

R

racism, ix, 17, 33, 115, 216
Rad, Gerhard von, 39, 47

Rauschenbusch, Walter, 5–7
Reconstruction, 86
"Religious Teachings of the Old Testament," 184
Remote One, 37
Republic, 10
"Revolutionary Petunias," 219
Rich, Judith, 182
Riggs, Marcia, 126, 217
Ring, Harry, 148
Rivera, Ernestina, 203
Riverside Church, 24, 161
Romero, Óscar A., ix, xiv, 2.19, 37, 184, 185, ch. 7
Roof, Dylann, 121
Rope and Faggot, 87
Ross, Rosetta, xvi
Rubinstein, Arthur, 32
Rukeyser, Muriel, 216
Rustin, Bayard, 16, 161n8

S

sacredness of persons, xi, 3, 14, 19, 20, 45, 46, 51, 67, 92, 96–97, 112, 120–24, 145, 148, 166, 171, 173, 195, 221–24, 232
"Saint Malcolm," 138
Sammy Lou, 219
Sarah Lawrence College, 216
Sarita, Doña, 212
Sartre, Jean Paul, 57, 111, 194
"Satan," 137, 141
Saul of Tarsus, 39, 168
Schleiermacher, Friedrich, 15
"School Strike for Climate," 244
Schwerner, Michael, 180, 180n82
Scott, Coretta, 160
Second Vatican Council, 23
Selma, Alabama, 24, 34, 35, 159, 231
sense of humor, 163
Sermon on the Mount, 201
Shabazz, Betty, 156
Shabazz, el-Hajj Malik, 137.
Shamanic Navigation (CD), 234
Shepherd's Diary, A, 189
"shero," ix, 81, 81n2

Shiphrah, 71
Shockley, William, 230
Shorty, 140
Simone, Nina, 115
Simons, Menno, 2
Sizemore, Barbara, 225
Slayton Lyceum Bureau, 92
Smith, Jane, 62, 63, 69
Snaith, Norman, 1, 23n1
Sobrino, Jon, 190, 200
Social Gospel Movement, 5
Soloranzo, Manuel, 189
"Some Things We Must Do," 184
Sophia, 142
Smith, Robert Seneca, 39, 61
Souls of Black Folk, The, 141
Spelman College, xvi, 216
Spinoza, 112
Spock, Benjamin, 170
Spurgeon, C. H., 38
Standing in the Margins, xv, 2
Stern, Carl, 32
St. John the Divine (cathedral), 115
Steuermann, Edward, 32
Stewart, Henry, 85
Stewart, Maria W., 2
Stitskin, Leon D., 166n27
Straus, Sylvia, 32
Student Nonviolent Coordinating Committee (SNCC), 216
Swa people, 234
sweeping allegation, 49–50, 100–102, 145, 150–53
sweeping exaggeration, 50
sweeping generalization, 49, 51, 110
Synagogue Council of America, 164, 174

T

Take Back the Night, 218
Tate, Claudia, 182
Tell Me How Long the Train's Been Gone, 113
Tennessee Supreme Court, 94
theotropism, 15
Third Life of Grange Copeland, The, 226

INDEX

Thomas, Norman, 170
Thunberg, Greta, 244, 245
Tillich, Paul, 167
To Grow in Wisdom, 29
Townes, Emilie M., 104, 105, 106, 217
"traits of ethical prophet," 4–5
"true Islam," 144, 148
"true test of worship," 7
Trump, Donald J., 13, 117, 127, 163, 177, 182, 220, 235
Truth, Sojourner, xiv
Turner, Mary, 87
Turner, Nat, 141
Tutu, Desmond, 4, 183

U

ubuntu, 4
Unitarian Church, 79
United Theological Seminary (Twin Cities), 16
Universal Negro Improvement Association, 139
University of Louvain, 210
University of Maryland, 162
"unmoved mover," 10, 174
"unpopularity of ethical prophets," 7–9
Uriah, 36

V

Vanderbilt University, xv, xvi
Vatican, 188
Vietnam War, 13, 24, 115, 161, 162, 166, 176
Vivian, C. T., 16, 161n8
Vollmer, August, 228, 229

W

Walker, Alice, ix, xiv, 18, 20, 37, 55, 114, 117, 124, 140, 184, 213, ch. 8
Walker, David, xiv
Walker, Joe, 133
Walker, Minnie Lou, 216
Walker, Rebecca, 217
Walker, Willie Lee, 216
Weems, Renita, 41
Weld, Theodore, 58, 78
Wells, Elizabeth Warrenton, 83
Wells, Jim, 83
Wells-Barnett, Ida B., ix, 17–18, 37, 50, ch. 3, 153, 183, 244
West, Cornel, 192, 231
West, Traci, xvi, 217
Weston, Nancy, 77
Where Have all the Prophets Gone?, xiv, 43
White, Walter, 87
Wholly Other, 37, 150
Wieman, Henry Nelson, 167
Willard, Frances, 91, 103
Williams, Adam Daniel, 159
Williams, Delores, 217
Winchester rifle, 90, 97
Witness, 5, 124–27
womanist, 20, 104, 216, 218, 219
Woods, Eliza, 95
World Council of Churches, 132
World Festival of Youth and Students, 216
World Peace Award, 174
Wright, Elizur, 77
Wright, Henry C., 63
Wright, Theodore, 58
Wyler, Sam, 166

Y

Yitzhak, Levi, 30
You Can't Keep a Good Woman Down, 218
Young, Andrew, 16, 161n8

Z

Zeus, 194
Zimmerman, George, 86

www.ingramcontent.com/pod-product-compliance
Lightning Source LLC
Chambersburg PA
CBHW022001220426
43663CB00007B/909